Structure and Agency in Everyday Life

Structure and Agency in Everyday Life

An Introduction to Social Psychology, Second Edition

GIL RICHARD MUSOLF

ROWMAN & LITTLEFIELD PUBLISHERS, INC.
Lanham • Boulder • New York • Toronto • Oxford

ROWMAN & LITTLEFIELD PUBLISHERS, INC.

Published in the United States of America
by Rowman & Littlefield Publishers, Inc.
A Member of the Rowman & Littlefield Publishing Group
4501 Forbes Boulevard, Suite 200, Lanham, Maryland 20706
www.rowmanlittlefield.com

P.O. Box 317, Oxford OX2 9RU, United Kingdom

Copyright © 2003 by Rowman & Littlefield Publishers, Inc.

British Library Cataloguing in Publication Information Available

Library of Congress Cataloging-in-Publication Data Available

ISBN 0-7425-2527-9 (cloth : alk. paper)
ISBN 0-7425-2528-7 (pbk. : alk. paper)

Printed in the United States of America

♾™ The paper used in this publication meets the minimum requirements of American
National Standard for Information Sciences—Permanence of Paper for Printed Library
Materials, ANSI/NISO Z39.48-1992.

To my mom, Lorraine Musolf

Contents

Contents

Preface to the Second Edition

Structure and Agency in Everyday Life is intended for undergraduate students in social psychology and in sociological theory classes where significant time is devoted to symbolic interactionism. It is also appropriate for advanced and/or graduate classes in social psychology/social theory.

Part of the work presented here stems from my dissertation, *The Social Origins of Symbolic Interactionism: Corporate Capitalism, Progressive Politics, and the Nature/Nurture Debate*. Only a very small part of the dissertation's treatment of the social context of symbolic interactionism appears here.

The main purpose of part I is to trace the theoretical and conceptual development of symbolic interactionism, which occurred during a period when American social thought underwent a transition from the dogma of biological determinism to the hegemony of social and cultural theory. Much of the book is a history of the increasingly sociological concepts of symbolic interactionists. Part II highlights some of the best work done by interactionists under the rubrics of society, self, and mind. Part III concentrates on socialization, gender, and the emotions. Part IV summarizes the interactionist perspective on deviance.

Symbolic interactionism is sometimes spelled out, sometimes designated as (SI). Also, William James, James Mark Baldwin, Charles Horton Cooley, William Isaac Thomas, John Dewey, and George Herbert Mead are categorized as early interactionists and/or symbolic interactionists. They have been classified as such since Herbert Blumer, in 1937, argued that a corpus of their interrelated ideas, tenets, and concepts constituted a perspective he termed symbolic interaction. James, Dewey, and Mead are also, occasionally, referred to as pragmatists. Scholars of such magnitude are not to be circumscribed under one appellation.

When these scholars wrote, "man" was the word used to define everyone. For aesthetic reasons and also because I assume that any sociology student is aware of the history of the sexist nature of the English language, I have not added *sic* when "man" appears. I use he or she, they, their, or humans and humankind, when referring to Homo sapiens.

The second edition has added sections on phatic communion in chapter 7, an examination of the explanatory utility of the personality concept in chapter 8, and a discussion on two similar emotions, resentment and *ressentiment*, in chapter 11. I deleted the sections on Goffman's *Frame Analysis,* the comparison between symbolic interactionism and the British School of Cultural Studies, and philosopher Maurice Natanson's work on *The Journeying Self.* I also eliminated the chapters on Chodorow and Gilligan and the chapter on socialization at midlife. I rewrote the section on John Dewey in chapter 4.

Many of the chapters contain previously published work. Part of chapter 1 was previously published as "Social Structure, Human Agency, and Social Policy," in *International Journal of Sociology and Social Policy* 23: 1-12, 2003. Part of chapter 3 was previously published as "William James and Symbolic Interactionsim," in *Sociological Focus* 27: 303-14, 1994. Part of chapter 4 was previously published as "John Dewy's Social Psychology and Neopragmatism: Theoretical Foundations of Human Agency and Social Reconstruction," in *The Social Science Journal* 38: 277-95, 2001. Part of chapter 6 was previously published as "Structure, Institutions, Power, and Ideology: New Direction in Symbolic Interactionism" in *The Sociological Quarterly* 33: 171-89, 1992. Part of chapter 7 was previously published as an article by Bernard N. Meltzer and Gil Richard Musolf entitled "Have a Nice Day! Phatic Communion and Everyday Life," in *Studies in Symbolic Interaction* 23: 95-111, 2000. Part of chapter 8 was previously published as an article by Bernard N. Meltzer and Gil Richard Musolf entitled "The End of Personality?" in *Studies in Symbolic Interaction* 22: 197-221, 1999. Chapter 10 was previously published as "Interactionism and the Child: Cahill, Corsaro, and Denzin on Childhood Socialization," in *Symbolic Interaction* 19: 303-21, 1996. Part of chapter 11 was previously published as an article by Bernard N. Meltzer and Gil Richard Musolf entitled "Resentment and *Ressentiment*," in *Sociological Inquiry* 72: 240-55, 2002.

Acknowledgments

I would like to thank Bernard N. Meltzer for allowing me to include the majority of each of three articles we have done together. I would like to thank Dean Birkenkamp for encouraging me to do a second edition. Additionally, I would like to thank the production staff at Rowman & Littlefield, especially Jessica Gribble, April Leo, Kirstyn Leuner, and Alison Sullenberger for helping me with the production layout of the manuscript.

1

Introduction to Symbolic Interactionism

The Argument

This project attempts to outline the perspective of symbolic interactionism (SI) and its conceptual contributions to how humans emerge as humans with selves, consciences, and the ability to engage in minded behavior. Its pervading theme is that behavior is neither biologically nor culturally determined but an emergent of the dialectical interplay of structure and agency. The ideas of SI emerged at a historically propitious time. In part I, a brief account of the social and intellectual context of that time is presented along with the major ideas and concepts of the founding framers of the perspective. The antideterminist stance that rejected biological and cultural determinism is still a guiding principle of contemporary interactionist research and theory building. The argument presented in part I as to why SI emerged when it did is so fundamental to the framework of this text that a preliminary statement is in order. The following paragraph enunciates that argument.

In the latter part of the nineteenth and the early part of the twentieth centuries, just how we emerge as human and what is the nature of human nature were among the most pressing problems in the social sciences. They were also of grave concern to policymakers. Given the recent resurgence of biological determinism and social Darwinism, perhaps they still are. An extraordinarily important point is that the debate over what it means to be human did not arise in a social vacuum. Thus the social context within which SI arose is an imperative question for the sociology of knowledge. Symbolic interactionism arose from a historically particular social setting: industrialization, urbanization, and immigration in the latter part of the nineteenth and early part of the twentieth centuries in the United States. It also arose from a social science and policy debate. The policy debate centered on the

1

nature of the state in modern society. On one side there was a Progressive move-ment for social reconstruction; another side was in favor of anti-interventionism, both governmental and philanthropic. The social science debate focused on the conceptualization of human nature in what has come to be known as the na-ture/nurture controversy. The social context and the arguments over the nature of human nature are closely intertwined.

The *social* nature of human nature and behavior is the thesis, which is pre-sented first in part I, and then conveyed throughout the text, especially as we analyze the social construction of gender.

The rest of this chapter briefly presents symbolic interactionism as a perspec-tive, indicating why first-generation interactionism ended with George Herbert Mead, the main ideas of symbolic interactionism, a succinct summary of the SI position on structure and agency, and an outline of the four parts of this book.

Symbolic Interactionism as a Perspective

The term symbolic interactionism originated with Herbert Blumer, who used it to characterize the theoretical perspectives of William James, James Mark Baldwin, Charles Horton Cooley, W. I. Thomas, John Dewey, and George Herbert Mead. Since these scholars are regarded as the progenitors of this school of thought by contemporary symbolic interactionists (Rose 1962; Manis and Meltzer 1975; Gordon and Gergen 1968; Blumer 1969; Stone and Farberman 1970; Meltzer, Petras, and Reynolds 1975; Hewitt 1991; Charon 1979; Karp and Yoels 1979; Rock 1979; Lewis and Smith 1980; Stryker 1980; Lindesmith, Strauss, and Denzin, 1991), we are provided with a generally recognized consensus as to what symbolic interactionists define as symbolic interactionism.

Symbolic interactionism is a unique perspective, a set of interrelated assump-tions and concepts that endeavors to explain social life. Social life is a broad and general term for the patterns of human interaction. It may cover anything from the simplest interpersonal exchange to the relationships between social institutions to the relationships between nations. Those who share a perspective share certain assumptions about social life, focus their attention on dealing with particular issues, and use certain concepts in analyzing those issues. Framing the issues are the questions of how people define social reality and the consequences of those definitions for everyday behavior. The issues are the nature of human nature, how humans are different from other species, how the individual develops into a human being with a self, a mind, consciousness, role-taking ability, and the capacity for human agency.

In what way does symbolic interactionism represent a perspective? First and foremost, I have used the term perspective because symbolic interactionists them-selves conceive of their work as such (in a fashion similar to the definition described above), rather than a theory. "Symbolic interactionism is a sociological social psychological orientation or perspective, i.e., a broad set of interrelated concepts, ideas, findings, and assumptions about the two-way relationship between man and the socio-cultural system, rather than a theory" (Schmitt 1974, 453).

A social theory is an effort to explain the relationship between two or more social phenomena. It must have logical propositions and be empirically testable. Whether symbolic interactionism comprises testable propositions has been the subject of much debate (Huber 1973).

What are the main substantive features of symbolic interactionism? Three scholars have defined what is common among most adherents, thereby providing an answer to what unifies the works of James, Baldwin, Cooley, Thomas, Dewey, and Mead (Meltzer, Petras, and Reynolds 1975, vii).

> The perspective known as symbolic interactionism comprises the following basic ideas: The influence that stimuli have upon human behavior is shaped by the context of symbolic meanings within which human behavior occurs. These meanings emerge from the shared interaction of individuals in human society. Society itself is constructed out of the behavior of humans, who actively play a role in developing the social limits that will be placed upon their behavior. Thus, human behavior is not a unilinear unfolding toward a predetermined end, but an active constructing process whereby humans endeavor to "make sense" of their social and physical environments.

More succinctly put, symbolic interactionism is a perspective that offers generalizations about how the individual develops a self and a mind, and the dialectical relationship of the individual who possesses a self and a mind to the society in which he or she lives.

What unites early symbolic interactionists is that their social ontology expressed a concern with phenomena such as the nature of human nature, the emergence of self, mind, and the indeterminacy of social behavior, and the indissoluble connection between society and self. Methodologically, interactionists devised research (ethnographies) that would illuminate the subjective side of symbolic interaction; for example, the influence of the definition of the situation on human behavior. This subjective understanding of others began in James and Baldwin but becomes more explicit in Cooley (sympathetic introspection), Thomas (definition of the situation), Dewey (deliberation), and Mead (taking the role or attitude of the other). Hinkle, in his 1967 study of Cooley and his 1980 study of the founding theory of American sociology, describes Cooley's social methodological orientation, which can be attributed to early symbolic interactionists generally (Hinkle 1980, 100).

> Personal, social knowledge concerns minds, consciousness, imaginations, and feelings—the internal and subjective. It is a form of knowledge requiring that the researcher engage in interpretation using the unique technique of sympathetic

introspection. Less precise, verifiable, cumulative, and susceptible to measurement, quantification, and statistical manipulation, its data are to be treated emergentistically, synthetically, and typologically.

Eventually this orientation led to the engaged social research of participant observation, one hallmark of the Chicago school. In this school, W. I. Thomas was the outstanding practitioner of this research method.

In analyzing the symbolic interactionist perspective I focus exclusively on the emergence and contemporary work of the "Chicago school" of symbolic interactionism, largely ignoring the "Iowa school" of symbolic interactionism (for a discussion of these schools, see Meltzer, Petras, and Reynolds 1975, 53-82). Time, space, theoretical coherence, and consistency are the primary reasons for this decision. In discussing contemporary interactionism, I concentrate on Erving Goffman because I consider him squarely within the Chicago school tradition, though a number of scholars have given his work the separate classification of "dramaturgical sociology."

Mead as the Culmination of Early Interactionism

Chicago school symbolic interactionists are unified by the development of a set of concepts that received its first full expression with the publication of Mead's works, especially his posthumous publication of *Mind, Self, and Society* in 1934. Early interactionism had several distinguishing features: "there tends to be much repetition; there is a strain to 'get it right,' that is, to be correct; there is much debate over orthodoxy" (Kuhn, 1972, 58).

We have now discussed the term perspective, what characterizes symbolic interactionism as a perspective, and why I focus on the particular thinkers that I do. It is now time to summarize the main ideas of interactionism.

Main Ideas of Interactionism

Revolting against formalism and any fixed structures of the mind, or any abstract, static concept of human nature, it was primarily the interactionists who set out to show that behavior was socially, not just biologically, influenced. People became human beings through taking the role of significant and generalized others, internalizing culture through socialization, and thereby developing selves, minds, consciousness, and intelligence, the last of which is an evolutionary, adaptive capacity to suspend the stimulus-response sequence and engage in agency. The self possesses creativity, choice, possibility, spontaneity, and novelty; thus, human conduct is not biologically determined. This quality of the self makes people more determining than determined. Through selective and symbolic responses to social objects on the basis of the meaning that those objects have for them, people create their own social worlds. Because of enculturation and socialization, social control is largely self-control. Individuals can solve problems in living through minded behavior; that is, intelligence, as an adaptive faculty, allows humans to define the situation, consider alternative courses of action, and then act. People are malleable, which allows the environment to impinge on the human being. Individuals have the potential to adapt to environmental impact and act back on their environment, thereby influencing it. Thus, humans have the capacity to influence the way the environment affects them. Consequentially, they have the capacity constantly to improve the human condition in general and the quality of life and opportunities available for each individual. Since the self is a social object, humans can act on it and reconstitute themselves. Because of the codeterminacy and interdependency between the social environment and humans, the self and the social environment are constantly in a dialectical process of becoming.

Through the above assumptions and the development of a whole host of concepts to be explored in this text, interactionists have argued for the social basis of human nature and behavior. Socialization endows actors with the unique human capacity both to symbolize objects and events expressed through language and to empathize with others. This capacity constitutes the basis of human nature. Influenced by Darwin's and Spencer's notion of adaptation and evolution, interactionists hold that people adapt to situations through action (adjustive responses) guided by definitions of the situation and the meanings that social objects have for them. Definitions of the situation and the meanings that social objects have for people are both socially embedded in their social relationships and are emergents of the social situation. Thus, one's situation in the world continuously evolves, that is, it is an emergent process. Our ability to define the situation and make an adjustive response based on that definition is the contribution of intelligence to the adaptive capacity of the species. One is always in the process of becoming; one's self and mind are ceaselessly evolving through one's interaction with the environment and with others.

The above interactionist argument presented a view of human nature diametrically opposed to the passive, immutable, biological, and instinct perspective that held hegemony in the early years of the twentieth century.

The interactionist emphasis on the emergent and indeterminant quality of social behavior is an argument against the instinct thesis of innate and immutable behavior. In the early twentieth century it was argued that human beings possessed the following instincts: "herding," "acquisition," "aggression," and "self-preservation." In 1924 L. L. Bernard, after an exhaustive review of the literature, *Instincts: A Study in Social Psychology*, had identified 15,789 instincts attributed to human beings. But instinct behavior is innate and immutable behavior that denies the possibilities of choice.

The above argument sheds light on the dialectical relationship among social context, political commitments, and conceptualization. The metatheoretical origins of symbolic interactionism are to be found in a particular historical social context and in Progressive era political commitments that called for social reconstruction. The theoretical origins are to be found in the nature/nurture debate.

Symbolic interactionism thus contributed to the view of the social nature of human beings, of what it means to become and be human. What emerged, and what now prevails, is a view of human beings, a view of human nature, that is conceptualized as an emergent of a dialectical relationship between social structure and human agency. This terminology is reminiscent of an old debate: determinism versus free will. We must make clear the SI relationship between structure and agency.

Structure and Human Agency

The problem of bridging the gap between microsociological and macrosociological levels has not been satisfactorily handled by any known theory. The result is that most theorists shift gears radically when they move from one level to the other. For example, many macrosociologists adopt a voluntaristic stance for microlevel analysis and a deterministic stance for macrolevel analysis. They are willing to grant that actors interpret definitions of the situation in interpersonal relations, but they convert actors into mindless robots on the societal/aggregate level. The challenge is both to avoid reification of social structure and to develop a consistent image of human beings. In any case, social structure must be taken into account. However, social structure is maintained and changed by what people do; it is not autonomous or self-regulating.[1]

Structure refers to the innumerable social facts over which the individual, *qua* individual, does not have much control and which he or she cannot escape. Race, class, sex, ideology, institutions, organizational hierarchy, groups, geographical location, period of history, mode of production, generational cohort, family, culture, roles and rules are all examples of social facts, the structural dimension of social life. We are born into situations that have existed before us and that will exist after we are gone. In general, structure refers to social arrangements, social relations, and social practices which exert enormous power and constraint over our lives. Social is repeated to emphasize that arrangements, relations, and practices are constructed, maintained, and altered by human beings. Structure can refer to—among other things—one's social location/status in class, race, gender, and other hierarchies so that the higher one's status the more power one has within any institution. Thus, structure organizes social positions hierarchically in all institutions so that power emanates from those who own the means of administration to make, and the means of violence to enforce, policy. Policy constrains everyone; subjects/citizens usually conform, though, of course, many do not; thus crime, deviance, and protest occur. Policyframers, whether corporate, legislative, judicial, executive, ecclesiastical, or, royal, can devastate lives. They are able to exercise meta-power, that is, some "actors can create future and distant social conditions for other actors" (Hall 2003, 36). Meta-power is a process that creates "inequality orders," that is, actors who deploy meta-power set in motion "conditions, organizational arrangements, [and] processes, . . . that shape categories and patterns of inequality and their intersections" (43). A few examples can illuminate this. When executives at General Motors decided it was good policy to close factories in Flint, Michigan, and move the plants to the Third World, the social dislocation of hundreds of thousands may have been the last thing on their minds. When the justices of the U.S. Supreme Court adjudicated that capital punishment does not violate the Eighth Amendment, then many prisoners were executed. When state legislators enacted Jim Crow statutes, then countless African Americans were disenfranchised, lost their civil liberties and civil rights, and became reenslaved to tyranny. If the president of the United States calls on the military to engage in war, then men and women serving in the armed forces will have to risk life and limb. The examples are endless.

The lava flow from the volcano of policy overruns everything in its path. Familial and economic shipwreck is frequently the result. An example of landlord policy from early Tudor England suffices to illustrate the constancy of social dislocation.

> [L]ords of the manor and great freeholders took commercial decisions with devastating consequences for communities, evicting tenants who were powerless to oppose when lands and lives were determined at the lord's will (Brigden 2000, 11). [T]he landowners enclosed land for pasture, driving poor farmers from the soil and families from their homes to wander and beg—sheep became "devourers of men" (3). [W]here before a hundred arable labourers had tilled and harrowed, now a few shepherds watched. (11)

Policy and power are plagues; oppression renders us susceptible to their contagion. Those easily infected are the downtrodden: the poor, weak, and exploited whose oppression is justified by ideology, which cloaks the power and inequality embedded in ruling-class policy.

But for all of that, it does not mean that we have no choice in our behavior even though, for many of us, the situations we find ourselves in are wretched, oppressive, exploitative, and rob us of resources and opportunities. First and foremost, "structures are not eternal, but exist in historical time and are the products of historical processes" (Parker 2000, 7). We human beings have collectively constructed the structures of our world and that world is alterable by human agency. As Foucault argues (1979), wherever there is power there is resistance. But, what is more important, wherever there is resistence there is the potential for social transformation. This "history-producing power of human agency" (Parker

2000, 10) at times ignites the world, setting structures ablaze.

Agency, then, refers to the fact that we make culture, history, and policy though not under conditions of our own choosing. Human behavior is embedded in, and emerges through, social interaction. Human beings are producers as well as produced, shapers as well as shaped, influencing as well as influenced. Social action is volitional, purposeful, and meaningful, even though social facts constrain life chances. Actors reflect, rather than respond by reflex. Agency emerges through the ability of humans to ascribe meaning to objects and events, to define the situation based on those meanings, and then to act. Endowed with agency, the oppressed can oppose structures such as those in the examples above; they can and have taken to the streets and won policy for themselves. Policy, then, can also be a cure for social dislocation. Innumerable policies have been enacted as a result of the collective definitions and actions of ordinary human beings who have opposed those with more power and resources and yet changed the structures (the social arrangements, relations, and practices) that affect their lives. For example, collective bargaining empowers us to advocate for wages, benefits, and improvements as a union; unemployment insurance assures that one has some immediate income after the loss of a job; minimum wage laws, child labor laws, and overtime pay protect the value of labor and childhood; Social Security makes it possible that one can someday retire; Medicare and Medicaid afford that the elderly and the poor can receive medical services; laws prohibit discrimination against one's sex, sexual orientation, race, ethnicity, nationality, religion, age, and so on; general assistance and food stamps provide that one can at least eat if destitute; product liability laws afford standing to sue if corporations manufacture products that injure, maim, or kill; as a result of the Civil Rights Movement and the women's movement, new congressional Civil Rights legislation was enacted and U.S. Supreme Court opinions were implemented to eradicate racist and sexist policy. The examples are, again, endless. No policy was handed over to the people by enlightened despots, philosopher-kings, or socially conscious CEOs; instead, amelioration was wrested through class, race, and gender struggles of human beings, through the history-producing power of human agency. People sooner or later may throw up rotten deals thrust down their throats and enact new deals. Social life is a dialectical struggle between structure and agency. One cannot predict the course of this struggle (Marx's failure) because it is the result of evolving collective definitions of the situation and collective history/action that emerges in interaction in everyday life—definitions and action that are, many times, unforseen.

The main reason that agency is diminished in popular culture and in social science literature is the overwhelming belief in determinism.[2] Many determinists argue for two ideas; (a) the way social arrangements, relations, and practices are is the way they are supposed to be and (b) the way we behave is determined by biology, genes, culture, structure, or some other source that constitutes an escape from responsibility. The first argument has a long ideological lineage beginning with social Darwinism; for example, it justifies present stratification as indefeasible: There's no sense in trying to change the status quo, to improve the lives of the poor, because the poor will always be with us; hence, "you're just paving a road to hell with good intentions." The second argument, not taking responsibility for our actions, has an even longer lineage. If criminals are genetically determined, if heredity is the cause of male aggressiveness, well, then, we certainly should not blame these people for behavior they have absolutely no control over. Crime, for example, is still explained by many social scientists as due to either heredity or culture. As a sociologist, I consider social circumstances and situations highly influential but not determinative. People have choices. Listen, for example, to one of the most famous criminals in all of English literature, Edmund, from *King Lear*. Determinism in the stars? Even Edmund knew that that was rationalization and evasion.

> This is the excellent foppery of the world, that when we are sick in fortune, often the surfeits of our own behavior, we make guilty of our disasters the sun, the moon, and stars; as if we were villains on necessity; fools by heavenly compulsion; knaves, thieves, and treachers by spherical predominance; drunkards, liars, and adulterers by an enforced obedience of planetary influence; and all that we are evil in, by a divine thrusting on. An admirable evasion of whoremaster man, to lay his goatish disposition on the charge of a star. My father compounded with my mother under the Dragon's Tail, and my nativity was under Ursa Major, so that if follows I am rough and lecherous.

I can only agree with Shakespeare's satire in that it is the "excellent foppery" of some social scientists, an admirable theory to lay people's goatish dispositions on the charge of biological or environmental determinism, dismissing human agency and responsibility in everyday life.

Snow (2001, 373-74) has summarized the interactionist position on structure and agency.

> [H]uman beings are viewed neither as hard-wired robots responding in a lockstep fashion to internal directives or codes nor as passive social actors behaving merely in accord with extant structural and cultural directives and constraints. Yet biological, structural, and cultural factors are not dismissed in the determination and explanation of behavior. Rather, . . . these factors [are] predispositions or constraints on action without automatically or necessarily determining the character of that action. [S]ocial actors take into account the structural and cultural constraints (e.g., roles, social expectations, norms, values) that impinge on situations in which they find themselves in the course of developing their respective lines of action.

Structure and agency are now becoming recognized as specious, or spurious, polarities; instead, they are inextricably intertwined in a nonquantifiable dialectic constituting constraint and emergence as two salient features of everyday life. To say that humans are both shaped and shapers means that structure and agency construct each other. We are the stuff of culture and institutions; humans construct the culture and institutions that shape them. This ongoing, interdependent process explains why culture, institutions, and the values, norms, beliefs, and behaviors of humans change reciprocally; they coevolve. There is no way to measure, in a quantitative sense, the force of either structure or agency—to say, for example, that structure explains 60 percent of the behavior in a situation and agency 40 percent, or some other such percentages. The basic problem of a structure-and-agency perspective is to create "a theoretical position that [gives] *sufficient* weight to *both* structure and agency" (Parker 2000, 13; emphasis in original). Doing so will prevent reification (viewing structures as enlivened, action-taking things autonomous from human efficacy) and reductionism and/or methodological individualism (viewing structures as merely nominal rather than as *sui generis* social arrangements, relations, and practices, which humans must take into account and negotiate so that in doing so such structures exert constraint and power over them) (Parker 2000, 35, 70); moreover, doing so helps avoid essentialism. "In essentialism, something either 'is' or 'has' agency or structure but not both" (Fuchs 2001, 26). Once we accept the structure-and-agency perspective, "it no longer makes much sense to assume the social world divides naturally, all by itself, into two separate and distinct realms that then must somehow be reconciled or reintegrated. The social is of one piece" (Fuchs 2001, 31). This is not an argument that sociologists should conflate structure and agency so that we remain uninformed over the contribution of each. They are still analytically distinct categories (Parker 2000, 72 and *passim*). Sociologists can examine hierarchy and the effect roles and rules have on behavior just as they can analyze how actors make secondary adjustments to those roles and rules, or use/exploit the system in any hierarchy. Such analysis calls for an interpretive rather than a positivistic sociology.

How structure and agency play out in any historical situation can be analyzed only a posteriori and not a priori. "Ask . . . which forces make something small bigger or what happens as a macrostructure, such as a bureaucracy, falls apart into local fiefdoms. These are empirical, not conceptual, questions, concerning not any agency/structure or micro/macro transition 'in general' but rather to be dealt with case by empirical case" (Fuchs 2001, 26; see also Parker 2000, 119). Which forces make something small bigger is exactly what Max Weber identified when he argued the effect of *The Protestant Ethic and the Spirit of Capitalism* on the rise of capitalism itself. The rise of capitalism, according to Weber, was an unintended consequence of the rational pursuit of productivity and prosperity as signs of grace, an idea implanted in Protestants by John Calvin's theology. Agency will be highlighted in some situations (or problems) while structure will be underscored in others. Such historical clarity is only retrospective. But the future can be seen, if at all, solely through a glass darkly. History is nonteleological. The unintended consequences of rational action can derail the plans of policymakers.

Irrational action also makes the predictability of everyday life precarious.

Structure and agency can also change their relative effects on each other. For example, the power of structure, at times, can seem insuperable, and the possibility of agency can seem inconceivable. Indeed, in czarist Russia, pre-1789 France, and the United States in the 1950s, Russian and French peasants and American blacks, respectively, were thought of as passive, the status quo resting assured in the garden of pleasure or, in the last case, oblivion. Indeed, Marie Antoinette flippantly replied, so the fable goes, that if the peasants were starving, why, then, let them eat cake. Nicholas II and Alexandra, oblivious to the starving outside their palace, were throwing million-dollar dances of death. White Americans were relaxing in the suburbs, confident that blacks had accommodated themselves to Jim Crow and segregation. What is crucial is that no one predicted the *emergent* social revolutions; agency was unfathomable. Yet, instead, agency was always there in emerging collective definitions of the situation and actions of resistance, arising and overthrowing structures of oppression. No matter what breakwaters we build to structure out social change, the time and tide of human agency may disrupt all.

Conceptualizing structure and agency as a dialectical process, it is hoped, contributes "to understanding the establishment of enduring, patterned forms of social relations and practices, and the contribution of human agents to such establishments" (Parker 2000, x). The problem for interpretive theorists is to present an account of constraint that includes hierarchy, roles, rules, power, ideology, and the like. The problem for structural theorists is to present an account of agency that includes consciousness, meaning, defining the situation, resistance, transformation, and the like. These two (traditionally) oppositional theory groups benefit social analysis the more they incorporate insights from each other, which, in some cases, has been occurring (Musolf 1992). Social theory explains the ontological state of everyday life; it is the argument of this text that a structure-and-agency perspective provides the best current explanation of social reality.

Structure and agency encompass the dialectic between social reproduction (stability) and social transformation (change). In this wide and universal theater, we find ourselves situated in woeful pageants; nevertheless, even though the stage of social action has been set, as actors (though structures make us all strut and fret) we always have some degree of choice over how we play out the scene. That is what endows social life with drama, emergence, and novelty.

I now briefly outline the book.

Outline of the Four Parts of the Text

Part I begins with a chapter on the social context of SI, which animated the social science and policy debates that led to the rise of interactionism and social reconstruction. It then proceeds to summarize the relevant ideas of James, Baldwin, Cooley, Dewey, Thomas, and Mead on the social nature of human beings.

Part II surveys the work of current SI theory, with chapters on society, self, and mind.

Part III focuses on socialization, gender, and emotions.

Part IV presents the SI position on deviance and concludes with a summary of the main ideas of SI.

Notes

1. This opening paragraph on structure and agency was written by Bernard N. Meltzer.

2. This discussion on determinism, though informed by thirty years of reading on symbolic interactionism, was theoretically enhanced by reading A. Kohn, *The Brighter Side of Human Nature: Altruism and Empathy in Everyday Life*, New York: Basic Books, 1990.

Part I

The Social Nature of Human Nature

2

The Social and Ideological Context of Symbolic Interactionism

The Historical Context

The following is a brief summary of some highlights of the social context of symbolic interactionism. It relies heavily on the work of the following historians: Beard 1914; Cravens 1978; Curti 1980; Degler 1970; Faulkner 1951; Goldman 1955; Hinkle 1980; Hofstadter 1969; Kolko 1967; Krout 1971; Morris and Greenleaf 1969; Szymanski 1978; Weinstein 1968; and Wiebe 1967.

The writings of the early interactionists are reduced in introductory sociology and social psychology textbooks to those of their classic concepts that are a part of every sociologist's vocabulary. But these concepts were engendered as criticism of the hegemony of biological determinism and a hereditarian psychology in a protracted series of theoretical and political debates over nature versus nurture; heredity versus socialization; the definition and measurement of intelligence; the inherent quality and determined fate of social classes, national origins, and race; the efficacy of mass education; the social policies of immigration and eugenics; the viability of democracy; the role of the state; and the prospects of social reconstruction.

Understanding these debates in their social context is indispensable to a comprehension of twentieth-century social theory and social policy in general, and the rise of symbolic interactionism in particular. Theoretical development must be historically informed by refusing to abstract solely from texts the concepts that are the hallmark of a perspective.

George Stocking (1968, 306-7) has stated that the nature/nurture debate established a social science view of human beings and their relationship to the social environment and culture.

By the middle of the twentieth century, it was commonplace for educated Americans to refer to human differences in cultural terms, and to say that "modern science has shown that all human races are equal." In fact, what science had shown was better put negatively than positively: there was no scientific basis for assuming that one race was inferior or superior to another. That assumption—part and parcel, if you will, of a different paradigm for viewing human differences—was not supported by the evidence. The data of human difference could be interpreted more satisfactorily, within another paradigm, as the product of cultural conditioning.

Stocking (1968, 307) goes on to argue that it was writers within the social sciences:

> rather than the racialist writers associated with the eugenics movement which [were] able to speak to Americans as the voice of science on all matters of race, culture, and evolution—a fact whose significance for the recent history of the United States doubtless merits further exploration.

Stocking's intellectual history sought to outline the contributions of Franz Boaz to the development of the culture concept and the anthropological perspective. Boaz was the leading intellectual theorizing against scientific racism. From Stocking's argument, it is implied that vast changes in the social and political context of American life were being undergone at the time of this reconceptualization of human nature.

The reconceptualization of human nature and behavior, to which symbolic interactionists contributed, took place within the larger social and political context of American life. Some of the large-scale features that were part and parcel of the social and political context were the growth of industrialization, immigration, and urbanization, the rise of the Progressive movement, the reorganization of graduate education, the emergence of the middle class and its culture of professionalism, and the reaction against formalism. Economy, polity, culture, and ethnicity were transforming America, leading to a broader conception of democracy and equality.

After the Civil War, the United States went through a rapid period of industrialization and westward expansion. The government came to play a large role in this industrialization, in the development of the railroad industry, for example. Industry became concentrated and centralized. The United States was moving from laissez-faire to corporate capitalism. Finance capitalism became the new center of power. Immigration provided the massive number of workers to labor for paltry wages during this period. The most important development in immigration for the shaping of the social and political context of America was the shift from northern and western European immigrants to eastern and southern European immigrants after 1890. These immigrants came not as farmers but as city dwellers to labor in the massive factory systems developing in American cities. The immigrants who came swelled the cities. Urbanization and industrialization grew together. At the turn of the century America was no longer the America of the independent farmer, but the America of the city dweller. The city formed the social context for much of sociological theory, for it was the slums and the social problems associated with them that led sociologists to a moral response that was an argument for social reform.

These social changes in American life led to the formation of an industrial working class and the rise of a new middle class and its culture of professionalism as numerous occupations came into existence. This led to a reorganization of graduate education, for these new professions required college diplomas and graduate degrees (Bledstein, 1976).

Capitalism and industrialization grew, but it was an unregulated growth. Captains of industry ruled the era. Eventually this unregulated growth and the social problems associated with industrialization, urbanization, and immigration led to the rise of the Social Gospel movement, Populism, muckrakers, and above all, the Progressive movement, a movement of social reform and governmental regulation. Social work—Jane Addams at Hull-House in Chicago was its epitome—became an ever growing profession advocating on behalf of the poor and disenfranchised. It was the beginning of the decline of the philosophy of laissez-faire, which had argued that government, the courts, and laborers had no right to any say in the affairs of business or the market. The tenet that government governs best that governs least was being challenged. But it was also the desire of corporate capitalists for social order that led to the growth of state interventionism.

The social context of laissez-faire capitalism, along with the above social transformations from the end of the Civil War in 1865 to the beginning of the decline of laissez-faire capitalism in 1897, is the crucial context for development of the ideas of evolutionary science and the social evolutionary theory of social change (Morris and Greenleaf 1969; Degler 1970; Peel 1971; Krout 1971; and Hinkle 1980).

Within this social context there arose the idea of social evolution. From social evolution there emerged social Darwinism, which justified laissez-faire capitalism, and later, around 1880, a competing idea that it was cooperation rather than competition that led societies to evolve and adapt, which supported social reconstruction. Biological determinism had been a fundamental aspect of American thought since its beginning. In fact, Lieberman (1970) traces the ideology of biological superiority and the conceptualization of race as a scientific taxonomy to the seventeenth century with the rise of European colonialism, slavery, and nationalism. Europeans conceptualized race as an ideology to justify the aforementioned social practices. They conquered, enslaved, and committed genocide remorselessly, believing non-Europeans were inferiors or members of subhuman species. Social Darwinism constituted an extreme form of biological determinism. Its basic idea was that certain people (whites) or classes (the rich) were biologically superior to others (the nonwhite and the poor). Society, just like the natural world, rewarded fitness with dominance, the survival of the fittest. Those who can compete and adapt to an ever evolving capitalism (which was defined as the natural economic condition of humankind) rise to the top and those who cannot compete and adapt fall to the bottom of society. Intervening in the lives of the unfit spawns societal ruin and debases the culture; moreover, amelioration was destined to fail since altering someone's biological inferiority is indefeasible.

With the incorporation of the American Social Science Association in 1865 and the American Economic Association in 1885, there also emerged the idea that the environment was crucial in the development of the human being. Thus, during the period of laissez-faire capitalism there already was an ongoing debate over the type of society America was to become and how one would conceptualize human beings and the nature of human nature. According to Harold Faulkner's study, *The Decline of Laissez Faire 1897-1917* (1951), one can date the decline of laissez-faire capitalism from 1897. This is illuminating and helps our understanding of the rise and fall of ideas, for the decline in intellectual thought that justified laissez-faire capitalism occurs at this time. Hofstadter dates the decline of social Darwinism in the first decade of the twentieth century (Hofstadter 1969), while Hinkle describes the decline of social evolutionary theory as occurring during 1915 to 1918 (Hinkle 1980, 300). From 1897 to 1917 a new social context emerges, the rise of corporate capitalism and the beginning of the liberal state (Kolko 1967; Weinstein 1968; Morris and Greenleaf 1969; Degler 1970; Krout 1971).

Corporate capitalism provided the backdrop for the continuing intellectual debate between hereditarians and environmentalists. This intellectual debate continued with the rise of Progressivism, the eugenics movement, Jim Crow legislation, both biological and psychological hereditarianism, the new genetics, the rise of cultural anthropology and comparative ethnography, and the rise of pragmatism and symbolic interactionism. Thus within this context there continued an intellectual struggle and debate over the type of society America was to become, either committed to egalitarianism, social mobility, and democracy or committed to inequality, rigid class stratification (racial and sexual stratification were largely ignored at this time, even by Progressive reformers), and plutocracy.

In the early twentieth century, the hereditarians were in the majority, and even many thinkers who advocated social reconstruction were hereditarians. But the symbolic interactionists were opposed to hereditarian arguments and in favor of social reconstruction. The biological hereditarian position based on *unit characteristics* held sway until it was undermined by genetics in the second decade of the twentieth century. Cultural anthropologists and comparative ethnologists were also establishing the basis for the separation of culture from biology and attacking the eugenics movement, which was based on biological hereditarianism (McKee 1993).

A third period of debate arises after World War I between the psychological hereditarians on one side (IQ testers) and nonhereditarian psychologists on the other. Nonhereditarian psychologists began to use control variables in their examination of the relationship between IQ, race, and class. They showed that the relationship disappeared when one controlled for variables such as education or residence. The interactionists were also developing arguments centering on *the effects socialization had on social behavior*. This debate also took place within the solidifying of the corporate capitalist state—though the corporate capitalist state does not fully take shape until the rise of the New Deal and the emergence of the military-industrial complex after World War II. The rise of early interactionism within this social context and these social science debates ended with the publication of Mead's major work in 1934. The intellectual shift is now more closely detailed.

The Intellectual Context

In the almost fifty years from 1890 to 1934, beginning with William James's monumental *Principles of Psychology* and ending with the posthumous publication of Mead's *Mind, Self, and Society*, American sociology was formed. During the last two decades of the nineteenth century, Lewis and Smith (1980, 4) point out that many sociologists were influenced by the evolutionary writings of Herbert Spencer.

> This doctrine, as applied to the field of sociology, conceives of social structures as the product of the interactions of individuals acting out of a desire to satisfy universal human needs of an organic or quasi-organic nature. Societies and individuals not socially organized in ways functionally compatible with these needs will eventually perish when forced to compete for resources with those more harmoniously adapted, thus providing the evolutionary thrust to human social history.

Many American sociologists accepted Spencer's evolutionary thesis and his individualism but did not accept his social Darwinism.

Social Darwinism, an ideology to justify the social inequality of the period, particularly class stratification and the system of laissez-faire capitalism that perpetuated it, flourished in America in the 1880s and 1890s. The wealthy were fit and prospering while the poor were unfit and degenerating. Since the fit benefited the species and society they should be permitted to thrive unencumbered (laissez-faire) while the unfit should be neglected so that they can die out. Thus social Darwinists argued that inequality was the result of natural selection and that both philanthropic and state interventionism to help the less fit (note, not the less fortunate or privileged) only prolonged the agony of a biologically inferior class and squandered the resources of the state. Inequality was not considered inequitable. Arguments were advanced that "natural" inequalities among people inevitably lead to a "natural" system of social stratification. Philanthropic and state interventionism was, therefore, meddling with the "natural" order of events (capitalism), threatening the survival of the species (upper-class whites). William Graham

Sumner, a diehard social Darwinist, expressed these beliefs in his book *What Social Classes Owe to Each Other* (1883) and in his article "The Absurd Effort to Make the World Over" (1894). Social Darwinism functioned to blame the victims of capitalism for their misery and to shunt attention away from the social circumstances of both the well-off and the impoverished that reproduce their respective superior and inferior social statuses.

Social Darwinism was short-lived, however; even in the 1880s it was challenged by American scholars influenced by European theorists, who supplanted competition with cooperation and mutual aid as sources of social evolution and adaptation. It was challenged by Lamarckians of the American Social Science Association, who called for social intervention. Moreover, it was challenged by Progressive era reformers who also called for social reconstruction. But the most important element in the downfall of social Darwinism was the advent of corporate capitalism, which undermined the need for an ideology to justify laissez-faire capitalism. Corporate capitalists saw the need for social responsibility and the creation of a regulated, interventionist, liberal state to create social order (Weinstein 1968, x). The concept of social evolution would remain, though it, too, came under attack in the early decades of the twentieth century with the advent of comparative ethnography.

Among those reformers who called for social reconstruction were the pragmatists. Beginning in 1890 with the writings of William James and continuing into the first three decades of the twentieth century with the writings of James M. Baldwin, W. I. Thomas, Charles H. Cooley, John Dewey, and George Herbert Mead, these social philosophers and sociologists, along with many others, challenged biological determinism. As Lewis and Smith argue (1980, 5), through their Progressive era politics they rejected the social Darwinist notion of anti-interventionism, and through their reconceptualization of the nature of human nature they rejected biological determinism.

> Spencer's philosophy of history was too materialistic to appeal unqualifiedly to American sociologists, many of whom had deep humanistic commitments stemming from earlier careers as ministers. They preferred a philosophy that preserved the naturalistic and individualistic overtones while nevertheless admitting the possibility of and, indeed, necessity for intelligently guided melioristic social reform. Pragmatism, especially the pragmatism of James and Dewey, offered precisely this philosophical combination.

The early symbolic interactionists came from the disciplines of philosophy and sociology. Symbolic interactionism is closely associated with the American philosophy of pragmatism; indeed, William James, John Dewey, and George H. Mead are considered pragmatists. Thus, the pragmatists (or early interactionists, I use these terms interchangeably) contested Spencer's philosophy on three fronts: they rejected the laissez-faire doctrine of economic individualism; rather than deterministic in their conception of human beings, they conceptualized human beings as volitional; and, theoretically opposing biological determinism, they reconceptualized the nature of human nature, postulating that human beings developed through selves and minds. Interactionists accepted and helped in developing what Hinkle and Hinkle (1954, v) have called voluntaristic nominalism.

The Importance of Socialization: Science and Politics

The symbolic interactionists argued that the human being was a social animal, a creature made social through socialization. Socialization gave every human being a self and a mind. With selves and minds, human beings could think, formulate plans of action, define the situation, and act. Always constrained by social structure, human beings yet had some choice in their behavior and were more determining than determined. The mature development of this thought in the works of George Herbert Mead led to the challenging of biological determinism and Watsonian behaviorism; it also contributed to the reconceptualization of human nature and behavior and thereby to the development of sociology.

Yet, even though social Darwinism declined, biological determinism was far from dead. Hereditarianism arose. Biological hereditarianism arose with the development of experimental biology in the works of August Weismann, Gregor Mendel, Hugo DeVries, Charles B. Davenport, and other experimental biologists. Psychological hereditarianism arose with the new psychology in the works of H. H. Goddard, Lewis Terman, Robert M. Yerkes, and many others. Psychological hereditarianism led to the invention of the IQ test as the measure of the innate self-worth of human beings. Within the disciplines of biology and psychology, it was argued that human beings were biologically determined and that their intelligence was fixed, unalterable, and that there was great variation in the intelligence of races. The hereditarian biologists and psychologists also gave impetus to the eugenics movement. In general, the eugenicists exploited the perspective of hereditarianism as scientific ammunition to justify programs such as restricted immigration, especially of eastern Europeans, and involuntary sterilization of those they argued were "less fit." Earlier, southern state legislatures had enacted laws, later tested by the U.S. Supreme Court, which adjudicated constitutional segregation and disenfranchisement. The most crucial cases were *Plessy v. Ferguson* in 1896, which declared constitutional the separate but equal doctrine, and the 1898 case of *Williams v. Mississippi*, which held constitutional the Louisiana concept of the "grandfather clause," disenfranchising African American males. With segregation and disenfranchisement constitutional, and drawing on scientific racism from the academy, southern legislatures in the early twentieth century passed numerous Jim Crow laws.

Hereditarianism would be challenged by symbolic interactionists through their reconceptualization of the nature of human nature and behavior (Hinkle and Hinkle 1954, 30). The hereditarianism of the early psychologists and biologists would be challenged by two other developments: the work of Franz Boas, who fostered the rise of cultural anthropology and the work of the new geneticists in the second and third decades of the twentieth century. It is crucial to note that it was the work of the geneticists, who could attack the basic assumptions of hereditarianism from within biology, that finally undermined it.

The Nature/Nurture Debate

A new perspective on the nature of human nature, emphasizing its emergent and transcendent characteristics, furnished a theoretical justification for social reconstruction. The early interactionists were a subset of social reformers oriented to a task that characterized sociologists generally, for the new knowledge generated by the study of society was oriented to, and indeed provided justifications for, social reconstruction.

> Sociology in general and theory in particular developed justifications which demanded that the field be consciously oriented to the social problems phenomena associated especially with the conditions of industrialization, urbanization, and immigration around the turn of the twentieth century (Hinkle 1980, 53). [Hinkle (1980, 23) continues:] This knowledge would permit social progress to become a conscious objective and would facilitate amelioration of those social conditions construed to be "social problems."

The notion that human intelligence, guided by socialization, is an active instrument in remaking the self and the world presupposes that individuals can make and remake themselves. This assumption was in stark contrast to biological determinism and instinct theory, the prevailing perspective on the nature of human nature in the early decades of the twentieth century, which implied passivity, fatalism, and resignation to people's lot in life and their inability to change their lives for the better. If human behavior and achievements were limited by biology and instincts, if human intelligence did not have the capacity to adapt to a changing environment, then social intervention through reform and education to socially reconstruct society was scientifically unsound and politically bankrupt.

The nature/nurture debate—the intellectual struggle between biological determinism and socialization, of which symbolic interactionism was a part—emerged within the context of the social transformations occurring in the late-nineteenth-century United States, primarily the influx of eastern European immigration. Some who were Progressives, such as E. A. Ross and John Commons, were more interested in social control and were also hereditarians. Development of the SI perspective on human nature was complex and emerged slowly, at first in the works of William James, who had concepts of free will and indeterminacy, but who also adhered to instinct theory and only late in life came to advocate for social reform. The emerging perspective advanced with the work of Baldwin, Cooley, and Thomas; it then advanced, much more profoundly, in the works of Dewey and Mead. Their efforts were to develop a perspective that thoroughly demonstrated the social basis and indeterminant nature of behavior and human nature.

Theories of Human Nature and Theories of the State

A theory of human nature provides theoretical justification for a theory of the state. In the nineteenth century, Herbert Spencer could argue that philanthropic and governmental interventionism was a waste of effort because the lot or fate of a human being is sealed in his or her anatomy. From his perspective on human nature, an anti-interventionist state is valid, though, of course, his premises were unsound. What theorists of human nature believed had much to do with what they saw. What they saw was the wretched condition of humanity brought about by social transformation.

The city slums and poverty influenced the hereditarians' argument that it was nature that was dominant in contributing to intelligence and poverty. It was a dialectical outgrowth among their interpretation of those social conditions, their political commitment to eugenics, and their conceptualizations. Beginning with James, but with strong statements by Baldwin, Cooley, Thomas, and, especially, Dewey and Mead, it was argued that nurture, the primary group, peer groups, significant others and the generalized other, and culture were central in the emergence of a person's self and mind. It was the interpretation of those social changes, along with opposing political commitments, that affected the conceptualization of human nature leading to the nature/nurture debate.

Social policy consequences would follow in the wake of each interpretation of human nature. The major thrust of the symbolic interactionists' response to hereditarian, determinant, and instinct reasoning comprised concepts that formulated a socialization perspective. Socialization was, at one time, a very political perspective. The symbolic interactionists' arguments were that all people were capable of learning, that all people could become citizens, that all people could participate in a democracy, that all people can be socialized to the prevailing culture. Today we take this for granted, but in the early decades of the twentieth century, to assume that eastern and southern Europeans had the same human nature as Anglo Americans, that they could become human through the very same processes that everyone else did, was a political and fiercely contested notion. The interactionist argument was that there is an indissoluble connection between society and self. Society makes or constitutes human beings as human beings make or constitute society; one does not exist in independence of the other. For the interactionists, even if one is a hermit, one takes society with one mentally, for action will always be based on a conversation of significant gestures with others, that is, thinking, deliberating, and forming plans of action with reference to significant others or the generalized other. Such minded behavior is inescapably social and the defining character of the human being.

Thus, through a sociology of knowledge model that reviews the dialectical interplay among social context, Progressive politics, the particular intersections of biography and history for the interactionists, and the conceptualization process, one is able to understand why interactionism emerged when it did, why it took one direction and not another, why it developed the set of concepts that it did. Directly out of the nature/nurture debate, the interactionists constructed an image of people's situation in the world as continuously evolving through adaptation by adjustive responses to the environment and others, which led to the emergent perspective on self and mind—a new perspective on human nature. Biology, culture, or the situation did not determine action or behavior, for there is a dialectical relationship among the situation, our definition of the situation, and our adjustive response or social behavior. This ability to define the situation embeds indeterminacy into all social action and allows for novel behavior. One's social behavior in a situation because one can take the role of many significant others as well as the generalized other, is probabilistic rather than determined by culture, biology, or social structure. The challenge the interactionists took was to establish the indissoluble connection between human beings and their social surroundings, that human beings are primarily social beings with emergent selves and minds that empower them to transcend the determinist claims of both biology and culture. We are not born human, we become human.

To summarize: The interactionists' interpretation of the social changes transforming America led to their Progressive views. Their Progressive views issued in their call for social reconstruction through education. Influenced by the social context background and Progressive politics, symbolic interactionism emerged directly out of the nature/nurture debate with a perspective on human nature that would support melioristic intervention and offer an alternative to biological determinism and instinct theory. The social conditions and the Progressive era politics of the times—working in dialectical fashion—led interactionists to reassess the nature of human nature and formulate a socialization perspective that is generally accepted in social science today. Thus, the concepts of symbolic interactionism are tied in, embedded directly, in the social and political context of that time.

3

William James and James Mark Baldwin

William James

It is proposed here that William James's contribution to SI, while acknowledged, is underutilized.[1] James's contribution, his concepts, are richer and more numerous than textbooks suggest. Even the most significant SI tenet, that people respond to objects on the basis of the meaning that they have for them, is to be found first in James.

One of the reasons for the inadequate treatment may be that many interactionists have not fully examined James's work. Even more to the point, James's shortened version of the two-volume *Principles of Psychology* (1890), entitled *Psychology: Briefer Course* (1892), is not mentioned in the major texts. In the foreword to the 1984 publication of *The Works of William James*, Frederick H. Burkhardt, general editor, has drawn scholars' attention to its advanced thought, and therefore my rationale for including this work to represent James's psychology. "James added important new material, made a number of revisions, and developed some concepts, like the famous 'stream of consciousness,' more fully, so that it represents James's latest thinking in the field" (Burkhardt 1984, v).

After a brief introduction to the tradition of functional psychology that James came from, I explore his key concepts. I mean by key concepts exclusively those that contributed to the development of SI. Needless to say, William James was a profound thinker who had many insights on arguments not related to SI.

Functional Psychology

James was an adherent of the principles of functional psychology. This perspective germinated from the psychology of capacities or individual differences.

25

In America the leader was J. McKeen Cattell, who had been "a student in Wundt's laboratory, [and] who had also worked with Francis Galton" (Curti 1980, 202). Cattell's coworkers were social scientists such as H. H. Goddard, Lewis Terman, and, later, E. L. Thorndike, among others. Functionalism sought to measure individual differences in the development of functions that help one to adapt to one's environment; functions that, according to Curti (1980, 202-3), would increase humans' ability to survive in an evolving world.

> Based on biological evolutionary theory, functionalism regarded mental activities, conscious and unconscious alike, as a continuing, dynamic adjustment on the part of the organism to the demands of life. With the assumption that the needs of the organism were met by sense perception, mental images, emotions, and thinking, functionalists tried to find at what stage in human development the need for each became sufficiently pressing to account for the appearance of a partial process or function. Functionalism thus emphasized motor activity in the ongoing search for adjustment to changing situations.

How individuals *adjust* to their environment, not how they are determined by it, was at the heart of James's early work. The social changes transforming America after the Civil War led functional psychologists to conceptualizations concerning the question of how individuals can adjust to the often overwhelming shock of rapid social change.

James's concern with how an individual makes a decision was to form the basis, for example, of Dewey's deliberation, Mead's taking the role of others, and of Thomas's definition of the situation. James argued against the simplistic associationist pain-pleasure psychology of decision making, advancing instead an argument in which consciousness was at the center of decision making (Curti 1980, 204). He was opposed to the "reflex-arc" concept or any "theory that reduced mental phenomena to electrical impulses" (Curti 1980, 205). He maintained that "interest and attention" and a "thought or idea" would intervene in any stimulus-response process (Curti 1980, 205). Ideas were the instruments that were to guide human beings in adapting to their environment. James thereby provided the beginning of a nonmechanistic, nonreductionistic conceptualization of human behavior, that is, the social basis of minded activity.

> An idea was not an abstraction but rather a self-conscious, animated part of a functional process of adaptation. Put still differently, mind was to be regarded not as the sum of sensations, feelings, and conations, not as an atomistic melange, but as a dynamic, organic, purposeful, and above all selective process *engaging* the whole being. (Curti 1980, 206; emphasis in the original)

Without a doubt, this view held by James provided the theoretical basis for transcending determinism. Note also the connection between the notion that an idea, or thought, helps us adapt to the environment and the pragmatic conception of truth. An idea, for James, was true if it paid, or had "cash value," that is, if it helped us cope with the environment. A true idea is one that will bring us success in our engagement with the world. Thus the pragmatic theory of truth may almost be called the evolutionary theory of truth: that is true that helps us adapt to an evolving world. James's major concepts, which are foundational to the perspective of SI, are now summarized.

Mind

The influence of Darwinian evolution on James is evident in James's conceptualization of mind. The intellectual journey to the *social* interpretation of humankind begins with his analysis of mind, or minded behavior, or what is now usually called self-reflexivity.

Michael M. Sokal, a James scholar, has stated: "for James, the mind—or consciousness, or thought—was to be studied as part of nature, with a focus on how it helped the human organism live in the world" (Sokal 1984, xii). The mind qualitatively advanced humans' adaptive capacity in helping them survive in the struggle for existence. Consequently, the stimulus-response model of human behavior was, for James, profoundly inadequate.

James explicitly refers to the human capacity for minded, purposeful activity as a product of evolution: "*mental life is teleological*; that is to say, that our various ways of feeling and thinking have grown to be what they are because of their utility in shaping our *reaction* on the outer world" (James 1984, 11; emphasis in the original). James also stipulates, in a dialectical manner, that that world, or environment, influences individuals. "*Mental facts cannot be properly studied apart from the physical environment of which they take cognizance.* Mind and world in short have been evolved together, and in consequence are something of a mutual fit" (James 1984, 11; emphasis in the original).

Thus, the human being and the environment are the coevolving result of a dialectical process of interaction, or as James put it, "special interactions between the outer order and the order of consciousness" (James 1984, 11). Each human faculty is a product of the process of evolution, of interaction between the human species and the environment. This process of interaction evolves human faculties to the point where they provide an adaptive function, which increases human survivability. "Our inner faculties are *adapted* in advance to the features of the world in which we dwell, adapted, I mean, so as to secure our safety and prosperity in its midst" (James 1984, 11; emphasis in the original).

Because of the human capacity for minded behavior, James insisted that psychology become a Darwinian natural science, concerned with the way human beings adapt to their environment and function in the world (Sokal 1984, xxiv). Such a science, he held, required a unique method of inquiry into human consciousness. As do many contemporary interactionists, he rejected the use of laboratory experiments for such inquiry (although, it must be emphasized, not for physiological studies).[2] James, in commenting on reaction-time experiments "constantly stressed how artificial the experiments were and how little they had to do with the way individuals actually thought" (Sokal 1984, xxiv). Decades later, both his Darwinian approach and his strictures against experimental study of minded behavior, would lead, at the University of Chicago, to a new model of human nature and a new method of studying human consciousness, namely, participant observation.

Stream of Consciousness

James's conception of mind as a "stream of consciousness" also strengthened the emerging reconceptualization of human behavior. For him, consciousness is an active teleological faculty, a continuous process, not a jointed, sporadic activity. As James (1984, 145; emphasis in the original) argued, "A 'river' or a 'stream' are the metaphors by which it is most naturally described. *Let us call it the stream of thought, of consciousness, or of subjective life.*"

Thus, humans are not simply reactive beings who respond directly to stimuli, but are constantly *active* in pursuit of both short-range and long-term goals. Moreover, the mind is active in creating the environment to which the individual adapts. The same objective environment can affect us differently at disparate times because *"consciousness is in constant change"* (James 1984, 141; emphasis in the original). Thus there is a symbolic nature to objects. *"There is no proof that an incoming current ever gives us just the same bodily sensations twice. What is got twice is the same OBJECT"* (James 1984, 142; emphasis and capitalization in the original). Thus, because consciousness is constantly changing, there is a "different way in which the same things look and sound and smell at different distances and under different circumstances" (James 1984, 142).

Not only does the environment influence us differently at different times, depending on our constantly changing consciousness but also, James pointed out, the environment is perceived differently by different people. Here James anticipates the concept of social worlds. "It would probably astound each of them beyond measure to be let into his neighbor's mind and to find how different the scenery there was from his own" (James 1984, 154). This view, of course, greatly influenced other interactionists, especially Cooley, who held that social life was mental.

According to James (1984, 154; emphasis in the original), the mind, or consciousness, thus plays an active role in selecting its environment. *"Consciousness is always interested more in one part of its object than in another, and welcomes and rejects, or chooses, all the while it thinks."* This describes the phenomenon of selective attention, and as a corollary, a selected environment. James became the first interactionist to argue that the teleologically active mind constructs its world.

Perception

In James's argument for an active mind that selectively attends to objects, one sees an embryonic formulation of the interactionist tenet that people respond to objects on the basis of the meaning those objects have for them. For James, we attend to objects on the basis of our interest in them. The importance of this canon to interactionism warrants quoting James in detail. "One of the most extraordinary facts of our life is that, although we are besieged at every moment by impressions from our whole sensory surface, we notice so very small a part of them" (James 1984, 192).

> We notice only those sensations which are signs to us of *things* which happen practically or aesthetically to interest us, to which we therefore give substantive names, and which we exalt to this exclusive status of independence and dignity. But in itself, apart from my interest, a particular dustwreath on a windy day is just as much or as little deserves an individual name, as my own body does. (James 1984, 155; emphasis in the original)

> The sum total of our impressions never enters into our *experience* consciously so called. . . . [But those impressions which do enter our experience] are those which are said to "interest" us at the time; and thus that selective character of our attention. (James 1984, 192-93; emphasis in the original)

> If one must have a single name for the condition upon which the impulsive and inhibitive quality of objects depends, one had better call it their *interest*. [W]hat-we-attend-to and what-interests-us are synonymous terms. (James 1984, 384; emphasis in the original)

The world that is out there is a social world, that is, "a world of objects thus individualized by our mind's selective industry" (James 1984, 156). The phrase "selective character of our attention" or, for short, selective attention, is to be duly credited to James.

Selective Attention and Selected Environment

Human beings thus live in a social, symbolic, phenomenological, and selected environment. Experience of the world that is actually out there is different for each one of us depending on what social objects interest us. "A thing may be present to a man a hundred times, but if he persistently fails to notice it, it cannot be said to enter into his experience. We are all seeing flies, moths, and beetles by the thousand, but to whom, save an entomologist, do they say anything distinct?" (James 1984, 156). The entomologist notices them, or selectively attends to them, because they interest him. Thus it is implicit in James's thought to say that we can tell the meaning that flies and moths have for the entomologist by the way he or she responds to them, that is, with interest. For the rest of us, flies and moths have no interest, and thus the meaning of our inattention.

James is not suggesting that the world is so different to all of us that order and patterned behavior are absent. He argued that cultural consensus exerted influence on what was of human interest. "Taking human experience in a general way, the choosings of different men are to a great extent the same. The race as a whole largely agrees as to what it shall notice and name" (James 1984, 158). Thus he recognized the existence of a normative order, that social norms help to shape what has interest, or meaning, to humans.

Emergent Behavior

Another argument, albeit implied, is derived from James's concepts so far: that behavior is characteristically an emergent, indeterminant, and situated process. Selectively attending to objects on the basis of our interest entails the notion that human beings live in a symbolic environment, one in which their behavior can readily change since consciousness and their situation in the world are in a dialectical process of flux. "But the whole feeling of reality, the whole sting and excitement of our voluntary life, depends on our sense that in it, things are *really being decided* from one moment to another, and that it is not the dull rattling-off of a chain that was forged innumerable ages ago" (James 1984, 209; emphasis in the original). Thus, humans have the ability to modify their behavior on the basis of past experience and innovative thinking. All of which leads to the conclusion that behavior is characteristically an emergent, and not a determined, predictable, and static response.

The Self

James's conception of the self laid the foundation for subsequent interactionist self-theory (Collier, Minton, and Reynolds 1991, 65). He developed a fecund theory of the self that comprised notions of the self as subject and object, as knower and known, and as both I and Me. Let us begin with his view of the three constituent "Me"s, which included the material Me, the social Me, and the spiritual Me (James 1968, 41).

The material Me, according to James, consisted of one's body and clothing, one's immediate family, one's home and accumulated property. But the material Me was also bound up with James's conception of instincts, as he held that an "instinctive impulse drives us to collect property; and the collections thus made become, with different degrees of intimacy, parts of our empirical selves" (James 1968, 42). Certainly, James's view of the material Me derives from his brilliant insights into the complexity of selves in an acquisitive, possession-oriented society. Certainly no adult who has experienced, or has known others who have experienced, the personal loss of a loved one, friend, or sentimental and valued property would discredit the argument. "There are few men who would not feel personally annihilated if a life-long construction of their hands or brains were suddenly swept away" (James 1968, 42). This profound understanding goes a long way to explain the desolation or general depression many experience when overwhelmed by personal loss, the emotions that are normally associated with bereavement.[3]

> Although it is true that a part of our depression at the loss of possessions is due to our feeling that we must now go without certain goods that we expected the possessions to bring in their train, yet in every case there remains, over and above this, a sense of the shrinkage of our personality, a partial conversion of ourselves to nothingness. (James 1968, 42)

James's conceptualization of the material Me reflects the beginnings (despite the recourse to instincts) of the shift away from a purely biological and psychological image of human beings to a social one: the self becomes conceived as much by its social inheritance as by its biological and psychological inheritance.

This movement toward a sociological conception of self was made more explicit in the concept of the social Me. Anticipating Goffman's impression-management frame of reference—as well as Cooley's looking-glass self—the social Me is the desire to receive recognition from those we encounter. Linked with this aspect of the self was James's formulation of the multiple social self concept: "a man has as *many social selves as there are individuals who recognize him* and carry an image of him in their mind" (James 1970, 374; emphasis in the original). James's (1970, 374; emphasis in the original) following statement, however, constitutes a clearer emphasis on the *group* sources of one's social selves:

> We may practically say that he has as many different social selves as there are distinct *groups* of persons about whose opinion he cares. He generally shows a different side of himself to each of these different groups. Many a youth who is demure enough before his parents and teachers, swears and swaggers like a pirate among his "tough" young friends. We do not show ourselves to our children as to our club-companions, to our customers as to the laborers we employ, to our own masters and employers as to our intimate friends. From this there results what practically is a division of the man into several selves; and this may be a discordant splitting, as where one is afraid to let one set of his acquaintances know him as he

is elsewhere; or it may be a perfectly harmonious division of labor, as where one tender to his children is stern to the soldiers or prisoners under his command.

James here anticipated Goffman's concept of "audience segregation" as well as the sociological concept of social roles. Further, he anticipated some of the work of Simmel; and, it can be argued, Mead's "generalized other" (albeit as a multiple phenomenon). The above quotation certainly makes plain that human behavior is influenced by those around one, that others exercise, in a sense, social control, and that one must take others into account when acting, that one must be able to assess social meaning.

At this point it is appropriate to quote Sheldon Stryker (1980, 23), who points out: "along with conceptualizing the social self as a derivative of relationships with others, James prepares the way for a view of self which emphasizes its multifaceted character. And he prepares the way for viewing that multifaceted self as the product of a heterogeneously organized society." James's conception of a multiple self does not, however, completely abandon the notion of the self as unitary. Conceiving some selves as more important in the individual's life than others, he held that "some degree of unity among a person's selves is achieved through their hierarchical ordering, with self-feelings and action tendencies being greatest for those selves high in the hierarchy" (Turner, Beeghly, and Poivers 1989).

The spiritual Me (the least important component, for our present purposes, of the triadic self) is our self at our most conscious reflection, or better, during our most conscious activity. As James points out, however, an important emotional element is present in this aspect of self: "The more *active-feeling* states of consciousness are thus the more central portions of the spiritual Me" (James 1968, 43; emphasis in the original). This feelings element of the self was further developed, of course, by Cooley.

These three components of the Me reflect James's trend away from conceiving individuals as solely biological and psychological beings and toward a view as social beings, as ones affected by the society in which they are socialized. Some of James's notions would not be accepted by contemporary interactionists, but the point is to underscore the direction in which James was leading a later generation of social psychologists.

James's concept of the I is, also, similar to the one later expanded upon by Mead. It is an active-self aspect, the conscious agent of our actions. "It is that which at any given moment *is* conscious, whereas the Me is only one of the things which it is conscious *of*" (James 1968, 46; emphasis in the original). An active I is one capable of change, a tenet that further moves us away from conceiving the self in static, biological terms.

The Social Basis of Self-Esteem

James also postulated a self-feeling that, as in Cooley's looking-glass self, can be one of pride or mortification. Which of these feelings one experiences at any given time depended on a pragmatic criterion, namely, success in the world: "the normal *provocative* of self-feeling is one's actual success or failure, and the good or bad actual position one holds in the world" (James 1968, 43; emphasis in the original). In fact, James adopted a formula for self-esteem:

$$\text{Self-Esteem} = \frac{\text{Success}}{\text{Pretensions}}$$

"Such a fraction may be increased as well by diminishing the denominator as by increasing the numerator" (James 1968, 45). We measure our worthiness by our success and status in the world. Even though those measures may be personal ones, society still will measure us with its own standards; therefore, our own concept of worthiness is bound to be influenced by the norms of society. Self-esteem cannot but have a social basis.

Recognizing that aspirations are inculcated through a normative order that emphasizes achievement, James began the understanding of the social construction of both the self and self-esteem.[4]

Instinct

Like most functional psychologists, James put forward the notion of instincts. William McDougall in his *Introduction to Social Psychology* (1908), developed the most elaborate instinctivist theory of behavior; yet, "the 20th-century psychological discussions of the role of inherited dispositions in behavior begins with the views of William James" (Krantz and Allen 1967, 326). James's (1984, 339) definition was: "Instinct is usually defined as the faculty of acting in such a way as to produce certain ends, without foresight of the ends, and without previous education in the performance." Instincts are not learned, they are genetically inherited, predetermined actions characteristic of the entire species. Of course, this undermines cultural variability in behavior, which comparative ethnographers would soon establish.

James's conception of instincts, however, was especially complex. For him (1984, 340) "every instinct is an impulse," and "man has a far greater variety of *impulses* than any lower animal" (James 1984, 342; emphasis in the original). Human instincts cease to be "blind" because of experience and self-reflexivity, that is, "owing to man's memory, power of reflection, and power of inference"

(James 1984, 342); thus, "his resultant actions will be much modified if the instincts combine with experience" (James 1984, 343).

In human beings, a purely instinctive response is also blocked by the fact that, as James asserts: "*Nature implants contrary impulses to act on many classes of things*" (James 1984, 344; emphasis in the original). These contrary impulses, he goes on to say, "lead to a life of hesitation and choice, an intellectual life" (James 1984, 345).

James also listed "two principles of non-uniformity," that can suppress instincts: the inhibition of instincts by habits, and the transitory character of instincts (James 1984, 345). The first principle states: "A habit, once grafted on an instinctive tendency, restricts the range of the tendency itself" (James 1984, 346). The second principle is that "*Many instincts ripen at a certain age and then fade away*" (James 1984, 348; emphasis in the original). James (1984, 349) argued that a modification of innate tendencies by habits, plasticity, and self-reflexivity was ongoing.

> Turning to human instincts, we see the law of transiency corroborated on the widest scale by the alternation of different interests and passions as human life goes on. With the child, life is all play and fairy-tales and learning the external properties of "things"; with the youth, it is bodily exercises of a more systematic sort, novels of the real world, boon-fellowships and song, friendship and love, nature, travel and adventure, science and philosophy; with the man, ambition and policy, acquisitiveness, responsibility to others, and the selfish zest of the battle of life.

If we read the above passage with the idea of socialization in mind, one might agree with the argument that James is implicitly describing socialization, but under the dominant intellectual trend to describe human behavior in instinctual terms. In any event, the above view was later reformulated by others into the idea of socialization throughout the life course.

James (1984, 352) further elaborates his view on the relationship among instincts, habits, and human behavior.

> In a perfectly-rounded development every one of these instincts would start a habit towards certain objects and inhibit a habit towards certain others. Usually this is the case; but, in the one-sided development of civilized life, it happens that the timely age goes by in a sort of starvation of objects, and the individual then grows up with gaps in his psychic constitution which future experiences can never fill. Compare the accomplished gentleman with the poor artisan or trades-man of a city: during the adolescence of the former, objects appropriate to his growing interests, bodily and mental, were offered as fast as the interests awoke, and, as a consequence, he is armed and equipped at every angle to meet the world. Sport came to the rescue and completed his education where real things were lacking. He has tasted of the essence of fighter, talker, dandy, man of affairs, etc., all in one. Over the city poor boy's youth no such golden opportunities were hung, and in his manhood no de-

sires for most of them exist. Fortunate it is for him if gaps are the only anomalies his instinctive life presents; perversions are too often the fruit of his unnatural bringing-up.

Sociologists today are concerned with the opportunity structure, or differential life chances, associated with class socialization. This passage from James, minus the instinct argument, could pass for an explanation of social behavior based on class-differentiated socialization; but James argues that the noticeable differences in social class behavior are due to opportunities to cultivate habits from instincts. Again, the important point is to discern the implicit contribution of James's thought to later sociological theory, which is exactly what later interactionists did.

We now turn to the concepts that overrode James's account of a purely instinctual human nature, habit and plasticity.

Habit and Plasticity

Through the process of evolution, our bodies evolved a plasticity to help us adapt and survive: *"the phenomena of habit in living beings are due to the plasticity of the organic materials of which their bodies are composed. Plasticity, then, in the widest sense of the word, means the possession of a structure weak enough to yield to an influence, but strong enough not to yield all at once"* (James 1984, 126; emphasis in the original).

This plasticity provides the physiological matrix of habits that guide much human behavior. "Each relatively stable phase of equilibrium in such a structure is marked by what we may call a new set of habits" (James 1984, 126). The concepts of plasticity and habit formation attacked the argument that biology and heredity are overpowering (or, even later, Freud's dictum that anatomy is destiny). What it means to human beings to possess plasticity is that we have some control over our lives; we are not merely passive—though we do possess a structure weak enough to yield—but active, volitional, able to respond.

James formulated his concept of plasticity in response to the biological and geographical determinism of Herbert Spencer (Meltzer, Petras, and Reynolds 1975, 7). The social order is not seen by James as oppressive, but the mechanism through which the creativity of human beings could be expressed (Meltzer, Petras, and Reynolds 1975, 7). The environment impinges on us; yet, the plasticity of our organic materials helps us to form habits so that we can adapt to that environment. "Habits are due to the plasticity of materials to outward agents" (James 1984, 127). Habits also increase our adaptive capacity so that we can act in the world without constantly thinking of what we are doing or, as James said, *"habits diminish the conscious attention with which our acts are performed"* (James 1984, 129; emphasis in the original). James (1984, 129) argues, then, that habits are unreflective action that develop as a part of learning; once learned they help us to act in the world without relearning everything de novo.

> Whilst we are learning to walk, to ride, to swim, skate, fence, write, play, or sing,
> we interrupt ourselves at every step by unnecessary movements and false notes.
> When we are proficient, on the contrary, the results follow not only with the very
> minimum of muscular action requisite to bring them forth, but they follow from a
> single instantaneous "cue."

Habits, then, are unreflective, but not necessarily mechanical, action; they allow
for situational adaptation. Camic (1986, 1046-47) constructs a definition of habit
at the higher end of the continuum that early psychologists, James among them,
were developing.

> In place of the idea of a fixed, mechanical reaction to stimuli, it has been held that
> habit creates a stable inner core that affords immunity from external sensations and
> impetuous appetites; that it is not by such stimuli as these, but by the ego itself, that
> habit is called into play and allowed to proceed, with leeway for situational adapta-
> tion; and that, however much habitual action may be removed from "hesitation and
> reflection," such action is still no more "mechanical" than action of the same type
> that emerges from wholly reflective processes.

Habit thus furnishes the human being with the possibility of learning and choice.

A continuum of conceptual development of habit can be seen from the biological sense of habit to the more advanced social uses of the concept, that is, from its
use in biology to its use in psychology to its use in sociology.[5] A close reading of
James's own description of habit and habitual action provides a theoretical basis
for thinking about influences, other than the biological, on human behavior.
Though it was Mead who later developed the concept of socialization through
role-taking, it is in James, to some degree, where the intellectual origins of the
socialization concept lie.

Is Socialization Implicit in the Concept of Habit?

In salient and subtle ways, one function of socialization is the social reproduction
of the class system. Our society has class-differentiated institutions of socialization, the schools serving as the most conspicuous example. Upper-class schoolchildren are socialized to become different social beings than are lower-class
children; indeed, they attend different institutions of schooling that are vastly
different social worlds (Kozol, 1991). The existence of private and public schooling, or within a system, the practice of tracking, serves the function of perpetuating social stratification. It is argued that these thoughts are implicit in James's
concept of habit, for James used the concept of habit to explain the social repro-

duction of class and class behavior.

At the lower end of the continuum, James's concept of habit is biologically and physiologically grounded. But the concept of habit formed, in many scholars, a continuum that started with a biological and physiological base but, at its higher end, expanded to social interpretations (Camic 1986, 1045-47). Miners, deck-hands, and fishermen learn to stay in their walks of life because they have been habituated (socialized) to, or as James said, because of habits, which are learned. Part of learning habits (or class socialization), is becoming conscious of your class position and an accompanying self-image and self-esteem, that is, what Cooley later called a looking-glass self.

Learning class-differentiated habits is thus learning to labor, and learning to view and feel about oneself (self-consciousness) in a way that prevents the social strata from mixing. James's theory of habit is thus also a theory of social order and social control. Certain people—for example, classes—have predisposed habits. Thus, habits function (as does socialization) to maintain social order. "Habit is thus the enormous flywheel of society, its most precious conservative agent. It alone is what keeps us all within the bounds of ordinance, and saves the children of fortune from the envious uprisings of the poor" (James 1984, 132-33). And for social control (James 1984, 133):

> It alone prevents the hardest and most repulsive walks of life from being deserted by those brought up to tread therein. It keeps the fisherman and the deckhand at sea through the winter; it holds the miner in his darkness, and nails the countryman to his log-cabin and his lonely farm through all the months of snow; it protects us from invasion by the natives of the desert and the frozen zone. It dooms us all to fight out the battle of life upon the lines of our nurture or our early choice, and to make the best of a pursuit that disagrees, because there is no other for which we are fitted, and it is too late to begin again. It keeps different social strata from mixing.

Habit is what brings the oppressed to tread within certain wretched occupations? Habit is what keeps the social strata from mixing? Habit is what saves the children of fortune from the envious uprising of the poor? James is here contributing to the shift away from biology toward an implicitly sociological understanding of human behavior; however, he has not developed a sociological understanding. For James, habits that had their origins in class differences were insurmountable. "Hardly ever can a youth transferred to the society of his betters unlearn the nasality and other vices of speech bred in him by the association of his growing years" (James 1984, 133). For the person of lower-class origins, "no matter how much money there be in his pocket, can he ever learn to *dress* like a gentleman-born" (James 1984, 133; emphasis in the original). James's notion of habit does not allow for constant self-change, as does the concept of socialization. Habit, at least in terms of class behavior, is "an invisible law, as strong as gravitation" (James 1984, 133).

Today a sociologist might replace habit with differential power—social, economic, and political—as the contributing factor in occupational stratification; power as the force that prevents the social strata from mixing and keeps the children of fortune (by classism, ideology, hegemony, etc., or, if necessary, more drastic means) from the envious, resentful uprisings of the poor. These sociological implications were exactly the ones taken up by later interactionists, especially Mead and Dewey, who were both Chicago Progressives, basing their call for social reconstruction on the nature of human nature.

Yet, outside of James's own class prejudices (he was a member of the upper class), he certainly believed we could acquire new behavior through self-consciously embarking on acquiring new habits. "In the acquisition of a new habit, or the leaving off of an old one, we must take care to *launch ourselves with as strong and decided an initiative as possible*" (James 1984, 134; emphasis in the original). Members of the working class may indeed desire to acquire the habits to improve their social condition, but the opportunity structure constrains such desires. It is lamentable that James did not recognize this, especially when he made the following statement: "It is surprising how soon a desire will die of inanition if it be *never* fed" (James 1984, 135; emphasis in the original).

Although James conceived of habit as an individual phenomenon, and although it is linked to his notion of instincts, what he implicitly described is the power of the normative order in regulating everyday behavior, that there are forces other than the biological that constrain, ones that induce social order and social control; yet habits, dialectically, make choice possible. "Habit could open the door to possible changes of conduct and social relations. His theory enabled James to stress the binding character of habits while opening the way to the possibility of developing new ones by the exercise of attention, choice, will, and persistent repetition" (Curti 1980, 207).

Free Will

Besides arguing that habits arm the individual with the power to transcend instinctual predispositions, James further attenuated his instinctivist views by contending that humans have free will; though, "voluntary movements must be secondary, not primary, functions of our organism" (James 1984, 358). Preceding any act of free will, he held, the human being is in a problematic situation, "that peculiar feeling of inward unrest known as *indecision*" (James 1984, 368; emphasis in the original). Further anticipating interactionist ideas, James (1984, 368-69; emphasis in the original) asserted:

> With the various objects before the attention, we are said to *deliberate*; and when finally the original suggestion either prevails and makes the movement take place, or gets definitively quenched by its antagonists, we are said to *decide*, or to *utter*

our voluntary fiat, in favor of one or the other course.

James has drawn a picture of a very active human being consciously deliberating courses of action. Minded behavior, or self-reflexivity, is constitutive of the human species. For him, mental life is a quintessential human capacity to think, define, interpret, choose, and then act. "The volitional effort lies exclusively within the mental world. The whole drama is a mental drama" (James 1984, 388).

We can discern in his conception of free will part of the Horatio Alger myth of laissez-faire capitalism. This underscores the theme of voluntaristic nominalism that Hinkle and Hinkle (1954) argued was the predominant theme of early sociology. But we must understand James's position within the intellectual context of the times. In providing a voluntaristic corrective to the prevailing hegemony of biological determinism, however, he resorted to a virtually unbounded and unbridled free will. This view, of course, has been displaced by the current conception that the human being experiences both freedom and constraint, in which social behavior constitutes an emergent among structure, power, and action.

James: Determinist or Voluntaristic Nominalist?

H. S. Thayer (1973, 232) speculates on the social sources of James's mutually contradictory ideas. James, who had traveled extensively in Europe, was wedded to two cultures.

> One part is the indigenous, evolving community begun in a wilderness, become colonized, and most of whose organization and mores were (and in very complex ways continue to be) determined by conditions of survival and, in due course, conditions of prosperity on the cleared land or seaport. The other part is the whole imported, variegated, intellectual, moral, and religious European tradition.

Influenced by these contrasting cultures, James's concepts of relatively fixed instincts and habits and of extreme plasticity and free will reflected this diversity. Merle Curti explains James's position: "William James was both an effective champion of the New Psychology and a trenchant critic. His ambivalent and contradictory positions did not greatly trouble him. He preferred to leave paradoxes dangling rather than to resolve them in misleading oversimplifications" (Curti 1980, 203).

Determinism and the Prospect of Science

James knew that the dominant trend in psychology was determinism. His contemporary psychologists also swarmed to positivism because that type of research promoted determinism, and determinism armed psychology so that it could defend itself as a science.[6] In any event, James held, as do present-day Chicago school interactionists, that the positivistic stance of determinism is incapable of dealing with the voluntaristic aspects of human behavior.[7] James's (1984, 392; emphasis in the original) following statement (in which "independent variables" refers to indeterminate elements of behavior) expresses this view.

> [The psychologist] wants to build a *Science*; and a Science is a system of fixed relations. Wherever there are independent variables, there Science stops. So far, then, as our volitions may be independent variables, a scientific psychology must ignore that fact, and treat of them only so far as they are fixed functions. In other words, she must deal with the *general laws* of volition exclusively; with the impulsive and inhibitory character of ideas; with the nature of their appeals to the attention; with the conditions under which effort may arise, etc.; but not with the precise amounts of effort, for these, if our wills be free, are impossible to compute. Psychology will surely never grow refined enough to discover, in the case of any individual's decision, a discrepancy between her scientific calculations and the fact. Her prevision will never foretell, whether the effort be completely predestinate or not, the way in which each individual emergency is resolved.

The rise of research universities provided an important context that led to positivism in the social sciences. Research universities promoted particular models of research, ones that had to "prove" their scientific status. The tag of "science" would help a new discipline institutionalize itself and achieve departmental autonomy over against the natural sciences which were already established and gatekeepers to upstart disciplines (Camic 1986, 1067). Psychology was eager to gain both scientific status and departmental institutionalization and autonomy; therefore, it molded its concepts after those of the most respected disciplines of the times. Thus, "American psychology followed the example of the new European[8] psychology and brought to the study of mental life the concepts and methods of Darwinian biology and experimental physiology—sciences then at the summit of the academic hierarchy" (Camic 1986, 1067).[9] The institutional norms of academic research in the new research universities meant that James's emphasis on the volitional and free-will aspects of behavior (largely unmeasurable, unquantifiable, and unoperationalizable, thus holding no claim to science and research dollars), would be largely ignored by his successors. "The philosophically trained pioneers of psychology left the scene to numbers of specialized researchers determined to push forward the campaign to institutionalize their eminently scientific discipline" (Camic 1986, 1067). Which is precisely why those whom James most influenced were those in sociology, rather than psychology. Cooley, Thomas, Dewey, and Mead advanced the implicit social conceptualization of human nature, and the emphasis on covert, or minded behavior, that James had begun.[10]

The Sociological and Political Implications of the Thought of William James

James's intellectual life span ended before the Progressive era. But James (1984, 393; emphasis in the original) did believe that human effort made a difference in our lives and morality.

> Of course we measure ourselves by many standards. Our strength and our intelligence, our wealth and even our good luck, are things which warm our heart and make us feel ourselves a match for life. But deeper than all such things, and able to suffice unto itself without them, is the sense of the amount of effort which we can put forth. Those are, after all, but effects, products, and reflections of the outer world within. But the effort seems to belong to an altogether different realm, as if it were the substantive thing which we are, and those were but externals which we *carry*.

James (1984, 394) continues that "thus not only our morality but our religion, so far as the latter is deliberate, depend on the effort which we can make."

These implications were drawn out by later interactionists who accepted and advanced James's perspective of a plastic and indeterminant human nature, but who also wedded that perspective on human nature with a progressive politics of social reconstruction. They believed in applying their theory on human nature directly to the type of society that would foster the full potential of all human beings.

Thus, James's contribution to SI is rich. The concept of socialization is implicit, but many others that are hallmarks of interactionism are fully developed: social worlds, selective attention, the social basis of self-esteem, the complexity of the self, the dialectic between environment and human volition, and the notion that consciousness shapes action. Other contributions were that the stimulus-response concept is inadequate and that, given the subjective aspects of human nature, a social scientist cannot rely solely on objective and quantitative methods.

James Mark Baldwin

Baldwin continued, in a much stronger way, arguments to develop a perspective on human nature that opposed conceiving behavior in solely biological and psychological terms. Through Baldwin's works, for the first time in sociology, the person became recognized as a fully social being (Martindale 1960, 317). Society socially constructed human beings (Noble 1967, 79).

Baldwin attacked Herbert Spencer's biological determinism as much for its scientific inadequacy as for its political agenda. Baldwin felt that if Spencer's conception of human nature were taken as true, then it would make futile "all attempts to remake man and society" (Noble 1967, 80). Most important of all, Baldwin was "the American who first gave a complete scientific rationalization to the theses of Progressive Democracy" (Noble 1967, 78).

For Baldwin, Darwinian evolution had bestowed on humankind intelligence, which provided an adaptive capacity to plan rational action, allowing humans to construct their own world (Noble 1967, 83). He used the concept of plasticity, much as did William James, and the concept of novelty, much as did George Herbert Mead later, to articulate this view.

Habit and Accommodation

In *Mental Development in the Child and the Race* (1894/1968), Baldwin advanced James's concept of habit, making it more social psychological than James's psychological and instinctivist conception. Human agency as a concept began to emerge. "What is the least that we can say about an organism's development? Everybody admits that two things must be said: first, it develops by getting habits formed; and second, it develops by new adaptations which involve the breaking up or modification of habits—these latter being called accommodations" (Baldwin 1968, 452).

The individual acts according to habits, but not ones that are innate or based on instincts; rather, the individual develops through habits that are socially learned. This comes to light clearly in Baldwin's (1968, 45) concept of accommodation: "Accommodation is the principle by which an organism comes to adapt itself to more complex conditions of stimulation by performing more complex functions." Basically, accommodation was, for Baldwin, a process of social learning. "Learning to act is just accommodation, nothing more nor less. Speech, tracery, handwriting, pianoplaying, all motor acquisitions, are what accommodation is, i.e., adaptations to more complex conditions" (Baldwin 1968, 455). We become who we are, developing habits, through a process of social learning.

Baldwin's study of the mental growth of the child and its ability to develop through habit and accommodation helped establish a field that became known as genetic psychology (Foote 1970, 325). Baldwin's argument that children develop cognitively through play informed Mead's play-game theory of self-development, the work of Jean Piaget, and such other interactionists as Norman K. Denzin, Spencer Cahill, and William Corsaro.

Suggestion, Imitation, and the Social Person

Continuing with his analysis of how the person develops, Baldwin advanced the concepts of imitation and suggestion. Imitation is a concept that is similar to

Mead's taking the role of the other. We develop selves by incorporating others into our selves, imaginatively. "My sense of myself grows by imitation of you, and my sense of yourself grows in terms of my sense of myself. Both ego and alter are thus essentially social; each is a socius, and each is an imitative creation" (Baldwin 1968, 321). Baldwin (1973, 66) emphasized that imitation is the creative part of self-development, but society, also, has a socializing role.

> The growth of human personality has been found to be pre-eminently a matter of social suggestion. The material from which the child draws is found in the store of accomplished activities, forms, patterns, organizations, etc., which society already possesses. These serve as ready stimulating agencies, loadstones so to speak, to his dawning energies, to draw him ever on in his career of growth into the safe, sound useful network of personal acquisitions and social relationships which the slow progress of the race has set in permanent form. All this he owes, at any rate in the first instance, to society. His business is to be teachable.

This conceptualization of self-development, a dialectical relationship between the individual and the environment, would later inform the concepts of the I and Me by George Herbert Mead. Through imitation and suggestion, Baldwin (1968, 324) argues, the self is constantly changing, constantly being socialized; again, major themes of symbolic interactionism.

> We never outgrow imitation, nor our social obligation to it. Our sense of self is constantly growing richer and fuller as we understand others better,—as we get into social co-operation with them,—and our understanding of them is in turn enriched by the additions which our own private experience makes to the lessons we learn from them.

Baldwin's concepts of imitation and suggestion helped enable a view of the self as independent of biological determinants. The self is an emergent in its dialectical relationship with society. Baldwin furthered the argument that human beings emerge through their interaction with society; that they are thus thoroughly social beings, and only social beings because of society. In the following quotation (Baldwin 1968, 144-45), we recognize a description of self-development that emphasizes socialization, that individuals develop their selves through their intimate social bonds with others, not through something that is innate, or predetermined.

> We have to say, therefore, that the child is born to be a member of society, in the same sense, precisely, that he is born with eyes and ears to see and hear the movements and sounds of the world, and with touch to feel the things of space; and, as I hope to show later in detail, all views of the man as a total creature, a creation, must recognize him not as a single body to act, or to abstain from acting, upon others similarly shut up in similar bodies; but as a soul partly in his own body, partly in

the bodies of others, to all intents and purposes, so intimate is this social bond—a service for which he pays in kind, since we see in his body, considered simply as a physical organism, preparation for the reception of the soul-life, the suggestions of mind and spirit, of those others.

As Baldwin (1968, 148) argued, one becomes a person only through one's interaction with society: "For the infant is an embryo person, a social unit in the process of forming." It takes time to develop, to emerge as a social being, to become human, for one is not these at birth: "For the social life is a late attainment" (Baldwin 1968, 148).

This development of self begins in childhood and goes through phases that anticipate the play and game stages of Mead. In *The Story of the Mind* Baldwin (1910, 16), outlined the developmental process of becoming a social person.

First, the epoch of the rudimentary sense processes, the pleasure and pain process, and simple motor adaptation, called for convenience the "affective epoch": second, the epoch of presentation, memory, imitation, defensive action, instinct, which passes by gradations into, third, the epoch of complex presentation, complex motor coordination, of conquest, of offensive action, and rudimentary volition. These, the second and third together, I should characterize, on the side of consciousness, as the "epoch of objective reference": and, finally, the epoch of thought, reflection, self-assertion, social organization, union of forces, cooperation; the "epoch of subjective reference," which in human history merges into the "social and ethical epoch."

The strong argument of human development, especially the importance of human consciousness, thought, reflection, self-assertion, and social organization, clearly marks a difference from the biological conception of human behavior. The emphasis that the last epoch in childhood development is the social and ethical epoch, that individuals learn to behave in a social environment, is crucial to a developmental and social view of human nature and behavior.

Making a profound change in the conceptualization of the self, from solely a biological and psychological construct to a social one, Baldwin's contribution to the perspective of symbolic interactionism is evident. We are thoroughly social beings because we can develop selves only through imitation and interaction with others. "I have become what I am in part through my sympathy with you and imitation of you" (Baldwin 1968, 325). It is this notion of sympathy with others that Charles Cooley would later expand upon in his concept of human nature.

And, whatever society is, that is bound to influence the type of person one becomes, for any society will circumscribe the types of people one can imitate and interact with. The interactionist tenet that there is an indissoluble connection between self and society is held by Baldwin. Society constitutes human beings, and human beings, through the actions of self and mind, constitute society. Here Baldwin anticipates Mead's view of the development of becoming human through taking the role of the generalized other. Though the notion is somewhat vague, we are developed, constituted, or "realized," according to Baldwin (1968, 467), by incorporating from society a "copy" and then acting back on society.

> The self is realized by taking in "copies" from the world, and the world is enabled to set higher copies only through the constant reactions of the individual self upon it. Morally I am as much a part of society as physically I am a part of the world's fauna; and as my body gets its best explanation from the point of view of its place in a zoological scale, so morally I occupy a place in the social order; and an important factor in the understanding of me is the understanding of it.

Social Heredity

In *Social and Ethical Interpretations in Mental Development* (1897), Baldwin expressed even stronger views on the social nature of human beings and the social nature of human nature than he had in 1894 in *Mental Development in the Child and Race*. Baldwin (1973, 60-61) developed the concept of social heredity.

> It is hereditary in that the child cannot escape it. It is as inexorably his as the color of his eyes and the shape of his nose. He is born into a system of social relationships just as he is born into a certain quality of air. As he grows in body by breathing the one, so he grows in mind by absorbing the other. The influence is as real and as tangible; and the only reason that it is variable in its results upon different individuals is that each individual has his physical heredity besides, and the outcome is always the outcome of the two factors,—natural temperament and social heredity.

Through the concept of social heredity Baldwin views behavior as having both a biological and a social basis. But he goes on to challenge the notion of instincts in people.

> The influence of social heredity is, in a large sense, inversely as the amount and definiteness of natural heredity. By this is meant that the more a person or an animal is destined to learn in his lifetime, the less fully equipped with instincts and special organic adaptations must he be at birth. (Baldwin 1973, 61)

With Baldwin's minimization of instincts and his emphasis on learning, we see how much he advanced the social view of human nature since William James. Baldwin did not, however, abandon biology; he clearly believed that the human being was a result of both "causes." Baldwin felt that the current debate was emphasizing one or the other to the detriment of an alternative view: *"that most of man's equipment is due to both causes working together"* (Baldwin 1973, 68; emphasis in the original). With this insight, Baldwin became the first major social psychologist of the twentieth century to articulate the dialectical relationship between biology and society.

Notes

1. The leading text expounding the principles of SI, *Social Psychology*, by Lindesmith, Strauss, and Denzin (1991), mentions James only three times. The same can be said for Hewitt's *Self and Society* (1991). The Karp and Yoels text, *Symbols, Selves, and Society* (1979) does not mention James at all, while the Charon text *Symbolic Interactionism* (1995) makes two references on the social self. Sheldon Stryker's text (1980) discusses James's concept of self and habit. Reynolds (1993) also limits his attention to the same concepts. The Meltzer, Petras, and Reynolds text, *Symbolic Interactionism* (1975), confined their focus to the concepts of habit, instinct, and self. Intellectual historians such as Curti (1980) have paid heed to James, but they have not been adequately familiar with the SI tradition to which James contributed.

2. "[James] kept working the facts of physiological psychology into his lectures on physiology, and in 1875, when he first offered his course on physiological psychology, he actually had a two-room demonstrational laboratory set up, where his students performed some of the psychological experiments that were regarded as basic" (Boring 1963, 162).

3. The above experience is certainly a psychological phenomenon, but we believe the argument that most social psychologists today would accept is that it has a sociological element as well. Socialization to accumulate private property and the view that a person of worth is a person of wealth is, we believe, a powerful explanation of why depressive states may overwhelm us when we suffer a loss of property. We may feel we are nothing when we suffer loss of property because we have been indoctrinated to feel and believe that we are only something, somebody, a fairly important somebody (a big deal) if we possess wealth and/or power. An ego importuning us to acquire property is the result of enculturation to a materialistic, possession-oriented social order. But, of course, the loss of others is more universal and psychological; grief is universal in all cultures and societies.

4. One example of James's influence is Robert Merton's notion of crime causation. Merton argued that criminals had the same aspirations as everyone else but that because they did not have the means to achieve those ends, criminals resorted to contranormative means to achieve normative ends. A low self-esteem based on failure to achieve aspirations set by societal standards provided the motivation to crime.

5. Eventually, the concept of habit would be dropped by sociologists because it was too intertwined with biology and psychology. A solely sociological interpretation of humankind was necessary if sociology was going to establish its own institutionalization and autonomy (Camic 1986, 1069-73).

6. As Edwin G. Boring explains, some researchers equate science with quantification. *"Quantification is favored by the desire of investigators to claim the prestige of science for their research.* Especially has this motivation operated among the psychologists, insecure because of their unscientific heritage from philosophy, and thus repeatedly insisting on the scientific validity of their new experimental psychology" (Boring 1963, 156: emphasis in the original). Interactionism was able to eschew determinism, sciencemongering, quantifi-

cation, and a concern with prediction and control, until the arrival of Manford H. Kuhn and his Iowa school of self-theory.

7. What constitutes an adequate methodology for studying human behavior is still highly debatable. For example, that debate erupted again in 1973; see Joan Huber (1973).

8. European influenced, yes; but, one country in particular. "Up to the end of the century America was consciously copying Germany, determined to make psychology physiological and experimental, energetically concerned with the founding of laboratories and the accumulation of psychological apparatus, crossing the ocean to get its doctor's degrees—mostly from Wundt's *psychologisches Institut* at Leipzig" (Boring 1963, 159; emphasis in the original).

9. Wilhelm Wundt definitely wanted his physiological psychology thought of as a science. "Using Fechner's empirical methods of studying perception, Wundt proposed to build metaphysics on a solid basis, thus making philosophy a science. To preserve his scientific status, he was forced not only to carry out a revolution in philosophy by replacing logical speculation with empirical research, but also to widely advertise the fact that he was in a different kind of enterprise than the traditional philosophers" (Ben-David and Collins 1966, 463).

10. James went to Germany, too, but because of personal misfortune did not study under Wundt and therefore may have been less influenced to make his psychology a science, influencing sociologists instead (Boring 1963, 162).

4

Charles Horton Cooley, W. I. Thomas, and John Dewey

Charles Horton Cooley

Charles Cooley is largely remembered for three major concepts: the looking-glass self, primary groups, and sympathetic introspection. Throughout his work runs the theme of antideterminism. "From the German social idealist Albert Eberhard Friedrich Schäffe he took the idea that society could be free from deterministic control by an external environment while it was at the same time the formative setting for human nature" (Curti 1980, 240). Cooley also greatly advanced analysis of the relationship between the individual and society, holding that they are inseparable.

Sympathetic Introspection

Sympathetic introspection is a methodological tool or, better, mental manipulation by which one imaginatively puts oneself in an individual's place or frame of reference in order to comprehend better the meaning of an individual's behavior. This is how we obtain an understanding about others. It is at once both subjective and idealistic. Cooley's epistemological idealism holds that social reality is ultimately mental, a work of the imagination, a construct that the mind is generally developing as a system (Hinkle 1967, 8). One of the assumptions of pragmatism, and later, SI, is that reality is shaped by the knower. Reality can only be reality-as-known by the individual perceiver. Thus, Cooley formulated his concepts within the domain assumptions of pragmatism. What we know of others originates from how able we are imaginatively to "sink into" another's frame of reference, under-

49

stand his or her subjectivity or mentality. Sympathetic introspection is analogous
to what W. I. Thomas called one's "definition of the situation," what Max Weber
called "*verstehen*," and what G. H. Mead called "taking the role of the other." Its
purpose is to try to comprehend the other. Cooley (1967a, 69) argues the result is
social knowledge or sympathy.

> [It is] developed from contact with the minds of other men, through communica-
> tion, which sets going a process of thought and sentiment similar to theirs and
> enables us to understand them by sharing their states of mind. This I call personal
> or social knowledge. It might also be described as sympathetic, or, in its more
> active forms, as dramatic, since it is apt to consist of a visualization of behavior
> accompanied by imagination of corresponding mental processes.

Cooley (1967a, 71) maintained that sympathy provides us with the inner experience we need for socialization, supplying the means by which we come to know
others and thereby develop a self.

> Every response we make is a step in our education, teaching us to act, to think, and
> to feel a little more humanly. Our brain and nerve complexes develop in the sense
> of our social surroundings. And at the same time our consciousness takes account
> of this inward experience and proceeds to ascribe it to other people in similar
> conditions. Thus by a single process we increase our understanding of persons, of
> society, and of ourselves.

We come to know others through sympathy, and we also can plan how to act, how
to adjust to any particular situation. Our behavior is social because we must take
others into account before we act. As Cooley (1967a, 72) argues,"What you know
about a man consists, in part, of flashes of vision as to what he would do in particular situations, how he would look, speak and move; it is by such flashes that you
judge whether he is brave or a coward, hasty or deliberate, honest or false, kind or
cruel, and so on."

In arguing that we can know others only if we incorporate a sympathetic understanding, Cooley is also attacking Watsonian behaviorism.Watson had made great
strides in challenging the hereditarian argument of an innate human nature. He
also argued in favor of limiting statements about human beings to overt activity, to
behavior. Cooley's response is that we must study people differently from our
study of animals. "We know animals mostly as a peculiarly lively kind of thing.
On the other hand, although our knowledge of people is likewise behavioristic, it
has no penetration, no distinctively human insight, unless it is sympathetic also"
(Cooley 1967a, 72). Studies of acts alone cannot give us a complete understanding
of human nature and social behavior.

> The social man is something more than the sum of standardized acts, no matter how
> many or how well chosen. You can grasp him only by the understanding and syn-

thetic power of your own mental complex, without which any knowledge you may gain from behavior tests must remain superficial and unintelligent. (Cooley 1967a, 73)

Cooley's (1967a, 73) distaste of personality tests, which were then used to characterize people in toto, led him to criticize intelligence tests. "Is it not a somewhat equivocal use of terms when we talk of measuring intelligence or personality? What we measure is the performance of standardized operations. To pass from these to the organic whole of intelligence or personality is always a difficult and fallible work of the constructive imagination" (Cooley 1967a, 73). Today Cooley's words speak as critically as they did nearly three-quarters of a century earlier.

Social theory that ignored human consciousness would lead to merely superficial analysis; "sympathetic introspection, or the understanding of another's consciousness by the aid of your own" could provide a deeper, though subjective, understanding of the other (Cooley 1967a, 76).

Cooley was quite aware that this sort of knowledge was less precise, verifiable, and cumulative. But to Cooley the question was: What does behavior mean? And the only way to assess the meaning of human behavior was through the study of covert action, consciousness, human agency, of how people defined the situation. "The human material is peculiar not only in its enormous abundance and variety, but in requiring, to deal with it, a radically different theoretical and technical equipment" (Cooley 1967a, 83). For Cooley "the imaginations which people have of one another are the solid facts of society and to observe these must be the chief aim of sociology" (Cooley, quoted in Jandy 1942, 109). In this concept we discern a further move toward a social conception of mind, a move that was completed with Mead.

The Looking-Glass Self

The fundamental significance of the ideas we have of others logically leads to Cooley's concept of the self: the self we construct is based on our imaginations of how others perceive us. A looking-glass self is the process by which we develop a self, a self-concept, and self-esteem. The often quoted definition of the looking-glass self involves "the imagination of our appearance to the other person; the imagination of the judgment of that appearance, and some sort of self-feeling, such as pride or mortification" (Cooley 1970, 380). The second tenet is the more important, for that is how our self-concept is formed, that is, by how we think others, especially meaningful or significant others, view us. Cooley (1970, 380) extended James's notion of the social basis of self-esteem.

The comparison with a looking-glass hardly suggests the second element, the imagined judgment, which is quite essential. The thing that moves us to pride or shame is not the mere mechanical reflection of ourselves, but an imputed sentiment, the imagined effect of this reflection upon another's mind. This is evident from the fact that the character and weight of that other, in whose mind we see ourselves, makes all the difference with our feeling.

In attaching importance to our concern with the opinions of others, Cooley also realized that these need not be immediately present, or personally known others, but may simply be imagined others. Cooley's insight provides the provenance of the imaginary reference group concept.

These [others] are not necessarily living persons; any one that is at all real, that is imaginable, to us, becomes a possible occasion of social self-feeling; and idealizing and aspiring persons live largely in the imagined presence of masters and heroes to whom they refer their own life for comment and improvement. (Cooley 1968a, 140)

The core of the self-concept is thus a feeling. "The distinctive thing in the idea for which the pronouns of the first person are names is apparently a characteristic kind of feeling which may be called the my-feeling or sense of appropriation" (Cooley 1968b, 87).

Cooley (1968b, 88) conceived self-feeling as developing synchronously with the expansion of our control over objects.

It appears to be associated chiefly with ideas of the exercise of power, of being a cause, ideas that emphasize the antithesis between the mind and the rest of the world. The first definite thoughts that a child associates with self-feeling are probably those of his earliest endeavors to control visible objects—his limbs, his playthings, his bottle, and the like. Then he attempts to control the actions of the persons about him, and so his circle of power and self-feeling widens without interruption to the most complex objects of mature ambition.

The self-feeling is thus associated with accomplishment, with purposeful activity. This notion is very similar to James's notion that self-esteem is the relationship between aspirations and achievement. Cooley has thus also constructed a pragmatic self-feeling. In fact, "to lose the sense of a separate, productive, resisting self, would be to melt and merge and cease to be" (Cooley 1968a, 141).

We also see the move away from our emotions as psychologically and biologically based solely on instincts; our emotions are socially constituted as well.

We are ashamed to seem evasive in the presence of a straightforward man, cowardly in the presence of a brave one, gross in the eyes of a refined one. We always imagine, and in imagining share, the judgments of the other mind. A man will boast to one person of an action—say some sharp transaction in trade—which he would be ashamed to own to another. (Cooley 1972a, 231-32)

Cooley articulated two other ideas on the self still debated in symbolic interactionism: (1) the self as multiple self, and (2) the self as a seasoned actor. Cooley's (1970, 382) idea in the former is attributable to the influence of James.

> The young performer soon learns to be different things to different people, showing that he begins to apprehend personality and to foresee its operation. If the mother or nurse is more tender then just she will almost certainly be "worked" by systematic weeping. It is a matter of common observation that children often behave worse with their mother than with other and less sympathetic people.

The second, anticipating Goffman's dramaturgy, is that we are all actors. Cooley (1970, 382), in referring to his daughter, states:

> At about fifteen months old she had become "a perfect little actress," seeming to live largely in imaginations of her effect upon other people. She constantly and obviously laid traps for attention, and looked abashed or wept at any signs of disapproval or indifference. At times it would seem as if she could not get over these repulses, but would cry long in a grieved way, refusing to be comforted. If she hit upon any little trick that made people laugh she would be sure to repeat it, laughing loudly and affectedly in imitation. She had quite a repertory of these small performances, which she would display to a sympathetic audience, or even try upon strangers.

Cooley quite evidently knew that people try to impress one another and to control the definitions of themselves that emerge through our competency or incompetency in social interaction. We must be constantly on guard, for even if we know that our image is positive in the eyes of others, such a state of affairs can dramatically change. Cooley's (1968a, 141) metaphor is apt:

> Perhaps we do something, quite naturally, that we find the social order is set against, or perhaps it is the ordinary course of our life that is not so well regarded as we supposed. At any rate, we find with a chill or terror that the world is cold and strange, and that our self-esteem, self-confidence, and hope, being chiefly founded upon opinions attributed to others, go down in the crash. As social beings we live with our eyes upon our reflection, but have no assurance of the tranquility of the waters in which we see it.

Cooley's concept of self was one so rich that it is still referred to in symbolic interactionism. Many of his insights on self have been elaborated on, especially by Erving Goffman and his notion of the dramatizing self, the self as impression manager.

The Individual and Society

Cooley (1972b, 160) maintained that "society and individuals are inseparable phases of a common whole, so that wherever we find an individual fact we may look for a social fact to go with it." The relationship between the individual and society is one of organic dependence. Spencer's influence on Cooley (1967b, 153) is evident.

> That is, we see that the individual is not separable from the human whole, but a living member of it, deriving his life from the whole through social and hereditary transmission as truly as if men were literally one body. He cannot cut himself off; the strands of heredity and education are woven into all his being. And, on the other hand, the social whole is in some degree dependent upon each individual, because each contributes something to the common life that no one else can contribute. Thus, we have, in a broad sense of the word, an "organism" or living whole made up of differentiated members, each of which has a special function.

Neither society nor the individual can exist without the other in this organic relationship. "The organic view stresses both the unity of the whole and the peculiar value of the individual, explaining each by the other. A well-developed individual can exist only in and through a well-developed whole, and vice versa" (Cooley 1967b, 153).

Cooley is offering strong arguments here against the hereditarian view, for he contends that individuals are social products. In fact, Cooley (1967b, 155) asks and then answers this question, and in doing so presents his view of the relationship between heredity and environment.

> Is the individual a product of society? Yes, in the sense that everything human about him has a history in the social past. If we consider the two sources from which he draws his life, heredity and communication, we see that what he gets through the germ-plasm has a social history in that it had to adapt itself to past society in order to survive: the traits we are born with are such as have undergone a social test in the lives of our ancestors. And what he gets from communication—language, education, and the like—comes directly from society. Even physical influences, like food and climate, rarely reach us except as modified and adapted by social conditions.

Even if one were to live as a hermit, one would carry society within the mind. "If you go off alone into the wilderness you take with you a mind formed in society, and you continue social intercourse in your memory and imagination, or by the aid of your books. This, and this alone, keeps humanity alive within you, as just so far as you lose the power of intercourse your mind decays" (Cooley 1967b, 155). Implicit here is the concept Mead would develop of the generalized other and of the influence communication has on the emergence of the mind. The group and, a fortiori, the society is thus vital and necessary in social development.

The Primary Group and Human Nature

Cooley's social origins may have helped him develop one of the core concepts in sociology, the primary group. Early in his career Cooley published a monograph, *Genius, Fame and the Comparison of Races*, "making a brilliant attack on the particularistic and dogmatic hereditary views of genius which Francis Galton championed" (Jandy 1942, 91). Like Galton, Thomas Carlyle had formulated a Great Man theory of leadership in his text *Heroes, Hero Worship, and the Heroic in History* (Jandy 1942, 91). This tendentious, aristocratic view of history, genius, class, and leadership was sure to be invidious to a person from a family that had achieved national prominence from humble beginnings. Charles's father, Thomas McIntyre Cooley, was the eighth child in a family of fifteen, but even though financial resources hampered him from securing an education, his ambition, industriousness, and psychic drive led him to become the country's leading constitutional lawyer (Jandy 1942, 10). For Charles Cooley, the notion that one had to accept one's position in life, rather than strive for upward mobility, was not only elitist and vulgar, but viewed individuals deterministically, as though the influence of biology and heredity were destiny. Charles Cooley could see from the upward mobility of his father that primary group socialization, that is, socialization within the family, was significant in developing one's self and mind, one's values and ambitions. Thus, to Charles Cooley, the most important and necessary of all groups is the primary group.

Primary groups are primary in the sense that they give the individual his or her earliest and most complete experience of social unity, and in the sense that they do not change in the same degree as more elaborate relations, but form a comparatively permanent source out of which the latter are ever springing (Cooley 1972b, 158). Out of the primary group, Cooley (1972b, 159-60) argued, emerges human nature.

> The view here maintained is that human nature is not something existing separately in the individual, but a group-nature or primary phase of society, a relatively simple and general condition of the social mind. It is something more, on the one hand, than the mere instinct that is born in us—though that enters into it—and something less, on the other, than the more elaborate development of ideas and sentiments that makes up institutions. It is the nature which is developed and expressed in those simple, face-to-face groups that are somewhat alike in all societies; groups of the family, the playground, and the neighborhood. In the essential similarity of these is to be found the basis, in experience, for similar ideas and sentiments in the human mind. In these, everywhere, human nature comes into existence. Man does not have it at birth; he cannot acquire it except through fellowship, and it decays in isolation.

Don Martindale has summarized five characteristics of Cooley's concept of primary groups: (1) face-to-face association, (2) unspecified nature of associations, (3) relative permanence, (4) a small number of persons involved, and (5) relative intimacy of participants (Martindale 1960, 345).

The primary group's cardinal function is the socialization process through which children develop their human nature. "Here Cooley broke unplowed ground in specifically explaining human nature in terms of the human organization that developed only in the experience of the individual in primary groups" (Curti 1980, 241). Adults are also socialized and continually resocialized by the primary groups they encounter, cultivating their capacities to both empathize and symbolize. For Cooley, human nature was not a biological given but was the result of socialization. Sentiments of all sorts are potentialities within the individual; however, for Cooley (1972b, 158), the sentiment of sympathy was fundamental.

> By human nature, I suppose, we may understand those sentiments and impulses that are human in being superior to those of lower animals, and also in the sense that they belong to mankind at large, and not to any particular race or time. It means, particularly, sympathy and the innumerable sentiments into which sympathy enters, such as love, resentment, ambition, vanity, hero-worship, and the feeling of social right and wrong.

This process of acquiring human nature within primary groups is considered universal (Thomas 1966, 57), though what a human being is to become (his or her content) does not then depend so much on native human capacity but on the type of society and culture he or she is born into, especially its opportunity structure.

Cooley's notion that one could not become a human being or develop human nature without these had received support from such cases as the *sauvage de l'Aveyron* and those of Anna or Isabelle (Elkin and Handel 1978, 22-31).[1] These cases have come to be known as social isolates or feral children. The first case is of a French boy who was found "wild" in the woods but brought under the care of Jean-Marc-Gaspard Itard—the founder of special education. The boy was named Victor. He was successfully, though only partially, socialized by Itard. Victor learned to write but never to speak. Part of what was human nature had decayed in isolation. Anna was a girl who had been locked up in a room since infancy with only occasional contact with other humans beings. She was found when six years old and died five years later without developing a basic human nature. Isabelle was another six-year-old who was found under similar circumstances, but through an intensive program did acquire aspects of her human nature. Isabelle, however, had had contact with her mother, though her mother was a deaf mute. The link between social deprivation and the development of a fully human self constitutes specialties within psychology and psychiatry. Such cases, and Cooley's perspective, underscore how strong was his argument that human beings are social, requiring the company of others.

Primary Groups and Identity Formation

Solidarity formation, too, is a function of the primary group, for example, primary group definitions of self and group in the social construction of identity can contravene negative definitions, that is, what I perceive society thinks of me and my group. Such an identity, however, may not be able to block or prevent negative sanctions from that society on the self or the primary group. For example, a minority family that defined their identity as possessing the same rights as any other members of the society might come into conflict with racists, who do not define the minority's status as equal to theirs. "The self-respecting man values others' judgments and occupies his mind with them a great deal, but he keeps his head, he discriminates and selects, considers all suggestions with a view to his character, and will not submit to influences not in the line of his development" (Cooley 1968a, 139). We must consider the source in reacting to those making adverse valuations of us. What others mean to us has much to do with how meaningful we consider their characterizations.

By using the example of minority groups we can illustrate how the primary group sustains solidarity and a positive identity. In-group peers can offer social support to a minority member suffering from negative societal evaluations. Significant others also function as a social shield from attacks on one's self-concept. People live in social worlds; thus, minorities can be intellectually inoculated from a "sick" environment. Cooley's enduring concepts underscore his contribution to SI.

W. I. Thomas[2]

The Definition of the Situation or the Thomas Axiom

"If men define their situations as real, they are real in their consequences" (Thomas 1966, 301). The way we define a situation leads to a particular plan of action, just as belief about a situation or object becomes that upon which we are prepared to act. Whether the belief is true or not, and whether the way we define our situations corresponds to the actual, objective state of affairs, is inconsequential for motivating action, since both accurate and inaccurate beliefs, or definitions of the situation, lead to action. Although the epistemic status of a belief is inconsequential in motivating action, it is not inconsequential for the action itself. Action that leads to failure or, as Dewey phrased it, "fails to clear up confusion, uncertainty, and evil," deviates from the norms of practicality and success.

W. I. Thomas (1966, 301) introduced the concept of "definition of the situation" by illustrating how belief can motivate action with tragic consequences.

A paranoid person, at present in one of the New York institutions, has killed several persons who had the unfortunate habit of talking to themselves on the street. From the movement of their lips he imagined they were calling him vile names, and he behaved as if this were true. If men define their situations as real, they are real in their consequences. The total situation will always contain more or less subjective factors, and the behavior reactions can be studied only in connection with the whole context, that is, the situation as it exists in verifiable, objective terms, and as it seemed to exist in terms of the interested person.

The implication is that to understand behavior in a meaningful sense, one must know how individuals define situations. One must understand how an actor interprets situations and objects in order to understand why that actor behaved in a situation or toward a certain object as he or she did. In the American idiom this is phrased: "Oh, yes, I see where you're coming from." The world becomes for us what we define it to be. But social structure and social organization are also important. To understand the subjective meaning of an individual's act—to understand why he or she defines reality in a particular way that leads to particular behavior—is also to try to uncover the social sources of interpretation/perception. Thomas does not emphasize the social influences on one's definition of the situation. Instead, his emphasis is that because one can define situations, one is not totally determined by the social structure or existential surround. Defining the situation allows one to break out of the conventional wisdom of the age and respond with novelty to the world.

Definitions, as we have seen, are not without their consequences. Thomas (1966, 166) knew that defining a situation in a way unshared by members of a group can be considered deviance and can lead to negative sanctions.

As long as the definitions of situations remain constant and common, we may anticipate orderly behavior reactions. When rival definitions arise we may anticipate social disorganization and personal demoralization. There are always constitutional inferiors and divergent personalities in any society who do not adjust, but the mass of delinquency, crime, and emotional instability is the result of conflicting definitions.

Thomas's concept of the definition of the situation is still widely used to explain human behavior in a way that rejects determinism, both biological and psychological, and puts behavior in the context of the meaning it has to an individual, which is socially constructed.

Philistine, Bohemian, and the Creative Person

Thomas also constructed a typology of how people define situations in response to the prevailing norms of the culture. A continual conflict between the individual, who wants to maximize new experiences, and societal demands for a maximum of stability create three types of behaviors or patterns (Thomas 1966, 169-81). The Philistine adheres to societal norms, like an automaton. He or she values security over new experience and individuality. The Bohemian lives in a normless state, somewhat analogous to anomie. He or she escapes from normative behavior through a tendency to drift from one place to another, by not having a stable set of significant or reference others (to use terms not yet employed by Thomas). While the two other types represent extremes in social behavior, the creative person represents symbolic interaction's paragon of behavior, that is, one confronted by social or cultural forces but able to transcend them through rationally redefining the situation. The creative person does not overconform to the norms (the Philistine) nor is he or she unsocialized to the norms (the Bohemian) but, instead, interprets the norms and chooses an appropriate plan of action. The ideal creative person is one who reflects the primary theme of the early interactionists, voluntaristic conduct.

The Culture Concept

W. I. Thomas also incorporated the concept of culture into his work, primarily by showing how Old World traits were dysfunctional to immigrants coming to America. In *The Polish Peasant* (1918-1920) with Florian Znaniecki, *Old World Traits Transplanted* (1921), with Robert E. Park and Herbert A. Miller, and *The Unadjusted Girl* (1923), Thomas spent much of his life's work "tracing the dependence of individuals on social life and culture and of culture and social life on the individual" (Martindale 1960, 348). In these works Thomas contributed to what would become SI research methods: the life history, the case history, ethnography, and what is now called by interactionists participant observation.

The city, primarily its seedy side, was the laboratory for Thomas's new type of empirical research. One was to explore the various social worlds of the incoming immigrants. This focus on the social worlds of the immigrant was also responsible for the later development of the concept of subculture in sociology, as well as the ecology school of deviance developed under the direction of Robert Park. Direct observation redirected attention to the meanings that actors gave to their deviant acts (Davis 1980, 57).

In *The Polish Peasant in Europe and America*, social disorganization was defined by Thomas and Znaniecki (1966, 4) as the absence of social control, that is, "a decrease of the influence of existing social rules of behavior upon individual members of the group." Thus, social disorganization referred to institutions "and only secondarily to men" (Thomas and Znaniecki 1966, 5). The theme emphasized by Thomas and Znaniecki is that one may live in an area of social disorganization but not necessarily suffer any individual disorganization, or, conversely, one may be individually disorganized but live in an area of social organization. One phenomenon is not coextensive with the other (Thomas and Znaniecki 1966, 5).

What Thomas and Znaniecki were emphasizing was the dialectic between structure and agency. Structure, such as the social disorganization of an inner-city neighborhood, may influence one's behavior. Influential as that structure may be, one still has some choice in deciding, for example, whether to engage in a life of crime.

Sadly, Thomas, along with his coauthors Robert E. Park and Herbert A. Miller, in *Old World Traits Transplanted*, were influenced by both the salubrious and the toxic aspects of early-twentieth-century culture. The influx of southern and eastern European immigrants adversely influenced some of their views, for they echo the fears of the mental testers and eugenicists. The immigrants, according to these views, did not have an inferior biology or an inferior intelligence, but an inferior culture. Thomas and his coauthors thought that these immigrants would breed too rapidly for American democracy. The social context of the times influenced Thomas, Park, and Miller's (1966, 198) theory, as it would any social theory. That is the main argument of the sociology of knowledge.

> If we should receive, say, a million Congo blacks and a million Chinese coolies annually, and if they should propagate faster than the white Americans, it is certain that our educational system would break down; we could not impart even the "three R's." We should then be in a state of chaos unless we abandoned the idea of democracy and secured efficiency by reverting to the "ordering and forbidding" type of state. This is the general significance of immigration to our problem of democracy.

We have to help the immigrant adjust properly, these authors claimed, for: "if visitors are disorderly, unsanitary, or ignorant, the group which incorporates them, even temporarily, will not escape the bad effects of this" (Thomas, Park, and Miller 1966, 197-98). Immigrants need not do better on intelligence tests but, rather, they had better learn American values. "They cannot be intelligent citizens unless they 'get the hang' of American ways of thinking as well as of doing" (Thomas, Park, and Miller 1966, 198). Thomas, Park, and Miller (1966, 197) were less fearful of polluting the gene pool than the culture pool. "We have on our hands this problem we are importing large numbers of aliens, representing various types, in the main below our cultural level." Therefore "we must make the immigrants a working part in our system of life, ideal and political, as well as economic, or lose the character of our culture. Self-preservation makes this necessary" (Thomas, Park, and Miller 1966, 198).

Thomas's and his coauthors' work on the influence of culture on human beings' lives, even though it incorporated a notion of cultural inferiority, helped in putting forth the culture concept, contemporaneously encouraged by Boas's students in anthropology. His work with Florian Znaniecki was regarded for a long time as the exemplar in the field of ethnographic sociology.

John Dewey

Beyond the Reflex Arc: The Stimulus as Symbol

In his critique of the reflex arc idea in psychology, Dewey was among the first, if not the first, to argue that a stimulus is not an objective phenomenon but is constituted by interpretation, that is, it is symbolic. "The stimulus must be constituted for the response to occur" (Dewey 1931, 245). A stimulus does not have an objective existence apart from actors who define it. "The conscious sensation of a stimulus is not a thing or existence by itself (Dewey 1931, 245), the stimulus is something to be discovered; to be made out" (Dewey 1931, 247-48). In addition, Dewey argued that the social context in which anything is experienced influences how that thing is defined. For example, something as simple as a noise is defined differently depending on the situation. "If one is reading a book, if one is hunting, if one is watching in a dark place on a lonely night, if one is performing a chemical experiment, in each case, the noise has a very different mental value; it is a different experience" (Dewey 1931, 238). These ideas would be expanded upon by others leading to the recognition of the enormous influence of not only social context, but also the interactive context, that is, the taking into account of others (present or mentally referred to) and their sway on human behavior. In subsequent work to be shortly examined, Dewey is formulating a perspective that will come, along with the work of others, such as G. H. Mead, to challenge the tenets of behaviorism, which was to have enormous sweep in the social sciences, especially psychology, in the early decades of the twentieth century.

Behaviorism, a reaction to unscientific (that is, nonpositivistic and introspectionist) psychology, negated consciousness or, at best, regarded it (and anything unobservable and thus unverifiable) as epiphenomenal. Mentalistic concepts, such as mind, were excoriated. Action is modeled as a simple stimulus-response sequence influenced by conditioning. Dewey argued that humans are not passive reactors to "objectively given" stimuli but are, instead, active interpreters of the symbolic nature of stimuli. Objects, communication, and interaction are infused with culturally derived symbolic meaning. Yet the meaning of objects, communication, and interaction, for any given actor, situationally emerges through the process of interaction with others within a historical and cultural context, rendering behavior diverse, contingent, and novel. Responses are always already culturally contextualized but, nevertheless, situationally contingent. Behavior is meaningful, purposeful, and intentional. In contrast to determinism, there is indeterminism.

Dewey's social psychology expanded tenets derived from those first espoused in psychological functionalism, for example, in the work of James Rowland Angell (1904). In criticizing behaviorism, the influence of Darwinian evolution and functional psychology on Dewey is profound; drawing from Angell, he emphasized the adaptive capacity of intelligence in human affairs, the ability to deliberate and make choices. Functionalism rejected simple stimulus-response couplets as an adequate explanation of social behavior; rather, it sought to measure individual differences in the development of functions that help actors adapt to their environment. Humans adjust through consciousness and intelligence, that is, minded activity, to their environment, thereby transcending structural and cultural constraints.

An agentic view of human nature, along with A. L. Kroeber's (1917) concept of the "superorganic" (the word taken from Herbert Spencer), which was to become anthropology's concept of culture, provided a theoretical justification that humans were not internally or externally determined and mindless but capable of subjectivity and choice, could internalize intelligent habits through education, and, consequently, could become competent to exercise responsibilities that freedom and democracy entailed (Baldwin, 1973; Cravens, 1978; Curti, 1980; Dewey, 1926; Gossett, 1969; Gould, 1981; Herman, 1943; Hinkle and Hinkle, 1954; Hinkle, 1980; Stocking, 1968). These arguments were theoretically and politically interwoven.

Dewey's theory contributed to and was part of a political, state-policy transition in America from a Lockean laissez-faire liberalism to a Rousseauesque welfare-state liberalism (Cranston 1967, 458-61). These ideas were themselves enveloped in the progression from competitive to corporate capitalism. Once steel-chained ideas such as instinct, social Darwinism, and determinism were dissolved, an intellectual foundation for freedom, educational reform, and democracy had been laid (Goldman 1955, 123-24). Thus Dewey's ideas, along with those of other pragmatists (e.g., George Herbert Mead), held that human beings were not determined by either biology or culture but thwarted by social circumstances, which were socially alterable through consciousness, pragmatic inquiry, and agency, leading to societal change and, reciprocally, self-change.

Vast social changes transforming the United States after the Civil War—industrialization, urbanization, and immigration—led functional psychologists to conceptualizations concerning the question of how individuals can adjust to the often overwhelming shock of rapid social change. For Dewey, intelligence developed through education led to instrumental habits that provided human beings with an adaptive function to meet the contingencies of everyday life. Individuals, endowed with minded behavior, had the adaptive capacity to make and remake themselves and, in addition, to reconstruct the institutions of society and all of culture, the very structures that influenced what we as a species could become. This idea proved to be foundational for American sociology and social policy. In sociology, it contributed to the perspective of symbolic interactionism, which emphasizes socialization, process, choice, consciousness, minded activity, defining the situation, joint action, role-taking, and role-making. In social policy, it underlaid Progressive reform in order to "replace an evolution that stopped at the present with an evolution that raced on; an environment that predetermined men and women with an environment that human beings manipulated to meet their needs; the dreary inevitabilities of Conservative Darwinism with the radiant hopefulness of Reform Darwinism" (Goldman 1955, 123). This political shift from laissez-faire to welfare-state liberalism was not only justified by a theory of human nature but also championed by a significant segment of the growing corporate economic structure interested in social order, regulation, and reform (Weinstein 1968; Wiebe 1967).

It is now time to examine Dewey's contributions to SI in more detail, which I shall do by focusing on his major work in social psychology, *Human Nature and Conduct* (1922/1957).

Agency and Social Reconstruction

From the opening pages of *Human Nature and Conduct*, Dewey's argument about human nature is coextensive with his notion of Progressive social reform.[3] Dewey presents an interactive view of human nature that is determined by neither instincts (a contemporaneously popular concept) nor the environment (an overreaction to biological determinism).[4] Dewey's perspective underscored the interaction between the biological and the social:

> We can recognize that all conduct is interaction between elements of human nature and the environment, natural and social. Then we shall see that progress proceeds in two ways, and that freedom is found in that kind of interaction which maintains an environment in which human desire and choice count for something. There are in truth forces in man as well as without him. (11)

Dewey's belief that we are influenced by the environment means that we should "maintain an environment" in which "human desire and choice count for something." Metaphors signify; Dewey's engineering metaphor implies that if human nature emerges through the institutions that socialize us, then there is an opportunity to change human nature by changing social institutions: "The issue shifts from within personality to an engineering issue" (11).

Dewey began his contribution to social psychology with a conceptualization of habits. Habit is an acquired predisposition to ways or modes of response, not to particular acts, except as, under special conditions, these express a way of behaving. Habit means sensitivity or accessibility to certain classes of stimuli, standing predilections and aversions, rather than a knee-jerk recurrence of specific acts (40-41). The way we act in a social situation (our habit) is a function "requiring cooperation of organism and environment" (17). "They are working adaptations of personal capacities with environing forces. All virtues and vices are habits which incorporate objective forces. They are interactions of elements contributed by the make-up of an individual with elements supplied by the outdoor world" (19).

Dewey's conceptualization is a guide as to how far human behavior had come to be seen as a product of the environment as well as a product of the organism. Human behavior is now seen as social behavior. "It is not an ethical 'ought' that conduct should be social. It is social, whether good or bad" (19).

Again we notice how Dewey's conceptualization of human nature grounded his political goals. "To change the working character or will of another we have to alter objective conditions which enter into his habits" (22). One cannot just advocate that people change; Dewey rejected not only biological determinism (which meant that people could not change) but also "a belief in metaphysical free-will" (which meant that people were free of social constraint in their choice of behavior) (20). His approach meant "that there are many recognitions of the part played by social factors in generating personal traits. We change character from worse to better only by changing conditions. . . . We cannot change habit directly: that notion is magic" (22).

A social evolutionary conception of habits that change with intelligent interaction with one's environment led Dewey to Reform Darwinism. From the premises of minded behavior as an instrument of adaptation and history as contingent, Dewey concluded that Progressive politics was sound (Boring 1963, 166). Notions of social inheritance and social evolution contributed to the conceptualization of social institutions as an emergent process through evolutionary change. If we are to change human beings through social means, then it requires evolving new forms, in this case, new habits. To evolve new habits, a different environment, primarily consisting of institutions and culture, is required.

Dewey's concept of custom is closely associated with the anthropological concept of culture. For Dewey, "customs or widespread uniformities of habit, exist because individuals face the same situation and react in like fashion. But to a larger extent, customs persist because individuals form their personal habits under conditions set by prior customs" (55). Uniformities of habit exist among people because they share a common environment. Those habits that are built up out of intelligent responses to that environment create a culture, or, for Dewey, a set of customs. Customs persist because we are socialized to them; they are there before we are born and they will exist after we are gone. In order for human beings to become social, to become members of their community, they must incorporate the customs of the group (55). The relationship between the individual and society (or for Dewey, the individual and customs) is a dynamic one. Individuals are changed as they interact with others, and the customs of all are changed in the process of interaction:

> Those established and more or less deeply grooved systems of interaction which we call social groups, big and small, modify the activities of individuals who perforce are caught-up within them [and at the same time] the activities of component individuals remake and redirect previously established customs. (57)

Customs, then, are merely "settled systems of interaction among individuals" (56). And it is by understanding customs, these settled though dynamic systems of interaction, that we understand human groups. That is to say, for Dewey to understand the human group meant that sociology was much more relevant than psychology (59).

Therefore, customs shape the individual. But that does not mean for Dewey that human beings are determined by customs. People always have some choice, and choice increases with the complexity of modern society:

> Because of present mobility and interminglings of customs, an individual is now offered an enormous range of custom-patterns, and can exercise personal ingenuity in selecting and rearranging their elements. In short, he can, *if he will intelligently adapt customs to conditions, and thereby remake them.* (70; emphasis added)

One is able to define the situation and respond with intelligent action. Custom supplies the storehouse from which to choose behavior. But behavior can be novel because people can always combine customs in unique ways or initiate noncustomary acts. Also, people can completely innovate acts. This does not mean that the individual can act any way that he or she wants to, at least not without consequences: "Customs in any case constitute moral standards" (70); a "breach of custom or habit is the source of sympathetic resentment, while overt approbation goes out to fidelity to custom maintained" (71).

Customs and institutions are built up through social interaction. Dewey used the custom of language to make his argument:

> Men did not intend language; they did not have social objects in view when they began to talk, nor did they have grammatical and phonetic principles before them by which to regulate their efforts at communication. These things come after the fact and because of it. Language grew out of unintelligent babblings, instinctive motions called gestures, and the pressure of circumstance.
>
> What is said of the institution of language holds good of every institution. Family life, property, legal forms, churches and schools, academies of art and science. (74)

Dewey also recognized that within any society there was a plurality of customs, a notion that would probably be found under the heading of subcultures in today's sociological terminology. In fact, Dewey even offered a class analysis of customs: "For segregated classes develop their own customs, which is to say their own working morals" (76). This diversity of customs leads to cultural conflict "between propertied classes and those who depend upon daily wage; between men and women; between old and young. Each appeals to its own standard of right, and each thinks the other the creature of personal desire, whim or obstinacy" (77). The point is that human agency constructs customs, that customs are symbols that different subcultural groups and different individuals variously interpret, explaining the diversity of subcultural and individual behavior; moreover, such notions rebut behaviorism and determinism.

Customs emerge through impulses, a concept somewhat similar to George Herbert Mead's notion of the I of the social self, in that both initiate novel behavior. "Impulses are the pivots upon which the reorganizations of activities turn, they are agencies of deviation, for giving new directions to old habits and changing their quality" (Dewey, 88). Because of impulse, there is a plasticity to self and society (97). Yet Dewey emphasized strong social structural aspects to impulses: "Social institutions and expectations shape and crystallize impulses into dominant habits" (115). That is to say, impulses have social, historical, and cultural elements.

Freedom and Antideterminism

All human beings are influenced by social expectations; it does not mean we are socially determined. Subject to social control, the individual through consciousness interprets objects, communication, and interaction: "As he looks, he sees definite things which are not just things at large but which are related to his course of action" (172). As an individual attempts to complete his or her course of action, he or she goes through a process of deliberation, which "is a dramatic rehearsal (in imagination) of various competing possible lines of action. It starts from the blocking of efficient overt action" (179). Through this process of deliberation, a person does not act in a stimulus-response pattern as do lower animals; rather, "choice is made as soon as some habit, or some combination of elements of habits and impulse, finds a way fully open. Then energy is released. The mind is made up, composed, unified" (181). Neither internal mechanisms nor social expectations determine (absolutely) human behavior. Through deliberation, human beings can respond to their environment selectively. They can use their minds to rehearse competing plans of action so that they can anticipate the consequences of each possible course. Another reason that the behavior of actors is not determined by social expectations is that humans assign meanings to objects, acts, and communication, responding to each situationally. Because a person sees definite things, not just things at large, there is a phenomenal, or symbolic, character to the world. What one object means to one person may mean something entirely different to someone else. And what something means to us may change situationally, hence behavior is contingent. Thus to anticipate how someone might respond in a social situation, what sort of behavior he or she may engage in, is futile without knowing the meaning that objects and events have for someone, and even then new meanings of objects and events can emerge in any given situation:

> The meaning of native activities is not native; it is acquired. It depends upon interaction with a matured social medium. In the case of a tiger or eagle, anger may be

identified with a serviceable life-activity, with attack and defense. With a human being it is as meaningless as a gust of wind on a mudpuddle apart from a direction given it by the presence of other persons, apart from the responses they make to it. (86).

Human beings' creativity in responding to their environment leads them to construct unique habits. Habits found instrumental in guiding purposive social interaction become customs. Habits, then, are associated more with individuals; customs with the group. The diversity of customs constructed through responding to an environment leads to a unique way of life, a culture that distinguishes one people from another. A patterned way of life, a social order, has emerged through processes of thought and meaning. The social order, society, is thus a social product built up through social interaction. The social order is never a "natural order," a product of inevitable human nature. Therefore, no social order—slavery, feudalism, or capitalism—can be justified as an inevitable manifestation of human nature. Deliberation and meaning make all social orders, cultures, and relationships dynamic, ever evolving, and contingent.

Social Constructionism and Antiessentialism

If human beings construct society, and that society constructs human beings, then not only are there a variety of historical and cultural expressions of being human but also the human being is not determined to be anything in particular. There is no human essence. The self has a variety of manifestations and is constantly in the process of becoming.

> There is no one ready-made self behind activities. There are complex, unstable, opposing attitudes, habits, impulses which gradually come to terms with one another, and assume a certain consistency of configuration, even though only by means of a distribution of inconsistencies which keeps them in watertight compartments, giving them separate turns or tricks in action. (130)

Humans develop social selves through their association with others. What we become and what we can be is contingent on our associations and, even more so, on the quality of the institutions of the larger society.

Contingent Selves, Contingent History

Dewey challenged both the conservative and the revolutionary views on human nature, presenting, instead, a social constructionist view of human nature that grounds social reconstruction. For Dewey, the conservative argument on the immutability of human nature commits one to the political practice of laissez-faire. The revolutionary errs in the opposite direction, believing in "the idea of the complete malleability of a human nature which originally is wholly empty and passive . . . the ground of proclaiming the infinite perfectibility of mankind" (101). According to Dewey, the idea that one can quickly change human nature by revolutionary changes in social institutions ignores the profound conditioning effect of socialization. In fact, it is through socialization that Dewey finds a third way: "Native human nature supplies the raw materials, but custom furnishes the machinery and the designs" (104). The gradual change of human nature by changing habits through these processes must begin before habits are ossified; therefore, it begins with the young (120).

Dewey fully realized that education and the school system would have to be altered, for they were institutions that served the prevailing powers, constituting mechanisms of indoctrination. Since its inception "schooling has been largely utilized as a convenient tool of the existing nationalistic and economic regimes" (120). Nevertheless, schooling is the answer to a progressively better society (92).

Social science specialties have emerged with the realization of how precious childhood socialization is, for example, within developmental psychology and the work of Jean Piaget in particular. Since we can change society by changing institutions that socialize the young, society is ours for the remaking. What we make of it is attributable to human design, not to an essential human nature. For example, Dewey points out that forms of oppression are usually justified by attributing social practices to human nature. Thus, Aristotle justifies slavery and many captains of industry justify capitalism, as expressions of inevitable human nature. Dewey argues that, instead, there are many ways to become human and to construct society, a "fact of history and also its lesson; the diversity of institutional forms and customs which the same human nature may produce and employ" (105).

Dewey's emphasis on choice and deliberation as a result of experience and learning (habit and custom) characterizes interaction in the human species; it still stands as a foundational rebuttal of determinism (lack of agency). Intelligence as instrumental is a fundamental premise of the argument that humans have evolved the adaptive capacity for cooperative, collective, or social telesis: "Pragmatism made the whole progressive program quite consistent with human nature, enticingly scientific, thoroughly democratic, Constitutional, and moral" (Goldman 1955, 124). Dewey developed "a psychology perfectly tailored to progressive needs" (122).

Dewey's argument that humans possess agency and a contingent human nature furnished a social-psychological justification for social reform through education. Education's function is to cultivate creative individuals with intelligent habits who, it is hoped, will apply those habits in pragmatic inquiry to transform society—specifically, through the expansion of democracy. Devising a curriculum that cultivates "critical intelligence"—so that through pragmatic inquiry students can reconstruct institutions, social practices, and values—liberalizes education and directs attention to solving social problems. Inquiry and policy are continually reformulated in the light of experience, that is, determining whether the policy produced efficacious results, a pragmatic criterion of truth. Democracy is the political palladium best suited to nurture individuals' growth in acquiring intelligent habits through education (Bernstein 1967, 384; Price 1967, 241).

Intervention through education was a hallmark of Progressive ideology. In order to ground a theory of social intervention, a new view of human nature was conceptualized, which argued that humans could influence their environment rather than resigning themselves to being false conscious victims of the ideology of biological and social determinism. Self and society became indivisible. Dewey's conceptualization prevailed not just because it appeared to social psychologists and sociologists to be a better explanatory model but because it also was harmonious with—in fact, it offered a social-science justification of—the emerging reformist welfare state. That is to say, a new conceptualization of human nature was circumfused in a power struggle between conservative and liberal policy makers. It also discredited Marxist strategies: "Intelligence and social planning represent the means for achieving a social form that assists in the realization of individual capacities, as against the method of class struggle" (Moreno and Fey 1985, 24). Dewey's incrementalist vision of social change epitomized Progressive statecraft that sought to steer clear of "the sort of struggle required to implement the revolutionary changes advocated by Marx [which] would lead to the destruction of civilized life" (24).

Unless human beings possess a nature that is adaptable and a self that is mutable, it makes no sense to implement Progressive social programs. Social Darwinist, eugenic, and hereditarian perspectives on human nature, purporting that the fate of social classes, minorities, and women is biologically and socially sealed, had argued that social programs to ameliorate the life-chances of the "unfit" were futile (Hofstadter 1969; Peel 1971). Social theorists who argued for an emergent human nature through adaptive intelligence triumphed over those who argued for determinism (Boring 1963; Cravens 1978; Curti 1980; Gossett 1969; Gould 1981; Hinkle 1980; Krantz and Allen 1967; Kroeber 1952; Lewis and Smith 1980; Noble 1967; Parrington 1927; Scheffler 1974; Shalin 1988; and White 1957). In terms of politics, this meant that social reconstruction triumphed over laissez-faire.

We now turn to the person who did more than anyone else to develop a sociological conception of human nature and behavior, contributing to the hegemony of the sociological perspective that George Stocking argued was evident on questions of human nature and behavior by the middle of the twentieth century.

Notes

1. The accounts of Victor, Anna, and Isabelle are taken from Elkin and Handel.
2. In this section on W. I. Thomas, all quotations are from the text, *W. I. Thomas on*

Social Organization and Social Personality, edited by Morris Janowitz (1966). Many of the selections in that text are works by Thomas that were coauthored with others. When such works were coauthored by others I note it in the quotations by citing all authors. In the references, however, one will not find these works by Thomas along with his coauthors. For scholars wanting to locate the quotation and its context, one must refer to the Thomas text, edited by Janowitz, which then clearly states which texts have been selected by him.

3. "[Dewey] formulated his views—as did every social science college text of the period—in dialogue with socialism" (Ross 1991, 168).

4. William McDougall's *An Introduction to Social Psychology*, published in 1908, was a leading text outlining the instinctivist perspective on human behavior. Behaviorists also discredited this perspective, arguing that conditioning was the paramount tenet in accounting for human behavior.

5

George Herbert Mead

It is now time to direct our attention to the ideas of G. H. Mead, the person who, above all, has influenced the perspective in sociology named by Herbert Blumer, in 1937, symbolic interaction.

Any order of discussion is arbitrary, but the one employed here is of an increasing complexity in concepts. I start with the simplest for the sake of clarity, hoping that this will facilitate comprehension of later, more complex concepts.

Gesture and a Conversation of Gestures

Mead's thinking on gestures was influenced by Wilhelm Wundt, who "isolated a very valuable conception of the gesture as that which becomes later a symbol, but which is to be found in its earlier stages as a part of a social act" (Mead 1972, 154). This earlier stage of the social act is a simple stimulus that elicits a direct, immediate, response. Here gestures have no meaning; there is no conscious attempt to guide or control one's action or the response of others. Simply put, the gesture is an automatic action.

> We have a situation in which certain parts of the act become a stimulus to the other form to adjust itself to those responses; and that adjustment in turn becomes a stimulus to the first form to change his own act and start a different one. The term "gesture" may be identified with these beginnings of social acts which are stimuli for the response of other forms. (Mead 1972, 155)

For example, in an animal, the gesture, growling, is a sign that is an initial stage of an act, attack; it serves as a stimulus leading another animal to make a response. A

71

series of these gestures, where a stimulus in animal A creates a response in animal B, which then serves as a stimulus to animal A, which makes a response, and so on, is what Mead (1972, 158) referred to as the unconscious or nonsignificant conversation of gestures. At this level, the meanings of gestures are not shared. The stimulus, growl, initiates the response of flight. The dog does not put itself in the place of the cat; the stimulus is not a shared understanding in the sense that it means the same to the initiator as it does to the respondent. It is to this level that animal action is restricted. It is communication at the prehuman level, absent consciousness and interpretation.

Gestures do not carry ideas with them. They do, however, carry, or are initiated by, emotional attitudes. "Anger expresses itself in attack; fear expresses itself in flight" (Mead 1972, 157). Attacks and flight are gestures, automatic responses. Nevertheless, "we cannot say the animal means it in the sense that he has a reflective determination to attack" (Mead 1972, 155). Perhaps the best way to understand the simple gesture is that it is not preconceived. When one has an idea behind one's gesture, one has made a conscious determination to act in a particular way.

Symbols

Before we can explain Mead's notion of significant symbols, it will help to define what we mean by a symbol. A symbol is a representation of something else that is arbitrary, social, and consensual. It is arbitrary because the symbol, red, means stop at a traffic light, but it could just as well mean go, if humans decided so. The designation that red will mean stop arose as a process of negotiation among human beings (perhaps between traffic engineers and the city council); thus, a symbol is social. A symbol is consensual in that we all understand what the symbol represents. But it does not mean that we all respond in the same way all the time. Most of us stop at a red traffic light; however, one might interpret the risk of being caught as slight and proceed through the red light.

The ability to symbolize gives rise to language, consciousness, and culture, through which we name objects—concrete, abstract, even imaginary ones. Through language we interpret the stimuli in our world, making them symbols, to which we then respond. Thus we do not respond to stimuli directly, but only indirectly. All Homo sapiens can respond indirectly to their world, since they all have the capacity for symbolization and language; just how they will respond hinges on how they interpret the stimuli of their world, that is, it depends on culture. Naming objects also means that we socially construct our world. Using symbols to create language and culture involves a qualitatively different ability in cognitive manipulation that, so far as we know, is solely possessed by Homo sapiens.

Significant Gestures/Symbols and a
Conversation of Significant Gestures

Mead had set out to establish that Watsonian behaviorism was misguided in that it approached the study of the behavior of animals and people with the same methodological assumptions, that is, that a scientific psychology should be restricted to the study of solely overt/observable behavior. Watson did not even think consciousness existed; for many other behaviorists it is considered epiphenomenal. Still other behaviorists concede consciousness and minded activity exist, yet consider them covert activity unsuitable to scientific investigation. It was through the concept of significant gestures that Mead distinguished between the behavior of animals and that of people, and thus between behaviorism and social behaviorism. Human beings gesture in a qualitatively different way from animals: "gesture [for humans] means idea behind it and it arouses that idea in the other individual" (Mead 1972, 157). Mead (1972, 157) means that the meaning of a significant gesture is shared.

> The observer sees that the attitude of the dog means attack, but he does not say that it means a conscious determination to attack on the part of the dog. However, should somebody shake his fist in your face you assume that he has not only a hostile attitude but that he has some idea behind it. In the case of the dogfight we have a gesture which calls out appropriate response; in the present case (someone shaking his fist in your face) we have a symbol which answers to a meaning in the experience of the first individual and which also calls out that meaning in the second individual.

Because significant gestures have shared meaning, we respond to them as others do. The fact that significant gestures are intersubjectively shared, even culturally shared, allows us to share in the experience of others, even the experience of others long dead, through their cultural artifacts and writings, for example. Significant gestures are an example of a more inclusive category, significant symbols. As Mead (1972, 157), argued, "Where the gesture reaches that situation it has become what we call 'language.' It is now a significant symbol, and it signifies a certain meaning." Significant symbols—language—constitute human intersubjectivity and communication since, in a process of social interaction, "objects of consciousness in symbol users and recipients" are shared (MacKinnon 1994, 2). Since actors share objects of consciousness, they also respond to social objects similarly. In the significant symbol, Mead believed he had found "a universal, objective principle that transcends the subjectivity of individual consciousness" (MacKinnon 1994, 1). Gesture-action at this level is a "conscious or significant conversation of gestures" (Mead 1972, 158).

Significant gestures/symbols confer a great diversity in, and control over, human behavior, behavior that is infinitely more complex, conscious, directed, and purposive than that of animal behavior. Language (or symbolization generally) constitutes complex forms of behavior and development. "People transform external stimuli into objects of consciousness or cognitions by invoking the social classifications provided by significant symbols" (MacKinnon 1994, 16). Since these classifications are social, derived from a common culture, we interpret and respond in similar ways; that is, there is a normative order. But behavior is not determined because interpretations, hence behavior, can change. Emergence and novelty are conceivable in any situation.

Significant symbols allow us to act in the present toward some future goal guided by our experience of the past. Through symbol manipulation we can act with the concrete world, the abstract world, or construct a fantasy world. "Only language could have broken through the prison of immediate experience in which every other creature is locked, releasing us into infinite freedoms of space and time" (Bickerton, quoted by Leakey 1994, 119). The fact that we can create worlds of our own making, far removed from the physical world, can lead to such things as insight, creativity, and mental illness. Thus, Mead opposed Watson's reductionist method of studying human behavior (zoomorphism), that is, his treatment of humans and their symbolic worlds as though they were no different from animals and their nonsymbolic world. The animal world is one of stimulus and response; the human world is one of stimulus, interpretation, and response. Whether you define this ability to interpret stimuli, transforming them into symbols, as consciousness, cognitive ability, thinking, and so on, all definitions share the notion that minded activity separates a stimulus from a response. Humans are able to do this because of their ability to symbolize. A qualitative difference in human cognition should surely require a qualitatively different, or at least more sophisticated, methodology. Participant observation is the method that interactionists use to study the symbolizing process, the way meaning emerges through social interaction.

The importance of the significant symbol to SI and human beings warrants a recapitulation. Significant symbols are the *sine qua non* of human behavior; our ability to use them distinguishes the human species from all others. They are shared objects of consciousness that lead to (1) communication and intersubjectivity, (2) a normative order, (3) a social order, since response/behavior is patterned, and (4) self-objectification through taking the role of the other—viewing oneself through the significant symbols of language—leading to self-consciousness.[1]

Vocal Gesture

It is through the concept of the vocal gesture that Mead elaborated his notion of meaning as emerging through a shared response to a stimulus. "The particular importance of the vocal gesture is that it affects the individual who makes it just as much as it affects the individual to whom it is directed. We hear what we say" (Mead 1972, 36). Mead means that we respond to our vocal gestures as others do.

The vocal gesture assumes—as do all significant gestures—that meaning is consensual. This allows us to control our behavior socially. We are able to anticipate the response that a vocal gesture may have on others, thereby framing what we say in order to elicit the response we desire. We are able to "see" our action from the point of view of others before we act. Not only can we see our action but also we can see our selves as others do, as an object, as a name or label. Thinking about and acting toward our selves as others do, self-objectification, gives rise to self-consciousness. The vocal gesture (language) is thus that form of minded activity that is most fundamental to the development of the self, for it allows us to take the role of the other.

Responding indirectly to the world through our interpretation of symbols, significant symbols and gestures, vocal gestures, and engaging in a conversation of significant symbols means that we symbolically interact with our world, a life of symbolic interaction.

Taking the Role or Attitude of the Other

The process through which gestures "arouse in an individual making them the same responses which they explicitly arouse, or are supposed to arouse, in other individuals, the individuals to whom they are addressed" (Mead 1972, 158-59), is the process of taking the role or attitude of the other. The taking of the other's attitude allows gestures to become significant: we understand the meaning of our gestures, and of the gestures of others by imaginatively placing our selves in the position and/or attitude of the other. A common consciousness of meaning emerges: "the individual's consciousness of the content and flow of meaning involved depends on his thus taking the attitude of the other toward his own gestures" (Mead 1972, 159). Communication and experience become shared; solidarity is more likely.

Through taking the role of the other we are able to plan our action/behavior giving consideration to others' possible responses to our action. Thus, reciprocally taking each others' attitudes influences each of our acts/behaviors reciprocally. For Mead, then, one important function of taking the attitude of the other is that of social control. If we know another's attitude, then what he or she expects of us will certainly influence how we act. Social control becomes self-control. And since our behavior is influenced by taking the role of others, we transcend any notion whatsoever of a biologically determined behavior; behavior becomes situational, calculating, volitional, and problematic; we must assess the meaning of others' significant gestures and respond with significant gestures of our own. And how we respond depends on how we define the situation.

Social Objects

Objects are human creations. Objects exist independently of us and become objects for us only when we experience them. We experience and give meaning to objects by acting toward them. No object has intrinsic meaning; the meaning of an object is designated by our response to it. Objects are different entities for different individuals; thus responses to them are diverse. Mead (1972, 193) is not solipsistic, for he does not deny the existence in nature of objects independent of our experience; instead, he is a reality constructionist in his notion that objects are different entities for different individuals.

> Nature—the external world—is objectively there, in opposition to our experience of it or in opposition to the individual himself. Although external objects are there, independent of the experiencing individual, nevertheless they possess certain characteristics by virtue of their relations to his experiencing or to his mind, which they would not possess otherwise or apart from those relations. These characteristics are their meaning for him. The distinction between physical objects or physical reality and the mental or self-conscious experience of those objects or that reality—the distinction between external and internal experience—lies in the fact that the latter is concerned with or constituted by meanings. Experienced objects have definite meanings for the individuals thinking about them.

We orient our action toward objects on the basis of the meaning the objects have for us, and that meaning emerges through the process of social interaction.

The groups one interacts with, whether one is a member in fact or an imaginary member, influence social meaning. Groups, as does the larger culture, help us define the situation, but such definitions are not obligatory. The interaction, say, between a parent and a child of an upper-class family regarding the object, college education, and the interaction between the parents and a child from a family not nearly as economically advantaged, are likely to be different in terms of the definitions placed on the object. Yet, the child of the upper-class family may reject a college education, while the child of the working-class family may do all he or she can to pursue a degree.

Language

Mead is emphasizing that objects are emergents through the process of symbolization—a process not achievable by animals. The animal world is determined, but humans, since they can create objects, can create their own worlds. The most important symbol system of all is language. Language allows us to name objects and to respond to them. "The social process, as involving communication, is in a sense responsible for the appearance of new objects in the field of experience of the individual organisms implicated in that process" (Mead 1972, 164). And "language does not simply symbolize a situation or object which is already there in advance; it makes possible the existence or the appearance of that situation or object, for it is part of the mechanism whereby that situation or object is created" (Mead 1972, 165). A common notion in our culture, and in others, is that what the word cannot express, the mind cannot know. The more language we possess (names, labels, vocabulary, metaphors, concepts, theories), the more we are able to perceive aspects of our social worlds and insights into our selves. We classify, organize, and respond to our world through language to such an extent that Lindesmith, Strauss, and Denzin (1991, 54) refer to this human characteristic as a "categorical attitude." We are a category-obsessive species, ever multiplying ways to conceptualize social objects. Language is *the* way we think about the world. Language and self-development are also closely related, as is made clear in chapter 10.

Language, since it is the epitome of abstraction, is a double-edged sword. We create the order of things and all that culture entails: literature, scholarship, an understanding of history, projections of the future, and communication between actors, primary groups, families, the larger culture, and even other cultures through language. Language allows us to see what we have not seen before, even though this object may have always been there. Language may also let us "see" things that are never there, as in cases of paranoid schizophrenia or those who suffer from hallucinations.

Sociologists and philosophers have explored this darker side of language, the way it can be manipulated to make us define the world in a way advantageous to those in power so that behavior is controlled: Marx on ideology and alienation, Michel Foucault on discourse formation, Althusser on ideological state apparatuses, and Gramsci on hegemony. Since language conveys the power to see the world, it conveys power to those whose language we use in seeing the world. Language can reveal or mask reality; it is political. The first task of the revolutionary is to discard the language of the rulers and invent a language of the oppressed.

To summarize Mead's ideas thus far: (1) The meaning of any object is designated by how one responds to it. (2) One responds to an object on the basis of the expectations that one holds about the object. (3) Expectations about objects are socially constructed through symbolic interaction; they are social emergents. (4) If the expectations about the objects provide "cash value," one will continue to respond to the object in a probabilistic manner; if expectations sour, response becomes problematic. Note the pragmatic influence: if it works, the object as you conceive it must be true. (5) Personal change (attitudinal and behavioral) occurs when we reconstitute the meanings of certain objects and thereby respond to them de novo.

A person who responds to Coke by drinking can after can has (1) a favorable image/meaning of the object; (2) perhaps based on the expectation that Coke is a refreshing drink; (3) constructed by, say, how one's friends talk about and use it, and the influence of the mass media; (4) and every time the person drinks a Coke he or she enjoys, it thereby reaffirms one's expectations; (5) though a trip to the dentist, who berates the person for being so careless with an irreplaceable possession as well as inflicting pain and the insult of a $1,000 dentist bill, may lead the person to reconstitute the meaning of Coke with the expectation that, if one continued to drink it, all one's teeth would rot, thereby changing the person's attitude and behavior vis-à-vis the object, Coke. This illustrates how social objects are emergent and subject to redefinition.

Meaning

Obviously, from the above discussion, the concept of meaning is closely tied to our understanding of objects. Meaning is a socially acquired propensity to act or respond in a certain way toward gestures or objects. These tendencies are social constructs, emerging through interaction with others. While meaning is a process of internalizing how others define objects or situations, it is not a passive process. Meaning is the response we make to a gesture or object or situation, not a mere stimulus-response, but a stimulus-interpretation-response.

The Social Act and the Emergence of Meaning

Meaning, for Mead, emerges within the three-phase process of the social act. "This threefold or triadic relation between gesture, adjustive response, and resultant of the social act which the gesture initiates is the basis of meaning" (Mead 1972, 167). These phases are described as follows: The *first* phase is the gesture, the initial process of the social act. The *second* phase: "Response on the part of the second organism to the gesture of the first is the interpretation—and brings out the meaning—of that gesture" (Mead 1972, 167). Symbolization is here a prerequisite, a necessary condition. We perceive, name, and interpret the stimulus through inextricable social influences: experiences, relationships, culture, and so on. The *third* phase is the completion of a given act by the initiator of the gesture. Mead, in developing this point, enunciated, perhaps, the most important tenet within symbolic interaction: *"The meaning of a gesture on the part of one organism is the adjustive response of another organism to it"* (Mead 1972, 168; my emphasis).

Meaning, of course, is something that changes as the individual changes his or her response to an object. Meaning is always being mediated through social interaction. For example, marriage or a college education may not be responded to favorably—a negative meaning—but through one's experiences, emotions, and interaction with others, a new meaning may emerge in regard to obtaining a college education or getting married. Because meanings are shared, there is cooperative behavior, shared expectations, and normative patterns of interaction; in short, social order. Meanings can change; leading to both personal and social change. A meaning-diverse society is demonstrated by various responses to gestures, leading to individuality, cultural, and subcultural variation, even deviance. Thus behavior is probabilistic, rather than determined. Indeterminacy is a salient feature of everyday life.

Selective Attention

As we discussed above, objects and meanings are social emergents. Social structures—social forces or constraints—are omnipresent; yet, they do not overpower the individual. Instead, people are able to select out those stimuli that are relevant to their ongoing acts. This theme of voluntaristic nominalism pervades Mead's (1972, 132-39) work.

> Our whole intelligent process seems to lie in the attention which is selective of certain types of stimuli. Other stimuli which are bombarding the system are in some fashion shunted off. We give our attention to one particular thing.
>
> Here we have the organism as acting and determining its environment. It is not simply a set of passive senses played upon by the stimuli that come from without. The organism goes out and determines what it is going to respond to and organizes that world.

This strong antideterministic stance must be seen in its contemporary setting, for Mead still had to win the battle against the biological determinists. Today a sociologist might say; In what sense does someone from the ghetto go out and organize their world? Mead's slighting of social structure is understandable when we remember that he was arguing for a reconceptualization of human nature and behavior, away from a vulgar, racist, classist, and sexist determinism that said that people were biologically trapped.

Through selective perception, reality becomes a social construction. Stimuli are present—objective—but how we perceive/experience them is socially constructed. "The particular color or odor that any one of us experiences is a private affair. It differs from the experiences of other individuals, and yet there is a common object to which it refers" (Mead 1972, 146). It is as though every object is a holograph toward which we all have different angles of vision. Mead does not view perception as idiosyncratic, however, but as an emergent of the social influences that surround us: others, culture, institutions. Both perception and meaning are intersubjective, that is, shared; otherwise, we could not communicate or engage in joint action.

Mead is contending that the concept of selective attention discredits Watsonian behaviorists. Human beings are qualitatively different because they can select out the stimuli to which they will respond, while animals cannot. This whole process or activity is a rational one: it is rationality itself. To select out those stimuli to which we respond and to indicate stimuli to others through significant gestures is rational conduct. "That is what you are doing when you act in a rational fashion; you are indicating to yourself what the stimuli are that will call out a complex response" (Mead 1972, 172). Action is intelligent action. We are able to choose what to do when confronted by problematic situations. We engage in reflective, introspective, decision-making processes. We are able mentally to design alternative scenarios to stimuli (that is, to imagine) by taking the role of the other, how our responses will be met (that is, evaluated by others) and what possible consequences our action may have. "All this is preliminary covert activity. Human intelligence . . . deliberately selects one from among the several alternative responses which are possible in the given problematic environmental situation. . . . And thus it makes possible the exercise of intelligent or reflective choice in the acceptance of that one among these possible alternative responses which is to be carried into overt effect" (Mead 1972, 176).

The problem here, to be taken up in a later chapter, is that this presents an overly rational conception of human beings. Mead had, as interactionists for some time to come (except for Cooley), ignored the nonrational and emotional component to behavior. Mead 1972, 199), however, recognized that much human behavior does not involve a self.

Selective Environment

It is through the activity of selective attention that we select our environment. Environmental relativity emerges. Since each individual selects his or her own stimuli, the corollary deduction is that the environment becomes relative vis-à-vis the individual: "The particular phase of reality that is there for us is picked out for us by our response" (Mead 1972, 190), "in this sense the environment of the individual is relative to the individual" (Mead 1972, 191).

Remember that Mead argued that the world is objectively there but that we experience the world cognitively, affectively, and behaviorally as subjective. In fact, Mead criticized Cooley's *Human Nature and Social Order* as solipsistic, of denying the existence of society (Mead 1972, 244). In defining what social psychology is—as opposed to reductionist Watsonian behaviorism—Mead states: "for social psychology, the whole (society) is prior to the part (the individual), not the part of the whole; and the part is explained in terms of the whole, not the whole in terms of the parts" (Mead 1972, 121). That society is prior to the individual is an important point, without which Mead's theory would lose a great deal of sociological significance.

The Self

The self is George Herbert Mead's paramount concept. The self develops through the individual taking the role of others toward himself or herself. The self is both subject and object. We are self-conscious when we treat our self as an object, when we scrutinize our self from the vantage point of another. We are able to evaluate our own behavior, to laud our self or to blame our self as others would do; indeed, we do so from the standpoint of specific others or the generalized other, a process of self-objectification. By taking the role of others we have internalized the norms and attitudes of significant and generalized others. This process of normative internalization makes us moral beings and distinguishes us as members of the community in the fullest sense, since the community is now within us. Without internalizing the norms of the community, we would become, in a very real sense, social pariahs.

The self is a developmental activity that is in contradistinction to "the physiological organism proper." "The self is something which has a development; it is not initially there at birth but arises in the process of social experience and activity" (Mead 1972, 199). Mead simply meant that the body is different from the self. "The body can be there and can operate in a very intelligent fashion without there being a self involved in the experience. The self has the characteristic that it is an object to itself, and that characteristic distinguishes it from other objects and from the body" (Mead 1972, 200). Our selves are operative only at certain times, at times when we are objects to our selves. The view that a body does not necessarily possess a self differentiates human beings from animals. "The intelligence of the lower forms of animal life, like a great deal of human intelligence, does not involve a self" (Mead 1972, 199). The ability to be an object to our self endows us with reflexivity: "This characteristic is represented in the word 'self' which is a reflexive, and indicates that which can be both subject and object" (Mead 1972: 201). Mead (1972, 202-3) continues:

> The individual experiences himself as such, not directly, but only indirectly, from the particular standpoints of other individual members of the same social group or from the generalized standpoint of the social group as a whole to which he belongs. For he enters his own experience as a self or individual, not directly or immediately, not by becoming a subject to himself, but only insofar as he first becomes an object to himself just as other individuals are objects to him or are in his experience; and he becomes an object to himself only by taking the attitudes of other individuals toward himself within a social environment or context of experience and behavior in which both he and they are involved.

The substance of this mechanism of role-taking is language, for "it provides a form of behavior in which the organism or the individual may become an object to himself" (Mead 1972, 203). "I know of no other form of behavior than the linguistic in which the individual is an object to himself" (Mead 1972, 206).

Another person does not have to be present for us to slip into his or her place, to take his or her role toward our self. Having this conversation with our self is thinking. "The very process of thinking is, of course, simply an inner conversation that goes on, but it is a conversation of gestures which in its completion implies the expression of that which one thinks to an audience" (Mead 1972, 206). A crucial note is that not all of our self is present in any one situation. Mead (1972, 207) underscored that the self that is presented is in a sense a situational self, the aspect of the self that is the most important in the ongoing interaction. In many routine situations, the self is not taken into account.

> What determines the amount of the self that gets into communication is the social experience itself. We carry on a whole series of different relationships to different people. We are one thing to one man and another thing to another. There are parts of the self which exist only for the self in relationship to itself. There are all sorts of different selves answering to all sorts of different social reactions.

The debate over whether Mead considered the self unitary or multiple is perhaps engendered here. Mead goes on to say that "normally, within the sort of community as a whole to which we belong, there is a unified self, but that can be broken up" (Mead 1972, 207). We also see here how much Mead's work was influenced by William James. The situational self helps us to function in a world when we encounter different groups or different reactions to our behavior. We present a self that is appropriate for the group or possible reaction we may encounter: "there can be different selves, and it is dependent upon the set of social reaction that is involved as to which self we are going to be" (Mead 1972, 207-8). When this happens we are not expressing our complete selves. Mead was trying to distinguish between fragmentary selves and complete selves. A number of elementary selves, Mead (1972, 208) argues, are specific to particular situations or interaction and the complete self that is a composite of all the elementary selves.

> The unity and structure of the complete self reflects the unity and structure of the social process as a whole; and each of the elementary selves of which it is composed reflects the unity and structure of one of the various aspects of that process in which the individual is implicated. In other words, the various elementary selves which constitute, or are organized into, a complete self are the various aspects of the structure of that complete self answering to the various aspects of the structure of the social process as a whole; the structure of the complete self is thus a reflection of the complete social process.

This passages shows how thoroughly the self is a social construction.

But there is also an abnormal self presented, that is, a self-dissociation. "The phenomenon of dissociation of personality is caused by a breaking up of the complete, unitary self into the component selves of which it is composed, and which respectively correspond to different aspects of the social process in which the person is involved" (Mead 1970, 209).

With the conceptualization of multiple selves and our ability to use each aspect of the self at will, depending on what the social situation calls for, we notice how successfully Mead has challenged biological determinism.

The Emergence of the Self

Drawing on Baldwin's earlier work in developmental psychology, Mead located the emergence of the self in two stages: play and game. Play is the rudimentary stage of role-taking. "Play in this sense is play at something" (Mead 1972, 214). One plays at being the various roles that children encounter: father, mother, firefighter, police officer, nurse, doctor, and the like. The child has no unified self as yet: "the child says something in one character and responds in another character" (Mead 1972, 215). At the play stage, role-taking is not sophisticated or advanced beyond that of a fragmentary taking of another's role toward oneself.

In the game stage one "must be ready to take the attitude of everyone else involved in the game and these roles must have a definite relationship to each other" (Mead 1972, 215). The individual is now able to engage in abstraction so as to consider the attitudes of others simultaneously. Only insofar as one becomes able to accomplish this will one be able to develop a complete self. If the individual does not take the role of the generalized other toward his or her behavior, he or she will not be a moral being, will not develop a conscience, will not have internalized the norms of the community. A very important function that is a result of role-taking will be vitiated: the loss of social control through self-control. "It is in the form of the generalized other that the social process influences the behavior of the individuals involved in it and carrying it on, that is, that the community exercises control over the conduct of its individual members" (Mead 1972, 219).

The individual thus develops conduct norms, has a guide to his or her behavior, and is able to achieve self-control, as the mechanism of self-control is the internalized norms of the community. Without this role-taking ability, the individual may develop in deviant ways.

An important theme in Mead, especially for the sociology of knowledge, is in the effect of the group on the structure of the self. Our selves are inescapably structured by the social groups we are part of; in fact, as we have already shown, one cannot develop a self until one has internalized the norms and expectations of our groups, of the generalized other (Mead 1972, 227-28).

Mead was not casting human beings in a deterministic mold, for even though the self emerges with the internalization of the community, the individual is always above and beyond the community in the sense that he or she selects stimuli/objects, defines the situation, considers alternative plans of action, and can act on the world, rather than passively respond to it. One does not respond to norms as a passive vessel. The individual confronted by any problematic situation is able to use various referents, but how he or she uses them in any combination may produce a novel social act. Also, through interaction with oneself one may formulate novel ideas, that is, ideas that differ from those of any groups. The individual is both determined and determiner, both conformist and radical (in the nonpolitical sense), thus society remains stable though ever in a state of flux. How is this accomplished? Mead argued that this is possible because there are two processes or activity phases of the self: the I and the Me. The I and the Me are not physical places within the brain but are merely constructs Mead conceptualized to help him understand human behavior.

The I and the Me

Mead presents a simple statement describing the I and the Me: "the I is the response of the organism to the attitudes of the others; the Me is the organized set of attitudes of others which one himself assumes" (Mead 1972, 230). The Me is society in microcosm; it is the self developed through role-taking. The function of the Me is goal direction, conformity, and stability. The Me functions to organize the individual's response to be compatible, but not identical, with community expectations. The response is not determined but a probabilistic expectation. The "response of the I is something that is more or less uncertain" (Mead 1972, 231). Thus, there is an indeterminacy of the self through the I. The function of the I is novelty, spontaneity, and creativity. "The I gives the sense of freedom, of initiative" (Mead 1972, 232). But the I is caught sight of only as a historical figure, for the second we think of the I we are in the phase of activity that is the Me. The following presents an overly rational sense of the act, ignoring for the moment—for analytical reasons—emotions and other acts where the self is not involved. There is a dialectical phase of activity between the Me and the I, whereby the I (thesis) calls out the Me (antithesis) and the resulting social act, often after we ruminate over several plans of action, is novelty (synthesis). Personal change (attitudinal and behavioral) is thus an inescapable characteristic of the dialectical process of the self.

Social control is one function of the Me, but this does not robotize us to respond to norms methodically, or as marionettes pulled to and fro by the norms of the community. The response of the I "raises us above the institutionalized individual" (Mead 1972, 239).

Mind

Mead rejected Wundt's concept of mind as the antecedent condition and prerequisite for the social process of experience.

[Rather, the social process of experience was prior] to the existence of mind and explain[s] the origin of minds in terms of interaction among individuals within that process. Mind arises through communication by a conversation of gestures in a social process or context of experience—not communication through mind. (Mead 1972, 162)

Language plays the most crucial role in the development of the mind. Significant symbols such as the vocal gesture are necessary human manipulations (cognitive prerequisites) for the development of the mind. Only as human beings developed communication through language as a result of evolution did the possibility of mind arise. "Out of language emerges the field of mind" (Mead 1972, 195). When we are able to indicate to our selves and to others, through the vocal gesture—language—what our response to objects will be, it is then that we have developed mind.

Mind is the ability and process of the human to select a response to an object or stimulus. The mind has the ability to select our stimuli and plan complete acts before we ever physically initiate those acts. The formation of the mind requires a physiologically necessary condition, a complex and advanced brain. But the brain and the mind are not identical.

The mind allows us to have an internal organization of the act before we physically initiate the act. Mead named this ability to respond to an object in a certain preplanned way our attitude (Troyer 1946, 199).

The mental attributes of human beings thus require a methodology appropriate to study them. This is why Mead so vehemently and rightly opposed any reductionist methodology such as Watsonian behaviorism. Human life is qualitatively different. The mind "is essentially a social phenomenon; even its biological functions are primarily social" (Mead 1972, 195). That mind emerges only through social interaction is a significant insight into the origins of mental production. Mead thus has a more grounded social theory of mind than any other social psychologist, viewing the mind as thoroughly socially constituted, a social emergent coterminous with and dependent on linguistic communication.

Mead's social theory of mind describes how the group is paramount in the construction of self and mind. One is inescapably of the group, though, through reflexivity, novelty, and adjustive response, one transcends the group. The objects of the environment give us freedom, for they do not wholly determine our world. Instead, through selective attention to objects on the basis of our current attitude, we organize what we respond to.

The Challenge to Behavioristic Psychology

From the opening pages of *Mind, Self, and Society*, it is manifest that Mead was reacting to the behaviorism of J. B. Watson. Mead maintained that Watson's reductionist conception of both behavior and mind was inadequate. Watson (like his later disciple, B. F. Skinner) reduced the study of behavior only to that which is observable; to say anything else he deemed unscientific. He continued that activities such as introspection and consciousness are untenable, mere speculation and metaphysics. Mead would agree that mind, consciousness, and introspection do not exist as entities: he did not reify his concepts. Nevertheless, he claimed that mind and consciousness do exist as activities. Mead viewed behaviorists as narrowly circumscribing action—as though there were no qualitative difference between animals and human beings. Behaviorists studied animals and generalized their hypotheses to human beings. "Behaviorism entered psychology through the door of animal psychology. There it was found to be impossible to use what is termed introspection. One cannot appeal to the animal's introspection, but must study the animal in terms of external conduct" (Mead 1972, 116).

Since introspection and consciousness are unobservable in animals, "it was possible to carry it [the behaviorist view] over to the human animal" (Mead 1972, 116). According to Mead, Watson's view was that what does not exist in the animal cannot exist in the human being. "John B. Watson's attitude was that of the Queen in Alice in Wonderland—off with their heads—there were no such things" (Mead 1972, 117).

The meaning of an individual's act was irrelevant to Watson—the overt behavior alone was studied. But for Mead that inner experience, meaning, can be reached through speech or language. "There is a field within the act itself which is not external, but which belongs to the act, and there are characteristics of that inner organic conduct which do reveal themselves in our own attitudes, especially those connected with speech" (Mead 1972, 120).

Mead's social psychology was thus antireductionist when juxtaposed against the behaviorism of Watson. Mead began with Watsonian premises, but he expanded them to include a more adequate and sophisticated image of human interaction. People are qualitatively different from animals and thus cannot be studied like animals. Thus mentalism was not the pejorative for Mead that is was for Watson or, later, B. F. Skinner.

> Social psychology is behavioristic in the sense of starting off with observable activity—the dynamic, ongoing social process and the social acts which are its component elements—to be studied and analyzed scientifically. But it is not behavioristic in the sense of ignoring the inner experience of the individual—the inner phase of that process or activity. (Mead 1972, 121-22)

One problem with Watsonian behaviorism was that of methodology. Behaviorists tend to be animal psychologists, and then, when impelled to say something about human beings, rather than elaborate their methodology, they reduce the individual, in procrustean fashion, to gloss over methodological inadequacies. Mind does not fit the animal psychologists' assumptions or methodology; thus, they are explained away as nonexistent in human beings (Mead 1972, 124). We see how thoroughly Mead challenged behavioristic psychology, advocating a distinctive methodology when studying human beings.

Society

Society is a series of institutions that are functionally interrelated and interdependent. Society is constituted by a multitude of institutions built up out of social interaction. And what is an institution? "The institution represents a common response on the part of all members of the community to a particular situation" (Mead 1971, 249). That is, we all share generalized ideas on how to respond to everyday situations, and usually we respond in the normative way. A large number of people living in proximity and sharing common attitudes about public behavior, with individual variations, constitutes society. These institutions influence us to think and act in patterned, though not wholly predictable, ways. We become discriminable from other groups. We are distinguished by our institutions: by how we as a society respond to the situations of everyday life. Other groups, communities, and societies evolved with different institutions, different ways to respond to the situations of everyday life, thereby contributing to different ways to be human, different cultures.

We internalize these institutions through socialization. Shared education, media, and life experiences socialize us to respond to situations in a distinct way, contributing to the development of a unique culture and society. "Thus, the institutions of society are organized forms of group or social activity—forms so organized that the individual members of society can act adequately and socially by taking the attitudes of others toward these activities" (Mead 1972, 250).

Society is prior to the individual, and the individual can become human only if adequately socialized to society's institutions. We become human through the process of internalizing the ways to respond to situations from the institutions that socialize us, that is how selves and minds develop. "Without social institutions of some sort, without the organized social attitudes and activities by which social institutions are constituted, there could be no fully mature individual selves or personalities at all" (Mead 1972, 250). Such social institutions as our family, church, school, and jobs socialize us, which means we incorporate or internalize their prescriptions of how to respond to the situations we encounter.

Mead went on to argue that we are never totally determined by the institutions that have socialized us. For example, the child is certainly socialized to the way his or her parents want him or her to respond (to behave) in certain situations, but what child is totally conformist? The "generation gap" and "teenage rebellion" are legendary instances of the self asserting its individuality. Certainly if we all conformed to the institutions to which we have been socialized, deviance of any sort would be eliminated. That, however, is obviously not the case. Social interaction is rife with everyday conflict. We rebel, to some extent, against all agents of socialization: parents, school, church, government, jobs, and spouses. Conformity may be expected but in fact individuals asserting themselves is normal in everyday life. Obviously, a dialectic between the institutions that have socialized us and our desire to express our individuality is the way we resolve many everyday interactional conflicts. This is basically the dialectic of behavior that Mead conceptualized as that between the I and Me of the self. Such realities as social power are, of course, always operative and need to be taken into account. Positive sanctions (or at least avoiding negative sanctions) that come by responding to situations as we have been socialized are certainly inducements to conform, but we assess situations and then act individually.

Mead's argument that we are determined neither by biology nor social forces underscores his commitment to voluntaristic nominalism. We make our own history, even if not under circumstances we choose. In a plural society socialization is general and diversified. Most social institutions—organized attitudes on how to act—allow for some degree of leniency, idiosyncrasy, and diversity. Tolerance, novelty, and change are themselves norms. For Mead, the purpose of education is to broaden our social horizons, to educate us against ethnocentrism and nationalism and in favor of cultural relativism and internationalism. "We all belong to small cliques, and we may remain simply inside of them. The 'organized other' present in ourselves is then a community of a narrow diameter. We are struggling now to get a certain amount of international-mindedness. We are realizing ourselves as members of a larger community" (Mead 1972, 253).

As Durkheim recognized, the more tolerance and diversity we allow, the more our society was open to social change. It is through education that we can foster the growth of a universal society by internalizing the generalized others of different cultures.

> The universe of discourse within which people can express themselves makes possible the bringing-together of those organized attitudes which represent the life of these different communities into such relationship that they can lead to a higher organization. The very universality of the processes which belong to human society opens the door to a universal society. (Mead 1972, 258-59)

This universal society would be a generalized other that all members of the world share. Everyone would be socialized to common institutions and thereby share a common understanding. Society will lose its conflictual nature because, as we shortly discover, Mead's (1972, 270-71) notion of conflict was one that arises because of different attitudes about how to act in social situations.

> The human social ideal—the ideal or ultimate goal of human social progress—is
> the attainment of a universal human society in which all human individuals would
> possess a perfected social intelligence, such that all social meanings would each be
> similarly reflected in their respective individual consciousness—such that the
> meanings of any one individual's acts or gestures (as realized by him and expressed
> in the structure of his self, through his ability to take the social attitudes of other
> individuals toward himself and toward their common social ends or purposes)
> would be the same whatever for any other individual who responded to them.

Mead's goals were cosmopolitan insight, tolerance, and (what would be referred
to today as) diversity. Socialization of the individual both to intrasociety and
intersociety normative structures does not mean that Mead had any concept of the
individual as oversocialized or as a determined creature doomed to be synonymous with his social context. Social institutions, Mead (1972, 251) argues, leave
room for and even promote individual freedom.

> [Social institutions] are not necessarily subversive of individuality in the individual
> members; and they do not necessarily represent or uphold narrow definitions of
> certain fixed and specific patterns of acting which in any given circumstances
> should characterize the behavior of all intelligent and socially responsible individu-
> als. On the contrary, they need to define the social, or socially responsible, patterns
> of individual conduct in only a very broad and general sense, affording plenty of
> scope for originality, flexibility, and variety of such conduct.

Thus the relationship between the individual and society is dynamic and dialectical. Mead does not theorize that the individual is totally determined or determiner.
His notion of the interplay between social forces and human subjectivity is similar
to Marx's. Human sociality for Mead meant the human beings can reconstruct
society in new ways, even though their selves and minds were constituted by that
very society. Society sets the social context for interaction. The weight of the
individual on society, Mead (1972, 251) contended, can also be felt.

> Human society, we have insisted, does not merely stamp the pattern of its organized
> social behavior upon any one of its individual members, so that this pattern be-
> comes likewise the pattern of the individual's self; it also, at the same time, gives
> him a mind, as the means or ability of consciously conversing with himself in terms
> of the social attitudes which constitute the structure of his self and which embody
> the pattern of human society's organized behavior as reflected in that structure.
> And his mind enables him in turn to stamp the pattern of his further developing self
> (further developing through his mental activity) upon the structure or organization
> of human society.

Mead did not mention the concepts of praxis and revolution; he was more concerned with bringing about self-change; nor did his concepts articulate the potential efficacy of human subjectivity and intention in the collective sense, as did Marx's. For Mead, social change is in large part self-change.

Social change is primarily a reconstituting of ways to think and act when faced with problematic situations. It is the minded behavior of acquiring new interpretations of the problems one faces. By selecting a combination of any of the infinite number of existing attitudes on how to act, or devising one's own attitude, one can constitute a new and unique way to act when faced with the inescapable problematic situations of everyday life. But his approach was to stress individual rather than collective action. Collective action is absent because Mead's concept of conflict in society was limited. He viewed conflict primarily as individual and interpersonal, rather than social. Individuals could think of solutions to the oppressive conditions they might find themselves in.

> Mind, as constructive or reflective or problem-solving thinking, is the socially acquired means or mechanism or apparatus whereby the human individual solves the various problems of environmental adjustment which arise to confront him in the course of his experience and which prevent his conduct from proceeding harmoniously on its way until they have thus been dealt with. (Mead 1972, 268-69)

The more problems the self encounters, the more opportunity the mind has to develop. For Mead, thinking about problems and problem-solving are social in that one takes others' attitudes into account and reconstructs them so as to solve a problem in living; but, as indicated, Mead's analysis was focused on individual action, on solving problems by oneself. He saw all problems in living as largely personal and overcome by creative thinking, not collective action. This underscores the Progressive rejection of violence and the threat to democracy and civil liberties that they argued might come about through revolutionary action. The power of the ruling class in inhibiting social change was not a major concern in Mead's view of society and social change. He assumed that we shall rationally, through intellectual tolerance and critical thinking, come to know others' institutions, their generalized beliefs, practices, and behavior. Moreover, he held, we shall recognize the rationality of incorporating a cosmopolitan perspective. Self-change and a universal generalized other adapted from the community of nations will lead to the universal society and the end of conflict (Mead 1972, 269-70).

But what is rational to one group or society is not rational to others, especially since the movement to universalism that Mead saw happening implies equality in economics, politics, and distributive justice. A universal society is unlikely to come about while those issues remain unsolved. Mead (1972, 277) recognized these irreconcilable conflicts; they were ones perpetuated by an inability of the parties to take the role of the other.

> Examples of social situations of this general type are those involving interactions or

relations between capital and labor, that is, those in which some of the individuals are acting in their socially functional capacity as members of the capitalistic class, which is one economic aspect of modern human social organization; whereas the other individuals are acting in their socially functional capacity as members of the laboring class, which is another (and in social interests directly opposed) economic aspect of that social organization.

But Mead failed to see how these overwhelming class struggles will retard the progression toward a universal society. He noticed such irreconcilabilities but failed to explore them more fully. Had he done so, he might have realized how limited was his view of social change and social structure.

Mead identified communication competence as the social mechanism that will allow us to transform the social situation so that all will be able to take the role of others. "The ideal of human society cannot exist as long as it is impossible for individuals to enter into the attitudes of those whom they are affecting in the performance of their own peculiar functions" (Mead 1972, 282). Thus, "as democracy now exists, there is not this development of communication so that individuals can put themselves into the attitudes of those whom they affect" (Mead 1972, 282). Communication competence, he maintained, must be democratized through the democracy of education. Unless we have a democracy of education allowing all of us access to the cultures of the world, we shall have no universal political democracy.

Methodologically, this implies the development of sympathetic introspection, role-taking, participant observation, and comparative ethnography to prevent a reductionist interpretation of human behavior. These views form the basis of microsociology, a foundation of sociology in general.

Certainly those sociologists who read Mead took from him the views that challenged biological determinism and contributed to the hegemony of the sociological view of human nature and behavior. In fact, sociology became institutionalized as it dropped its association with biological concepts such as habit (Camic 1986, 1077). Sociologists who continued development of the socialization concept, such as Thomas, Park, Faris, Znaniecki, and even Parsons, wanted no contamination from biology (Camic 1986, 1076). In fact, so removed from biology did sociology strive to become, that one critic has charged that later sociologists went too far. "Just as Watson made habit virtually everything in social life, so in casting the concept aside, sociologists were, in effect, allotting habit no role in the social world worth even speaking of. It was not long before nonreflective processes were wholly eclipsed" (Camic 1986, 1072).

In concluding part I, several ideas warrant mention. Mead and other interactionists responded to the scientific claims of the biological determinists, their conceptualizations forming, in part, the nurture part of the nature/nurture controversy. In the process of reconceptualizing human nature and behavior, the early interactionists made unique and profound contributions to the perspective of socialization and the discipline of sociology. Their thinking was at the center of a transformation in social thought that constituted a perspective in social science's, and eventually the American public's, image of human beings and social behavior. This period also saw a transformation in American capitalism in which the corporate ideal of regulation, order, and reform was restructuring the institutions of the economy and polity. The development of a corporate capitalist liberal state, in which business interests would still dominate, was at the heart of the twentieth-century transformation in society, politics, theory, and culture.

As mentioned in the introduction, social theories typically justify state policy. That is why the triumph of the nurture perspective is so important to American democracy. Of course, America still has, and is likely always to have, a power elite. Formal structures such as federalism, constitutionalism, checks and balances, separation of powers, and judicial review (all to be deeply revered) have not prevented upper-class white males (and a few females) from ruling. But America did not go the route of Germany, which used racist biology and anthropology to justify state-run genocide. Neither would America use discredited evolutionary theory, such as Lamarckianism (the inheritance of acquired characteristics), exemplified in the work of Trofim Lysenko, to prop up a totalitarian Soviet state desperate for a scientific justification that they were on the right side of history. Instead, in America, the New Deal would be undertaken. Long-delayed and not-yet-completed civil rights laws for minorities, and all others who suffer categoric discrimination, would ignite as an issue. The self as a social product that could constantly change necessitated an environment that would facilitate inner-and other-directed transformations in the self. Disadvantages of social structure were seen as removable obstacles, not determinants, of human potential. A dialectical self meant that neither biology nor structure was destiny.

A caveat is warranted. Biological determinism is hydra-headed. Chop off the head of such an argument in a Spencer or Goddard in the early twentieth century and it rises fiercer in midcentury in the voice of Lewis Terman; chop off that head and it rises today in the writings of a Charles Murray or a Richard Herrnstein. Biological determinists will be flogging their dead horse as long as we have social inequality, for it provides, as scientific racism, the ideological justification for a meritocracy.

Though it is far from as compelling in the academic community as it once was, biologically based racism and sexism is still prevalent in the minds of the American public. Inequality is as prevalent as ever. For many Americans, the prevailing view of social problems is still couched in terms of individualism, abnormal psychology, or some genetic defect (for example, the XYY chromosome defect to explain violent males), or hormonal imbalances (too much testosterone to account for violent males or career-oriented females). Disputes rage over institutional discrimination, structures of domination, equality of opportunity, and retributive justice. Policy has recognized only slightly structural disadvantages by establishing voting rights legislation, affirmative action, and race and sex norming. They have hardly made a dent in the American stratification system. For any political aspirant, it still means walking down the *Via Dolorosa* if one advocates income and wealth redistribution.

Note

1. Anything that reduces the number of significant symbols that we share threatens communication and the normative and social order. Social stratification and cultural polarization, intertwined processes, are contributing to such a reduction. "Without communication there is no community" (Ross 1962, 156).

Part II

Macrosociological Structures

6

Society: The Structural Context
of Interaction

The order of analysis follows the suggestions by Faris (1936), Troyer (1946), and Meltzer (1967) that the proper sociological order of analysis is society, self, and mind.

Society encompasses two chapters. Chapter 6 explores the structural context of interaction while chapter 7 summarizes its microfoundations. Though I have analytically separated society, self, and mind into different chapters, it is impossible to analyze one without making occasional comments on the other two.

During the 1970s, symbolic interactionism (SI) was heavily attacked. Most of this criticism argued that SI failed to incorporate conceptions of structure, power, and institutions (Meltzer, Petras, and Reynolds 1975).

In the past fifteen years SI has attempted to accentuate aspects of social life previously deemed slighted. Some studies that had addressed the structural features of complex organizations examined only the micropolitics of negotiation; however, a review of recent studies, organized under the rubrics of negotiated order, master institutions, structure, and power and ideology, illustrates that, since about 1975, SI has focused on both constraint and human agency. Many scholars in the SI perspective emphasize cultural domination and resistance, human agency, and the variety of ways power and inequality are reproduced, allowing a regime, or the powerful, to rule by consent.

Communication is a social process whereby human beings create symbolic forms. Carey's argument is that macrosociological links bind communication and community. "If we follow Dewey, it will occur to us that problems of communication are linked to problems of community, to problems surrounding the kinds of communities we create and in which we live" (Carey 1988, 33). Making the link between microsociological communication processes and macrosociological community structures, interactionists have also expanded their definition and exploration of power. The type of "community structures" explored in these SI studies—police stations, prisons, medical schools, airlines, bill-collecting firms, universities, and extramarital affairs—are hierarchical and oppressive, communication within them manipulative, subversive, and alienating. But as these articles emphasize, the meaning of interaction, despite social constraint (hierarchy or culture), is still a function of joint action and definitions of the situation.

Thus, interactionists have taken seriously 1970s criticisms, many from American Marxists, which have enhanced their view that social life is rife with constraint and agency. These critics stimulated interactionists to consider their theoretical shortcomings (astructural bias primarily) and to pursue a macrosociological framework (Meltzer, Petras, and Reynolds 1975). This expanded view of power and ideology within SI is leading to a more comprehensive view of social life that cannot ignore the structural constrains on the processes of everyday interaction and communication. Finding macrosociological links between communication and community, recent SI research is attenuating the astructural bias, but in a way that maintains its theoretical tradition by focusing on indeterminism and the social construction of meaning.

Chapter 6 reviews the move to a more dialectical view of social life (that incorporates human agency and social constraint) evolving within SI. Because of the significance of power, structure, and institutions in everyday life, and the criticism that SI has ignored these features, I focus on the negotiated order, the master institutions of the economy and media, the structural categories of race and gender, and power and ideology.

The Negotiated Order

Concern with human agency and resistance to domination, especially in the way actors in asymmetric relationships engage in negotiation[1] to subvert authority, is a major SI interest.

A basic way organizations constrain humans, and humans react in subverting authority, is through roles and rules. For example, organizational rules lead frontline police officers making narcotics arrests to reconstruct the meanings organizational goals have (Manning 1977). Rule interpretation and subsequent behavior are contextual, for "the interpretive contexts within which rules in a police organization will be understood are not fully *shared* between the segments of an organization" (Manning 1977, 48; emphasis in the original). Because rules are not fully shared, a great number of tacit understandings allow work to be accomplished. The myth that rules are shared allows those with power to sanction lower-level police officers when questionable action comes under departmental review. As "rule-violation encounters are rituals which reaffirm the power and authority of the organizational segment above the rank of sergeant," countervailing power comes from those at the investigative level to withhold information that would lead to sanctions (Manning 1977, 58). Thus, because rules must remain tacit so that organizations can effectively function, a structured power struggle wages between representatives of organizational levels, especially if behavior comes under departmental review. Negotiation to subvert organizational constraints is ongoing; power struggle is incessant.

One way organizations maintain power is through invisible encoding procedures. Decoding the "invisible assumptive tenets and understandings" that two police organizations use to interpret incoming calls for help unmasks organizational power (Manning 1982, 235). A call's meaning derives from how the police respond to it, and based on their conventionalized encoding practice, glossed as interpretation, they may choose, perhaps fatally, not to respond.

This ability to define the situation, in this case, the incoming call, shows how organizations monopolize the "centrality of the power that inheres in the ability to control, define, transform and reproduce the codes of life, and to reflect them back to people as versions of themselves and legitimate state power" (Manning 1982, 239). This is analogous to what Marxists have said for over a century: those who own the means of production own the means of mental production; hence, their definition of the situation is usually accepted as legitimate and official.

But even in total institutions, such as maximum-security prisons, "negotiations relocate power in ways that tacitly decouple aspects of authority" (Thomas 1984, 215). Administrators and guards need information, which becomes a bargaining chip for amenities. Negotiation—compromise, exchange, corruption, conning, hassling, and intimidation—alters the balance of power between guards and prisoners to accomplish social order. Negotiation empowers those at the bottom of total institutions with "mechanisms for altering the asymmetrical hierarchical power relations" (217). The need for social order "dramatically alters the hegemonic power structure" (227).

Structural constraints, however, always limit negotiation (P. Hall and Spencer-Hall 1982; O'Toole and O'Toole 1981). P. Hall and Spencer-Hall compared the negotiation processes in two school districts, outlining facilitating and impeding conditions: Numerous structural variables, such as the superintendents' administrative style and differences in the active interest, knowledge, and interaction within the boards of education, contributed to the negotiation power of one school district and the impotence of the other. Structural constraints can also restrict interorganizational negotiation: "Political control, funding, professional dominance, religion, [and] ethnicity," (O'Toole and O'Toole 1981, 31) were among the circumstances affecting the success of an interdepartmental goal to unite eleven agencies as one rehabilitation complex.

Negotiation can also affect an organization's career by reframing purposes and goals. A nonprofit organization averted extinction by negotiating a new reality that redefined its mission, clients, funding sources, payment and operation methods, and board membership criteria (Altheide 1988). The most important structural variable was resource mobilization, especially recruitment of powerful community board members. Clearly, the negotiation of meaning is a vital organizational asset to meet contingencies or emergencies.

Several recent SI studies, then, analyze the struggle between organizational power and its human subversion. SI's illustrations that negotiation is a product of constraint and human agency thematically resonate with S. Hall's view of social life. As Grossberg (1986, 63) puts it, "Hall occupies the middle ground between those who emphasize the determination of human life by social structures and processes, and those who, emphasizing the freedom and creativity of human activity, fail to recognize its historical limits and conditions."

SI research that portrays how master institutions affect everyday interaction and human consciousness further develops this power tension. I begin with research on the economy.

The Economy as a Master Institution

Hochschild's book, *The Managed Heart: Commercialization of Human Feeling* (1983), draws on Marx, Mills, Goffman, Freud, and SI's conceptualization of emotion to introduce the concept of emotional labor, which "requires one to induce or suppress feeling in order to sustain the outward countenance that produces the proper state of mind in others" (7). In capitalism, one new service is to keep customers happy, a form of alienated labor that requires deep acting, to disguise artificiality. Hochschild argues, correctly I believe, that even as industrial labor vanishes, Marx's analysis of alienated labor describes the emotional labor of service production, the commodity being "trained management of feeling."

Describing the negotiation of roles and rules, Hochschild enumerates new demands—feeling rules—service-producing organizations place on employees. She argues the negotiation of feeling rules in private life is constrained in public life by organizational feeling rules and role expectations.

In scientific management, Taylorism, management of employee time and motion fostered alienation. Roles and rules constrained interaction, but feeling rules remained flexible. In professional jobs, the negotiated order perspective shows how flexible roles and rules are. Nevertheless, Hochschild's research reveals that, for women primarily, part of the work normative order is a new role expectation, emotional display. Feeling rules require workers to manage and commercialize their emotions, a new form of alienation and a new object of knowledge to manage scientifically. The organizational constraint on the emotions and behavior of flight attendants and bill collectors parallels that foisted on well-to-do automobile dealers.

The automobile industry allows corporate elites to enforce a pricing policy that leads to a criminogenic market structure (Farberman 1975), arguing they need to sell in large numbers to achieve economies of scale, as well as avoid direct competition. They financially pressure new-car dealers to accomplish their purpose, forcing them to be high-volume, low-profit-per-unit enterprises. Manufacturer control of the number of cars supplied the dealer and the profit allowed per unit is the key social fact of the market structure that leads to a chain of criminal acts. Dealers react to this pricing policy by committing numerous frauds, including "fraudulent warrantee statements to the manufacturers," "service repair rackets," kickbacks used-car wholesalers pay used-car managers of new-car dealerships, and state fraud through tax evasion.[2]

The Media as a Master Institution

The media affect social interaction as a generalized referent for how to act (Altheide 1985, 18). Media organizing principles and procedures have produced a "media self" as "more and more of one's identity [becomes] tied to products and styles" (1984, 178).

That the media as a master institution socially construct reality, make them a political force (Altheide 1984, 1985). Although Altheide detects major problems with the "dominant ideology thesis"—that the ideas of the ruling class are the ruling ideas—he considers the media a "dominant cultural form" and "social force" that socializes people to the "values, beliefs, meanings, and symbols that define our social world" (1985, 13). Information and events are fitted to a media logic; the media's power can "transform the spatial and temporal dimensions of events" (Altheide 1985, 21).

Altheide (2002, 230) has done empirical work to show how the media have "forged a fear-generating machine that trades on fostering common public definitions of fear, danger, and dread." "The[ir] message is that our lives are dominated by fear, that fearful stuff surrounds us, and the world is really frightening" (245). This discourse of fear centers on children. Innumerable news agency reports (increasingly in the late 1980s and mid-1990s) describe the tragedies that either befall or are perpetrated by children. We either need fear children or what is done to them. Children's stories are turned into instruments by political agencies in order to manufacture "a discourse of control" (231). That discourse of control centers on both protecting children and the public from them, justifying social control agencies enacting "social policies that promote state control and surveillance" (247). Mass communication organizations define the source of fear and manufacture a culture of fear. Thus news agencies share complicity in elevated levels of social control; their fear generation transforms them into proxy social control agencies. State social control agencies manipulate this rampant fear to increase their power over society. "Directing fear in a society is tantamount to controlling that society" (247). The really frightening outcome is that social control agencies have discovered the perfect instrument in fear over children to garrison a panoptic/police society. A nation scared out of its wits "can justify excess in protecting children, and increasingly . . . can excuse excess in punishing them" (248).

Media can manufacture desire as well as fear. Corporations, through marketing strategy and media campaigns, whet humans' desire to transform mundane reality (Farberman 1980). Capitalism manufactures demand through media advertising, saturating our consciousness with fantasy. We want to become—and spend a great deal of money trying to become—something other than what we are, a process of "situation identity transformation." Further, the ability to manufacture a consumer consciousness that keeps us salivating in hot pursuit of fantasy experiences and products does more than daily reconstitute the corporate economy; it is political and social control that defuses *ressentiment*. We will focus on *ressentiment* in the section on emotions.

Similarly, Wolf (1986), expanding Shibutani's[3] argument, reveals how oppression is legitimated and notions of inferiority channeled into the oppressed. Powerful elites, who control the media, suffuse the airwaves with images of the working class, poor, and minorities as inferior; the oppressed internalize such depictions, as active but falsely conscious participants in their own oppression. Wolf proffers the notion of "reflexive legitimation, a process by which the external structure of oppression is internalized" (1986, 228).

Legitimation means the "process by which an oppressed group comes to accept the dominant-subordinate relationship" (Wolf 1986, 221). For the poor, minorities, and women, the process of internalizing the normative order through taking the role of the generalized other, in which self, mind, and identity emerge, leads to "the internalization of inferiority vis-à-vis the dominant group or of one's place in the system as appropriate or both" (222). Wolf thus explains how a capitalist or any regime can legitimate oppression through channeling meaning—in this case, by internalizing inferiority. The goal is to manufacture consent which produces accommodation to the way things are and reduces resistance since the system is seen as just. The best way to make such an accommodation a fait accompli, Wolf argues, is to have the subjugated internalize a definition of reality (ideology) favorable to the political elite. If the oppressed defined the situation as one of no justice, then political turmoil may ignite, that is, no peace.

Structures of Race, Gender, Power, and Ideology and Discourse

One's social location in racial and gender hierarchies is one of the most powerful aspects of structure that still oppresses women and minorities. Both are still victimized by structural arrangements and deleterious definitions. Recent SI elaborations underscore how both racial and gender hierarchies and the social construction of gender and race reproduce inequality in everyday interaction and social relations. These studies attend to structure and illuminate the macrosociological links between communication and community. But agency (resistance and struggle) is always involved.

Race

Before we look at current research, however, a myth about SI should be dispelled. Many who criticize SI for not focusing on the historical and structural features of race relations fail to explore Herbert Blumer's work. Even interactionists forget their mentor's important works on this subject (Lyman 1984; Lyman and Vidich 1988; Maines 1988, 1989). As Lyman notes, Blumer not only has been ignored; he in fact provides a historical, structural, and institutional account of race relations. Blumer's dissent from both order and conflict perspective social prognostications "that industrialization inevitably undermines the traditional or established order," so far proves correct (Lyman 1984, 114). No industrial society has to date abolished the racial order, and certainly ethnic group oppression in eastern Europe supports Blumer's view.

Recent SI research explores the struggle against oppression; it also examines the effort to redefine collective image. A small section of Strauss's book, *Negotiations* (1978), focuses on the negotiation to reduce ethnic inequality. He acknowledges the importance of power and structure, defining power not only as a structural but processual property (Strauss 1978, 209).

When mobility is fixed, of course, relatively little opportunity for negotiation exists between the powerful and powerless. Strauss cites this structural condition in Kenya among European settlers, Asians, and Africans during the colonial period. Power descended structurally from whites to Asians to Africans.

By the 1950s, both Asians and Africans were more effectively organized, which "began to alter the old balance of political power" (Strauss 1978, 219). The goal of self-determination—a negotiation process—structurally relates to group position. Improved structural position increases negotiation ability. Thus, a structural context always has a corresponding negotiating context. In Kenya, where overt and silent conflict, manipulation, rule by coercion and coercive law reign, negotiation nevertheless is part of the social order (223), a primary theme of Strauss's book: "A social order—even the most repressive—without some forms of negotiation would be inconceivable" (ix). But equally important is that negotiation is a process that can foment systemic change.

The elite's ability to define the image of minorities, an ideological struggle, provides one way to reproduce inequality. Negotiation to redefine the image is an ongoing struggle. The emergence of a new negotiated image of blacks and whites is embedded directly within the historical and changing structure of racial inequality in both the United States and India (Killian 1985). Drawing on and expanding the work of Blumer and Goffman, Killian shows the sensitivity of such negotiations to even slight changes in the structure of black/white relations. Thus, Killian argues, whites have suffered stigma reversal, "the imputation of guilt and moral inferiority to the members of a dominant group on the basis of descent when the moral justification of the group's position of advantage is being redefined" (9). He suggests this directly relates to "changes in the relative power of the two [racial groups which] seem basic to the development of such challenges" (9). But that power shift has brought limited gains.

But even this slight power realignment has redefined images, which may affect further negotiations. Killian argues that even though whites still dominate, this renegotiated image poses a legitimacy crisis for whites, deemed politically and morally bankrupt, without justification for their continued privilege and rank.

Lee (1980) also explores the negotiation of collective images, a process embedded within a context of unequal ethnic group power and access to valued resources. Colonization and independence, Lee points out, shaped the structural relations among three major West Malaysian ethnic groups (Malays, Chinese, and Indians).

The specific issue negotiated within this context centered on the enactment of a National Language Bill, which established the Malay's language, Bahasa Malaysia, as official language. A countermove sought to establish a Chinese language university, Merdeka University. The bill's enactment and government failure to support establishment of the university sparked fear of eroding opportunity and mobility for Chinese and Indians.

Diverse elements within the Chinese community, for related but different reasons, rallied around the denial of a Chinese university to ensconce the image of discrimination, them as underdogs. The university effort failed, but they did negotiate an underdog image important for future struggles.

SI illuminates the power of culture and communication to both reproduce and struggle against racist and sexist social practices at all levels. By culture, I mean S. Hall's notion of "the grounded terrain of practices, representations, languages and customs of any specific historical society which have taken root in and help shape popular life" (S. Hall 1986a, 26). The multitudinous cultural institutions and communication practices "play an absolutely vital role in giving, sustaining and reproducing different societies in a racially [and sexually] structural form" (26). For Hall, elites' control of the ability of culture and communication to define reality and thus reproduce privileged social worlds, constitutes their power. As these studies show, their social position yields elites that power, and manipulative communication directly links to hierarchical social structure. But SI research also illuminates that struggle against such structures, power, and ideology is ongoing.

Storrs (1999) portrays the resistance and struggle of mixed-race women living in a racist society. Whiteness has traditionally been defined as representing the superior race and any (even one drop) of "black blood" has been defined as a mark of blackness and inferiority. Yet the women that Storss interviewed redefine the racial order: "Contrary to dominant racial assumptions about the superiority of whiteness, these women perceive their identities as potentially 'spoiled' not by their non-whiteness, but by their whiteness—their lack of non-white racial purity and their appearance of being 'too white'" (188). Anything is open to being redefined. One of Dewey's cardinal premises underscored earlier, is that the stimulus is symbolic, which means that the meaning of any object is collectively defined and hence can change. Storrs (188) recognizes this: "whiteness is not a static identity, but, instead, is in flux because individuals challenge its meanings" Mixed-race women (this group anyway) engage in "identity work" as a form of resistance to prevailing definitions of whiteness as superior. Whiteness, to them, is meaningless, empty, and oppressive. "These women reject their white ancestry and culture because of their interpretation of this culture, and their ancestors, as racist, patriarchal, and discriminatory [; instead,] non-whiteness for [these] women is perceived and discussed using positive attributes: spiritual, caring, and nurturing" (196). Storrs reports that these women attempt to pass as nonwhite by using symbolic markers (hair color and style, makeup, dress and demeanor, and narratives drawn from resistance ideology of a personal history of oppression and discrimination, of encountering whites as evil and nonwhites as good) (200-204). As is obvious, discourses of resistance, analogous to discourses of oppression, employ racial essentialism: "the belief that races are real, invariable, immutable, fixed, natural, and empirical" (203) that "values and personalities are naturally and essentially rooted" (207). Storrs (208) has interwoven both structure and agency, pointing out how "institutional forces constrain and shape individual identities" through, for example, one's position in the racial hierarchy and the affect of racist ideologies on attitudes and behavior. Yet mixed-race women as "[i]ndividuals and groups are active agents in the contestation and construction of racial categories and identities" through, for example, "their negative characterization of whiteness" (208). They "reverse the stigma" of nonwhiteness and stigmatize whiteness.

Nagel's (2001) research also shows how institutional forces impose definitions of essentialist sexualities associated with race, ethnicity, and nationality. "Sexual ascription is an extremely powerful and loaded means to juxtapose *our* racial, ethnic, or national group against *their* racial, ethnic or national group" (126; emphasis in original). Imputed sexualities is another way that those with the power to define the public consciousness construct the "other," that is, use "ideological material out of which racial, ethnic, and national boundaries are constructed" (126). The "sexual components of ethnic constructions contribute to the profane potency of ethic slurs and prejudices" for these ethnic constructions are saturated in the images of "racial pollution or invasion" (129). The Census Bureau's "pronouncements are pregnant with sexualized images linking race and reproduction. They make immigration demographic patterns sound like the spread of a deadly epidemic" (128). Ideological images of "welfare queens," "teenage mothers," and black felons such as Willie Horton are intended to bring to public consciousness "racialized images of immoral and excessive sexuality" (129). Imputed "sexuality works to justify systems of inequality and domination" (136), powerful stereotypes in the construction of a racist, sexist, nationalist order.

Nagel brings to light that there are even more tragic results of racist sexualizing: that the other is always a sexual other, an object upon which to vent rage, hatred, and violence. We act on the basis of our definitions of others; once we have dehumanized and objectified them, anything is possible. "In countries around the world, rape often is seen as a polluting action, a way to soil the victim actually and symbolically, sometimes extending beyond the moment of violation when victims are mutilated or when pregnancies or births result" (133). These are the situations in everyday life where structure is at its most powerful.

The above bring to light the brutality, cruelness, and inhumanity of racism, of openly racist ideology and social practices. Yet Trepagnier (2001) argues that racism is more deeply embedded in the consciousness and social practices of American society than that, that there exists a "silent racism." It "refers to unspoken negative thoughts, emotions, and attitudes regarding African Americans and other people of color on the part of white people. Silent racism results from misinformation and negative ideas about minority groups that permeate the culture" (142). Silent racism is different from the overt, "everyday racism" that permeates American institutions, it does not refer to "discriminatory statements or actions taken against" people of color (144). Silent racism is practiced by people who do not believe that they are racist, thereby perpetuating institutional racism since their actions go unexamined. However, as Trepagnier (145) argues, drawing on the Thomas Axiom (if one defines a situation as real, it is real in its consequences), "[d]efinitions imbued with silent racism produce racist actions." "As white people construct their definitions of situations, they use the silent racism embedded in their perspectives. The actions that proceed from definitions and perspectives imbued with racism are the everyday racism that constitute institutional racism" (146). Trepagnier wants to eliminate the binary categories of racist and not racist, arguing instead that in a society and culture where we are socialized by "parents, teachers, peers, and media" to "learn the negative thoughts, emotions, and attitudes that comprise silent racism" it is more accurate to say (following Blumer in 1939) that there is a continuum, "that white people are racist in varying degrees" (146).

Trepagnier studied a group of primarily young, educated (college degrees) white women who believed that they were not racist. However, ironically, in the midst of group conversations the members realized, when challenged by others, that they employed unwitting racist stereotypes and paternalism (patronizing attitudes). Everyone, including the author of the study, found that silent racism was embedded in their consciousness and social practices. Trepagnier concludes that racism is so deep within the American psyche that even those who detest racism unconsciously practice it, which makes racism hard to eliminate. "Because silent racism is hard to detect, it does its damage undisturbed, obscuring the link between individual racism and institutional racism" (159). Trepagnier's research illustrates the macrosociological link between communication and community.

Gender

Patriarchal society structures gender inequality in interaction through traditional patterns of male dominance and higher socioeconomic status, reproduced even in extramarital relationships (Richardson 1986, 1988). Such constraints as time, space, privacy, self-investment, expectations of temporariness, and the "demographic bind" (there are not enough men to go around) contribute to interaction that reinforces rather than challenges traditional patterns of power and dominance.

The opportunities for women to meet men at work and their receptivity to affairs with "occupational peers" are both greater now than in the past. Eschewing the "kept mistress" identity, these women experience independence, pursue activities such as an education and career, explore their sexuality, or raise their children alone. But women involved with married men become disempowered and disillusioned—ironic, for they enter these affairs to gain more independence than they perceived available in traditional marriage.

Men in the relationship control the world of home and affairs. Single, feminist women engaged in extramarital affairs, who may want to deconstruct traditional patterns of gender inequality, end up reproducing differential sexual gratification, self-esteem, and power. The overarching constraint of gender structures the status inequality of extramarital as much as marital relationships.

Police department workplace politics also reproduce gender inequality, in a number of ways: environmental cues that structure "territorial arrangements" to reinforce stereotypical gender roles (that is, certain places are "owned" by men, and women who encroach are regarded as deviants or receive verbal and nonverbal gestures casting them as service or sexual provider); dehumanizing verbal cues (for example, broad, girl, lady, bitch, and lesbian); joking relationships and verbal putdowns; gossip; nonverbal cues, such as men touching women but not vice versa, by which "women are reminded that they are both sex objects and subordinates"; and sexual harassment (Martin 1978).

Martin's research shows that women also suffer the politics of exclusion—from information exchange networks, informal social life, getting close to officials for sponsorship, socialization, and promotion. This impairs their role performance and institutional mobility. In a patriarchal society, gender handicaps women at work, sexualizes the workplace, and reinforces subordinate status. The unsurprising result is that women may suffer a negative self-image and thwarted occupational role performance.

Hammond further illustrates the macrosociological communication/community link by noting that women medical students must build special vocabularies of motive to counter male peers' suspicions that they are not serious, competitive, motivated, qualified candidates for the physician occupation (Hammond 1980).

Men, as dominant, can and constantly do question the "gender fitness" of females in medical school. Women must create past and present gender fitness biographies to gain peer acceptance. For example, they may argue that they are not different from men or that traditional nurturing qualities make them superior. Women's task of proving gender fitness and capability to be a physician renders medical school one long, continual status-degradation ceremony.

Murray (2000, 135) also examines how workplace organizations reproduce gender hierarchy, but, in addition, she notes how men and women "actively contribute to child care's gendered occupational status." Murray studied two child care centers. Child care is an occupation where 94 percent of the employees are women, yet where men dominate in administration. Murray is interested in the accounts and vocabularies of motive that workers, especially men, deploy to explain their presence in a "low-paid, low-prestige gendered occupation" (138). As we saw in the section on race, understanding of social life, self, and others is constructed out of the available discourses in the culture. "What workers think, feel, and express verbally and behaviorally (and thus symbolically) at the interactional level is profoundly shaped by social structural processes and historically constructed meanings about child care and women's work" (138). The question that haunts these workers when asked by others is why would anyone choose an occupation where the financial and prestige rewards are minuscule? "The women workers drew on either sex role socialization or innate biological forces to explain their presence in this occupation, and the men talked about political and academic motives" (147). Women accounted for being a child care worker due to the maternal instinct, their ability to have babies, they needed the money or other reasons that diminished their choice. "The need to explain away their agency arises from workers' awareness of the occupational status of child care and outsiders' perceptions of them as (unskilled) babysitters" (149). However, men saw themselves as "active agents in their employment selection" (151). But both male and female accounts to explain why one stays in such an occupation end up reproducing gender hierarchy, of reinforcing the stereotype of low-paid, low-prestige work as women's work and that emotional rewards are equitable compensation for low pay. The irony is that "developing a vocabulary of motive that privileges feeling rewards over financial ones in effect robs them of the rhetoric to demand more compensation and, by implication, more status for their occupation" (157). Child care workers are active agents in their own oppression, mostly because they are subjugated by the sexist discourses that frame their perception. They accept rather than develop a critical consciousness to oppose them.

Conversational interruptions between patients and female physicians also reveal gender's master status in our society (West 1984).[4] Parsons's notion that physicians' status and role usually provide control of patient-physician interaction holds, except when the doctor is female: male physicians make 67 percent of the interruptions in private conversations with patients, female physicians only 32 percent. Interruptions subvert authority and control. They vitiate females' performance of the physician role and can harm the patient, for authority and control are important to diagnosis and treatment (Wolinsky, quoted in West 1984, 94).

If females cannot maintain control and authority even at the pinnacle of culturally validated statuses in the United States, how much greater must they suffer in occupations less culturally validated? West's research shows that scripts do not determine statuses, roles, and communication, even in a status, physician, Parsons uses to model scripts' determining qualities. Instead, status, role, and communication are constrained by their macrosociological links to a sexist society's hierarchical social structure.

Power

SI empirical research explores, as the foregoing implies, the ways that power and inequality are reproduced, and that negotiation of reality, or definition of the situation, is politically constructed to maintain hegemony and power. We now turn to conceptualizing an interactionist definition of power.

"[P]ower is generally seen as multifaceted, relational, processual, and contingent while being dialectically embedded in situations, organizations, and institutions" (Hall and Wing 2000, 317). This interactionist definition highlights both structure and agency. Increasingly, interactionists implore researchers of everyday life not to ignore the past that is responsible for much in the present. "If we ignore the past, history, and the consequences of prior social action, we miss much about how power persists through shaping situations and organizations, constituting rules, categories, and meanings, and distributing resources" (Hall and Wing 2000, 318). Additionally, in attending to structure, "it is imperative to show how social forces, processes, and influences actually make a point of entry into the social life of groups and actors" (Hall 1997, 398-99).

"Metapower" is the analysis of the processes through which social organization makes a point of entry into the everyday lives of actors at various levels. Actors who have it create "the conditions and contexts in which other actors may find themselves" (403). Superordinates in all institutions can create conditions and consequences that affect actors everywhere. Metapower allows the ruling class, "dominants," superordinates, in general, those who have institutional resources to "organize situations in which subordinates act together without the presence of the former" (405). Additionally, power is to be "invisible . . . so that it is maintained and reproduced without its obvious exercise but with the expected results" (407).

Elites shape the social conditions in which others must act in a variety of ways:

structuring interaction; creating culture; establishing roles; monitoring activity; controlling time, space, and demeanor. [Additionally, elites] structur[e] communication to limit the ability of subordinates to communicate with one another, structur[e] payoffs to stimulate competition between subordinates, and promot[e] ideologies that foster identification with the superordinate in contrast with peers (405). [In every way, manner, shape, and form elites] seek to institutionalize power by defining "the game" and the "rules of the game." (407)

Hall identifies five processes that maintain and reproduce metapower: (a) strategic agency is a process in which institutionally high-status actors create the "social conditions and relations for other agencies," which is usually done by making policy (408); (b) rules and conventions allow those who establish them to shape "both a cause and a rationale for behavior" (409); (c) structuring situations, relationships, and activities is a process that occurs through "the formation of committees, task forces, project teams, councils, or commissions," where selection of members and the chair, and establishing goals and communication set the agenda for all those concerned (410); (d) creating culture, discourse, charters and missions "focuses upon shaping the symbols and discourse to assure valued intentions and actions" (411); and (e) delegation, whereby one tries "to produce cooperative or compliant behavior, often by getting others to embrace the intentions of their superiors" (413). However, Hall, following Foucault, realizes that "with tendencies for domination, there are also possibilities for resistance" (407), accentuating that agency is always a part of structure.

Hall in earlier work (1985; 1972) also argues that the powerful manufacture ideology to justify their status and dominance. Government officials persuade citizens they know best what is "good for society," the "commonweal," or, as so often put, the "national interest." They promulgate goals in a universal language that belies particular class-interest goals, that is, the ruling ideas are the ideas of the ruling class masked to appear universal. The powerful dominate the structure of social relations, the forms of deference and demeanor, and the regulation of time and space. They institutionalize procedures and rules which they can nevertheless abrogate with impunity. Lastly, Hall also considers false consciousness: "the third face of power reifi[es] a culture and structure so that subordinates are unaware of their manipulation and exploitation" (1985, 341). We will explore this last theme in the section on ideology.

The following research is some of the best at exploring the multidimensional faces of power. Hosticka (1979) and Molotch and Boden (1985)[5] focus on how reality making directly ties to structure and power. Those who own the means of communication construct the definition of reality, "invok[ing] routine conversational procedures to accomplish power" (Molotch and Boden 1985, 273). These control methods, especially subverting human agency, because largely unnoticed, exploit greater access to the interpretation of events; turntaking, topic and interruption control; and leading questions to define such aspects of reality as "the description of what happened, the evaluation of what ought to happen, and the prescription of what is going to happen" (Hosticka 1979, 607). Through this cultural domination in an ongoing, usually unrecognized fashion, men dominate women; counselors and teachers, students; doctors, patients; lawyers, clients; courtroom interrogators, witnesses; and parents, children. Power, then, pervades everyday life, hardly limited to ruling-class use. Those with power shape reality and culture via ideology to maintain social control.

Kahne and Schwartz's (1978) research shows how the constraints of time, locus of client/counselor exchange, persons involved, and social network unacknowledgedly influence psychiatric diagnoses. They reveal that these contextual features of interaction must be considered to prevent a sterile and distorted view of social behavior.

Two studies illuminate power's processual aspects and linkage to organizational structures (Luckenbill 1979; Travers 1982). Collective action involves power and thus "asymmetrical interaction, a conflict of interests, and the intentional production of compliance" (Luckenbill 1979, 107). Travers's study of punks, who desacralize themselves, and nurses, who sacralize themselves, illustrates that people can produce ritual power in interaction by dress and demeanor. Punks' visual construction of a mutilated and repelling image also expresses cultural resistance. "Style has meaning" (Hebdige 1979). But SI shows that power inheres in joint action and thus is not limited to the ruling class. Dress, demeanor, and communication have a macrosociological link, in the case of the punks, to resist structures of domination.

Ideology and Discourse

SI is developing a strong notion of the power of ideology and discourse in everyday life. S. Hall's (S. Hall 1986b, 29) notion of ideology has been employed by many within the interactionist tradition.

> The problem of ideology concerns the ways in which ideas of different kinds grip the minds of masses, and thereby become a "material force." It has especially to do with the concepts and the languages of practical thought which stabilize a particular form of power and domination; or which reconcile and accommodate the mass of the people to their subordinate place in the social formation.

The ability of economic and political elites to maintain their power and social order is bolstered by mass acceptance of their definition of reality. It is conceptually accepted within the interactionist community that *"power is the ability to define a situation for self and others"* (Altheide 2000, 5; emphasis in the original; see also Musolf 1992). The foregoing SI research has showed that organizations—medical schools, police stations, and universities—also struggle to define image in an ideological battle tied to protecting power and privilege. "The ability of the ruling bloc to secure its economic domination and establish political power [depends upon its] ideological struggle to win the consent of the masses to its definition of reality" (Grossberg 1986, 69). But SI shows how broad this tendency to define reality is among powerholders of all types. It thus mines a whole new research area focused on the political economy of meaning and reality, a theme Norman Denzin takes up (explored shortly).

SI also brings a unique insight into how ideology and discourse figure in all facets of everyday life. It extends the research agenda beyond "traditional state and politics" into the everyday social worlds where we are assaulted and dominated but also struggle and triumph. SI argues that communication has macrosociological links to hierarchical social structures and that social structures, besides economic and political institutions, need empirical investigation. That is what SI has done by empirically researching race and gender. Ideology and discourse also help maintain the racial and gender orders.

The most persuasive way that silent racism is inculcated into the minds of Americans is through the same way that the general racist discourse is conveyed, through the "media and the cinematic racial order" (Denzin 2001, 244), through "complex and fragmented media landscapes. These landscapes shape and define a society's discourses about race and race relations" (247). But discourse in general, and about race specifically, is broader than media landscapes. It is through a culture's total discourse that human subjects are constituted, the subjectification process. We are made into subjects by the formative efficacy of our culture's discourses which we internalize and absorb to the point that we think them "natural"; they provide the fundamental categories of understanding through which we perceive and think. "[D]iscourse is an order of concepts, schemata, constituted objects, systems of representation, and so forth, with its own internal structure and relations which impose themselves on subjects as the medium of their thinking" (Smith 1996, 178). This means that "[c]onsciousness, subjectivity, the subject, are hence always embedded, active, and constituted" by a culture's total landscape of discourses (172). Discourses constitute us as subjects by shaping our consciousness, the ways we think, perceive, feel, and, consequently, behave. We act on the basis of our interpretations, interpretations interactively constructed from a culture's discourses. "The mass media and popular culture provide significant symbolic meanings and perspectives that individuals may draw on in specific social situations" (Altheide 2002, 230). If a culture's discourses are racist, sexist, and classist, then our subjectivities are subjugated to those ideologies; moreover, we can actively behave, though unwittingly, in reproducing society's and/or our own oppression, as we saw in Trepagnier's and Murray's research. Again, we see the macrosociological links between communication and community. "Cultures command, convey, and ultimately are constituted by the discourses they reflect and invoke" (Altheide 2002, 247). It is important to emphasize that we constitute the discourses and culture that shape us. A culture's discourses influence but do not determine our perspectives or behavior. We can change a culture's discourses, resist subjugation to racist ideologies, as is ongoing in American culture. Humans do vigilantly interrogate their own and public discourses and actively construct and subsequently internalize discourses that increasingly (though with seemingly glacial speed) shape public consciousness to oppose oppression in all its variegated forms. American society is a place where ideology and discourse, through innumerable talk shows and other media formats, are incessantly interrogated ad nauseam. The result is that public consciousness is ever evolving as we reconstitute it daily. As can be extrapolated from Trepagnier, it is a lifelong project to acquire a critical consciousness, since ruling-class discourses are so deeply embedded and naturalized as the only way to think that in the very process of thinking we are nonracist, racist background assumptions undergird our concepts. However arduous and painful, this lifelong struggle is the defining moment of agency and the human spirit; it encapsulates the meaning of living by Socrates' precept that the unexamined life is not worth living. But transforming consciousness is an iceberg of egocentricity unless coupled to an avalanche of action that changes structures according to ever more egalitarian principles. Certainly the raison d'être of sociology and policy is not only to understand the self and the world but also to change them for the better.

This leads us to consider Norman K. Denzin's recent work, for more than any other interactionist, he embraces the notion of ideology and discourse, urging SI to espouse a political economy of meaning.

Denzin on the Ideology of Power

Denzin (1989a, 1989b) examines cinematic texts as one of the major ways ideologies perpetuate. He believes film epitomizes the power of cultural representations to shape lived experience. Communication is power and inherently ideological, reflecting its authors' worldview. Patriarchal bias pervades Western cultural representations. Control and production of images/voices reproduces images and ideologies that favor powerholders. They depict "'natural occurrences' and 'what-goes-without-saying,'" reifying gender stereotypes and sustaining "the traditional belief that 'objective' accounts of the social can be given" (Denzin 1989a, 38).

But texts invite oppositional interpretations. Denzin calls for "subversive" textual analyses to articulate the obscured voices of, for example, women in film and to illustrate that before decoding, films (and all cultural texts) reproduce cultural ideologies, particularly stereotypes about men, women, the family, and (in Denzin's studies) alcoholism. The subversive reading provides an alternative and/or opposition to powerholders' staged, dominant, and ideological reality/writing.

This new project meshes SI with cultural studies. "Cultural studies must always be radical, subversive and irreverent, always seeking to locate how the hegemonic, ideological structures of late postmodernism perpetuate particular conservative, scientific, individualistic images of societies and their cultural meanings" (Denzin 1991, 30).

Though acknowledging Blumer's argument that "films do shape content," Denzin does not posit culture in cause and effect, or determinist, terms. This reveals the influence of Derrida's deconstruction project. Denzin refrains from any object/subject dualism that views mind and behavior as determinate of culture. He elaborates his stance (1990, 1991) by arguing that to see cultural objects as determinates implies a "sender-receiver" communication model. Such a model reifies cultural representations, assumes they have a "determinate set of meanings communicated in a legible, clear manner" (1990, 1578). The assumption that cultural texts have objective, consensual meanings, obscures the political nature of both interpretation and resistance.

Denzin acknowledges an ideology and a political economy of meaning, but "individuals come out and create their own situated interpretations of themselves, their emotions, gendered sexuality, political beliefs, and intimate social relationships" (Denzin 1989b, 13). He enlists these two positions—(1) meaning is indeterminate and must be contextualized within the subject's own history of lived experience; and (2) a critical SI cultural studies project must "deconstruct and explode the repressive political economy of signs and meanings that invade and structure contemporary life," to give SI a new direction to follow. This research project "will show how language and its codes have become manipulated commodities within the cultural terrain of postmodern life" (Denzin 1990, 1579). Thus, Denzin's research agenda is threefold: "examine the field of cultural meanings and their production within the logocentric, political economy of the everyday world"; provide subversive readings that voice opposition to dominant ideologies; and maintain the indeterminacy of meaning (Denzin 1991, 31). His project presents one direction for a critical SI. There are many other new directions influencing symbolic interactionism, such as autoethnography, postmodernism, and cultural studies. They are beyond the scope of the present text.

Interactionists reviewed here are, in effect, decoding a political economy of meaning. They accept that social and cultural forces shape life, but rather than given, or determinate of attitudes and behavior, they are mediating influences, to be empirically investigated as to how the individual interprets them, assigns meaning, and then responds with the "history-producing power of human agency" (Parker 2000). This renders attitudes and behavior understandable in light of the history of lived experience, yet allows analysts to decode the ideological/political economy of cultural production, present subversive readings, and comment on the accuracy of those defining the situation, that is, to engage in deconstruction.

Human Agency and Resistance

Denzin's project to offer oppositional textual interpretations provides groundwork for social change. SI now constantly emphasizes that humans are actors, not just objects. SI research has shown that social change strategies inhere in negotiation, especially when we know that organizations can be made responsive to protest and dissent. "The structures of social orders to some extent are always breaking down and being reconstituted" (Maines 1979, 524). For those committed to negotiated social change, this means not forgetting "that social structure should also be regarded as a dependent variable, can be examined as a product of interaction, and is created, maintained, and changed through interactive processes" (527). Organizations can be said to sow the seeds of their own destruction. "There is a tension among the parts of an organizational structure which continually threatens to lead to the creation of structural modifications" (Maines and Charlton 1985, 302).

P. Hall (1987) favors strategic analysis of organizational constraints to mobilize countervailing power. He enumerates the categories of collective activity, network, conventions and practices, resources and power, temporality and processuality, and grounding relevant to understand both structure and change aspects of organizations.

Humans, as selves and minds, are not isolated, cynical, and apathetic "cultural dopes" or robots (Cicourel 1972; Garfinkel 1972; S. Hall 1986a, 1986b). Organizations comprise relationship networks that can, through collective behavior, constitute power, thwart formal roles and rules, and mobilize countervailing resources (Fine and Kleinman 1983, 106).

Negotiation principles also hold that "social order is constructed through meaningful, self-other interaction" (Fine and Kleinman 1983, 97). Essential "to [any] social structure is the centrality of actors' meanings; [that is] [m]eaning is equally important to social organization because it shapes stability and change within social structures" (98). Thus, the supposition that negotiation can change organizations and that collective meaning, consciousness, and the definition of the situation are central to the making of history, suggests a new SI research direction. Negotiation within organizations for roles and rules is far from social reconstruction, however. Also, negotiation may yield only system adjustments, not radical change.[6] This is where SI still must work to make its perspective further possibilities of systemic social change. Critical ethnographies that develop a discourse or ideology to empower people and help them transform institutions could assist (McCall and Becker 1990, 9).

Visano suggests (1988) that critical interactionist studies, though not aimed at social reconstruction, can provide "analyses of class struggles, the subordination of women, domination/emancipation, or political economy" to make the oppressed "aware of their predicament, to suggest how suffering can be alleviated, and to make authority relations problematic" (240). The studies here reviewed begin this move to a critical interactionist perspective. Analysis of the reproduction of cultural ideologies, the political economy of meaning, and the hierarchy of relationships within communication are new directions for SI. The challenge is to develop a theory "that will recognize both human agency and the production of knowledge and culture and will at the same time take into account the power of material and ideological structure" (Weiler, in McCall and Becker 1990, 7).

The reviewed studies best attempt to mesh structure, process, and agency. SI studies of the media as an institution show that the meanings people assign events in part result from the communication industry's symbol manipulation; that powerful elites run that industry; and that those in power seek to socialize people to, and have them identify with, their definition of social reality, the problem of ideology. The above studies also reveal how power and ideology are reproduced, as well as resisted, (Wolf 1986; Smith 1996; P. Hall 1997; P. Hall and Wing 2000; Denzin 2001); organizational roles and rules (Manning 1977, 1982; Thomas 1984; P. Hall and Spencer-Hall 1982; O'Toole and O'Toole 1981; Altheide 1988); gender and race hierarchies (Hammond 1980; Martin 1978; Richardson 1986, 1988; Denzin 1989a, 1989b; Storrs 1999; Nagel 2001; Trepagnier 2001; Murray 2000); forms of interaction (West 1984; Luckenbill 1979; Travers 1982; P. Hall 1972, 1985); definition of the situation (Hosticka 1979; Molotch and Boden 1985; Kahne and Schwartz 1978); collective images (Killian 1985; Lee 1980; Strauss 1978); the media as a master institution (Altheide 1984, 1985; Denzin 1989a, 1989b, 1990, 1991; Farberman 1980); and market structures (Farberman 1975; Hochschild 1983).

Clearly SI is attempting to explore the dialectical features of constraint and human agency in social life. As it attends power, structure, institutions, and ideology it furthers a more comprehensive and critical view of social life.

Notes

1. Maines and Charlton (1985) argue there has been an SI tradition of focusing on organizational constraints.

2. Similar work on the economy as master institution was done by Norman K. Denzin, "Crime and the American Liquor Industry." *Studies in Symbolic Interaction* 1 (1978): 887-918.

3. See Tamotsu Shibutani, "Reference Groups as Perspectives," in *Symbolic Interaction: A Reader in Social Psychology*, ed. Jerome G. Manis and Bernard N. Meltzer, 159-70 (Boston: Allyn and Bacon, 1967).

4. An anonymous reviewer suggests that West would probably not identify herself as an interactionist. However, I believe her analysis is, at least, compatible with SI.

5. Molotch and Boden are closer to ethnomethodology than to SI, though this piece is compatible with SI.

6. A reviewer reminded me of this.

7

The Structures of Social Interaction

Interaction and Its Microfoundations: Communication, Coordination, and Consensus

Though a plethora of books and articles have been written on the self, relatively fewer studies (from the symbolic interactionist perspective) have concentrated on society. Herbert Blumer's "Society as Symbolic Interaction" (1967) and "The Sociological Implications of the Thought of George Herbert Mead" (1966a), as well as C. K. Warriner's *The Emergence of Society* (1970), are probably the best-known interactionist treatments of society. Erving Goffman, through both participant and nonparticipant observation, has presented empirical research on society. We elaborate on Goffman's work shortly. I begin by first analyzing "society" as Blumer and Warriner define it.

Contrary to the theorizing of Talcott Parsons and other functionalists, interactionists argue that society is not held together by a "core-value system." Interaction is rife with conflict and antagonism. Such strife stems from value heterogeneity. Larger patterns of conflict, such as class struggle or revolution, may not be ongoing, but self-interested, value-assertive interaction is. Blumer (1966a, 544) issues a caveat to those who view society's cement as a core-value system. "To seek to encompass, analyze, and understand the life of a society on the assumption that the existence of a society necessarily depends on the sharing of values can lead to strained treatment, gross misrepresentation, and faulty lines of interpretation." People may act together for a variety of reasons that have nothing to do with a sharing of values. On the surface it may appear that people must share values to interact, but power, convenience, self-interest, and the like may be the magnet rather than a presupposed value consensus.

If society is not held together by a core-value system, what is it composed of? Blumer's (1964, 241) answer: joint action.

A society is seen as people meeting the varieties of situations that are thrust on them by their conditions of life. These situations are met by working out joint actions in which participants have to align their acts to one another. Each participant does so by interpreting the acts of others and, in turn by making indications to others as to how they should act. By virtue of this process of interpretation and definition joint actions are built up; they have careers.

What is meant by joint action? Blumer uses the term to replace Mead's concept of "social act." It refers to action by more than one person, that is, action in which two or more persons participate. "Joint actions range from a simple collaboration of two individuals to a complex alignment of the acts of huge organizations or institutions" (Blumer 1966a, 540). Joint action thus does not come about through a common value system; instead, "the participants fit their acts together, first, by identifying the social act in which they are about to engage and secondly by interpreting and defining each other's acts in forming the joint act" (Blumer 1966a, 540).

Society or symbolic joint action, then, has five aspects, which I paraphrase from Blumer's paper (1966a). (1) Society is "an ongoing process of action," not a "posited structure of relations"; (2) the concepts of society as interaction must concentrate on "joint action into which the separate lines of action fit and merge"; (3) joint action has a career or history; (4) joint action is generally stable due to common definitions of the situation; and (5) joint action is also open to novelty and uncertainty; thus, human behavior is probabilistic, not deterministic. Blumer underscored interaction and deemphasized structure, that is, "human society must necessarily be seen in terms of the acting units that form it" (Blumer 1967, 144). Interaction should be viewed as "interaction between people and not between roles" (Blumer 1966a, 543). Blumer (1966a, 543) defines interaction as more open-ended, more active, than is implied by the passive-vessel model of socialization that structural functionalists present.

> [Thus symbolic interactionists] see society not as a system whether in the form of a static, moving, or whatever kind of equilibrium but as a vast number of occurring joint actions, many closely linked, many not linked at all, many prefigured and repetitive, others being carved out in new directions, and all being pursued to serve the purposes of the participants and not the requirements of a system.

In order for society to emerge, three necessary interaction conditions must be fulfilled: communication, coordination, and consensus. We examine communication first.

Communication

In order for us to establish communicative competence, our acts have to be representational, that is, they must stand for or represent ideas and be relational—that is, entail mutual awareness among the actors that an act is occurring (Warriner 1970, 126-27). Communication has primitive forms such as gesturing, but language is the differentiating form of communication among humans. Language (written or spoken) is the apex of symbol evolution. "It is not that man has symbols because he has a language, rather he has a language because he is able to symbol" (Warriner 1970, 84). Language brings about one necessary condition for society. "It is only as men use their capacity to symbol as a tool of communication that they create the essential ingredient of society" (Warriner 1970, 133). Language, like any significant symbol, is an arbitrary but intentional construction by an active human mind. Language allows us to transcend the stimulus-response world of the lower animals. Language, and the general capacity to symbolize, means that we no longer respond to a noumenal world (a world that is "objectively" out there) but to a phenomenal one (a world that is socially constructed) (Warriner 1970, 81).

But a phenomenal world makes communication problematic. If communication is to be achieved, our acts must be confirmed; that is, even though language is a common referent we must still infer the proper intention/meaning of a speech-act so as not to miscommunicate. We do this through observation. We engage in *inference-confirmation* through observing whether "the other does indeed perform the action consequences of the meaning inferred" and "by making meanings objective in [our] conduct" (Warriner 1970, 110). And "these acts of confirmation by both actors complete the communication process. Each actor then knows that the other knows that he knows what the other 'had in mind'" (Warriner 1970, 110). The meaning of words and deeds must be caught by all participants; otherwise, we merely send confused messages to others, an example of communication incompetence. A reciprocity of perspectives must be established for every successful communication encounter.

Communication thus necessitates reference, inference, and confirmation (Warriner 1970, 112). The meaning is dependent on and emerges out of the situation: "evidence suggests that it is more appropriate and accurate to see meaning as lying in the situation rather than in the actor" (Warriner 1970, 91). Whether we infer the correct meaning in the situation or not is what makes communication problematic. Incorrect inferences lead to unconfirmed meaning, miscommunication.[1]

The goal of correct *inference-making* is expressed by the phrase "learning to read between the lines," or "I see where you're coming from." George Orwell's word "doublespeak" has made us aware of the distortion in much political speech. And the recent popularity of books on body language and nonverbal communication suggests a recognition of the need to read these forms of communication as though they were texts to be interpreted. Goffman referred to what we wittingly and unwittingly transmit as a distinction between expressions "given" and expressions "given off."

Consensus

What this mutual understanding means is that "communication involves a totally new phenomenon, that of collective meaning" (Warriner 1970, 154). Collective meaning is synonymous with consensus. Consensus does not mean value-consensus: "joint action need not involve or spring from the sharing of common values" (Blumer 1966a, 544). Consensus means interpretive, or inferential, consensus. "What is most immediately apparent about this structuring is that it is collective, consensual, conventional. The actors in any particular group understand what these acts are" (Warriner 1970, 17).

We must use symbols common to the participants in the interaction. Perception must be shared, that is, each actor must recognize "the identity of purpose and meaning among the several actors, and of the mutuality of action in response to the signs jointly perceived" (Warriner 1970, 93). Consensus over meaning is thus necessary for communication.

Coordination

Communication and consensus allow humans to interact and create their environment through coordination. Coordination and cooperation in human affairs are the rewards of communication. "Society is that coordination of action which is created and sustained by the collective representations—the meanings which emerge from interaction, which are shared by a particular collection of actions in particular systems of interactions" (Warriner 1970, 126). Sharing perspectives, or the reciprocity of perspectives, (intersubjectivity) is what makes interaction, and *a fortiori*, society possible. "[People] can act with other[s] because they have come to share notions as to what they will do" (Warriner 1970, 198). "[People] do not constitute a society unless what they do is in concert" (Warriner 1970, 97).

Mannheim's (1936) notion of a particularization of perspectives is an excellent way to view the limits of any one theory or theorist. This is true in the case of Blumer and Warriner. The influence of institutions, bureaucracy, class, race, gender—in general, social constraint—is, if not missing, understated. Zeitlin (1973, 218) argues that Blumer's theory of society deemphasizes structure more than Mead's ever did.

Here Blumer has abandoned Mead's dialectical philosophy and has presented in its place a one-sided interpretation that denies altogether social relationships, social structure, and social organization. Society from this standpoint, becomes a plurality of disembodied, unconstrained selves floating about in amorphous situations.

For Blumer, neither social structure nor culture overwhelm human interaction. Mead, as we have demonstrated, argued that culture was moving in a cosmopolitan, international direction, the development of a normative structure that would function similar to a universal generalized other. Mead saw culture as a powerful force influencing—though not determining—social behavior.

Warriner's concept of society at least stresses the need for coordination and consensus in order to negotiate interaction successfully, showing an understanding of the bureaucratic constraint that "organization men" must accommodate themselves to the goals of the institution.

Let us now examine to what extent Goffman's view of society has taken into account bureaucratic constraint and new forms of social structure and social organization. But, first, am I begging a very big question? Is Goffman a symbolic interactionist?

Goffman: A Symbolic Interactionist?

Goffman, it appears, has been somewhat slippery to classify. One critic of contemporary sociological theory views Goffman's works as falling "somewhere between the symbolic interactionist and phenomenological traditions" (Zeitlin 1973, 191). Others aver that "he stands squarely in the Durkheimian functionalist tradition, a more empirically oriented Talcott Parsons" (Collins and Makowsky 1972, 212). Others argue that he is a theorist not concerned with content, but forms, "Simmel's most faithful contemporary descendant" (Jary and Smith 1976, 923). Concurring with that position Manning (1980, 271) contends: "his primary debt is to formal sociology as seen in the work of Mauss, Durkheim, Simmel and more recently in his affection for a citation from structural semanticists." Still other critics (Meltzer, Petras, and Reynolds 1975, 70-71) identify him as tied to the Chicago school of symbolic interactionism, but they also state:

> [W]e find in his work no explicit theory, but a plausible and loosely organized frame of reference; little interest in explanatory schemes, but masterful descriptive analysis; virtually no accumulated evidence, but illuminating allusions, impressions, anecdotes, and illustrations; few formulations of empirically testable propositions, but innumerable provocative insights.

I would agree with these immediately preceding authors that Goffman has no "explicit theory" or "empirically testable propositions," and that he is a symbolic interactionist tied directly to the Chicago school.

Goffman's early work is clearly preoccupied with a symbolic, dramaturgical interaction, and how we present a performing self. His later work (especially

Frame Analysis) supersedes (theoretically) many of the issues of symbolic inter-actionism. With this foreknowledge as critical armor, we hope not to present any false theoretical tidiness by restricting Goffman solely to the symbolic inter-actionist tradition. As one commentator's stricture declares, too many have "un-thinkingly locate[d] Goffman in a tradition established by Mead and perpetuated by Blumer" (Ditton 1980, 13).

Though Goffman has branched into the wider theoretical horizon of ethno-methodology, phenomenology, and even semiotics, his roots are symbolic inter-actionist. Goffman's argument is diametrically opposed to the trait theorists of early-twentieth-century psychology; he concentrates, instead, on the "very com-plex exchange of symbols and meanings between at least two people" (Cuzzort 1969, 183).

Goffman's metaphor of life as a theater is an analysis of self with an admittedly unsystematic congeries of methods (some of which are systematic). Goffman's approach, perhaps best summarized in *Presentation of Self in Everyday Life* (1959), is certainly compatible with SI methods. "The illustrative materials used in this study are of a mixed status: some are taken from respectable researches where qualified generalizations are given reliably recorded regularities; some are taken from informal memoirs written by colorful people; many fall in between" (Goffman 1959, xi). Goffman's method in other works is that of both nonpartici-pant and participant observation, shying away from the positivist tradition of social surveys or laboratory experiments. *Asylums* (1963) is a classic ethnography.

Goffman's dramaturgical framework expands a Shakespearean metaphor into a general theory of social interaction. As Shakespeare metaphorized in *As You Like It* act II, scene vii: "All the world's a stage, And all the men and women merely players: They have their exits and their entrances; And one man in his time plays many parts, His act being seven ages." Goffman's comparable metaphor is: "The perspective employed in this report is that of the theatrical performance; the principles derived are dramaturgical ones" (Goffman 1959, xi).

Goffman's Image of Humans

We need to differentiate between how Goffman views everyday interaction and how we as subjects envision the world. Readers of Goffman may misconstrue his views to mean that his subjects (that is, all of us) view the universe as a "big con." As Messinger, Sampson, and Towne (1970) argue, however, Goffman does not impute to his actors (that is, all of us) intentional conning or conscious manipula-tion. Life as drama is a heuristic device, rather than a denunciation of human superficiality. Goffman "*is not suggesting that this is the way his subjects under-stand the world*" (Messinger, Sampson, and Towne 1970, 695; my emphasis). Impressions are simply the units of analysis. "The dramaturgic analyst seeks to describe the ways in which "impressions" are created, sustained, and ruptured under the condition that the actor is "unconscious" or only dimly "conscious" that this is a part of the business he is in" (Messinger, Sampson, Towne 1970, 696). Human beings do not consciously try to create a "stage" performance; rather, the social analyst uses this metaphor to describe impression management as though people were actors on a stage. People do not see life as a theater of manipulation and indeed feel alienated from their selves and interaction if they feel they are putting others "on" (Messinger, Sampson, Towne 1970, 698).

What the authors are trying to emphasize is that the actor should not be seen as consciously putting on a mask, a persona, under which his or her true self is hidden. The self the actor presents is his or her authentic self. The mask/persona metaphor connotes an intention to deceive, hoodwink, to present a false or spurious presentation, to "put on airs," and so on. Obviously, people do engage in presenting images of themselves that are intended to deceive, but these are deviant presentations (for example, those by confidence persons), not the normal or the normative. Much of Goffman's work, however, especially in *Frame Analysis*, does seem to subscribe to the notion that we are conscious of being actors and that we are very aware of our performances *qua* performances. For the type of work required in today's social institutions, impression management is a requirement, and the performers are conscious of exactly what they are trying to do.

In the following sections we analyze Goffman's two major writings on society: *Asylums*, 1961, and *Behavior in Public Places*, 1963. *Asylums* is concerned with behavior inside total institutions; *Behavior in Public Places* examines how we constitute society by establishing communication, coordination, and consensus.

Total Institutions

Goffman's trenchant analysis in *Asylums* of "total institutions" examines behavior under certain constraining conditions. The total institution operates like a "state," and its administrators and staff are "governors" (Goffman 1961, 77). Total institutions are structures of domination that do not brook inmate resistance. They include prisons, mental hospitals, naval vessels, monasteries, convents, P.O.W. and concentration camps, and military bases. Goffman's (1961, 124) first essay is an attempt to systematize "the underlying structural design common to them all." Goffman's (1961, xiv) formal definition of a total institution is "a place of residence and work where a large number of like-situated individuals, cut off from the wider society for an appreciable period of time, together lead an enclosed, formally administered round of life."

Relying primarily on a year's fieldwork at St. Elizabeth's Hospital, Washington, D.C. (a mental institution), Goffman's method of participant observation yields an understanding of the inmates' social world; it captures and presents their definitions of the situation. In my opinion, it is one of the finest examples of fieldwork done by a symbolic interactionist.

The behavior of inmates reveals a sordid state of affairs. In the total institution their behavior is constantly observed and programmed; an incessant "panoptic gaze" is operative, to use a term by M. Foucault. The result of incarceration is "a series of abasements, degradations, humiliations, and profanations of self" (Goffman 1961, 14). The self is systematically mortified, a destruction of self bordering on annihilation. The person entering a total institution is stripped of all roles and self-possessions. Only the role of inmate is hammered into his or her psyche. "Role dispossession" is only one aspect of "personal defacement that comes from being stripped of one's identity kit"; other horrors are "personal disfigurement that comes from direct and permanent mutilations of the body such as brands or loss of limbs" (Goffman 1966, 21). Such role deprivation or self-reduction is absent on the outside: "In civil society, an individual pushed to the wall in one of his social roles usually has an opportunity to crawl into some protected place" (Goffman 1961, 70). But such an escape inside the total institution is impossible, for no role except the inmate one is viewed as legitimate; "one's fall from grace is continuously pressed home" (Goffman 1961, 67).

The self is attacked by a predatory staff until the inmate is resocialized (succumbs or submits or surrenders) to the ideal self the staff is trying to forge. This ideal self is advocated to the inmate and propagandized to the outside world as in the best interests of the inmate. Goffman unmasks this therapy by revealing that such a self is merely to serve the benefit and convenience of the staff. Actually, "total institutions seem to function as storage dumps for inmates, but they usually present themselves to the public as rational organizations designed consciously, through and through, as effective machines for producing a few officially avowed and officially approved ends" (Goffman 1961, 74). The conflict between avowed "human standards" and "institutional efficiency" is resolved on the side of the institution. The institution must, however, confront "staging problems," a presentation of institution and staff to the outside as not violating any of the wider society's values over involuntary confinement. This is especially true for regulatory officials who could expose failings and violations to the extent of having the institution closed down and the staff publicly condemned or perhaps charged with criminal offenses.

To prevent such an occurrence, dramas of "institutional displays" are enacted where an ideal but mantled, misrepresented world is presented to the public. These dissimulations are usually holiday ceremonies where the public at large is invited to come in and see for themselves that all is on the up and up. Inmates are given more freedom at these times, and the public is allowed to glimpse only those things the staff promenades them through. During the ceremony a suspension of staff hostility is required, and the inmates are even allowed to satirize and make fun of the staff. "Whether through a sly article, a satirical sketch, or overfamiliarity during a dance, the subordinate in some ways profanes the superordinates" (Goffman 1961, 109). But as Goffman (109) rightly points out, "the very toleration of this skittishness is a sign of the strength of the establishment state."

Through savage assaults on the self, the inmate undergoes "disculturation" to such an extent that he or she may be unfit or incapable of surviving on the outside, that is, if the inmate is ever allowed to leave (Goffman 1961, 13). And if the inmate does leave, he or she has acquired stigmatization (Goffman 1961, 63) whereby the individual's welcome back into the wider society is a cold one at best.

The coerced behavior of the inmate is one of perpetual self-degradation and demoralization, acts of obedience, deference, submission, servility, a continual groveling of self until it has lost its human shape and form. These acts and postures of humiliation destroy the self-concept the individual formerly held. Any notion that the inmate is capable of autonomy or "executive competency" must be eradicated from the mind, if not the memory itself. Self-determination and self-expression are mutilated, if not vanquished. The daily round of activity is one where the self is assaulted and harassed by the staff with no chance for defense or retreat. Unconditional surrender is the only option the staff offers. The staff are umbrageous people who summarily respond to any untoward action with, if lucky, truculence, or, if unlucky, physical punishment. Such scourging toward the inmate's self results in a pusillanimous and inferior self-concept, while the staff present themselves as self-defined superior beings. "One of the main accomplishments of total institutions is staging a difference between two constructed categories of persons—a difference in social quality and moral character. The institution encourages the assumption that staff and inmates are of profoundly different human types" (Goffman 1961, 111).

The inmate understandably begins to view himself or herself as inferior, as worth only the value the staff accords, if any. Why? The self is mutable; it is as worthy or as worthless as the reference groups or others from which the self is viewed. The self is not a static entity but a processual one, changing synchronously with the definitions with which the self is labeled. Consequently, the self may succumb to the view that his or her oppressors have of him or her. Inside total institutions the self interacts with antipathetic others, everyone whose role the self takes is viewing the self with disgust and abhorrence. Antilocution is frequent. Thus, not to become crestfallen due to the inability to find others (outside of other patients, with whom the self may not interact for reasons of ratifying the negative label) with a positive view of the self is an almost insuperable affair. The self is seen through the eyes of others, and when those eyes engender inescapable torment, can we blame the self for abnegating its claim to sanity, for becoming a proselyte to madness rather than a Prometheus against it? Behavior naturally becomes routinized and somnambulist; people becomes automata and zombies.

To this incessant brutalization and oppression of self, the inmate must construct, or lapse into, a mode of adaptation. The self does what it can to survive. One form of adjustment is "situational withdrawal," a complete separation of self from everything "except events immediately around his body and [he or she] sees these in a perspective not employed by others present" (Goffman 1961, 61). This line of adaptation is often irreversible.

An "intransigent line" is a second strategy, whereby the inmate "intentionally challenges the institution by flagrantly refusing to cooperate with staff" (Goffman

1961, 62). This is only a temporary line of adjustment, for either the individual changes to another mode of habituation or is "broken" by the staff.

"Colonization" is a third mode of transformation whereby the individual builds up a "relatively contented existence" (Goffman 1961, 63). The inmates are sent out to sample the outside world, but because of its hostility or their failure to survive on the outside, the inmates feel their best chance is on the inside. They have found safety and security from a hostile universe, and "they may find it necessary to mess up just prior to their stated discharge to provide themselves with an apparently involuntary basis for continued incarceration" (Goffman 1961, 63).

"Conversion," a forth mode of acculturation, is where the inmate takes the role of the staff toward himself or herself and the other inmates, thereby succumbing to the staff's view of him or her and the rest of the inmates. The convert identifies with the staff rather than his or her fellow inmates: "the convert takes a more disciplined, moralistic, monochromatic line, presenting himself as someone whose institutional enthusiasm is always at the disposal of the staff" (Goffman 1961, 63). The person may try to present a self that is compatible to both inmates and staff, a "two facedness," one face presented to the fellow inmates and another to the staff. This form of adaptation is likely to be seen through by other inmates and labeled a "selling out." The epitome of the role adaptation is the "trustee" who eventually comes to "identify with the aggressor" (Goffman 1961, 93).

Such demoralized behavior can be understood only within the context of a total institution. Total institutions are thus the organizational response of a society to members it deems in need of "humane" and self-correctional "care."

The Moral Career of a Mental Patient

How does a person come to be an inmate in a total institution, especially a mental hospital? Goffman adapts the concept of *"career"* to portray one's experience of becoming hospitalized. The adjective "moral" refers to "the regular sequences of changes that career entails in the person's self and in his framework of imagery for judging himself and others" (Goffman 1961, 128). The moral aspect of this career is that the patient will come to see himself or herself as no longer a success but as a failure, an incompetent human being. The entire social organization of the hospital is set up to drive home an image of personal failure. The self can quite easily perceive that the surroundings are degraded and this vitiated environment comes symbolically to represent an externalized image of the vitiated self. As Goffman (1961, 148) states: "the self arises not merely out of its possessor's interactions with significant others, but also out of the arrangements that are evolved in an organization for its members." Thus, the patient's "assignment to a given ward is presented not as a reward or punishment, but as an expression of his general level of social functioning, his status as a person" (Goffman 1961, 149).

The person's self is "framed" (no pun intended) by the immediate milieu of the hospital ward. An isomorphism is effected between inmate self and social surround; that is to say, the institution of the mental health system is a structure exerting consraint and power over one's self and identity. The moral career of a patient falls into three stages: prepatient, inpatient, and ex-patient. Each one of these phases is guided by "career contingencies," variables that influence how the civilian is processed, by whom, for what reasons, and, finally, circumstances leading to both his or her ingress into and egress from a mental hospital. Contingencies are the immediate "causes" of one's incarceration, rather than the mental illness itself.

If the person is not a self-referral, he or she is processed, unwillingly, along the route leading to incarceration. The reasons for the initiation of this process is a complaint over the prepatient's contranormative behavior. In order for this untoward behavior to become socially relevant someone must engage in a complaint. This is the social beginning of the patient's career "regardless of where one might locate the psychological beginning of his mental illness" (Goffman 1961, 134).

The next stage is that a whole host of agents and agencies become involved in the "passage from civilian to patient status" (Goffman 1961, 135). The first of these agents is the "next-of-relation" who is trusted by the as yet naive patient. The next-of-relation usually sets the wheels of incarceration in motion by arranging a joint visit to the psychiatrist. In this visit the as yet civilian is likely to view the experience as an "allenative coalition," that is, the psychiatrist and next-of-relation presenting one definition of the situation and he or she, alone and unaided, presenting an alternative definition of the situation. The civilian realizes at the meeting that his or her status is on precarious grounds and that "a prior understanding between the professional and the next-of-relation has been put in operation against him" (Goffman 1961, 138). "The moral aspects of this career, then, typically begin with the experience of abandonment, disloyalty, and embitterment" (Goffman 1961, 133).

The next step is a series of "mediators," agents and agencies who recommend a specific course of action. These usually take the now famous form of "status degradation ceremonies." If the civilian's career contingencies are so fated, he or she winds up in the hospital "stripped of almost everything" (that is, rights and liberties) (Goffman 1961, 140). The patient turns to the next-of-relation for help in finding a way out; the agents turn to the same person for authorization to incarcerate the person, for the patient's own well-being, of course.

Once the patient is on the inside—the inpatient phase—he or she engages in role-distancing. He or she may avoid any interaction with other patients that would ratify the reality of the patient's world and his or her newly acquired degraded status. After acceptance of his or her plight, the patient embarks on constructing a "sad tale" to vindicate the incarceration, that is, to impute it to betrayal by others or to the inevitable result of uncontrollable circumstances. The "patient's apologies" are an attempt to disconfirm the only too overwhelmingly ratified reality that he or she "is, after all, a mental case who has suffered some kind of social collapse" (Goffman 1961, 151). The reality of being a mental case is "piercingly, persistently, and thoroughly" (Goffman 1961, 149) driven home by the setting, the house rules, and the confronting of the patient with the history of his or her misdeeds.

The case record functions as the institution's legitimation (apologia), assuring to its members and all those who may come to scrutinize the case that the patient's claim to be a competent human being is a false one. The patient is powerless and knows it. Therefore, one must make one's meek adjustment as best one can, to resign oneself, "to practice before all groups the amoral arts of shamelessness" (Goffman 1961, 269).

The Underlife of a Public Institution

Goffman's essay on the underlife of a public institution is one of the most theoretically integrated works incorporating the concepts of structure and agency. It does what I believe every sociology needs to do: it incorporates (1) the reality of social facts sui generis that externally confront the individual independent of his or her will, and (2) it dramatically shows that individuals possess both selves and minds, the ability of human agency. It is a dialectical paragon of people's struggle against an oppressive social situation.

Goffman's limnings on "secondary adjustments" is an account of just how people make their own history, but certainly not just as they please. Most organizations require from its members some "commitment" and "attachment"; but also most people deviate from total engrossment in the institutions or organizations of which they are members. Institutions not only exact member commitment and attachment to their values but also explicitly judge or grade their members according to the roles they perform in the institution. There is a correspondence, or homology, between one's role in an institution and one's value (from the perspective of the institution) as a human being. Therefore, one would expect that those who know the value of themselves to the organization will either act favorably or disfavorably to the value the institution places on their person. Executives may become "married to their work," and those who clean the urinals may avoid their jobs (when not financially coerced) like the plague. Those whom the institution favorably values will usually exhibit self-investment in their roles, and those whom the institution labels dubiously (though not necessarily negatively) will exhibit role-distance.

One's self, all the more so when negatively valued, will draw sustenance from sources other than one's institutional role, especially if one is unable to escape from the institution that promulgates a self-mortifying label. In such social situations, one will do one's best to build a self and world at odds with the prevailing judgment of one's worth as a human being.

A mental hospital is an example of an institution in which an inmate's self is negatively valued and he or she cannot escape the hostile valuations. One can at

best temporarily evade these evaluations by self-distancing oneself from the negative label and role suffered within a malignant environment. One's strategy is,
then, to make "secondary adjustments" to one's inextricable predicament. "Secondary adjustments represent ways in which the individual stands apart from the
role and the self that were taken for granted for him by the institution" (Goffman
1961, 189). Secondary adjustments can be both individual and collective, disruptive and contained. Goffman centers on ones that are individual ("collective means
of working the system seem not too common in mental hospitals" [Goffman 1961,
215]) and contained (that is, do not try to change the institutional structure radically). In a mental hospital secondary adjustments are pursued by both staff and
inmates. I comment on only the secondary adjustment of inmates.[2]

One of the ways of "making out" in a mental hospital is to gain acquisition of
material sources from which to construct meaningful objects. Thus, one appropri-
ates "make-do's," artifacts already made but whose use by inmates is illegitimate,
or one reconstructs the artifact for some other use. Another way of overcoming
repressive conditions is a whole host of activities under the rubric of "working the
system" (Goffman 1961, 210). This involves such activities as getting on sick call,
all types of "food-getting" strategy, scavenging, engaging in social interaction with
outsiders (that is, normals), and obtaining a pleasant job assignment. The job
assignment itself could be worked in various ways, that is, the worker is in a
position to appropriate "the fruit of his labor" (Goffman 1961, 210) or to associate
with desired company: higher staff personnel or females with males, and vice
versa.

Another way of making out is to sequester oneself away in a free space. Social
space in a mental hospital is either off-bounds or under surveillance, but a free
space allows one to escape the panoptic gaze of oppression. Patients engineered
free spaces for each ward and service, and also ones that "drew patients from the
whole hospital community" (Goffman 1961, 233). Besides public free spaces,
there evolve restricted group and private territories. The competition for scarce
resources pits the inmates against each other; structures of domination by more
powerful patients over weaker ones compound the brutality. Private coercion
becomes normal; an alien universe becomes a combative one as well.

Other ways of coping are working facilities for private ends, the development
of transportation systems, the construction of "shadow" economies through some
medium of exchange, usually cigarettes, the endearment of social exchange for
solidarity and mutual aid, and the flowering of bonded relationships, especially
ones that offer protection (that is, patron relationships).

Goffman also intimates that hospitalization itself may be one way of working
the larger system; that is, "some patients come into the hospital to dodge family
and work responsibilities, or to obtain free some major medical and dental work,
or to avoid a criminal charge" (Goffman 1961, 215).

In general, the patient's underlife is a conglomeration of "removal activities"
that temporarily distance his or her self from the judgment of the staff and blot out
the all too oppressive reality of one's wasteland environment (Goffman 1961,

309). They are counter self-judgments and world-building activities, ways the patient demonstrates that he or she "has some selfhood and personal autonomy beyond the grasp of the organization" (Goffman 1961, 314).

One's secondary adjustments are purposeful and meaningful acts of "ritual insubordination," "recalcitrance," and "insolence," acts that de-identify, de-commit, and disaffiliate one's self from the negatively valued institutional role one is coerced to perform. They are techniques of self-survival, ways the "I" asserts freedom under a regime. In the dialectical struggle between tyranny and freedom, the self is a "stance-taking entity," its constitution, its emergence, is every part due to standing "against something" as well as derived from commitment and attachment to something.

But Goffman (1961, 306) notes that this dialectical struggle between tyranny and freedom is a "vicious-circle"; a catch-22 is operative.

> Higher management may construe this alienative expression as just the sort of symptomatology the institution was established to deal with and as the best kind of evidence that the patient belongs where he now finds himself. Mental hospitalization outmaneuvers the patient, tending to rob him of the common expressions through which people hold off the embrace of organizations. Signs of disaffiliation are now read as signs of their maker's proper affiliation.

Self-assertion will not win the patient a viable, healthy self. Only in becoming self-less, by yielding to the psychiatric and institutional view of self, will the patient be viewed as convalescing, as engaging in therapeutic self-help. "This self-alienating moral servitude, which perhaps helps to account for some inmates becoming mentally confused, is achieved by invoking the great tradition of the expert servicing relation" (Goffman 1961, 386).

The psychiatrist, staff, and institution are set up to serve the mentally ill, and they are empowered to define the situation legally, to determine the who, what, when, and where of everything pertaining to the patient. "None of a patient's business, then, is none of the psychiatrist's business, nothing ought to be held back as irrelevant to his job. No other expert server with a system to tinker with seems to arrogate this kind of role to himself" (Goffman 1961, 358). The service model, when applied to the treatment of the mentally ill, has been perverted: "Instead of a server and the served, we find a governor and the governed, an officer and those subject to him" (Goffman 1961, 353).

The plain and simple fact Goffman (1961, 360) elucidates is that "a mental hospital is ill-equipped to be a place where the classic repair cycle occurs." "Mental hospitals institutionalize a kind of grotesque of the service relationship" (Goffman 1961, 369). The patient's "cure" is often in spite of hospitalization, rather than because of it (Goffman 1961, 382).

What Goffman has been illuminating is that the person has been diminished to a body, an object defined in need of repair or service, not solely for the benefit of the patient but for the protection and comfort of the community: "to be a patient is to be remade into a serviceable object" (Goffman 1961, 379), but this redefining of the person as "a kind of physiochemical machine" (Goffman 1961, 340) is to legitimate a power over the patient in which the patient is defined as either too incompetent or too sick to know what is for his or her own good. Defining people as objects of investigation/manipulation, and the rise of institutions, which thereby have complete authority over them, are not unrelated occurrences.[3]

Goffman has thus provided one of the best accounts of life on the inside of one of society's total institutions, an analysis of behavior centered on defining failures in face-to-face interaction in terms of social issues, rather than just personal problems.

Goffman, as opposed to Blumer and Warriner, emphasizes much more strongly the impact of twentieth-century social institutions on human behavior. He has shown how powerful social organizations can be in influencing behavior; how total institutions, and by implication, other institutions to a lesser extent, can destroy our essence as human beings, our ability to even communicate. Let us explore further how institutions can cause failures in communication.

Certainly, in terms of patient-staff interaction, the nonratifying stance each participant takes in regard to the other's institutional role eventuates in communication breakdown. The psychiatrist demands that the patient ratify/admit that the patient is mentally ill, rightfully held, and that the psychiatrist is a sincere, genuine, and competent server trying his or her best to help the patient recover. The patient, on the other hand, demands that the psychiatrist ratify his or her definition of the situation, that the patient is not insane, is unlawfully held, and that the whole establishment is immoral rather than salubrious to his or her mental and physical well-being. There is, then, a considerable failure in the components of communication: reference, inference, and confirmation. They both talk past each other (Goffman 1961, 368).

On the one hand, there is the "prideful man declining to exchange communications with someone who thinks he is crazy," and on the other hand, the psychiatrist who must respond to hostile aspersions: "not as directly usable statements of information but rather as signs of the illness itself, to be discounted as direct information" (Goffman 1961, 367).

Communication breakdown is institutionalized through each participant's unwillingness to take the role of the other. Empathetic ability does not emerge. Since each participant possesses a jaundiced view of the other, tendencies to view oneself from the other's frame of reference are destructive of one's self-concept. It is hard to take the role of a psychotic person; it is perhaps even harder to take the role of one's oppressor. Therefore to regard oneself as sane, the patient must refrain from taking the role of the psychiatrist; and equally understandable, to regard oneself as humane and not some vicious jailor, the psychiatrist must refrain from taking the role of the patient.

Let me make this more explicit. I want to discriminate between, or analytically separate, two components of taking the role of the other. Specifically, I want to separate analytically *knowing* the role of the other toward oneself and taking the role of the other toward oneself. Of course, the patient knows the psychiatrist's view of him or her, and the psychiatrist knows the patient's view of him or her; otherwise, they would not possess such jaundiced views of each other. But to take the role of the other in the sense I am using it here, means to accept the other's definition of oneself as both accurate and legitimate. Perhaps a better terminology would be internalizing the role of the other toward oneself. This distinction is compatible with Mead's notion, discussed earlier, that understanding emerges through the development of a universal generalized other.[4] Unfortunately (but I don't see how it could be otherwise), in this situation, this will be solely an asymmetrical process. If the patient is to be released, he or she must take/internalize the role of the psychiatrist toward himself or herself and swallow that painful definition as both accurate and legitimate. The psychiatrist is never under any obligation to take/internalize the role of the patient; however, to know the role of the patient toward oneself allows the psychiatrist, it is hoped, to adjust his or her response appropriately. The psychiatrist has to demonstrate to the patient that the patient's definition of the situation is unreasonable and unfounded, a misapprehension. If the psychiatrist is not tender (being tender would seem to be a professional requirement) then he or she is guilty of communication incompetence. Trust-in-the-other is problematic,[5] and trust is crucial, especially for the patient. The patient must trust that the psychiatrist will prescribe a course of treatment that will regenerate a normal, or better, normative self.

What may occur is a legitimation crisis: the patient refuses to acknowledge the validity or authority of the psychiatrist's institutional role. The political analogy I believe correct, for the psychiatrist does indeed represent a state (or at least is backed up by the coercive power of the state), and the inmates are a subject population. Goffman (1963, 109) has commented on this legitimation crisis in terms of inaccessibility for face-engagements, a strategy by which social encounters are circumvented:

> To acknowledge a staff overture is partly to acknowledge the legitimacy of the staff person making the overture, and if he is a serious worthy person then so must be his implied contention that the individual with whom he is initiating contact, namely, oneself, is a mental patient properly confined to a mental ward. To strengthen one's feeling that one is really sane, it may thus seem reasonable to disdain encounters in which the opposite will be assumed—even though this results in exactly the kind of conduct, namely inaccessibility, that confirms the hospital's view that one is mentally ill.

The parties thus suffer acute social alienation, for if there is to emerge mutual regard, a mutual experiencing of the other, then reciprocal role-taking is required. This social barrier is the first obstacle that must be obliterated if any improvement in the situation is to occur.

The communication problem of the psychiatrist (trustworthiness) may be helped if he or she can convince the patient that it is not in the psychiatrist's self-interest that the patient is incarcerated (Aronson 1976, 62). The communication problem of the patient (credibility) unfortunately can be surmounted only by the patient's acting in a normatively prescribed manner, by staging competent role performances. "It is possible to try to describe the sense in which an individual defined as insane is seen as an incompetent, faulty actor" (Goffman 1974, 115). The competing definitions of the situation lead each combative party to tell "exemplary tales" to others to assert the validity of their own interpretation of the situation. Stories of tragic accidents, mistakes, and incompetencies abound. The staff recites the account of the patient let go too early who murdered; the patient sobs the woeful tale of someone wrongfully incarcerated whose life was wasted. Each party is at war to discredit the other. A distorted, perverse reality is thus socially constructed. The staff, perhaps unwittingly, engages in acts whereby "reality must be considerably twisted somewhat as it is by judges, instructors, and officers in other of our coercive institutions. A crime must be uncovered that fits the punishment, and the character of the inmate must be reconstituted to fit the crime" (Goffman 1961, 384).

The institutional perversion of reality is the socially relevant one, for it is the institutional definition of the situation that is accepted by the wider society as the legitimate one. The power to define reality is in the hands of the gatekeepers, who ease our conscience by assuring us that their view is indeed the way things are. We defer to their expertise; thereby both society and gatekeeper are put at ease at the expense of those who, out of sight, are out of mind.

Goffman's work on *Asylums* is an example of how contemporary social institutions and social organizations influence and structure behavior. He has articulated how structures of domination pervert social interaction. The mental hospital—a service industry—illuminates the negative side of society dominated by large-scale organizations that can be malignant. Goffman's analysis articulates the power of large-scale bureaucratic structures. To a much lesser extent we must all live out our lives within institutions, though most of them are not set up to destroy us. But analyzing how the most powerful of these complex organizations—total institutions—structure our lives lends insight into the way all organizations in some way determine our everyday patterns of behavior.

The Normative Structure of Public Behavior

Goffman's book on *Behavior in Public Places* (1963) delineates the communication conduct norms that regulate the traffic of social intercourse. There are rules and regulations for initiating, sustaining, and disengaging from communicative contact with our fellow human beings. These rules, or the normative order of public behavior, stipulate when and when not to communicate, where and where not to communicate, and with whom to and whom not to communicate. These prescriptive and proscriptive communication conduct norms are of the "'nega-

tively eventful' kind, which give rise to specific negative sanctions if not performed, but which, [if they are] performed, pass unperceived as an event"
(Goffman 1963, 7).

These precepts are the glue of public order, they regulate the face-to-face
interaction of everyday life. They are the rules and regulations that apply to those
with whom we are unacquainted, those with whom we meet during the circuit of
our everyday itinerary. The dichotomy between public and private places is important here, for different rules and regulations are operative at different places.
"Public places refer to any regions in a community freely accessible to members
of that community; private places refer to soundproof regions where only members or invitees gather" (Goffman 1963, 9). Civility is due our fellow inhabitants
of public places, no matter how fleeting and superficial the face-engagement. They
are, however, middle-class notions of decorum and civility. Goffman thus seeks to
describe the middle-class social norms that are operative whenever two or more
individuals are copresent in a public place. Such a coming together of individuals
is entitled a "gathering," and gatherings are Goffman's basic unit of analysis.

The "pattern of conduct" that takes place during any gathering varies with the
social context of the gathering. The social context of any gathering is the larger
social occasion. Social occasions structure the pattern of conduct—the normative
order—of any particular gathering. There may be many or only a few gatherings at
any particular social occasion, but the interaction engaged in will be influenced, to
a large extent, by the larger social occasion. Social occasions are then social facts
that are exterior to us and constrain us independent of our will. For Goffman
(1963, 19), the social fact of a social occasion functions to domesticate the wild in
us.

> Each class of such occasions possesses a distinctive ethos, a spirit, an emotional
> structure, that must be properly created, sustained, and laid to rest, the participant
> finding that he is obliged to become caught up in the occasion, whatever his per-
> sonal feelings. These occasions, which are commonly programmed in advance,
> possess an agenda of activity, an allocation of management function, a specification
> of negative sanction for improper conduct, and a pre-established unfolding of
> phases and a highpoint.

Each social occasion prescribes a range of tolerable activities—"situational
properties"—that we have to conform to; otherwise, depending on the type and
magnitude of the deviation, we may find ourselves in serious trouble. Social
occasions are usually least troublesome when they are mutually exclusive. Problems in public order can arise when multiple social occasions occur within the
same "physical space." Therefore, the most critical social occasion must take
precedence, which in our society and almost all others is keeping the peace of
public places. This is so important that a whole occupation (the police) is devoted
to the task.

Unfocused Interaction

Unfocused interaction concerns the communication conduct of brief encounters, encounters so brief that they may be only the glance, the quick look, and so on. They are moments when we quickly assess or typify someone sharing public space with us.

Nevertheless, the management of presence is not a trifling matter. Bungling our presentation of selves, or even worse, an incapacity or collapse at being able to present a situationally appropriate self, may lead to commitment proceedings. The mental hospital is largely filled with those who consistently wore an improper mask to the social ball of public places.

One of the basic ways we express our aliveness to the situation is through "body idiom." Nonverbal communication is nonstop; we are always conveying something about ourselves through a "vocabulary of body symbols" (Goffman 1963, 35). Our demeanor, bearing, and deportment signal to others who and what we are before we ever begin to speak. "Body idiom, then, is a conventionalized discourse" (Goffman 1963, 34). It is as regulated by social norms as is verbal discourse.

Another way to demonstrate presence is to demonstrate that we are involved in the situation. It is a normative requirement that we take into account the situation at hand and make the appropriate adjustive responses. Of course, we may merely display "effective" involvement in a situation when, in fact, we are away. Thus "involvement shields" are required so as to express at least a pretense of involvement.

Involvement shields allow our spirits to escape backstage when our bodies are front stage. Through the use of involvement shields we assert some freedom over the social facts that constrain ourselves. Tyranny can be hoodwinked, for "we deal not so much with a network of rules that must be followed as with rules that must be taken into consideration, whether as something to follow or carefully to circumvent" (Goffman 1963, 42). Masquerading involvement constitutes an unknowable portion of everyday interaction. But the fact that there are even portable involvement shields such as newspapers and magazines suggests that a wanderlust is close to our hearts. Though we are social animals, we are solitary creatures as well.

We are not continually dominated by the need to manifest involvement. Involvement shields are a subterfuge, but there are legitimately sanctioned ways to loll and loiter, to some extent. There are main and side involvements. A main involvement is one that "absorbs the major part of an individual's attention and interest," while a side involvement is one we may "carry on in an abstracted fashion without threatening or confusing simultaneous maintenance of a main involvement" (Goffman 1963, 43). There are two other important distinctions concerning involvements. Dominant involvements are ones that make a priority claim upon us, ones we must acknowledge. Subordinate involvements are ones that we need give only pro forma attention to (Goffman 1963, 45). Thus, while at our jobs the dominant involvement is our required work, though if the foreman is absent, we may shirk our responsibility and engage in horseplay. At this time the horseplay will be both a subordinate and a main involvement. Thus the four categories of involvement are not mutually exclusive. The norm of being involved or having a purpose to our social behavior is, however, strong. Therefore, at times, lolling and loitering "can be deemed sufficiently improper to merit legal action" (Goffman 1963, 56). Overinvolvement is also deviant behavior. Discovery by others will cause embarrassment. We are thus required to conduct ourselves carefully, to balance our social behavior between under-and overinvolvements.

Even objects of involvement are normatively regulated. We can become involved with our own bodies—auto-involvement—only to a certain extent. Eating, dressing, picking one's teeth, combing hair, and the like, are all normatively regulated. The extreme form of auto-involvement is masturbation, which is allowed only when the self is securely secluded. Other forms of auto-involvement are "creature releases." The individual who engages in them must apologize, for they express our "animal nature" (Goffman 1963, 68). Creature releases are ways the individual expresses that he or she has lost situational presence. "Aways" are another way we leave the situation; they are momentary daydreams, reveries, or preoccupations. When in an away, the individual is aware that he or she is drifting and, if need be, can respond when called upon. We can inform others through the proper cues that we are momentarily withdrawing situational presence. If others do not sense that we know that we are away, however, or if we are unable to "snap back to interactional attention" (Goffman 1963, 76), then our involvement will have become "occult." It is not necessarily the contranormative behavior itself that leads others to become suspicious of our frame of mind, but our inability to be alive to situations and gatherings at large. Of course, it should also be said that with regard to the behavior itself, what is defined as an occult activity by one group may be normal to others. Thus labeling deviant behavior is always, to some extent, ethnocentric and political. Those who have the power to define the situation always avail themselves of the opportunity to do so. These last two points, of course, have attained the status of truism in the sociology of deviance.

Perhaps the most prevailing norm in public places concerning individuals who cross each other's path is "civil inattention." Goffman's (1963, 89) definition: "[W]hat seems to be involved is that one gives to another enough visual notice to demonstrate that one appreciates that the other is present (and that one admits openly to having seen him) while at the next moment withdrawing one's attention from him so as to express that he does not constitute a target of special curiosity or design." An example of this is our behavior when entering, or already inside, an elevator. The right to civil inattention is one that transcends the social status, class, or social characteristics of the other person encountered (Goffman 1963, 86). Civil inattention is granted to those who behave properly. The withdrawing of civil inattention, however, say, by staring at others, is one of the first and most easily employed mechanisms of social control (Goffman 1963, 88).

Focused Interaction

People can change unfocused interaction to focused interaction by initiating an encounter, or face-engagement. This state of affairs emerges when two people share a "mutual activity," when they focus "cognitive and visual attention" at each other (Goffman 1963, 89). Communication of a more intense and higher order is now allowed to pass back and forth among actors. Though speech is not specifically required (for example, the focused interaction among prespeaking children), the conversation is the touchstone (Goffman 1963, 90). Since the norm of civil inattention causes us to refrain from eye-to-eye contact, such contact is usually a signal that someone wants to initiate a face-engagement. If we respond in a positive manner, then the request has been ratified, a face-engagement is under way. We usually begin by talking about inoffensive subjects, a bag of "safe supplies" carried mentally allows us to warm the engine of conversation. Counterbalancing the norm of civil inattention, then, is the norm of being "accessible" for face-engagements. If we express our inaccessibility or "refusal to enter proffered engagements," we are signaling in a not so subtle way an alienation or hostility to the gathering; or if we are mentally incapacitated to extend such a request, this may confirm others' belief that we are mentally ill (Goffman 1963, 107). Just as there are entrance cues for face-engagement, so are there exit cues when one or more participants of an encounter want to disengage.

The norm to be accessible for face engagements is strongest among those with whom we are acquainted; not to be open is a severe affront, colloquially called a "cut." Even to those whom we may despise we should acknowledge recognition, if only to pay respect to the gathering at large. The fact that most of us are aware of this norm as it pertains to acquaintances leads us to avoid introductions to others or places where introductions are most likely to occur. Once introduced to someone, the norm to acknowledge acquaintanceship may situationally structure unsolicited and unwanted interactions. Thus we would be deviant not to engage in interaction with those whom we know, even if only superficially, "while unacquainted persons require a reason" for us to pay attention to them (Goffman 1963, 124). In the one case we thereby avoid cutting the person and in the other avoid violating the norm of civil inattention.

There are, of course, many public roles that are open and exposed, allowing others to approach them at will: cab driver, priest, police officer, gas-station attendant, and so on. Many of these roles also allow their incumbents to approach anyone of us at will (for example, the police officer). Many places in American society are also defined as open and exposed so that anyone therein is vulnerable to communicative contact, for example, "bars," "taverns," "cocktail lounges," and "club cars" (Goffman 1963, 134).

Every gathering establishes "communication boundaries," ways of separating or segregating those who are participants of an encounter from those who are bystanders. Bystanders are under the norm to provide civil inattention to the encounter and not exploit the communication possibilities that exist. One must affect not to overhear what might be said only a few feet away. Many places, such as elevators, are difficult to establish communication closure within. In fact, the bystander may be affronted by those who treat him or her as a nonperson by engaging or continuing in a conversation when it is impossible for the bystander to escape. Participants are thus under normative constraints to talk about unenticing, innocuous affairs, to space themselves so as to demonstrate that an encounter is under way, and to damper the sound level of their discourse. Both participants and bystanders, then, owe obligations to each other.

Obligations are also owed the gathering at large. Just as is individual over-involvement, group overinvolvement is also contranormative. Individuals must pay their respects to the gathering at large. They must not be allowed to withdraw into their own private world. Also, underinvolvement must not be flagrantly displayed by profane speech or violent quarrels. For example, two people who hate each other but who have been invited to a common gathering are expected to keep a civil tongue to each other. This can be seen, for example, at parties where colleagues meet. Colleagues who despise each other and their respective work will nevertheless air the most superficial pleasantries to each other in order to pay respect to the host and the social occasion.

Underinvolvement is also displayed if at a social party we play the role of the loner, or if others cast us into the role of wallflower. Thus at social gatherings and at parties an accessibility to any encounter is to be maintained. Open topics of conversation are the norm. To make the best of a situation, then, one will have to balance what is owed the immediate encounter with what is owed the gathering at large. Contranormative behavior affronting either one can turn the best-laid plans into a social fiasco. Encounter "drift" is, of course, likely to occur, each set of people finding their own areas of interest, which differentiate them from other gatherings within the social occasion. To such an extent this will be beneficial to the social occasion. Groups may, of course, use involvement shields to conceal the extent of their drift, just as individuals do. As long as the chargé d'affaires, the manager of the social occasion, is perceptive of these drifts and diplomatically counters any overmeandering, as long as no one makes a "scene" or rudely engages in encounter or gathering leave-taking, so long as no one is stuck too long in an unwanted encounter, or deserted by one's assumed gathering partner, all might go well.

The intensity of the normative order of social occasions varies. Some social occasions are normatively very "tight," others are quite "loose." Whether similar social occasions will be tight or loose depends on a number of variables: culture, subculture, the region of the city (suburb/inner city), the age, gender, and social class of the participants, and so on.

One of the themes Goffman takes up here (and amplifies in *Relations in Public*) is the "decline of civility" (Manning 1976), that is, the ungluing of the normative structure of public places. Goffman's perception is accurate and critical; to the extent that we are becoming a more atomized, urbanized mass society, any semblance of a community of individuals disappears. Our increasing disregard for the norms of social occasions is direct evidence of the alienation and anomie suffered by urbanites. It is a regrettable state of affairs, part of our dubious inheritance in the latter decades of twentieth-century Western capitalism.

Christopher Lasch (1979, 53) has made an insightful comment on Goffman's portrayal of everyday interaction in public places, one with which he agrees.

> In a lawless, violent and unpredictable society, in which the normal conditions of everyday life come to resemble those formerly confined to the underworld, men live by their wits. They hope not so much to prosper as simply to survive, although survival itself increasingly demands a large income. In earlier times, the self-made man took pride in his judgment of character and probity; today he anxiously scans the faces of his fellows not so as to evaluate their credit but in order to gauge their susceptibility to his own blandishments. He practices the classic arts of seduction and with the same indifference to moral niceties, hoping to win your heart while picking your pocket.

Many violations are, of course, intentional. We may want to display resentment and hostility flagrantly to a conversation, class, community, organization, or institution. Whether this will be judged appropriate or not depends on the group defining the situation. At times such behavior may even compliment the violators, for example, the mentally ill incarcerated in an asylum, who, by displaying such disregard may be asserting their humanity rather than exhibiting misanthropy. Abusive talk to such people (in my opinion) as Nazis, or the KKK would seem to be another example. To the extent that the situation is oppressive, then resistance to the oppression is laudatory. The social protests of college students in the 1960s in another example. They considered exposing social injustice more important than the convention of civility (Slater 1970, 55). In this sense the disruption of civility constitutes concern for others.

But what Goffman is describing is that disregard for others is becoming a normal, patterned way of interaction. Perhaps we have become so acclimatized to a decline in civility that we expect such treatment from and respond in kind to our fellow interactants. We now seem regularly to engage, unconsciously, in a violation of each other's "civil rights." The norm of reciprocity has considerably waned. We have all become the means to each other's alienated ends. At a time when the centralization of social control is rampant—Foucault characterizes contemporary society as a disciplinary, panoptic one—we have responded by lashing out against our fellow citizens rather than the system at large, perhaps an indicator of the real impotence of publics and people.

Communication conduct norms and other situational properties hold the public and social order together. "More than to any family or club, more than to any class or sex, more than to any nation, the individual belongs to gatherings, and he best show that he is a member in good standing" (Goffman 1963, 248). The decline in civility as a subset of the larger phenomenon, "the eclipse of community," has been a long-standing sociological issue. As Alvin Gouldner (1970b, 379) has stated: "such social order as exists for Goffman depends upon the small kindnesses that [people] bestow upon one another; social systems are fragile little floating islands whose coasts have daily to be shored up and renewed." "There is communicated a sense of the precariousness of the world and, at the same time, of zest in managing oneself in it" (Gouldner 1970b, 380). One hopes that as captains of social occasions and gatherings we will retain a savoir-faire while our social ship sinks ever so slowly into the sea.

Goffman has characterized the various ways our everyday interaction is affected by the social structure and normative order of public places. Not only in total institutions but also in everyday public behavior the individual no longer dominates situations as much as he or she is dominated by them; even while traveling in a bus or riding an elevator social order is the priority, and it is a delicate social order: norms must be internalized, roles properly played, equilibrium maintained. Freedom in social interaction is not as abundant as it once was; even momentary "aways" must be carefully "staged" so as not to disrupt social gatherings. We must resort to "involvement shields" to escape the almost big-brother monitoring of working within large-scale, bureaucratic corporations. Goffman has shown that there is a complex social structure to everyday face-engagements; and that not only bureaucracies are built around the roles of structured interaction but also that even everyday encounters have roles and rules that require successful performances.

In terms of social interaction, Goffman has described the dialectical relationship between the individual and the new social institutions of American society—ones increasingly concerned with social order and social control. The individual now expresses his or her self, if possible, inside the bureaucracy, not the open frontier. The concepts of the early symbolic interactionists arose within the social context of a recently passed laissez-faire capitalism. Goffman's concepts are embedded in the society of corporate capitalism and the "organization man."

Efficiency of economic life was the triumph of early capitalism. As capitalism evolved, efficiency expanded—Weber's process of rationalization—to other institutions embodied in the bureaucratic ethos. Capitalist forms (for example, norms of efficiency and economic practices such as redefining objects or services as commodities) penetrate previously noncapitalistic social and cultural practices. Child care, as an example, has been redefined as a commodity in the service economy. This has caused changes in social practices and cultural definitions of childhood socialization. Now, even before kindergarten, many children will be partially socialized within a larger institutional setting, that is, early childhood socialization will rely less on primary groups and more on secondary groups. This state of affairs can be for the better or for the worse. Goffman has shown the way professionalization in the social sciences and medicine has led to a rise in power over the individual. More and more of our lives are lived out inside of organizations. And everyday public behavior is becoming more institutionalized. C. Wright Mills (1951, xii) has made one of the better comments concerning the power that contemporary institutions have over our lives versus life at an earlier time.

The nineteenth-century farmer and businessman were generally thought to be stalwart individuals—their own men, men who could quickly grow to be almost as big as anyone else. The twentieth-century white-collar man has never been independent as the farmer used to be, nor as hopeful of the main chance as the businessman. He is always somebody's man, the corporation's, the government's, the army's; and he is seen as the man who does not rise. The decline of the free entrepreneur and the rise of the dependent employee on the American scene has paralleled the decline of the independent individual and the rise of the little man.

Goffman's concept of society has portrayed this development as well as the various ways we fight back. He as ethnographically shown (as Foucault argued was the case) that wherever there is power, there is resistance.

Phatic Communion:
Bringing Unfocused Interaction into Focus

by Bernard N. Meltzer and Gil Richard Musolf

We now try to show how actors, through the use of phatic communion, bring unfocused interaction into focus, which may be as fleeting as a brief encounter or the beginning of a more sustained interaction sequence. Goffman is, again, a major contributor to our understanding. About 75 years ago, Bronislaw Malinowski (1943; first edition 1923) coined the phrase "phatic communion" (from the Greek *phatos*, spoken). By this phrase Malinowski referred to:

> the use of language in pure social intercourse; when the object of talk is not to achieve some aim but the exchange of words almost as an end in itself. . . . A mere phrase of politeness . . . fulfills a function to which the meaning of its words is almost completely irrelevant. Inquiries about health, comments on weather, affirmations of some supremely obvious state of things—all such are exchanged, not in order to inform, not . . . to connect people in action, certainly not in order to express any thought. (312-13)

And:

> Are words in phatic communion used primarily to convey meaning, the meaning that is symbolically theirs? Certainly not! They fulfill a *social* function and that is their principal aim, but they are neither the result of intellectual reflection, nor do they necessarily arouse reflection in the listener. Once again we may say that language does not function here as a means of transmission of thought. (315, emphasis added)

Subsequently, other scholars (chiefly linguists) have characterized phatic communion (sometimes termed "phatic communication") as follows: "making conversation for the sake of it" (Burton 1980), "language for the sake of maintaining rapport" (Crystal 1987), "talk . . . where speakers' relational goals supersede their commitment to factuality and instrumentality" (Coupland, Coupland, and Robinson 1992).[6] Moreover, since much of everyday conversation comprises phatic elements, popular designations abound, such as: "just being sociable," "casual conversation," "small talk," "chewing the fat," "shooting the breeze," "shmoozing," "yakking," and "chit-chat."

Linguists have found Malinowski's concept a productive source of theoretical formulations and research enterprises. Much of their recent work has centered upon the consideration of politeness, chiefly the strategies for maintaining face for oneself and others. In contrast, most sociologists and social psychologists, with the very notable exception of Erving Goffman, have virtually ignored the subject.[7] Although some sociologists have studied conversational openings and closings—which typically entail phatic utterances—they have tended to consider the phatic function only indirectly, incidental to other aspects. Examples of such studies are those by Miller, Hintz, and Couch (1975); Leichty (1986); Schegloff (1988); and Sacks (1995), in which no explicit mention of phatic communion is to be found. It is no surprise, therefore, to find that the term "phatic communion" is absent from the vocabulary of sociology. We find the foregoing facts especially puzzling in light—as will be shown later—of the contribution phaticity makes to the fundamental sociological question, "What is the nature of the social bond?" or, as Goffman put the question, "How does social reality sustain itself?"[8]

That Goffman addressed the subject of phatic communion (although never using the term itself) is readily evident. His key concerns, power and ceremony, subsumed the analysis of etiquette, of the ritual order. The phatic element is, of course, part of the ceremonial order of encounters. Moreover, Goffman, familiar with the field of linguistics (in which he published papers), recognized that some linguists were engaged in projects paralleling his own. Thus, his many relevant writings on the interaction order figure prominently in this section.[9]

This section adopts as its analytical perspective an explicit focus upon the phatic element in social interaction. In doing so, it attempts to fill-in some of the lacunae in the sociological treatment of phatic communion through a survey of noteworthy conceptual and empirical writings, primarily by linguists. The survey seeks to integrate the mutually-insulated treatments in the voluminous linguistics literature and the scant sociological literature on the topic. We begin with various conceptions about the nature of phaticity, touching upon both consensually-accepted and debated characteristics, as well as upon such derivative concepts as interaction rituals and politeness. Next, we consider its social significance, describing its general and specific functions in social life. We then deal with contextual influences upon its modalities, examining ideas and empirical findings about the effects of diverse social and cultural elements upon phatic communion. Finally, we suggest some aspects of both its dependence upon and impact upon macro phenomena.

The Nature of Phatic Communion

We have seen that the defining features of phatic communion have been conceptualized as (a) its nonreferential character and (b) its emphasis on social ties. What other, subsidiary characteristics have been noted? This section offers answers to this question.

Goffman (1971, 93) asserts, "From the fact that greetings are found among many of the higher primates, as well as in any number of preliterate societies and all civilized ones, it would be easy to conclude that something like access rituals are *universally* found in societies" (emphasis added); (also see Miller and Hintz [1997], 93). At least two scholars (Hymes 1974; Crystal 1987), however, have challenged the universality of phatic communion: Crystal (1987, 11), claims that in some groups (including the Paliyans of southern India and the Aritama of Colombia) members say little and prefer silence; Hymes (1974, 127) makes a similar statement about the Wishram Chinook of the Columbia River. However, Senft (1995) questions these claims and calls for further research on the matter.

Malinowski's neologism emerged from his study of meaning in nonliterate languages, especially among the Trobriand Islanders. This source limited his focus, perforce, to face-to-face conversations. Most linguists have followed his lead by treating phatic communion as, exclusively, a speech phenomenon. Quirk (1962, 59), for example, writes of "a use of language which relates only to speech, to spoken and not written language." On the other hand, McArthur (1992) and Crystal (1987) indicate that phatic expressions are conventional in the salutations and farewells of letters ("Dearest friend," "Sincerely yours") and in commercial greeting cards. Also, some scholars (e.g., Pavlidou 1994) have included *telephone* conversations within the purview of phatic communion, and e-mail, obviously, is a recent medium. We see no compelling reason for restricting the concept solely to speech; however, as Crystal (1987, 178) points out, "the immediacy of speech makes it ideal for social or 'phatic' functions." Hayakawa (1947, 62) expresses a somewhat similar view, pointing out that breaking bread together, playing games together, and working together are ways of establishing communion, "but talking together is the most easily arranged of all these forms of collective activity."

As we earlier suggested—and shall later show in some detail—phatic communion functions to affirm and reaffirm social bonds. This use of language, Wardhaugh (1993, 171) astutely asserts, "serves humans much like 'grooming behavior' serves many animals," bringing them together and helping to maintain social relationships. In a similar vein, Chaika (1982, 32) tells us that phatic expressions are akin to patting dogs on the head as a way of letting them know we care.

Malinowski (1943) and many linguists (e.g., Steible 1967; Marsh 1989) equate phatic communion with polite, friendly speech, which implies tie-binding consideration of the feelings of others. As we shall show in the next section of this chapter, polite conversation has recently become the focus of much scholarly work on phatic communion. Schneider (1988), in fact, equates phaticity with politeness. It is clear, however, that while politeness manifests itself on both the communicative and non-communicative levels, phaticity is found only on the former level. Encompassed by such speech—again, according to Malinowski and *some* linguists—is idle gossip, in the sense of "free, aimless social intercourse" (1943, 313). However, Schneider (1981) argues that gossip must be excluded from phatic communion because much gossip is, inescapably, intended to be referential, or informative (thereby violating a defining characteristic of phaticity). It would appear to us, on the other hand, that specific instances of gossip may be considered phatic to the extent that they foreground relational goals. Thus, a distinction can be made between aspects of the use of utterances that may be referred to their function as phatic communion and aspects that may be referred to their referential function.[10]

Numerous depictions of phatic utterances are available. Such expressions are typically formulistic or stereotyped,[11] composed of clichés and platitudes, noncommittal or perfunctory, minimally self-involved, avoidant of comments that are too personal, given to saying what one is expected to say, and marked by subordination of literal or "real" meaning. This last characteristic implies the presence of two levels of meaning, the semantic and the situational, surface, or apparent meaning. The parallel with irony and with such exchanges of insults in black-American society as "the dozens," "signifying," or "joning" is evident: the surface meaning is not intended to be taken seriously. Given this feature of phatic communion, second-language listeners often face the same problems of comprehension as they may with idiomatic words and phrases (e.g., does one offer a full reply to an acquaintance's "How are you today"?). Clearly, phatic communion requires—as in any effective communication—that the listener share the speaker's *intended* meaning, that interactants participate in a process of mutually sustaining a definition of the situation. As Goffman (1969, 9) puts the matter:

> Indeed, the very sense of a message depends on our telling whether it is conveyed, for example, seriously, or sarcastically, or tentatively, as an indirect quotation, and in face-to-face communication this "framing" information derives from paralinguistic cues such as intonation, facial gestures, and the like—cues that have an expressive, not semantic, character.

Although we have, thus far, dealt only with the verbal medium of phatic communion, one need hardly be reminded that substitutes for verbalisms are to be found in handshakes, smiles, hugs, kisses on or past cheeks, slightly prolonged eye contact, and the like. Also, various writers (e.g., Laver 1975; Lyons 1977) have considered such paralinguistic, kinesic, proxemic, and visual accompaniments as involuntary eye movements, gestures, posture, and tone of voice. As we indicated earlier, Goffman (1967), too, stressed the importance of glances, gestures, and positioning—along with verbalizations—in meeting ritual requirements that signal willingness to interact.

This discussion of the features of phaticity would be incomplete if we omitted mention of what Haverkate (1988, 399) terms "pseudo-phatic communion." This refers to instances where "the speaker pretends to achieve no other aim than displaying a socially appreciated form of interactional behavior, while, in actual fact, his behavior serves to reduce negative face effects in [an] ultimate request." Haverkate cites the example of greeting a friend with a compliment and, later, requesting a favor. Somewhat similar conduct is described by C. Wright Mills (1951) in his discussion of fake-friendly sales techniques in the pseudo-*Gemeinschaft* he calls "the great salesroom," or the marketplace. Hochschild's (1983) depiction—inspired, she acknowledges, by Mills' writings—of the ever-smiling, but self-estranged, airline attendants' emotion work also exemplifies the manipulative use of phatic expression. We need hardly indicate that everyday life today is marked by a surfeit of such use.

The literature, understandably, is replete with negatively valued aspects of phaticity. Pejoratives like "dissimulative," "inauthentic," "insincere," "vacuous," "banal," "idle gossip," "idle discourse," "small talk," "chit-chat," "cocktail chatter," "a mere exchange of words," and similar characterizations—on both the scholarly and popular levels—trivialize and derogate such discourse. In this connection, Strong (1988) asserts that the central argument in much of Goffman's work, the ceremonial order of the encounter, the etiquette that can be observed in most social occasions, is far from being a trivial matter. Referring to this etiquette (which is inclusive of phatic behavior), Goffman (1971, 64) writes:

> [Interaction rituals] are among the most conventionalized and perfunctory doings we engage in and traditionally have been treated by students of modern society as part of the dust of social activity, empty and trivial. . . . [W]henever an individual rubs up against another, he is likely to say hello or excuse me. Surely it is time to examine "Hello" or "Excuse me," or their equivalent. Moreover, . . . conversational encounters of the more extended kind are typically opened and closed by these devices, if not built up in terms of them.

In the past generation several linguists (Laver 1975; Marsh 1989; Cocchi 1992; Coupland, Coupland, and Robinson 1992) have also warned against minimizing its social importance. Our next section discusses the more positively valued aspects of phatic communion.

The Social Significance of Phatic Communion

One of its defining characteristics—the establishment or maintenance of social ties, however tenuous—constitutes the major social importance of phatic communion. This characteristic has been specified in several ways by various writers: language for the purpose of creating social contact (Jakobson 1960; Schneider 1981; Marsh 1989; Akindele 1990); utterances that aim to bond hearer to speaker

(Malinowski 1943); ritual courtesy that attests to civility and good will (Goffman 1971; Edwards 1976); speech that acknowledges someone's existence (Edwards 1976; Coupland, Coupland, and Robinson 1992); and such specifications by Goffman (1976) as conventionalized acts in which one portrays regard for another to that other and ceremony that affirms basic social arrangements and ultimate doctrines about humans and their world. Although both sociologists and anthropologists have long been aware of this relationship between ritual and social solidarity, their attention to phatic communion has been indirect and minimal rather than explicit and detailed.

Several component functions come into play in the various stages of encounters. Laver (1975) writes of three such functions in just the opening phase of interpersonal encounters: (1) a *propitiatory* function, by defusing the potential hostility engendered by silence in situations where speech is conventionally expected; (2) an *exploratory* function, by allowing the participants to develop what Goffman (1959) terms a working consensus about their encounter; and (3) an *initiatory* function, by enabling the participants to collaborate in getting the interaction underway. All of these functions facilitate what Rommetveit (1974) designated the "architecture of intersubjectivity," which is necessary to communication. Needless to say, however, openings often comprise the entirety of encounters.

For Goffman (1971, 63), the bonding function of greetings (and other "ritual offerings") is suggested in the following statement:

> When . . . one individual provides a sign of involvement in and connectedness to another, it behooves the recipient to show that the message has been received, that its import has been appreciated, that the affirmed relationship actually exists as the performer implies, that the performer himself has worth as a person, and finally, that the recipient has an appreciative, grateful nature.

In the closing phase of encounters, phatic communion serves, as Laver (1975) indicates, to mitigate a potential sense of rejection. It does so in two ways: (1) by enabling a cooperative parting, in which appropriate reassurance from the person who is leaving assuages any feelings of rejection by the person being left; (2) by consolidating the relationship through emphasizing the enjoyable nature of the encounter, mutual esteem, the promise of a continuation of the relationship, assertion of mutual solidarity, and the like (231), illustrated by the comments "As usual, it's been good talking to you. Let's do lunch someday." Leichty's (1986, 233) studies of social closings among dyads found that ending statements typically include elements quite similar to those just listed, namely: (1) summary statements of cognitive or affective material from the interaction, (2) continuity statements affirming the endurance of the relationship beyond the present, (3) well-wishing statements, (4) statements justifying the ending of the encounter, and (5) positive versus negative statements. Goffman (1963, 79) felicitously sums up the phatic character of many closings:

when [conversational encounters] come to be terminated, a supportive ritual will
. . . occur, namely some sort of farewell display performed during leave-taking. . . .
The interpretation is standard: the goodbye brings the encounter to an unambiguous
close, sums up the consequence of the encounter for the relationship, and bolsters
the relationship for the anticipated period of no contact.

It is clear, then, that phatic communion enables "the detailed management of
interpersonal relationships during the psychologically crucial margins of interaction" (Laver 1975, 217). That is, it facilitates a psychologically comfortable transition from silence to interaction, and then back to silence (233). Thus, phatic utterances are messages that serve to initiate, prolong, or terminate communication.

Idle talk, chit-chat, and gossip tend to provide the content of those medial
phases of interactions that are marked predominantly by phaticity. In the course of
such conversations—and, in fact, of other conversations—participants may employ what Goffman (1981, 28) calls "keep-going signals" in order to perpetuate
the encounter: "Gee, gosh, wow, hmm, tsk, no!" When the chief aim of conversation is not to exchange information but to keep the conversation going, participants may interpolate bits of information, but sociability tends to outweigh referential remarks.

Running through all phases of encounters, of course, is another function of
phaticity: the communication of indexical information about the identities and
attributes of the interactants (see Laver 1975). Such information influences the
nature of the particular interaction and of any ensuing action.

It is when we are on either the giving or receiving end of offenses against the
rituals of phatic communion that we are most likely to become cognizant of their
tie-binding role. That people generally feel obliged to avoid silence in situations
of copresence has long been noted. In an ethnocentric (and classist) statement,
Malinowski (1943, 313) asserted: "To the primitive mind, whether among sav-
ages or our own uneducated classes, taciturnity means not only unfriendliness but
directly a bad character." Similarly, Akindele (1990, 3) finds that, among the
Yoruba, failure to greet another in appropriate contexts tends to induce bad feelings, especially among close friends and relatives, to the extent that it can give rise
to suspicion of sorcery or witchcraft. In most societies, of course, this failure to
break silence in "sociability" contexts generally leads to such designations as
"rudeness," "social error," "unfriendliness," "unsociability," "egregious behavior,"
"snub," or "cut," and to such feeling-responses as distance, alienation, distrust,
dislike, fear, or ill will—not to mention puzzlement, at times, about the source of
the offender's omission. As Hintz and Miller (1995, 360) state: "When routine
greetings are not constructed, there is a sense of absence, even alarm. 'What's
wrong?' 'Could I have said something?'" Chaika (1982, 32), Goffman (1981,
150), and Sacks (1995, vol. 2, 360) have, also, treated this matter. Of course,
many of us have had the experience of avoiding the necessity of greeting someone—or even of refusing to shake hands with someone—with whom we do not
wish, at least at a given time, to associate. On such occasions, the phatic function

of the avoided or refused token is, certainly, clear to us.

Our comments on the discourteous acts of withholding phatic utterances leads directly into considerations of "face," a concept that lies at the heart of theories of interaction ritual and of politeness (see, for example, a collection of papers edited by Coulmas 1980). Drawing heavily upon Goffman's work, Brown and Levinson (1978, 1987) define politeness as the maintenance of face, the avoidance of embarrassment of oneself and other co-present actors. Most of their studies explore numerous strategies for avoiding face-threatening acts (FTA). Using tape-recorded conversations in three different languages (English, Tzeltal, and Tamil), they develop what they consider universal FTA strategies, such as the following: attend to the listeners' interests, wants, needs, and goods; use in-group identity markers; joke; make offers or promises; assume or assert reciprocity; include listeners in joint activity. As we shall note in part of the next section, other politeness scholars (e.g., Coupland, Coupland, and Giles 1991) have considered FTA strategies involving such specific groups as the elderly.

Contextual Influences on Phatic Communion

What kinds of situations, relationships, and other constraints impinge upon phatic events? This question falls within the domain of pragmatics, defined by Crystal (1980) as the study of language from the standpoint of the user, particularly the choices she or he makes, the constraints she or he encounters in using language in social interaction, and the effects this use of language has on the other interactants. We turn now to a consideration of this matter.[12]

Cross-cultural studies have revealed some differences in the use of phatic language. An analysis of telephone calls in Greece and Germany (Palidou 1994), for example, found that Greeks are twice as prone to employ phatic expressions than Germans. Further, while Greeks tend to use phatic utterances regardless of possible threats to face, Germans incline toward such language chiefly in order to reduce face threats connected with the reason for the call. Other studies (Tannen 1980, 1981) report that Greeks are more disposed than Americans toward both indirectness and involvement in conversation. Additional cross-cultural (e.g., Silva 1980; Byrnes 1986; Godard 1977) and intensive single-culture studies (e.g., Bazzanella 1988; Ghiga 1989) have been reported.

Also, social class subcultural influences on phatic language are reported by Meltzer (1994, 297n15) in a study of a poverty-stricken village in the Dominican Republic:

> [There is a special response] to the common greeting, "How are you?" (*¿I Como está?*). Rather than politely replying "Very well" ("*Muy Bien*") . . . most villagers simply say, "Struggling [to survive]" ("*luchano*"), "Alive" ("*Vivo*"), "Regular" ("*Regular*"), or some similar statement. As one 60-year-old . . . man observed, "Only the rich are 'very well'" (*Solamente los ricos están 'muy bien.'*)

Another contextual element is that of the prior relationship between inter-actants. Linguists disagree on some aspects of this issue. While Wardhaugh (1985) holds that much of the dialogue between closely bonded participants tends to be phatic in nature, Marsh (1989) expresses the common view that small talk (used synonymously with phatic communion) takes place only between strangers. Schneider (1988, 287) leans toward the latter view in his assertion that "[a]s a rule, the share of phatic elements in a conversation decreases, the closer the inter-personal relationship." This less restrictive view comports with our everyday experiences and observations: we may exchange superficial, uninvolved greetings and farewells with both a bartender and a friend, but, in the time between greeting and farewell, our talk with the friend is more likely to be serious and referential than mere "talk for the sake of talk."

The immediately preceding sentence can serve to introduce the point that the marginal phases of discourse—openings and closings—are generally considered most productive of phatic communion (see Laver [1975]; Burton [1980]; Schnei-der [1981]). Hence, the literature on our subject abounds in studies of these phases. Many of these concern the impact of statuses and roles upon modes of phatic discourse. Among the Yoruba, for instance, the type and structuring of greetings are, according to Akindele (1990, 2), affected by age, gender, and occu-pation. Thus, conventionally, younger persons initiate greetings in deference to older persons. (For a study touching upon Italian gender differences in phatic expressions, see Bazzanella 1988.)

Probably the most comprehensive set of studies of the phatic element in con-versations involving older people has been completed by J. and N. Coupland and their various associates (Coupland, Grainger, and Coupland 1988; Coupland, Coupland, and Giles 1991; Coupland, Coupland, and Robinson 1992; Coupland, Robinson, and Coupland 1994; and many others). Using a politeness perspective, Coupland, Coupland, and Giles (1991) list several "interactional goals" of elderly people: (1) (minimally) to elicit engagement and a range of positive responses from an individual interlocutor, from praise ("I lead quite a busy life although I'm eighty-six") to sympathy ("I'm not very well these days; I'm seventy"); (2) to stake a claim, at the intergroup level, for owed respect, attention, or care"; (3) to enact a set of relative evaluations, for example of the life position of an elderly speaker in relation to other elderly people . . . or to other reference individuals or groups; (4) to defuse a potentially threatening situation; (5) relatedly, to transfer age from the implicit to the explicit agenda, thereby defusing the threat imposed by uncertainty; (6) to try to come to terms with the balance between one's own chronological age and contextual age, and reduce one's own uncertainty about present states and future possibilities (71-72).

These goals enter the picture in discourse relating to age identity, age disclo-sure, intergenerational encounters, doctor-patient visits, and other situations. For example, studies have been conducted of the responses elderly patients make to "How are you?" greetings by physicians (Coupland, Coupland, and Robinson 1992), the presence of "face" elements even in such instrumental, transactional encounters as medical consultations (Coupland, Robinson, and Coupland 1994), and the face-threatening character of requests, criticism, expression of thanks, and apologies (Coupland, Grainger, and Coupland 1988).

Laver (1975, 1981) has written intensively about the effects of relative social status (and power) on phaticity in England. He begins his insightful discussion by differentiating *self-oriented* comments, (referring to the speaker, e.g., "This heat is too much for me"), *other-oriented* comments (referring to the listener, e.g., "How was your weekend?"), and *neutral* comments (referring to neither, e.g., "It's a nice day"). He then proceeds to delineate the following patterns of opening remarks in symmetrical and asymmetrical status relationships: (1) When a nonsolidary inferior speaks first to an acknowledged superior—"upwards" interaction—she or he tends to employ the self-oriented category of comments, but no the other-oriented. The inverse is true in "downwards" interaction, the nonsolidary superior using the other-oriented category when initiating conversation. Thus, "conventions seems to support a position where the superior is prepared to 'invade' the psychological world of the inferior, . . . (Laver 1975, 224). This latter statement is supported by Goffman's (1963, 74) assertion, "Often greetings will . . . affirm a differential allocation of status, specifically attesting that the subordinate is willing to keep his place." (2) Speakers, regardless of relative social status, are on "safe," uncontroversial, unassertive ground when they use the neutral category (Laver 1975, 224). (3) If the relationship is solidary, the speaker (whether inferior, superior, or equal in social status) has a free choice of category (223).

Laver (1975; 1981) also observes that "territoriality" is a constraint (at least in Great Britain and America) on who initiates an exchange of phatic utterances. A participant who is moving toward a stationary other, regardless of the physical site, tends (unless there are overriding special reasons) to begin the exchange.[13] Several reasons underline this likely pattern, according to Laver: (1) The speaker recognizes that, in a sense, the static listener is in a closer psychological relationship with the immediate territory than she or he is, and that in a way the listener can be deemed the "owner" of the territory; (2) She or he acknowledges his or her awareness of the fact of his or her "invasion" of the other's space; (3) She or he declares, in effect, that his or her intentions are pacific, and offers a propitiatory token; and (4) By implicitly inviting the other to participate in verbal interaction, the speaker asserts a claim to sociolinguistic solidarity with the listener.

Summary and Conclusion

This discussion has directed explicit attention to a subject that sociologists have tended to treat implicitly: phatic communion. Our survey of writings on phatic communion has considered the character of this taken-for-granted, everyday phenomenon, including its probable universality, its occurrence in various vehicles of communication (face-to-face speech, telephone messages, letters, and e-mail), its overlap with gossip (in the sense of idle discourse), its bilevel meaning, its paralinguistic equivalents and accompaniments, and pseudo-phatic acts. We have then directed attention to the positively valued aspects of phatic communion, that is, its function in affirming and reaffirming the social bond, touching upon this function in conventional openings, closings, and medial phases, and pointed out the implications of snubs or cuts. Moreover, we have shown the close connections between, on the one hand, face-saving strategies and, on the other, processes of phatic communion, interaction ritual, or politeness. We have also dealt with situational influences on phatic communion, describing findings of cross-cultural studies and a social-class study, considering the question of whether phaticity prevails to a greater extent in exchanges among strangers and acquaintances or among friends, and reporting studies on the effects of various social attributes upon phatic exchanges.

We conclude by suggesting that phatic communion carries implications for the micro-macro link. In the past generation, various sociologists have commented upon a trend of convergence between the micro and macro levels, which we now briefly review.[14] Two edited volumes on the subject (Helle and Eisenstadt 1985 and Alexander et al. 1987) conclude that we must recognize "the connection between large-scale societal structures and the everyday experiences of individuals" (Helle and Eisenstadt 1985, 7). Similarly, Brown and Levinson (1987) hold that interpersonal interaction seems to be both determined by and a determinant of various aspects of large-scale social facts. Putting the matter in a somewhat different way, Munch and Smelser (1987, 358) assert: "[M]icro theories invariably involve definite assumptions about the macrocontent in which interactional processes are embedded (and therefore have a macrocomponent) and . . . macrotheories invariably involve assumptions about individual motivation and interaction (and therefore have a microcomponent)."

Still another way of characterizing the link is provided by Collins (1987), who conceives macrostructures as comprising aggregations of microencounters and contends that every microencounter takes place within macrostructures that have emerged from previous aggregations of microencounters. (For additional views in the same vein as the preceding ones, see Duranti and Goodwin 1992 and Giesen 1987.)

Finally, while it is true that Goffman was not particularly interested in the macro world, he clearly acknowledged the power of the ties between it and the micro world (see Strong 1988). Seeing a "loose coupling" between the interaction order and the larger social order, he asserts (1961, 8): "An encounter provides a world for its participants, but the character and stability of this world is intimately related to its selective relationship to the wider one. The naturalistic study of encounters, then, is more closely tied to studies of social structure on one hand, and more separate from them, than one might at first imagine."

Looking, first, at the impact of the structural or institutional order on the interaction order, Goffman (1961) points to language and cultural knowledge that interactants draw upon, as well as the influence of status, authority, seniority, gender, class, and ethnic background, which are selectively filtered in and out of encounters (see Layder 1977, 215-19, for an excellent discussion of this topic). Describing this relationship as the reproduction of the macroorder by the microorder, Giddens (1984, 69) argues: "The fixity of institutional forms does not exist in spite of, or outside, the encounters of day-to-day life but is implicated in those very encounters." Our preceding section on "Contextual Influences on Phatic Communion" provides several illustrations of this claim.

Turning now to the reverse side of the picture, it is necessary to indicate that students of face-to-face encounters, in general, and phatic communion, in particular, have tended to overlook this aspect of the micro-macro link. However, some scholars have shown greater awareness in the matter. Nisbet (1966, 98), for example, paraphrases Simmel, arguing that "dyads, triads, and other timeless, constitutive elements of the social bond . . . have a profound effect upon the direction of change and the structures of the larger associations in society." The dyad and the triad are "the molecular elements of society." More recently, Maines (1979, 527) has commented similarly: [S]ocial structure should also be regarded as a dependent variable, . . . can be examined as a product of interaction, and . . . is created, maintained, and changed through interaction processes." Another scholar, writing from a similar perspective, specifically indicates the role of politeness: "[P]oliteness . . . is basic to the production of social order, and a precondition of human cooperation, so that any theory which provides an understanding of this phenomenon at the same time goes to the foundations of human social life" (Gumperz 1987, xiii).

Goffman (1983) provides us with a concrete instance of a connection between the interaction order and social structures, showing how a face-to-face gathering gave rise to a broad social movement. He recounts how a steel-band carnival that began as a multiethnic block party in the Notting Hill area of London ended up in the inception of the political organization of London's West Indians. Thus, what started as an annual Bank Holiday social affair eventually became a politically self-conscious social movement.

Summing up, we can say that phatic communion plays a significant part in the processes that keep people together in groups; and, reciprocally, larger social processes are important in shaping the form and content of phatic communion. If this is indeed the case, sociologists should feel doubly impelled to study phatic communion.

Notes

1. J. L. Austin has studied this notion comprehensively: "for some years we have been realizing more and more clearly that the occasion of an utterance matters seriously, and, that the words used are to some extent to be 'explained' by the 'context' in which they are designed to be or have actually been spoken in a linguistic interchange" (Austin 1978, 100). And "we must consider the total situation in which the utterance is issued—the total speech-act" (Austin 1978, 52). Jürgen Habermas has also comprehensively elaborated a theory that communication requires the achievement of four validity claims: "anyone acting

communicatively must, in performing any speech action, raise universal validity claims and suppose that they can be vindicated. Insofar as he wants to participate in a process of understanding, he cannot avoid raising the following—and indeed precisely the following—validity claims: (a) *Uttering* something understandably; (b) Giving (the hearer) *something* to understand, (c) Making *himself* thereby understandable; and (d) coming to an understanding *with another person* (Habermas 1979, 2; emphasis in original).

2. A criticism of Goffman's work on this aspect has been registered by Gouldner: "Goffman does not deal with how men seek to change the *structure* of these organizations or of other social systems, but, rather, with how they may adapt to and within them" (Gouldner 1970b, 381-82; emphasis in original). Thus, "Goffman's rejection of hierarchy often expresses itself as an *avoidance* of social stratification and of the importance of power differences, even for concerns that are central to him, thus, it entails an accommodation to existing power arrangements" (Gouldner 1970b, 379; emphasis in original).

3. Foucault (1979, 138) has studied the history of this phenomenon as it concerns the rise of the social science and medical disciplines. "What was then being formed was a policy of coercions that act upon the body, a calculated manipulation of its elements, its gestures, its behavior. The human body was entering a machinery of power that explores it, breaks it down, and rearranges it. A 'political anatomy' which also was a 'mechanics of power,' was being born. It defined how one may have hold over others' bodies, not only so that they may do what one wishes, but also so that they may operate as one wishes, with the techniques, the speed, and the efficiency that one determines. Thus, discipline produces subjected and practiced bodies, 'docile' bodies."

4. I thank Bernard N. Meltzer for pointing this out.

5. One of the reasons this trust-in-the-other is not forthcoming may be communicative incompetence. Communicative competence must be oriented to reaching an understanding and establishing a relationship. The failure to reach an understanding—which initiates staff-patient alienation—is due to a failure of the hearer of a speech-act to trust the speaker. But this reservation to trust the speaker—the psychiatrist—may be due to the speaker's incompetence to speak in that special way necessary when trying to establish a relationship with the mentally ill. Habermas puts the burden of communication on the speaker. Specifically, the psychiatrist might be charged with having failed in establishing two validity claims. "To [1] express his intentions in such a way that the linguistic expression represents what is intended (so that the hearer can trust the speaker); [2] To perform the speech act in such a way that it conforms to recognized norms or to accepted self-images (so that the hearer can be in accord with the speaker in shared value-orientation)" (Habermas 1979, 29). Habermas implicitly underscores the necessity to take the role of the other to achieve a relationship between speaker and hearer. "I shall speak of the success of a speech act only when the hearer not only understands the meaning of the sentence uttered, but also actively enters into the relationship intended by the speaker" (Habermas 1979, 59). Thus to the extent that the psychiatrist cannot induce the patient to take the role of the psychiatrist, the psychiatrist has failed in his or her speech act.

6. La Barre (1954) and Austin (1962) use the term "phatic" in ways that depart from the more common usage. La Barre uses "phatic communication" to refer to the expression of feeling (through poetry, for example), while Austin provides the following cumbersome and obscure definition of his "phatic act": "the act of uttering certain vocables or words, that is, noises of certain types belonging to *and as* belonging to a certain vocabulary, in a certain construction, i.e., conforming to and as conforming to a certain grammar, with a certain intonation, etc." (92, emphasis in original).

8. To illustrate, an excellent treatment of eighteen modes of conver-

sation—Perinbanayagam's *Discursive Acts* (1991)—makes no explicit reference to phaticity.

9. As Stewart (1998) expresses it, "How do people manage to live and act together?"

10. In a sense, "phatic communion" and "interaction rituals" are almost synonymous. Both designate expressive elements in discourse. However, while "phatic communion" embraces only efforts to build and maintain social ties, Goffman's (1981, 20, emphasis added) term more broadly encompasses: "a special class of quite conventionalized utterances, lexicalizations whose controlling purpose is to give praise, *blame*, thanks, support, affection, or show gratitude, *disapproval, dislike*, sympathy, or greet, say farewell, and so forth."

11. This statement can be linked to the more general view that "every communication has [both] a content and a relationship aspect . . ." (Watzlawick, Beavin, and Jackson 1967, 62; also see Bateson 1958).

12. Given the routinized character of phatic communion, such acts do not necessarily involve explicit indications to oneself of relational intentions.

13. We do not maintain that the structure of social situations and the normatively pertinent rituals *determine* the phaticity of an encounter. Rather, they exert *influence* upon this aspect. Whether interactants use phatic utterances, which ones they use, and how they respond to the use of such utterances by other participants—all depend heavily upon the ongoing construction of the act at every juncture in the encounter. Coupland, Coupland, and Robinson (1992) and Coupland, Robinson, and Coupland (1994) recognize this fluidity, presenting studies of the negotiation and monitoring of phatic comments and responses.

14. Sacks briefly describes another spatial element in phatic exchanges:

> One kind of interesting feature of the accomplishment of greetings-only interactions, where people are approaching each other on a street, in a hallway, etc. is the way in which parties are able to withhold doing greetings until they reach some space relative to each other so that they can do greetings. . . . For the most part, people do it well, engineering that thing so that they do not pass each other face to face having ended the interaction. . . . [F]or if one party starts a greeting at such a distance from the other as to involve that the other returns the greeting while they are still approaching each other, then more than greetings will perhaps have to be done. (Sacks, 1995, vol. 2, 192-93)

Such calculation of spatio-temporal coordinates attests to the care actors take in the construction of encounter rituals.

15. The pervasiveness of phaticity at the interpersonal, or macro-, level in everyday life should be borne in mind.

8

Contemporary Conceptions of the Social Self

The self is the major SI concept. Since Mead's formulations on the self, a number of other statements on the self have attained the status of classics. The texts to be reviewed here are in that category, yet systematic attention to them (except for Goffman's work) has not been forthcoming. These authors also present three different conceptions of the self. Goffman's project introduced a profound augmentation to the interactionist canon, the development of the dramaturgical perspective. Strauss's project emphasized the identity transformation the self can be subjected to, which has inspired, and continues to inspire, much work within this area of SI. He also paid more attention to social structure than previous interactionists.

Goffman: The Dramatizing Self

The world as phenomena is a theme that emerges with Goffman's *Presentation of Self in Everyday Life* and continues with his *Frame Analysis*. We present selves, near-theatrical performances, by which we dramatize the otherwise humdrum of everyday interaction. Two types of expression characterize our symbolic dramatizations, the expressions that we *give* and the unwitting expressions that we *give off*. Expressions that we give are of a verbal character, and expressions that we give off are "symptomatic of the actor," which may either be consistent with or contradict the expressions that we give. The individual manipulates his or her performances so as to control "the conduct of others, especially their responsive treatment of him" (Goffman 1959, 3). Interaction is a struggle over the control of

155

the definition of the situation. The actor dramatizes a self that he or she wants the audience to accept, and the audience is constantly observing both expressions given and ones given off to ascertain the validity of the self that the actor is trying to legitimate. Thus there is an undercurrent of opposition inherent in social interaction.

It is not that actors are constantly trying to stage "false" appearances or that audiences engage in a perpetual debunking of pretense, but that a *norm of circumspection* is operative in which a leeway of deviation is allowed before negative sanctions are invoked. This range of tolerable deviation is itself a norm, one we may call the *norm of civility*. A constant opposition pulls at audiences. On the one hand, a norm of civility allows actors to perform their roles with some measure of deviation or idiosyncrasy; on the other hand, the *norm of circumspection* warns us to be suspicious when actors appear too incompetent or out of character. It is as though we are given performance credits or capital (the norm of civility) which we cannot draw on or spend with too much pretense without bankrupting the norm. If we put on "too many airs," or give a suspicious performance, the norm of circumspection will guide us to invoke negative sanctions. We do not like to be embarrassed, made fools of, or conned, and that is precisely the preventive function of the norm of circumspection. "When these disruptive events occur, the interaction itself may come to a confused and embarrassed halt" (Goffman 1959, 12). The actor's definition of the situation is vitiated, validity claims are unsustained; the actor is unmasked, exposed as the fraud, the humbug. Such a spurious performance will usually entail embarrassment, tension, and anxiety, and perhaps verbal and/or physical conflict may ensue.

Interaction is precarious and fragile, and a concerted effort by both actor and audience is required to ensure successful encounters. The two norms, civility and circumspection, allow interaction to be patterned; they also provide for leeway in behavior. Goffman refers to this as a "working consensus," a *modus vivendi* for everyday encounters. "Together the participants contribute to a single definition of the situation, which involves not so much a real agreement as to what exists but rather a real agreement as to whose claims concerning what issues will be temporarily honored. Real agreements will also exist concerning definitions of the situation" (Goffman 1959, 9-10). What is ongoing, then, between interactants is a process of role bargaining, each participant lending support to the other's role claims. As participants in interaction, we are both audience and role performers, and we give each role performer audience support, expecting the same in kind. A norm of reciprocity is thus operative, guiding us to accept others' role claims and for them likewise to accept ours. But the norm of circumspection cautions us from accepting any role claim. We are not civil to the degree of being made dupes. The focus of Goffman (1959, 4) is primarily on expressions given off, that is, "the more theoretical and contextual kind, whether this communication be purposely engineered or not."

Goffman, concerned with the symbolic and dramatic aspects of delivery (that is, how we perform, act out, or orchestrate words and deeds), has drawn on the Thomas axiom, replacing situation with performance: if people define performances as real, they are real in their consequences. This admittedly pragmatic, instrumental criterion, unifies Goffman's work with that of earlier Chicagoans. Performers must have a "belief in the part they are playing." The rise of postmodernism has increased sociologists' concern with delivery, performances, representation, simulacra, and the way in which the symbolic nature of everyday life facilitates these social practices.

Performances

Performance is a dramaturgical variable. We may take our masks so seriously as to be taken in by them ourselves; or we may be cynical about our acts and the audiences who fall for them. There is, then, a continuum between sincerity and cynicism. All our dramatizations fall between these two poles. Our belief is not static, but dynamic; we may begin by performing our roles sincerely but end up being cynical, or begin by being cynics and end up with adamant conviction. But sincerity is fundamental as a projection; the actor may be sincere or cynical, but "if a performance is to come off, the witnesses by and large must be able to believe that the performers are sincere. This is the structural place of sincerity in the drama of events" (Goffman 1959, 71). Whether the actor is indeed sincere is "within the subjective understanding of the actor. It is impossible to detect it from the outside" (Cuzzort 1969, 180-81).

Cuzzort (177) has presented a typology of projections or dramatizations derived from Goffman's book. Cuzzort's concept of "content" refers to what Goffman's defines as expressions given. "Symptomatic behavior" refers to the

Table 8.1 Cuzzort's Table

Content	Symptomatic Behavior	Audience Reaction
Positive	Positive	A person with control over both levels of expression will be highly effective.
Positive	Negative	Despite content mastery, such a person may lose his audience because of incongruities in his performance.
Negative	Positive	This person may prove acceptable so long as he can conceal the existing incongruity.
Negative	Negative	This person will be highly ineffective.

notion of expressions given off. The two middle types are ones where social justice does not triumph. In the second example, the actor is likely to experience audience repudiation. A norm of civility may be operative for some time, but because of an inept, jejune performance the norm of circumspection will supplant the norm of civility and the actor may lose face. The third type is the classic case of the con person. The person has no legitimacy or authority for performing the role, but because of his or her mastery of the part, or the gullibility of the audience, the con person experiences a happy, and usually all-too-profitable denouement. The audience has been duped, hoodwinked.

We use a myriad of props to assist our performances. To begin with, our dramatization involves the presentation of *fronts*, that is, "the expressive equipment of a standard kind intentionally or unwittingly employed by the individual during his performance" (Goffman 1959, 22). Fronts involve setting or scenery to express ourselves in the most favorable light. They include our personal fronts as well, such attributes as appearance and manner. We strive to achieve "some coherence among setting, appearance, and manner" (25). These are then skillfully manipulated by the actor so as to achieve *dramatic realization*, that is, an attempt to have the actor's definition of the situation ratified or validated. Goffman (33) illuminates that actors are concerned with achieving dramatic realization when a salient aspect of their self is involved.

> Thus a professional [person] may be willing to take a very modest role in the street, in a shop, or in his home, but, in the social sphere which encompasses his display of professional competency, he will be much concerned to make an effective showing. He will be concerned not so much with the full round of the different routines he performs, but only with the one from which his occupational reputation derives.

Actors dramatize roles directly proportional to the saliency of their selves that are expressed in those roles. Our self-awareness that we will be evaluated in certain roles, our occupational ones, for example, prompts us to increase the effectiveness of our dramatization. Roles where no salient aspect of self is involved are likely to lead to a directly proportional decrease in dramatization. Our dramatizations thus vary with the degree of self-saliency in roles, coupled with the knowledge that we will be evaluated by others. This, of course, induces us to focus attention on our selves, engendering self-awareness and a performing self that characterizes everyday interaction in a culture that places a premium on display. A constant feedback process is thus operative among self-saliency in roles, evaluation by others, self-awareness, and dramatization.

Thus it is obvious that we try to present an *idealization* of our selves, to portray our selves in the most admirable of ways. If such an idealization of self is accepted by others, the rewards are positive evaluations that more than likely will increase self-saliency, self-awareness, and dramatization. These idealizations of roles are normative: "when the individual presents himself before others, his performance will tend to incorporate and exemplify the officially accredited values of the society" (Goffman 1959, 35). This leads to the unfortunate cases of "negative idealization," such as college girls playing dumb so as to affirm the "natural superiority" of the male. Those who violate these role expectations are deviant performers.

Goffman is influenced by James's multiple-self theory. We have as many selves as groups we must perform in front of. "The self, then, as a performed character, is not an organic thing that has a specific location, whose fundamental fate is to be born, to mature, and to die; it is a dramatic effect arising diffusely from a scene that is presented" (Goffman 1959, 253). Rather than conceptualize this as multiple selves, perhaps a better conceptualization is that there are, again, many aspects to our selves, some having more saliency in one situation, or scene, while other aspects of our selves have more saliency in other situations, or scenes (Stryker 1980). In order to appear self-consistent, we must be careful not to perform discrepant selves in front of the same audience. To prevent such a mishap we employ "audience segregation" (Goffman 1959, 49). In a society in which we belong to many groups and organizations, each of us having a unique geometrical pattern (in Simmel's sense), audience segregation allows us to go about our daily affairs by obviating conflict among others who may be dismayed or angered with us for belonging to certain groups and organizations.

Goffman also adheres to Mead's I and Me constructs of self. The dialectical interplay between the I and the Me is potentially disruptive to role performances, for an unremitting dialectic brews between the two processes of self, threatening our "expressive coherence." "As human beings we are presumably creatures of variable impulse with moods and energies that change from one moment to the next. As characters put on for an audience, however, we must not be subject to ups and downs" (Goffman 1959, 56). The socialized Me must coerce the I into acting properly in front of audiences: "a certain bureaucratization of the spirit is expected so that we can be relied upon to give a perfectly homogeneous performance at every appointed time" (Goffman 1959, 56). Thus, dialectical interaction is ongoing in the self. When we are eloquent and effective, the Me is operative; when we bungle, commit some faux pas, or gaffe, the I has heckled our own show.

Goffman is in agreement with the symbolic interactionist notion of nominalism. Many sociologists reify their concepts, but Goffman is able to demystify this by stating that "a status, a position, a social place is not a material thing, to be possessed and then displayed; it is a pattern of appropriate conduct, coherent, embellished, and well articulated. [It is] something enacted and portrayed" (Goffman 1959, 75). Concepts are merely names we give to processes and activities. The concepts are not real, but activities are. Activities or processes are observed and then given a name, but in the process we begin to treat the concept as real and forget that it is just a convenient tag, a shorthand referent to typify an activity or process.

Teams

Goffman (1959, 80) argues that "the team and the team-performance may well be the best units of analysis to take as the fundamental point of reference." The team is composed of a performer and audience, which may even be represented by the same individual. A team analysis is the insightful way to probe dramaturgical interaction. Teams function as units; that is, they cooperate to create and maintain a definition of the situation. Thus, before one another, team members cannot maintain fronts. Team performance presents new dangers. One team player, by bungling his or her part, may give the whole show away, the result being audience repudiation of all team members. Thus, team members must be circumspect over the conduct of their troupe. Team members have to "get their act together," "get their story straight" as the sayings go. The case where this comes easily to mind is politics. Members of an executive branch must present a consistent story on policy issues; otherwise, the public is likely to be confused and the team members embarrassed. Disagreements may also show a sign of team weakness or disloyalty, which could then be exploited by an opposition party. A united front presents us with a reassuring reality: "The team members all agree, therefore, they must be correct." We are all members of teams, and they require us to be secretive about our fronts, scenery, and dramatizations. Thus Goffman's image of humans is not a favorable one, though he is not trying to derogate or belittle us, but merely point out the exigencies of interaction survival, trying to illuminate the techniques of face-saving strategy. Nevertheless, "we must all carry within ourselves something of the sweet guilt of conspirators" (Goffman 1959, 105).

Regions and Region Behavior

Goffman draws some spatial distinctions here. A "front region" is the "place where a performance is given" (Goffman 1959, 107). A performance at the front region conforms (to be successful) to normative standards, to "matters of politeness," and "decorum." When the actor is at the front region, expressive consistency among setting, manner, and role expectation is required. The performer here must be prudent, especially if the audience is fastidious or evaluative. Job interviews are an example of this type: performances where we must be at our best. The other location is a "back region." "A back region or backstage may be defined as a place, relative to a given performance, where the impression fostered by the performance is knowingly contradicted as a matter of course" (Goffman 1959, 112). The backstage is where we prepare our performances or go to relax after a performance or during an intermission between performances. It is the dressing room where the self is made up, the rehearsal hall where we perfect our dramatizations. The backstage is off-limits to an audience member of the front stage. This is vital, for all sorts of trade or team secrets are kept, discussed, and perfected backstage. The audience must not "catch on" to the act. We would lose face, or the team be embarrassed or discredited, if the audience were to gain knowledge of how the act was performed. This is analogous to the magician whose legerdemain is a wonder or marvel to a naive audience but leaves us crestfallen once we know how the trick was done.

The ideal place for the social psychologist or sociologist is to gain entrance to the passageway between backstage and front stage, to observe the dynamics of self-creation: "One of the most interesting times to observe impression management is the moment when a performer leaves the back region and enters the place where the audience is to be found, or when he returns therefrom, for at these moments one can detect a wonderful putting on and taking off of characters" (Goffman 1959, 121). Thus one's socialization to a profession is a chance to observe (if conscious of these matters) how the self is to be dramatized. One of the more revealing would be a marginal position, say, where one was at times a member of the audience but at other times the sidekick to the performer. The role of graduate assistant in large universities is such a marginal position. The graduate assistant gets "in the know" through the shop talk by his or her professor. In the professor's office just before class the assistant learns what the professor really thinks of students, the precarious legitimacy of testing, grading; the constant worry and fret over teaching methods, books; how films fill in when the professor is unprepared; the trepidation of catching anyone at cheating; the antagonism of classroom lawyers; and so on. Then a remarkably different self unfolds. Cold, calculating, and reassured, an authoritative figure sprouts along the corridor to the lecture hall. As the graduate assistant accompanies his or her professor to the lecture room, he or she is able to observe one of those rare glimpses of a "wonderful putting on and taking off of character." The professor assures the audience of his or her expertise, erudition, and the students' possibilities for enlightenment. The students are satisfactorily awed. Such spiels are conspicuously foregone in graduate seminars.

Discrepant Roles

The problem of discrepant roles is that of the audience acquiring "destructive information about the situation that is being defined for them" (Goffman 1959, 141). "Information control" must be practiced at all times. This usually means keeping secrets, which Goffman classifies into three types. "Dark secrets" are ones that contradict the definitions of the situation or the performer. "Strategic secrets" are ones we use in competition, ones in opposition to others as individuals, groups, or businesses. "Inside secrets" are team secrets, the secrets of the profession.

Discrepant roles allow a person to gain access to secrets under false pretenses. There is the "informer," who gains access to the backstage by persuading team members he or she is a teamplayer. The informer then sells or gives away "the show to the audience" (Goffman 1959, 145). There is the "shill," who acts as though he or she "were an ordinary member of the audience but is in fact in league with the performers" (Goffman 1959, 146). Agents who check up on performers are "spotters." And those who would like to steal an act but do not get access to the backstage, hence just observe as members of an audience, are "shoppers." A "go-between" is someone familiar to two competing teams who impresses both teams that he or she will keep each team's secrets. Examples are arbitrators, lawyers, and counselors. Another person in the know is the "service specialist" who usually has helped construct the show. Thus to ensure information control all these people have to be held in check, have to be pleased or prevented from acquiring destructive information that will discredit the performance.

Communication Out of Character

Earlier I mentioned the marginal position of a graduate assistant who has a role as a sidekick to a professor and at other times is a student. It is in the role as sidekick that the assistant is able to hear "communication out of character." Specifically, usually in the professor's office, he or she hears what Goffman labels "treatment of the absent" where professors reproach absent students in general for a decline in scholarship, yet through selective recall reminisce on the achievements of their own college days. Sometimes team members convey to each other communication out of character but do so in such a way that the audience remains unaware. This is "team collusion," which is "any collusive information conveyed in such a way as to cause no threat to the illusion that is being fostered for the audience" (Goffman 1959, 117).

Another type of communication out of character is "realigning actions." These are a more intense form of team collusion. The performer takes risks in terms of losing face or having the definition of the situation disrupted. One of the most common, according to Goffman, is the realignments we enter with other married couples while at a party. We can then tell stories—secrets—about our teammates, inviting our audience to the backstage drama of married life.

The Art of Impression Management

The arts of impression management are used to counter disruptive information, to stabilize the definition of the situation. Many inconsistencies occur in trying to maintain expressive coherence: unmeant gestures, gaffes, boners, faux pas, slips of the tongue, a too spontaneous "I," and so on. These are embarrassing and precarious moments, for the definition of the situation is fragile. Both performer and audience try to prevent such mutually anxious moments. As long as a "scene" is not created that leads to irremediable damage of the definition of the situation, actors and audience can protect one another and stabilize a working consensus over social reality.

Actors or performers employ defensive measures such as (1) dramaturgical loyalty, whereby "they must not betray secrets of the team when between performances" (Goffman 1959, 212); (2) dramatic discipline, whereby the performer "remembers his part and does not commit unmeant gestures or faux pas. He is someone with discretion; he does not give the show away by involuntarily disclosing its secrets" (Goffman 1959, 216); and (3) dramatic circumspection, whereby team members "exercise foresight and design in determining in advance how best to stage a show" (Goffman 1959, 218).

The audience employs protective practices such as tact. They do not voluntarily enter back regions; they disregard blunders through "tactful inattention." When a performer is a novice, the audience is generous with patience and tolerance. A combined defensive and protective procedure is one that Goffman labels "tact regarding tact." This means that "if the audience is to employ tact on the performer's behalf, the performer must act in such a way as to make the rendering of this assistance possible" (Goffman 1959, 234). These measures of impression management operate to sustain a working consensus between performer and audience, a consensus necessary to maintain a single definition of the situation "in the face of a multitude of potential disruptions" (Goffman 1959, 254).

If we are presenting a self that is false or are trying to sustain a role for which we are incompetent, we are susceptible to discrediting. If such occurs, we will be in need of "cooling out," for we will have become marks to our own illusions of grandeur. "A mark who requires cooling out is a person who can no longer sustain one of his social roles and is about to be removed from it; he is a person who is losing one of his social lives and is about to die one of the deaths that are possible for him" (Goffman 1952, 462). We have been exposed: "The mark must therefore be supplied with a new set of apologies, a new framework. A process of redefining the self along defensible lines must be instigated and carried along" (Goffman 1952, 456). It is the arts of impression management that try to prevent such occurrences.

Goffman and Contemporary Social Institutions

Goffman's concept of self reflects the new bureaucratic world and the exigencies of working with other people. The bureaucratization of the self, the need for audience segregation, consistent selves, teamwork, and impression management are requirements of social institutions in which the performance of roles in a bureaucratic organization is the norm of everyday interaction. As Gouldner states, this new middle class does not reflect the dominating self of laissez-faire capitalism but instead "the new bourgeois world of 'impression management' is inhabited by anxious other-directed men with sweaty palms, who live in constant fear of exposure by others and of inadvertent self-betrayal" (Gouldner 1970b, 382). Goffman has depicted the interaction adaptations to the constraint of being on display within a bureaucratic society.

No one has identified the social sources of the performing self better than C. W. Mills. He sees the performing self—the roles that people can display—as a result of the structural transformation from the world of the small entrepreneur to a society based on salesmanship. In this new order, the employer buys behavior, such as the ability to sell or handle customers (Mills 1951, 182). Hochschild (1983), drawing from Mills and others, formulated her concept that in today's labor market, one must also adhere to "feeling rules" and perform "emotion work." Again, in our postmodern world, the concern with delivery, representation, and performances only increases. Style supplants substance.

Goffman wrote the training manual for occupations and other status positions in which the concomitant roles must be dramatized. Symbols, appearances, mystification, and dissemblance (instead of substance), count. Anxiety-riven role chameleons market a performing self to a showtime culture obsessed with display.

Strauss: The Searching Self

Arguing that symbolic interactionism is the most sociologically oriented social psychology, Strauss sets out to incorporate neglected structural influences on social behavior into symbolic interactionism, that is, "to juxtapose and fuse symbolic interactional and social organizational perspectives into a workable, suggestive social psychology" (Strauss 1969, 11). He has centered on the concepts of identity and identity transformation.

Language and Identity

One of the ways everyone presents himself or herself is through a name. The reaction of others to our names functions as a mirror of self-evaluation. Others either express approval, indifference, or disapproval on learning our names. Presenting or having our name presented to others is usually the first act of self-introduction. Our name functions as a social object by which others may initially typify us. Being introduced as the Reverend or Dr. so-and-so calls out a different response than being introduced as the maid or butler. Naming is an act of placing a person in a social situation, an act of identification. A person's name functions as context setting so that during social interaction others can categorize or typify the person and adjust their responses accordingly, thereby keeping interaction non-problematic. For, "if the actor feels he does not know what the object is, then with regards to it his action is blocked" (123).

Of course, more identification is needed than just a name to know how to respond to an individual; that is what the initial stage of interaction tries to accomplish. The only person we would know enough about by just hearing their name is a celebrity; such then is a definition of a celebrity: a person whose name needs no further identification.

Self-Appraisals and the Course of Action

Because the self is both subject and object, it is under continuous scrutiny by others and its self. Our acts of the past and present are constantly appraised and criticized in calculating future plans of action. The result is a dynamic, indeterminate self. The self is constantly changing in response to its environment, appraisals by others, and self-appraisals. "The I, as subject, in reviewing its Me's as objects, continually moves into a partially uncharted future; thus new I's and Me's necessarily emerge" (124). Our self and consequently our behavior are capable of changing, of transforming over the course of our lives; as our self undergoes change so does our response to the world, generally. Behavior, rather than predictable, is probabilistic. One strong reason our behavior is probabilistic is that the environment is incessantly changing. Also our definition of that environment can undergo change. What the world is can be redefined. The world, like any social object, is named, categorized, or typified. Any change in our definition of the world initiates a corresponding change in our behavior, an alteration in the way the self responds to the world. This view leads Strauss to the appropriate conclusion that we are in "danger" of "dispossession," that is, we can lose the world we may have believed in so complacently. But we can also "discover" new worlds. Our social relationship to our environment is precarious, the self is ever in danger of alienation from the world, or is experiencing ecstasy in discovering a new one; an almost archetypal pattern of spiritual death and rebirth.

Interaction

In order to organize a line of action toward others it is necessary to engage in "motivational assessments" of their behavior. We undertake a "search for motives" to answer to ourselves why others, or even why we, perform certain actions. The attribution of motives is an ongoing activity (at least, subliminally) practiced by all participants in a social situation. Motives assigned to the self Strauss terms "motive avowal," while motives assigned to others he terms "motive imputation" (52).

People avow or impute motive depending on their perspectives, their reference groups. Each perspective or reference group provides the self with a vocabulary of motives from which motivationally to assess our own or others' behavior, and therefrom to continue or refrain from certain lines of action in the future.[1]

One of the most powerful structures of interaction is our social position, that is, our status in groups, organizations, and institutions. Our positions affect the way we act, for each status has a particular role we enact in the groups, organizations, and institutions with which we are affiliated. Sometimes only one group, organization, or institution influences two actors in a social situation, "single-structural interaction." At other times many groups, organizations, and institutions influence interaction, "multistructural interaction" (74).

Because we have many statuses and roles we move from "one status base to another during the interplay" (74). This status switching is termed a "multi-structured process" (74). Sometimes this process is not freely enacted but forced upon us. Others force us to act out or confine ourselves to a certain status. Such "status forcing" can occur with either superiors or subordinates, but, of course, guided by different rules. Status forcing is not always a "deliberate set of operations" but an ongoing affair, for each of us "can be, and continually is, the unwitting agent(s) of such status-forcing" (82). Status forcing is similar to alter-casting, that is, casting others in roles you want them to play. These are mechanisms of interactional control.

Another mechanism of interactional control is status claiming, which is parallel to Goffman's work above. We claim a certain status and desire others to respond accordingly. Whether we are assigned the status we claim is an uncertain and precarious affair. Status claims are issued when interaction is unstructured, when identity is unknown, when we need to assert who we are. "In more strictly structured interaction there are mutual expectations" (87). Expectations are involved when participants recognize each others' status or role; it is a matter of consensus, validation, ratification. A status claim is an actor's *attempt* to ratify or validate a status projection: "there are claims and counter-claims, claims and denials, claims and acceptances" (87). When others do not ratify our claims, we have lost face, we are unable to sustain our definition of the situation, to make effective our status-projection. This denial of identity usually results in anger, embarrassment, or withdrawal.

Transformations of Identity

I believe Strauss has offered the most comprehensive theoretical analysis to date of identity change from a symbolic interactionist viewpoint. Rejecting the notions that the self is determined in early childhood through late adolescence, thereafter remaining static, Strauss develops a theory of *adult* identity change. Identity change is a process of reconceptualizing one's social universe, a change in one's terminological framework that reorders our world and has marked effects on our behavior.

> Shifts in concept connote shifts in perceiving, remembering and valuing,—in short, radical changes of action and person. [Strauss continues, these] terminological shifts necessitate, but also signalize, new evaluations: of self and others, of events, acts, and objects; and the transformation of perception is irreversible; once having changed there is no going back. One can look back, but he can evaluate only from a new status. (92)

A transformation in identity is thus a transformation in perspective and world outlook. As individuals change their perspective they change (1) their identities, (2) their definitions of social reality, and consequently (3) their behavior. As we acquire a new identity, we respond to a new reality.

An empirical study of a shift in terminological framework is provided by Becker's study on the change in perspective toward marijuana. People are not predisposed toward the drug. In order for people to acquire an identity as marijuana users they need to perceive the drug as an object of pleasure and recreation. This definition can *emerge* only through interaction with reference others who define the experience as a desirable one. Becker (1967, 422) has argued that shifts in conceiving the object lead to shifts in the self and consequently shifts in behavior.

> If a stable form of new behavior toward the object is to emerge, a transformation of meanings must occur, in which a person develops a new conception of the nature of the object. This happens in a series of communicative acts in which others point out new aspects of one's experience, present one with new interpretations of events, and help one achieve a new conceptual organization of his world, without which the new behavior is not possible.

The self—in an identity career—goes through many "turning points," which are either consciously recognized or so gradual as to go "virtually unnoticed" (Strauss 1969, 93). At some time, however, we realize that we have acquired new selves. We notice the distance between our old and new self. Many such self-transformations are institutionalized. Movement or passage from one status to another is anticipated and prepared for, giving "continuity" to institutional patterns that stabilize the social order. Rites of passage are the classic example. Such regulated patterns of initiating recruits into professions or occupations are accompanied by "coaching." Those who preceded us perform mentor roles that guide us through the ladder of succession, making sure we are prepared for each rite of passage, competent for each promotion; making sure we have the right qualifications, values, fortitude; that we "know the ropes." We are continuously socialized into new identities.

Other identity changes are more personal, more worked-out-by-the-self alone rather than through institutional socialization. In these less-institutionalized patterns of transformation the self must signal others that a self-change is evolving. We try to assure others that our claims of self-change are genuine. We send out "cues," we distance ourselves from our former identity, we claim/assert and present new selves and act in ways to have our definition of self ratified, though, of course, others may not grant legitimacy to our identity claims. For example, the nonvalidation of the identity claim of being "a trustworthy, reliable person" made by an ex-convict is usually denied, a tragic affair that may bring about the self-fulfilling prophecy of "once a criminal always a criminal." "I've turned over a new leaf" the ex-convict states, "hire me"; but, the employer states or thinks, "I don't believe you." "I must starve or steal," thinks the ex-convict. So it goes.

Our cognizance of identity change is dependent on how we define our life history, that is, the terminology we use to typify, categorize, order, and reorder past events and evolving interpretations of the "meaning" of our lives. "Each person's account of his life, as he writes or thinks about it is a symbolic ordering of events. The sense that you make of your own life rests upon what concepts, what interpretations, you bring to bear upon the multitudinous and disorderly crowd of past acts" (145).

Our lives will be perceived as continuous or discontinuous. This perception is not so much dependent on actual experience but on subjective definitions, on conceptual frameworks. "Terminological assessment is crucial to feelings of continuity or discontinuity" (146). "The subjective feeling of continuity turns not merely upon the number or degree of behavioral changes, but upon the framework of terms within which otherwise discordant events can be reconciled and related" (146). Our lives undergo many redefinitions of the situation. Meanings of past acts are ever-evolving through a reinterpretation of events and purpose from the present. This sense-making is necessary to understand who we were and who we are. The sense making process of constructing individual identity is analogous to the historical sense-making and identity construction of groups, organizations, and nations. A common terminology leads to a shared interpretation, understanding, and symbolic membership with the past.

Strauss and Contemporary Social Institutions

C. Wright Mills (1951, 255) has provided an analysis that can be used to gain an insight into the social sources of many of Strauss's concepts. For example, status claiming is due to the fact that most of us are denied status at work. The bureaucracy where everyone knows who you are or can easily find out is no place to assert pretensions. Away from work people can inflate their selves in the anonymous corridors of mass society. Mills's ideas converge with those of Goffman, who noticed the adaptations people made inside the bureaucracy. Mills focuses on how an insufferable bureaucratic structure, which denies status pretensions, motivates people to seek status elsewhere.

Thus part of the excitement of the weekend and once-a-year vacations is a way of leaving the residence, the job, the small town, where one's inferior status is known; one is free to strut with aplomb in high-priced restaurants, theaters, and resorts (257). Such symbols as expensive clothes, rented sports cars, and prestigious hotels help one to foster a false presentation of self. "The staffs as well as clientele play-act the whole set-up as if mutually consenting to be part of the successful illusion" (257-58).

Strauss's concepts of status claiming and status projection articulate new work practices within corporate capitalism, especially within the sales organization. Mills gives an excellent example of how the sales organization trains its personnel to project a particular status depending upon the audience. "Since the consumer is usually a stranger, the salesman must be a quick 'character analyst.' And he is instructed in human types and how to approach each: If a man is phlegmatic, handle him with deliberation; if sensitive, handle him with directness; if opinionated, with deference; if open-minded, with frankness; if cautious, handle him with proof" (185). Strauss's argument that interaction situations are dominated by self-appraisals is an accurate description of the job skills necessary to work in a bureaucracy. Primary groups do not necessitate a rigid and limited expression of self. And even in many secondary groups interaction is more relaxed. Only in occupational roles must one be continually alert to one's presentation of self. The reason is the monitoring of superordinates, colleagues, and subordinates necessitate unrelieved self-appraisal. The service sector of corporate capitalism where one works with people (clients, prospects, and patients) rather than things only intensifies the need for self-appraisals.

The concepts of motive imputation and motive avowal also describe the bureaucratic phenomenon of office politics. Office politics involves imputing motives to career competitors, usually in a negative way, and avowing positive motives to one's own actions. But in order for us to make such imputations or avowals we must be located in a social structure where we have proximity to others, where we can observe interaction, and where enough tension exists among occupational roles that accountability and professionalism engender either motive avowals or imputation; such a place is the bureaucracy.

Strauss's concepts of self-change, identity transformations, and continual social change also describe the flexibility an individual must have if one is to achieve career advancement. As Michael Crozier, a student of bureaucracy, states, a successful organization requires "a flexible individual always ready to compromise and generally more socially-minded than his more assertive counterpart of thirty years ago" (Crozier 1969, 358).

In terms of continuity with the early symbolic interactionists, Strauss is closer to Mead in his treatment of self than any other symbolic interactionist. But Strauss has also greatly expanded on Mead's theory by introducing a number of interrelated concepts that portray the self as affected by the social changes of the past fifty years. Such concepts as single-structural interaction, multistructural interaction, multistructured process, and status forcing articulate the types of interaction characteristic of a bureaucracy, whether it be the corporation, government agency, or the military. We act out our lives, at least in part, in terms of the various expectations that correspond to occupational roles and organizational goals.

Structures of Economy and Media on the Social Self

Many of the themes introduced, or that can be inferred—the diminished self, the alienated self, the bureaucratized self, the questionable depth to which we can know others, and the reduction of persons to roles through typification—expound changes in people that reflect their social embeddedness within the complex organizations of corporate capitalism. C. W. Mills, following David Riesman, was one of the first to illuminate the influence of this changed institutional structure and culture on human behavior. Contemporary institutions and culture are influential constraints that have led to a diminished and alienated self within service-oriented, bureaucratized, corporate America. Mills's portrait of these changes (previously discussed) illuminates the indissoluble connection between social context, new patterns of behavior, and social theory. The bureaucratization of the self through the reduction of interaction to that between role occupants rather than complete persons is a social institutional change that has caused contemporary interactionists to view the self as more diminished and alienated.

Mead, James, and W. I. Thomas saw the self as a more powerful one, able to overcome obstacles, assert its will, and accomplish goals less encumbered by social forces. The absence of constraint in the early theoretical works is striking when compared to the diminished capacity of the self as a typified role occupier and performer in contemporary analyses.

The rise of big business, big government, and big labor are the social forces that constrain the contemporary self (Mills 1951, 68). The laissez-faire social structure was conducive to the assertive self, the rugged individualist. Now the white-collar occupations housed within bureaucracies constitute role performers rather than complete selves. "In three or four generations the United States has passed from a loose scatter of enterprises to an increasingly bureaucratic coordination of specialized occupational structures. Its economy has become a bureaucratic cage" (58). The consequence for the self is that "the capitalist spirit itself has been bureaucratized and the enterprise fetishized" (107).

The diminished and alienated self inside a bureaucracy is also the product of the *detail division of labor*. Mills drew attention to this phenomenon, for both industrial and service labor, twenty-five years before Harry Braverman, a contemporary neo-Marxist. Drawing on insights from both Marx and Weber, Mills underscores how the self is reduced to mechanical functions and denied agency. Within bureaucracies, both ownership of the means of production and rationality (the decision-making process) have been expropriated from the workers. "No longer free to plan his work, much less to modify the plan to which he is subordinated, the individual is to a great extent managed and manipulated in his work" (225-26). Reduced to a cog in a bureaucratic labor-process, the emphasis shifts from doing or making things to performances and appearances. "Be calm, judicious, rational; groom your personality and control your appearance; make business a profession" (81). The end of meaning in work engenders a narcissistic preoccupation with the meaning and appearance of self.

Social encounters with anonymous others in urban areas demand constant minded activity. Goffman has warned us that we must interpret the proper meaning of others' actions, assess their intentions, decipher their motives; in fact, in some situations our lives may depend on accurate framing. We need to be alert to rekeyings, whether and when to shift upkey or downkey in order to "drive" safely through everyday encounters. The mind must be in a constant conversation with self. We had better take into account potential dangers: threatening stares or other nonverbal communication, violations in civil inattention and social spacing, and so on. As one critic has commented: "social relationships thus become an interaction of espionage agents, each seeking to convince the others that he really is what he claims to be, and each seeking to penetrate the other's cover" (Gouldner 1970b, 382). Gouldner goes on to state that "Goffman lays bare the elaborate strategies by which men ingeniously contrive to persuade others to buy a certain definition of the situation and accept it at face value. It is a clever unmasking of the clever and, at the same time, a how-to-do-it manual of the modern utilitarianism of the new middle class" (384). People have become amoral "gamesmen adroitly making their moves, not in accord with inward consultation, but in shrewd anticipation of the other's counter-move" (387).

Certainly one did not always have to be so cautious in social encounters. The rural community was a relatively safe place for framing the situation. Small towns are legendary in terms of everyone knowing what is going on; not so with the anonymity of urban life. Goffman has thus documented the results of social change, of how the mind must operate in an urban, bureaucratic world where we are required to engage in performances, since work now centers on working with people and symbols, rather than with things. Such work requires the constant defining and redefining of events.

The contemporary concern with framing and reframing social objects perhaps has its social basis in the institution of the economy where corporate capitalism must constantly appear to sell the same old commodity as something new and different. Fashion and packaging drive sales volume (Mills 1951, 164).

This manipulation of commodities has now led to a manipulation of others in everyday social interaction. "What began as the public and commercial relations of business have become deeply personal: there is a public-relations aspect to private relations of all sorts" (187). Thus, framing and reframing situations and social objects are an institutionalized part of corporate capitalism, a great sales-room that has engendered distrust and suspicion and led to alienation from others and ourselves. What unites us is a "cash nexus," rather than any bonds of community (188).

Goffman's concern with framing and reframing, manipulation, being conned, laminations of social reality, trying to assess what it is that is going on, is thus directly related to the major institutional force in our society, the economy. Goffman has shown the survival skills of minded behavior necessitated by corporate capitalism. But not only the economy is at work here. David L. Altheide (2000) has shown how the media has become a social force that perpetuates performances beyond all previous bounds.

The late twentieth century has witnessed an increasing invasion of popular culture into everyday life and it "plays a significant role in shaping audience expectations and criteria for self-presentations for themselves and others" (11). Everyday life is saturated in and surrounded by media formats to the extent that "the logic of advertising, entertainment, and popular culture become taken for granted as a 'normal form' of communication" (11). "The consequence of mass-mediated experience is ubiquitous, pervasive, and total. It affects the process and style of interaction, language use, and structure of accounts" (16). Hollywood has made us all accustomed to "the suspension of disbelief by the audience member" so that self presentation becomes infused with the "swagger of persona, entertainment, and action" (11); consequently, "the distinction between fantasy and reality disappears" (16) and "[i]dentity is wide open for claims makers" (23). Our identities become just another piece of merchandise that we shill just as advertising promotes corporate products (13). "Identity increasingly became something with which to play—like a toy" (20).

If popular culture is the new generalized other that dominates our consciousness, as Altheide argues (and I agree with him), then that presupposes a self and identity that can be jury-rigged to follow the temporary fads, foibles, and obsessions of popular culture. With such institutional forces as the economy and media shaping the self, it behooves us to ask, can the concept of personality provide an adequate explanation of social behavior in contemporary society?

Self or Personality?

By Bernard N. Meltzer and Gil Richard Musolf

In recent years we have formed the distinct impression that symbolic interactionism is in the process of abandoning the concept of personality. Such abandonment would mean, of course, the counterintuitive flouting of widely held assumptions, both popular and scholarly, about the dynamics of human behavior and interaction.

History of Personality

We offer a brief reminder of the early history of the personality concept (see Hunt 1993, 311-49). Early in this century, Freud provided a lasting impetus to personality theory with his holistic psychoanalytical orientation. By the 1930s, however, many psychologists began to exhibit a pronounced preference for a conception of personality that would yield—in contrast to the impressionistic insights of psychoanalysis—quantitative measurements. Gordon Allport's (1937) *Personality: A Psychological Interpretation* provided the idea of *traits*, measurable units of personality. These units denoted consistent, trans-situational patterns of thinking, feeling, and acting. As Theodorson and Theodorson's dictionary of sociological terms (1969, 297) defines it, a trait is a "relatively consistent and enduring pattern of behavior or other aspect of an individual's personality which is manifested in many situations and which can be used to distinguish one personality from another. Honesty and aggressiveness are examples of personality traits." Employing this frame of reference, Cattell (1946) and Eysenck (1947) developed paper-and-pencil tests to measure various bipolar traits, such as Cattell's dominance-submission, radicalism-conservatism, and emotional sensitivity-toughness. Currently, as McCrae and Costa (1997) point out, many psychologists are convinced that most personality traits can be encompassed within five basic dimensions: extroversion or surgency, agreeableness versus antagonism, conscientiousness, intellect or openness to experience, and neuroticism versus emotional stability (also see Hampton 1995; Digman 1990; and Montag and Levin 1994). On the other hand, other psychologists (e.g., Almagor, Tellegen, and Waller 1995; Benet and Waller 1995) are promoting what they term "the big seven model of personality description." The model, which overlaps somewhat with the preceding list, includes: positive valence, negative valence, positive emotionality, negative emotionality, agreeability, dependability, and conventionality. Presumably, almost all personality traits can be subsumed under these designations.

Sociology and Personality: Preliminary Comments

The central point of the foregoing rapid survey is that personality theory and its integral concept of traits have relied heavily upon the notion of consistency and stability in individual conduct. Many sociologists have exhibited interest in these ideas, especially in connection with the socialization process but also as a way of socially classifying individuals. Thus, the classic Thomas and Znaniecki work, *The Polish Peasant in Europe and America* (1918-1920), refers to Philistine, bohemian, and creative characters. In like manner, thirty years later, Riesman, Glazer, and Denny's *The Lonely Crowd* (1950) centers upon inner-directed, other directed, and tradition-directed types of character. More recently, some sociologists have referred to such "personality types" as the bureaucratic personality, the authoritarian personality, the charismatic personality, and many others.

Sources of the Decline of Personality[2]

Until recently, most sociologists found the concept of personality useful for their purposes (Meltzer and Musolf 1999). Still, from the inception of social psychology, sociologists and psychologists have differed in the levels of their enthusiasm about the concept. Thus, the first textbook in social psychology by a psychologist (McDougall 1908) employed the term, while its contemporary in sociology (Ross 1908) ignored it.

The current process of abandonment of personality parallels the earlier fate of instinct, drive, and race. Like these extinct concepts, personality has been characterized by a multiplicity of referents and listings. Just as L. L. Bernard (1924) discovered 14,000 different instincts in the literature of psychology, Allport (1937) listed 4,500 traits of personality. Although later psychologists have used factor analysis to derive shorter lists of the putatively basic, or most important, traits, the resultant lists (e.g., the 16P Factor Inventory, the Big-7 Model, and the 5-Factor Model) continue to vary both in number and—although overlapping somewhat—in composition. This diversity is reflected in the various definitions sociologists have given personality—commented upon previously—as further illustrated by the following: "traits which determine the role of the individual in the group" (Park and Burgess 1921); "the organization of biological, psychological, and sociological factors which underlie the individual's behavior" (Roucek and Warren 1951); "an organization of attitudes which are, in effect, the internalization of the individual's role recipes" (Hickman and Kuhn 1956); "the totality of the definitions, including plans of action, of an individual" (Vernon 1972); "the total of all the roles a person has played and is now playing as this social experience tends to form his or her attitudes and beliefs" (Hardert et al. 1977).

Challenges to the Personality Concept and Theory

The following pages offer our speculations about the sources of the decline of personality. We shall present three broad categories of these sources: (1) theoretical developments in sociology, (2) the group dynamics of the paradigm shift, and (3) relevant social influences.

Theoretical Developments

One of the earliest direct attacks upon personality was Reinhardt's (1937) challenge of personality traits, which, he held, overemphasize the individual as the locus of behavior and underemphasize the social-situational and cultural bases of behavior. About thirty years later, the psychologist Walter Mischel (1968) revived what has become an enduring controversy—the person versus situation debate—over this same point. Questioning the trans-situational character of trait-behavior, Mischel held that human conduct is largely situation-specific. In general, psychologists have tended to counter this claim, holding that personality theory does *not* completely overlook the situational component in behavior (see, for example, Kenrick and Funder 1988). It should come as no surprise to sociological social psychologists, however, that this component is most often treated by psychologists as of secondary, if not epiphenomenal, importance. This virtually context-free view matches the layperson's approach to comprehending the acts of associates: interacting with a given individual in a narrow range of situations (e.g., business or professional colleagues), the layperson may tend to overgeneralize the acts as springing from cross-situational "traits of personality."[4] In any event, as Harre and Lamb (1986) point out, the study of personality "has increasingly come to be regarded . . . as synonymous with the study of traits" (366). Moreover, as our survey of sociological works revealed, the situations evoked by users of the personality concept often were treated as *objective* circumstances, not as the constructions of actors. Illustrative of this state of affairs are discussions of personality in relation to early marriage (Rockwell, Elder, and Ross 1979), to visual dominance (Ellyson et al. 1980), and to elementary schooling (Entwisle et al. 1988)—each of which either omits reference to definitions of the situation or appears to take them for granted. Similarly, social structure and personality studies typically deal with macrolevel sociocultural contexts that are treated as objective sets of conditions.

It is our suggestion that the desertion of personality (and traits) by most sociologists is not a product of methodical deconstruction. Rather, there has been a gradual accretion of alternative analytical frames of reference for understanding behavior and interaction, as the following paragraphs indicate.

Several sociological concepts provide the emphasis on situations that most usages of personality lack. "Role," for example, is inextricably linked with relationships and with situations, thereby implying a challenge to the behavioral consistency across situations embodied in personality and personality traits. We have in mind here primarily the social psychological concept of role, rather than the social structural one. While the structural conception is that of a fixed cluster of coercive norms, the social psychological conception comprises a more or less flexible set of both constraints and opportunities. In conventional sociology, of course, roles imply a degree of stability, uniformity, or consistency, but clearly not cross-situationally. William James's (1890) often-quoted illustration makes this point lucidly:

> Many a youth who is demure enough before his parents and teachers, swears and swaggers like a pirate among his "tough" young friends. We do not show ourselves to our children as to our club-companions, to our customers as to the laborers we employ, to our masters as to our intimate friends. (294)

Later developments in the role concept furthered the subversion of personality. For example, Turner's (1962) expatiation of "role-making," with its emphasis on the constructed, negotiated character of role-enactment, strongly challenged the assumption of internal, decontexualized determinants of conduct. Even earlier, the recognition of role-dissensus by Gross, Mason, and McEachern (1958) helped to undermine the notion of fixed sources of behavior and interaction. Nevertheless, our survey revealed to us the coexistence, in many sociological works, of both role and personality. Thus, a popular topic of research has been the interplay between roles (especially occupational roles) and personality. Several writings, for instance, have investigated the part personality attributes play in the selection and performance of roles (e.g., Rossides 1993), while others have examined the impact of roles upon personality—reflected in the slogan "The role shapes the man." Still other works have considered roles as *components* of personality. As implied above, on the other hand, current interactionists tend to conceive of roles as somewhat flexible frameworks within which acts are constructed.

Role-identity and situated identity (McCall and Simmons 1966; Stryker 1968)—sometimes referred to as the subjective component of role—conceptualized additional sources of situational, role-linked variability in conduct. Recent feminist theory (e.g., Butler 1990; Meyers 1997)[5] carries this notion of variability even further. Such theory (for the most part, postmodern) rejects prevalent conceptions of gender as performative (i.e., enacted) within a cultural context marked by substantive, naturalistic, essentialist views of gender and by powerful norms prescribing heterosexuality and patriarchy. Gender, the theory holds, should not be construed as a stable identity, but as an identity tenuously constituted in time through a stylized repetition of "feminine" acts. The appearance of *substance* is, then, a role-performance that both the social audience and the actors themselves come to believe and perform. Gender "reality" is thus created through sustained social performance, which means that the very notion of a true and perduring masculinity or femininity is part of the ideology that conceals gender's performative character as well as performative possibilities for the proliferation of alternative gender configurations.

This reconceptualization of gender identity as multiply constructed (through ongoing discourse) opens up possibilities of agency, or autonomy, that are absent from views of identity as foundational, fixed, and structurally determined. However, the proposed view challenges any presumption of a coherent, unified subject with a stable identity who endures over time, thereby eschewing the utility of personality traits in explaining or understanding social acts.

The foregoing ideas have significant implications for feminist identity politics. The prevailing insistence upon the unity of the category of "women" ignores the multiplicity of cultural, social, political, and other intersections within the category. The limits of identity politics are indicated by the fragmentation within the feminist movement and the opposition toward the movement from women whom that movement inadvertently excludes while purporting to represent them. Some feminists have, therefore, proposed discussions in which variously positioned women articulate their diverse identities within the framework of an emergent, fluid coalition.

Current theories of the media-identity relationship, also, contribute to conceptions of identity and behavior as fluid, mutable phenomena. Gergen (1992 and 1996; for similar views, see Grodin and Lindlof 1996; Kellner 1992) for example, argues that media-saturated selves and identities—bombarded by radio, television, movies, computers, and the like—are characterized by pronounced instability, spawning behavior that is as inconsistent and transitory as media messages themselves. From this standpoint, the stability and consistency inherent in the concept of personality play no important part in social behavior.

The interactionist conception of self is, in our judgment, another probable source of the virtual disappearance of personality. It is our conviction that, to the extent that other theoretical frameworks allow for the influence of this conception, they can be expected to look askance at the concept of personality. The following ideas about self are presented in brief compass, as most sociologists (particularly symbolic interactionists) will doubtless find them familiar. Implicit in self (as interactionists conceive it) is an inescapable situational (i.e., interactional and structural) accentuation that eschews the notion of built-in predispositions toward uniform behavior across situations. (For explicit discussions of the centrality of situations in social conduct, see Goffman 1963; Goffman 1974; and Seeman 1997.) As with role, however, the concept of self has often coexisted with that of personality in the works we reviewed. A common conjoining of these two concepts takes the form of conceiving self as "the core of personality" (see, for example, Hoult 1974, 45; Robertson 1987, 121). Such syncretism frequently reflects a noninteractionist conception of self as a fixed entity.

The very disparate character of the concepts of personality and self are readily evident. To begin with, the former implies a deterministic view of human conduct as the result of preexisting internal dispositions, as opposed to the emergentist view of the latter. That human acts are emergent, rather than determined, needs no proof among interactionists—at least those of the Chicago School. As Blumer (1969) underscored repeatedly, joint activity and individual conduct "are not mere expressions or products of what people bring to their interaction or of conditions that are antecedent to their interaction" (10). It is hardly necessary to point out, then, that exponents of the interactionist view of self—unlike trait theorists—attend closely to the inner phase of human acts (wherein the process of act-formation is at its richest), taking the standpoint of those they study rather than endeavoring to infer traits either from personality inventories or from overt behavior.

Relatedly, personality and self differ also in that, while personality comprises an essentialist conception of a mental structure comprising durable traits within the actor purporting to explain the actor's specific actions, self is conceived as processual, fluid, and creative, enabling the construction of acts in the course of their ongoing execution. In this matter, the relatively new theoretical orientation of social constructionism joins with symbolic interactionism to oppose any view that social phenomena should be conceived as expressions of "essences" within individuals.

Another closely related antithesis between personality and self resides in a shortcoming of the former—not shared by the latter—that Pervin (1985), a psychologist, points out: "A problem with the trait concept is that it is a static concept and does not provide for an understanding of dynamic processes" (92). We shall return to this point in a later section when we consider the impact of rapid social change upon the dynamics of social conduct. Further, in contrast to the asocial character of many personality traits, the interactionist view of self necessarily involves taking others into account in both individual and joint activity. This necessity relates to the role-taking and role-playing constituents of acts. Also, as we have previously noted, the nature of the situation in which an act occurs may be deemed of limited relevance by exponents of personality; but, the situation defined by the actor is conceived as an eluctable context for the process called "self." Such situations may range, of course, from those at the microsocial level of interpersonal relations to the macrosocial level of institutional and societal conditions. And, finally, as implied in each of the foregoing differences, self-directed conduct inescapably entails interpretations and meanings—which are not intrinsic to trait-driven behavior. The following felicitously phrased characterization of the self points up our conception of it and of its contrast with personality:

Looked at sociologically, the self is [not] a solid, given entity that moves from one situation to another. It is rather a process, continuously created and re-created in each social situation that one enters, held together by the slender thread of memory. (Berger 1963, 106)

The shortcomings of personality traits as bases for explaining or understanding human behavior have led one psychologist to utter the following hope: "I look forward to the day when personality theories are regarded as historical curiosities" (Farber 1964, 37; cited in Kenrick and Funder 1988, 24-25). That similar sentiments are fairly prevalent in sociological social psychology should be quite evident by now.

Group Dynamics of the Paradigm Shift

In moving away from a reliance upon personality and personality traits, soc iologists highlight several domain assumptions that revolve chiefly around the interactionist conception of self, as described above. Thus, both substantive and methodological shifts—composing a different paradigm—are stressed. We have seen, however, that some recent sociological works have continued to use the personality paradigm. As Kuhn (1962) asserts:

During the transition period there will be a large but never complete overlap between the problems that can be solved by the old and by the new paradigms. But there will also be a decisive difference in the modes of solution. (85)

The shift from a personality paradigm to what we can term a "self paradigm," has been largely a "silent" one: as indicated early in this chapter, no debate over the relative merits of the two concepts and their respective paradigms is available in the literature of sociology. Yet, a subtle and implicit contention has taken the form of mutual critiques of entire theoretical frameworks and methodologies between symbolic interactionists and their opposition, primarily in the positivist camp. Latour (1987), Callon, Law, and Rip (1986), and Pickering (1993) are students of the sociology of science who describe the group dynamics of developments in disciplines. Stressing the interaction among scientists or scholars, not the purported relationship of knowledge claims to nature, they attend to the literary/rhetorical effects of scientists/scholars to establish their claims by persuading, negotiating, and badgering their audiences to accept their usefulness. (For a different approach to this subject, accenting the importance of opinion leaders in promoting fashions in science, see Sperber [1990].) Those among us who are old enough to have witnessed the series of debates, at annual meetings of the American Sociological Association, between Herbert Blumer and, over the years, George Lundberg, Samuel Stouffer, and Paul Lazarsfeld, can attest to the vigor of the contention. Needless to say, most published discussions of symbolic interactionism—whether by its proponents or its opponents—rehash many of the views argued by these icon sociologists. The protagonists in these discussions frequently, although only implicitly, take sides on the personality paradigm.

Within sociological social psychology, as House (1981, 525) points out, two "increasingly distinct and isolated domains or faces" dominate: the focus upon social structure and personality and the symbolic interactionism perspective. Although these approaches differ appreciably, both theoretically and methodologically, they have, largely, abstained from direct assaults upon each other—unlike earlier opposing camps in sociology. Substantively, both focus upon the differentiating feature of their subdiscipline—the social context of behavior—but while symbolic interactionism has traditionally given greater attention to microsocial conditions, the social structure and personality orientation has stressed the macrosocial level. Needless to say, one of the latter orientation's key concepts, "personality," renders the orientation susceptible to many of the adverse criticisms presented earlier.

Another contrast between the two faces of sociological social psychology is, of course, the quantitative accent in one and the qualitative prominence in the other. Reflecting the latter emphasis in symbolic interactionism (and other, less prominent perspectives), one notes an increase in the number of sociological journals that are devoted to qualitative investigation: *Journal of Contemporary Ethnography*, established in 1987 (formerly *Urban Life and Culture*, established in 1972, and *Urban Life*, established in 1975); and *Symbolic Interaction*, *Studies in Symbolic Interaction*, and *Qualitative Sociology*, all established in 1978. All of these periodicals have promoted the utilization of techniques of research congenial to the displacement of personality by self.

Relevant Social Influences

We continue our speculations about sources of the decline of personality by reviewing the impact of recent social trends upon current conceptions of social psychological phenomena. These trends have been designated in various ways, including postindustrialism, postmodernism, the electronic era, and so on. In describing the trends we shall not assume that a set of objective social changes, per se, impinges directly and undefined upon human conduct and interaction.

It may be useful, at this juncture, to remind ourselves that the decline of certain theories in sociology is readily attributable, at least in part, to the inability of such theories to account for social change. Treating social structures as stable, functionalism ignored the processes by which they came into being, changed, and vanished (see Gouldner 1970; Boutilier, Roed, and Svendsen 1980). As we shall soon show, personality theory tends to partake of a similar deficiency in accounting for changeability in the behavior of individuals.

A number of scholars—chiefly postmodernists and constructionists—have taken note of what they conceive to be recent alterations in the ways humans adapt to societies marked by rapid technological changes, transformations in social institutions, and alterations in forms of social interaction (see, for example, May 1996; Denzin 1991; Dickens and Fontana 1996). Interestingly, almost all of these scholars refer to purportedly required changes in *selves*. Thus we find works dealing with the mutable self, the protean self, the minimal self, the ambivalent self, the saturated self, the empty self, the fragmented self, the malleable self, the nomadic self, and so on. These terms designate what are held to be the "new" demands of a dramatically dynamic society,[7] as assumed in the following asser- tions: "the self's capacity for shifts and reversals" (Lifton 1993, 4); "self as multi- ple, not fixed, and always under construction with no overall blueprint" (Hollinger 1994, 113); "rapid shifts in modes of self-reference so as to cope most effectively with . . . varied *situations*" (Zurcher 1977, 10; emphasis added). Is it mere chance that accounts for the use of "self" rather than "personality" in these designations of a fluid, flexible, and readily adapting process? If our earlier designation of person- ality as comprising relatively durable cross-contextual traits is recalled, one can readily grasp the unsuitability of the concept to the phenomena depicted above.

This section has been an effort to account for the decrease in the use of person- ality by sociological social psychologists. Various theoretical developments have been shown to address the failure of the concept to take fuller account of the contexts of human acts. The concepts of role and self have probably helped to point up this deficiency. Role-making, role dissensus, and situated role identities sharpened the awareness of situational elements in acts, and both postmodern feminist conceptions of gender identity and theories of media-identity relations pointed to the mutability of human behavior. Self has done its part in the assault upon personality and personality traits by drawing attention to the emergent char- acter of acts, their construction, the social-relational implications of self, defini- tions of the situation, and the necessity to attend to meanings.

Kuhn's (1962) ideas on shifts in paradigms informed our further speculations about the apparent desertion of personality by most sociologists. That the use of the concept persists among some social psychologists—particularly students of social structure and personality—indicates that the defection is not complete.

Finally, an examination of societal trends that may relate to our topic engaged our attention. The most important of these, for our purposes, has been the acceler- ating pace of social and cultural change. A proliferation of concepts relating to a presumably recent transformation of the self has reflected—and perhaps contrib- uted to—the decline in personality.

The Future of Personality

We have seen that all of the types of works surveyed, without exception, exhibit decreases in concern with personality. Dictionaries and encyclopedias of sociology, introductory textbooks, a mainstream social psychology journal, textbooks of symbolic interactionism, and, especially, periodicals devoted to symbolic interactionist papers—all show this decrease. Does this augur ill for the future of personality?

Two prominent but opposing conditions in sociological social psychology bear upon this future. One of these, substantive in nature, is the interactionist conception of conduct as fluid, dynamic, and constructed. The other, primarily methodological, is the positivist emphasis on presumed objectivity and quantification.

Acting upon a conjecture that interactionist ideas, particularly that of the self, have been moving into the gap left by the decline of personality, we tabulated the use of "self" in the *Social Psychology Quarterly*. Our findings are that the past decade has witnessed an increase, albeit slight, over earlier years—19.3 percent of all articles versus 16.6 percent. It appears, then, that an increasing number of social psychologists may be assigning greater analytical utility to the self than to personality. Linked with this theoretical movement has been the previously noted increase in qualitative research, that is, the use of participant observation, narrative, ethnographic, and other case-study methods.

On the other hand, the positivist penchant for correlational and "causal" analyses may encourage some social psychologists to persist in their interest in personality traits. In a classic paper, Blumer (1969) refers to "the logical need of variable analysis to work with discrete, clear-cut, and unitary variables" (136). The trait concept nicely fits these specifications, thereby maintaining the unremitting attention of some scholars. The specialty of social structure and personality, as previously noted, is probably most representative of this type of interest. Studies in this specialty seek to explore the reciprocal relations between, on the one hand, macrosocial structures and processes and, on the other, the personal makeup and functioning of individuals—such studies addressing an important aspect of the macromicro link. Concerned with commonalities within, and differences among, collectivities and cohorts of individuals, social structure and personality researchers tend to focus upon quantifiable attributes of aggregates.[8]

Given the very likely continuing concurrence of the symbolic interactionist and structure and personality perspectives, the future status of personality in sociological social psychology is not entirely clear. We are hesitant to predict the "end," the "death," of personality. Rather, we can expect, on the one hand, an increasing general displacement of personality by interactionist ideas. This expectation is suggested by our tabulations, as well as the independent observations by Boutilier, Roed, and Svendsen (1980, 12) and Turner (1995, viii) of an increasing appreciation of symbolic interactionism in social psychology. On the other hand, we expect the persistence of enthusiasm for the personality concept among scholars in the social structure and personality tradition, who remain relatively impervious to the general trend. For those who view the two mutually insulated, leading orientations in sociological social psychology as *complementary*—one stressing ethnographic studies and the other aggregate data—their continued coexistence is not seen as problematic.

It is probable, also, that a small number of sociologists—given to eclectic or atheoretical stances—will continue to deal with both personality traits and such key interactionist concepts as self, oblivious to their irreconcilable domain assumptions.

This chapter also highlights the major theme of this book: that the self cannot be biologically determined, since it is continually evolving and adapting to its environment. It was a fundamental tenet of functional psychology (see chapter 1) that the mind is the agency that aids in adaptation. As society and culture change, the self changes, adapts, and evolves. The supreme achievement of the mind, which is to say of humans qua humans, is that since it can alter behavior and the nature of the self, human beings can adapt to social and cultural changes.

Notes

1. The concept of motive imputation is also known under the appellation of attribution theory. Attributing motives to another's behavior is a shorthand method of categorizing people according to a moral continuum. It satisfies our need to judge (often in the most superficial and cursory of ways) those with whom we come into contact and thereby provides us with a stock response. One function of motive imputation is thus response discretion. "Attribution theory deals with the rules that most people use in attempting to infer the causes of the behavior they observe. The theory also deals with the different kinds of situations that produce different kinds of attributions" (Aronson 1976, 177). Because the time available for response discretion is limited it leads to the social problem of stereotyping: the rapid deployment of comfortable unexamined motives to people's actions.

2. This section and the following one focus primarily upon sociological social psychology, the field in which the topic of this chapter is most germane.

3. We are employing the conception of "paradigm" provided by Ritzer (1980, 189): "A paradigm is a fundamental image of the subject matter within a science. It serves to define what should be studied, what questions should be asked, and what rules should be followed in interpreting the answers obtained." As we shall soon endeavor to show, the domain assumptions implied by personality differ significantly from those of symbolic interactionism.

4. Newspaper columnist Ellen Goodman (June 24, 1997) describes the general public's tenacious hold on this view that individual behavior reflects fixed, trans-situational attributes. She notes the common references to a neighbor or friend who has committed a heinous crime in such words as the following: "He was such a quiet boy." "This isn't like

him." "Such an act is entirely out of character for him." Some "specificists" (emphasizing the situational component in social conduct) join with "generalists" (emphasizing traits) in acknowledging at least some instances of consistency in conduct. Thus, Bem and Allen (1974) hold that some people are more consistent than others; Kenrick and Stringfield (1980) suggest that consistency is greatest for publicly observable behaviors; discussing identity theory, Wiley (1995, 367) ascribes to it the view that "the demands of the setting are assumed to be predominant except when there is an overwhelming need to maintain a particular identity across situations"; and Strauss (1969) asserts that indeterminancy is not likely to be present when "a path of action has been well traversed" (36).

5. The following paragraphs on feminist theory draw heavily on Butler (1990), and to a lesser extent, on Meyers (1997).

6. Obviously, the foregoing comments about self do not apply as fully to self as measured by the Twenty Statements (or Who Am I) Test; such a conception of self is more structured than processual, less contextualized than what we have described. Nor, for the same reasons, do our comments apply to such trait-like concepts as self-concept, self-image, and self-esteem.

7. Statements of this kind raise a question that is linked with "the problem of imputation" in the sociology of knowledge: Can we account for the influence of certain social conditions on the thinking of *some* scholars of social behavior but not of others?

8. An interesting mini-mystery involves two essays by a major contributor to the social structure and personality corpus. In a survey of the specialty, appearing in *Social Psychology: Sociological Perspectives* (Rosenberg and Turner 1981), House (1981) employs the term "personality" numerous times, while sparingly using such alternative phrasings as "individual psychology and behavior" and "psychological attributes." Fourteen years later, in a brief introduction to part III, "Social Structure, Relationships, and the Individual," of *Sociological Perspectives on Social Psychology* (Cook, Fine, and Homer 1995), he radically reverses these proportions, making scarce use of personality and quite numerous uses of "individuals," "individual psychology and behavior," "psychological and interactional processes," "self," and several other alternative words and phrases.

9

Mind

I now examine various concepts associated together under the heading of "mind." Some of the concepts have been briefly touched upon before when I discussed the concept of self and during the discussion of the early interactionists. They now receive an in-depth analysis. Mind, along with the self, are the two foremost concepts in SI. This chapter primarily focuses on the works of many SI scholars instead of summarizing the views of specific thinkers, such as I did in the chapters on society and self.

The mind is a process of self-interaction, a conversation of significant gestures with the self; minded activity is thinking, planning, formulating, judging, interpreting, and assigning meaning to social objects. Just as functionalists had presented an oversocialized concept of people, for a long time, before the attention to the sociology of emotions (presented in the next chapter), symbolic interactionists presented an overrationalized conception of people in modern society.

Four important concepts: identification, reference groups, role-taking, and self-indication help explain the process of minded activity. Identification and reference groups are similar enough that I treat them together.

Identification and Reference Groups

One way an actor constructs his or her moral self is by engaging in moral action. Respectability presentation requires a reputation for being a moral self, for eschewing activities that might in any way derogate one's self. What needs to be explained is that, if in a plural society moral meanings are relative and flexible, then how does one know which action will be considered moral, which disreputable? Why do actors choose one course of action, not another; why do actors present one account of their behavior rather than another? Who, in effect, is the actor's moral conscience or voice? Who advises actors as to where, when, and what to do? And after any action is undertaken who advises actors as to the appropriate reasons for "why" the action was performed, for why the actor did what he or she did, if valuative inquiries are pressed? The questions here are those of conscience and motivation. The answers given by symbolic interactionists involve identification and reference groups.

The first problem of what action to engage in is solved once actors know whose opinions about themselves count, whose expectations they must satisfy. The opinions and expectations that count are those of the persons, groups, or organizations that actors identify with, that is, their normative reference groups or others from whom individuals gain an identity. These are the individuals or groups from whom actors internalize their values and then mentally refer to when constructing a definition of the situation to guide problematic encounters and to formulate accounts or vocabularies of motive for questioned action. Whether the group or organization is one in which one is a member or merely aspires to, and whether the group/organization is real or imaginary are immaterial; this allows a range of choice broader than Kuhn's "orientational other," which is limited to those with whom we physically interact (Kuhn 1967, 181).

According to Nelson Foote, we act on the basis of our identities, of who we believe we are. Our identity is a source of our motivation. And our identity is formed largely by the reactions of others to our self, as is implicit in Cooley's concept of the looking-glass self. "We mean by *identification* appropriation of and commitment to a particular identity or series of identities. As a process, it proceeds by *naming*; its products are ever-evolving self-conceptions—with the emphasis on the *con*—, that is, upon ratification by significant others" (Foote 1967, 347; emphasis in original). Identification, then, involves taking others into account (as well as a whole world of objects and ongoing activities) before commitment to any plan of action.

Identity is, in part, an emergent of interaction, especially interaction with significant or referent others. Acting on the basis of one's identity (identification), then, involves acting in concert (mentally) with identified-with others: "identification is the process whereby individuals are effectively linked with their fellows in groups" (Foote 1967, 353). Identification with others inculcates in us a vocabulary by which we define situations. "Men discern situations with particular vocabularies, and it is in terms of some delimited vocabulary that they anticipate consequences of conduct" (Mills 1967, 357).

Thus, to present a moral self we construct plans of action in which we anticipate approval and refrain from plans of action that would elicit censure, placing our moral self in jeopardy. As Mills states, "acts often will be abandoned if no reason can be found that others will accept. Diplomacy in choice of motive often controls the diplomat" (Mills 1967, 358).

The goal of respectability management, of maintaining a moral self, is to sustain one's character vis-à-vis one's identified-with others and, of course, the laws of the land. If one is engaged in conduct that is generally contranormative one must be circumspect as to who learns of such behavior. One discloses oneself only to those from whom one anticipates approval. Such was the finding by Weinberg in his studies of nudists. A nudist tells Weinberg (1970, 379): "Everyone we talked to reacted favorably. But if we didn't anticipate a favorable reaction we wouldn't have talked to them. I'm very careful about who I tell. If I thought it would affect our relationship, I wouldn't tell them."

But, at times, we deviate inadvertently (for example, carelessly speeding) or consciously and commit actions that to someone in power to demand them requires an explanation.

The symbolic interactionist concept of reference group is very similar to the concept of identification. Following Shibutani, a reference group "is that group whose outlook is used by the actor as the frame of reference in the organization of his perceptual field" (Shibutani 1967, 163). From this perspective an actor "defines objects, other people, the world, and himself. He can visualize his proposed line of action from this generalized standpoint, anticipate the reactions of others, inhibit undesirable impulses, and thus guide his conduct" (Shibutani, 1967, 162). The behavior of an individual is usually patterned and consistent, for even though an actor identifies with more than one group, the "reference groups of most persons are mutually sustaining" (Shibutani 1967, 167). Kuhn agrees: "One supposes the others on which his self-conception crucially rests are only rarely or occasionally such as to put him under cross-pressures" (Kuhn 1967, 177).

We are not arguing here for any type of group determinism; rather, a dialectic process is ongoing between the me and I. As Margaret Aasterud Williams (1970, 552) states, a dialectic interaction "may go on between the individual and the reference group in arriving at a mutual viewpoint." And Foote concurs: "The operation of values in the formation of responses to situations is advisory, not executive" (Foote 1967, 351). Social action is an emergent; knowing others' reference groups does not mean we can predict behavior, it remains probabilistic at best.

One reason is that conflicts and issues of loyalty do arise, though "only in situations where alternative definitions are possible" (Shibutani 1967, 167). Such a situation can be termed role conflict, or better, identity conflict, a stressful situation that increases with modernization. "In secondary, secular, and urban structures, varying and competing vocabularies of motive operate coterminously and the situations to which they are appropriate are clearly not demarcated" (Mills 1967, 363). The problem is perhaps resolved by allying oneself with the more significant other or reference group, or using a particular significant other, such as in "What would my mother say?"

Ralph Turner, a symbolic interactionist, has also written on what structures and motivates human behavior. His ideas are similar to Foote's and Shibutani's. He believes ego's interaction with others is determined by ego's self-conception. Self-conception is different from behavior, appearance, or multiple self-image. Self-conception is almost isomorphic with identity: "the picture that carries with it the sense of "the real me"— "I myself as I really am" will be called self-conception" (Turner 1968, 94). Knowing who we are influences interaction, for we direct our acts on that basis. I should do such and such because I am so and so, or I had better refrain from such behavior for I am not that kind of person: "The individual function of the self-conception is to *supply stable and workable direction to action* by providing a criterion for selective attention to the social consequences and reflections of ego's behavior" (Turner 1968, 105; emphasis in original). The self-conception "rests ultimately as a guide to the interpretation of one's own gestures" (Turner 1968, 97).

We also desire our self-conceptions to be ratified/validated in the eyes of others through the self-images we project. In "identity-directed" action we strive to maintain a cognitive consistency between self-conception and self-image, that is, how we appear at any concrete moment of interaction to others and to ourselves. We must be alert to both agreements and disagreements between self-conception and self-image as it is recorded in the eyes of others. If we fail—and others as mirrors reflect this—our self-conceptions will dwindle. Others' responses are a check on pretentious and grandiloquent notions. "Each person's self-conception is a selective working compromise between his ideals and the images forced upon him by his imperfect behavior in actual situations" (Turner 1968, 94). In a trenchant phrase by Turner, what we end up with is a "reality-edited self-conception" (Turner 1968, 98).

Interaction is influenced not only by our identity, reference groups, self-conception, or "true self" but also by who we believe the other person to be. Gestures are interpreted in terms of the person who makes them. "Gesture interpretations are normally based in considerable part upon an idea or 'picture' of the gesturer. It is difficult to interpret a person's gestures confidently unless one knows something about him" (Turner 1968, 96). Minded activity is a constant typificatory process. This was the vital point that Strauss was making by underscoring the importance of ascertaining the identity of the other through naming. A name and a few vital bits of information (occupation, age, sex, religion, and so on) allow a tentative typification by which we can make interaction less problematic. We desperately need to classify, to have, as Turner (1968, 97) calls it, a person-conception.

> Person-conceptions are necessary to give stability to interaction while reducing the extent of disruptive noncongruence which results from assuming that a given gesture means the same thing to all who employ it. Person-conceptions guide behavior by enabling ego to assign the meaning to alter's gesture which ego requires in order to formulate his next gesture.

Awareness Contexts

Glaser and Strauss have emphasized that in respectability management, or just general interaction, our awareness of others' identities influences and guides our behavior, and that behavior may be used to expand or contract awareness degrees (Glaser and Strauss 1972). The awareness we have of others' identities may be open (we know the true identity of each other), closed ("one interactant does not know either the other's identity or the other's view of his identity"), a matter of suspicion (an interactant suspects the other's identity or the other's view of his or her identity), or a situation of pretense (both interactants are aware of the other's identity but pretend not to be) (Glaser and Strauss 1972, 449).

Identification and Social Control

One way to understand how powerful identification is in guiding behavior is to notice how this social psychological insight has been politically applied (usually by oppressors) as a technique of social control. The techniques of motivating behavior through identification are now being used as political weapons and as a way to raise corporate profits. No wonder it has become such a prolific concept during the era of corporate capitalism. Barnet and Müller (1974, 178) provide just one example.

> In *mestizo* countries such as Mexico and Venezuela where most of the population still bear strong traces of their Indian origin, billboards depicting the good life for sale invariably feature blond, blue-eyed American-looking men and women. One effect of such "white is beautiful" advertising is to reinforce feelings of inferiority which are the essence of a politically immobilizing colonial mentality.

Clearly, as Barnet and Müller (1974, 177) continue, socializing others to identify with the oppressor, here, a form of internalized racism, functions as powerful social control.

> Studies of the impact of TV in Peru suggest that the poor embrace the TV culture because it offers new fantasies that permit escape from the rigid class structure of their country. It is hopeless for them to aspire to middle-class status in their own society, but vicarious identification with the clean-cut operatives in *Mission Impossible* costs them nothing.

It costs them nothing but their political freedom and continued oppression. Such identification-management by oppressors is well understood. It also functions to keep corporate profits high at the expense of one's health. Through identification with the American way of life, the Third World is suffering from "what nutrition expert Jelliffe calls 'commerciogenic malnutrition'" (Barnet and Müller 1974, 184).

Socializing others to identify with your definition of the situation has been and is a subtle method of social control. Once subordinates interiorize how to define the situation from the point of view of those with whom they have been encouraged to identify, the need for more blunt methods of social control have been obviated. Social control by brute force is precarious at best, as it always poses the threat of resistance, of revolutionary action. Social control by changing the subordinates' attitudes or identity is more thorough and provides security; it renders impotent the subordinate's ability to analyze with a class consciousness ruling class' declarations and actions. This SI insight is analogous to Antonio Gramsci's (1971) concept of hegemony, that is, that a whole way of life is imaged as natural (through the agencies of socialization, especially education and the media) so as to manufacture and maintain consent among the oppressed, to reproduce the social order; in fact, to have the oppressed an accomplice in reproducing their own oppression (Willis 1977).

Another way identification fosters social control and engenders relative deprivation is by prompting us to identify not with peers but with the remarkable talents of the few. This has come about in the past thirty-five years through the structural influence of the communications industry, especially TV and film. We use celebrities as referent others.

> The media give substance to and thus intensify narcissistic dreams of fame and glory, encourage the common man to identify himself with the stars and to hate the 'herd,' and make it more and more difficult for him to accept the banality of everyday existence. (Lasch 1978, 21)

Media-induced inferiority (the media are also a looking glass through which we judge ourselves) can lead to devastating consequences for self-esteem, for as we fail to live up to unachievable goals, we label ourselves not as seekers of the impossible but as failures as human beings, as bums unworthy of existence.

> [The media] has made failure and loss unsupportable. When it finally occurs to the new Narcissus that he can 'live not only without fame but without self, live and die without ever having had one's fellows conscious of the microscopic space one occupies upon this planet' he experiences the discovery not merely as a disappointment but as a shattering blow to his sense of selfhood. (Lasch 1978, 22)

Media escapism bamboozles; we do not attack a social system that fails to provide a decent and humane environment, that fails to ensure an equitable distribution of resources, including the cultivation of self-esteem. Instead, images of the *Lifestyles of the Rich and Famous* socialize us to think individualistically, to identify with material success and manufactured perfection; but, when reality edits this delusion, disaster results.[1]

Needing to project, or believe in a self-image of perfection, can have suicidal consequences. Sylvia Plath, a poet who committed suicide at age thirty, is an example. In her "Letter to a Demon" published in the *New York Times*, April 18, 1982, the wish for perfection is evident.

> I cannot ignore this murderous self; it is there. I smell it and feel it, but I will not give it my name. I shall shame it. When it says: you shall not sleep, you cannot teach, I shall go on anyway, knocking its nose in. Its biggest weapon is and has been the image of myself as a perfect success: in writing, teaching and living. As soon as I sniff nonsuccess in the form of rejections, puzzled faces in class when I'm blurring a point, or a cold horror in personal relationships, I accuse myself of being a hypocrite, posing as better than I am, and being, at bottom, lousy. I have a good self, that loves skies, hills, ideas, tasty meals, bright colors. My demon would murder this self by demanding that it be a paragon, and saying it should run away if it is anything less. I have this demon who wants me to run away screaming if I am going to be flawed, fallible. It wants me to think I'm so good I must be perfect. Or nothing.

Unfortunately, Plath's demon was too powerful.

Thus, from a sociology of knowledge perspective we discern how social changes—the communication industry and its image of the performance of perfection—is tied to the social practices of humans and thereby the concepts of symbolic interactionism. We now identify with celebrities and internalize narcissistic patterns of behavior.

I want to make another point about identification and social control. I have shown only the negative side, but there is also a very positive side to this technique, and its application is in the socialization of the child. We do not want our children to obey us out of fear, we want them to identify with us and thereby accept our definitions of situations. Slater (1970, 22) suggests that we cultivate a loving relationship with our children and hope they will appropriate the values we cherish.

> Love-oriented techniques require by definition that love and discipline emanate from the same source. When this happens it is not merely a question of avoiding the punisher: the child wishes to anticipate the displeasure of the loved and loving parent, wants to be like the parent, and takes into himself as a part of himself the values and attitudes of the parent. He wants to please, not placate, and because he has taken the parent's attitudes as his own, pleasing the parent comes to mean making him feel good about himself.

Identity and reference groups are two processes of minded behavior that predispose (though do not determine) humans to act in certain ways. They are contingent variables, ones we bring to a situation. But the most important processes of minded behavior are those that emerge within the situation. They are role-taking and self-indication. Obviously the two contingent processes influence how we take the role of others and how we define situations. But they are not determinate, otherwise we would be able to predict behavior by knowing a person's reference groups and his or her identity. As has been indicated, a dialectical process occurs between identity, reference groups, and the immediate situation. By taking the role of the other or defining the situation, novel behavior may emerge. Therefore, in any situation the most important processes influencing behavior are not what the actor *brings to* the situation but what *emerges from* the situation.

Role-Taking

How do we communicate and then act with others in mind, whether those acts are individual or joint actions? Mead argued that to communicate and act with others in mind, to try to assess and understand others and the reasons for their behavior, we need to take the role of the other, that is, to engage in the minded process of role-taking, a concept virtually synonymous with Cooley's concept of sympathetic introspection. The taking of the other's attitude allows gestures to become significant: we understand the meaning of our gestures, and of the gestures of others by imaginatively placing our selves in the position and/or attitude of the other. A common consciousness of meaning emerges: "the individual's consciousness of the content and flow of meaning involved depends on his thus taking the attitude of the other toward his own gestures" (Mead 1972, 159). This sharing of meaning—intersubjectivity—is what makes communication, community, and culture possible. We experience solidarity and build social worlds. Social order and society become possible.

One's mind must anticipate the actions of others so that all concerned can act in ways that will ensure cooperation and fluid interaction. Meaning and intention must be inferred. "Role-taking in its most general form is a process of looking at or anticipating another's behavior by viewing it in the context of a role imputed to that other. It is thus always more than a simple reaction to another's behavior" (Turner 1956, 316). Blumer (1969, 70) argued that this assessing of the other's role vis-à-vis one's own role made joint action possible. "Each participant necessarily occupies a different position, acts from that position, and engages in a separate and distinct act. It is a fitting together of these acts and not their commonality that constitutes joint action." Through role-taking joint action and thus social order become possible. Role-taking is imagining how others will act out the roles of the social positions they occupy. This is important because it informs us of how others will act toward us (Coutu 1951, 180). Role-taking illuminates how interaction is always social, for through such a process the group, or generalized other, are in effect, copresent in our actions.

Taking the others' perspective fosters communication. It informs us of the others' definition of the situation and their views on relevant social objects under discussion, that is, we learn the meaning others attach to social objects through their communication, their general response to objects. For example, I am at a social occasion, a party, and I come up to a gathering of a few individuals. I listen to someone reviling welfare and "creeping socialism," by which I infer his or her political views. Through role-taking I recognize the person as someone with conservative attitudes. This informs me that if I express my views (which are negative) on capitalism (which I was just about to do), contention and "hot air" will no doubt arise. I may decide to do this anyway, or, paying respect to the gathering at large, I may gulp my drink in order to have an excuse to leave the situation and find more "sociable" persons with whom to interact. I have made an adjustive response. Of course, if I had expressed my views first, the other person would have had the same options. The point is that adjustive responses are made when others act, responses that usually facilitate rather than impede, interaction. Turner (1962, 23; emphasis in original) maintains: "Interaction is always a *tentative* process, a process of continuously testing the conception one has of the role of the other. The response of the other serves to reinforce or to challenge this conception. The product of the testing process is the stabilization or the modification of one's own role."

Lets take up our example again. I will have walked away from the other person thinking that he or she is politically naive and insensitive (from my perspective). Of course, the person may be quite humane and politically astute. But what I come away with will be some sort of stereotype of the person. Ralph Turner states the reason why: "role-taking involves selective perception of the actions of another and a great deal of selective emphasis" (Turner 1962, 28). "Role-taking is always incomplete, with differential sensitivity to the various aspects of the other-role" (Turner 1962, 34). Role-taking always entails the possibility of misinterpretation and miscommunication, a daily feature of everyday interaction. Thus Turner accepts the epistemological imprecision of knowing/understanding others.

But say I was not so passive, but instead, a more assertive fellow. Or say I was a political opportunist or a sex-starved young man, and the person opposing welfare was a beautiful and enticing young woman. Well, then, I may abjure my perspective and my reference groups. I can temporarily adopt her standpoint for exploitative reasons. Excitement is in the air. Apostasy never looked so good. The point is that the situation may influence our behavior more than what we bring to the situation.

Another important point that Turner (1956, 322) makes about role-taking is that it also involves evaluating one's self from the perspective of someone else, that is, reflexive role-taking. This, as Cooley underscored in his notion of the looking-glass self, can confer upon humans a range of emotions from pride to mortification. With names and labels (language), we are able to step outside of our selves as subjects and see our selves as others do, that is, as objects. We become conscious of our selves and separate our selves from others. Turner (1956, 324-25) provides an example of a salesman who becomes disaffected with himself after he engages in reflexive role-taking. "The high-pressure salesman who is exploiting the attitudes in the other-roles to the full may suddenly begin to identify with the attitudes of that other and be rendered incapable of continuing his sales talk."

Turner has thus considered three aspects of role-taking: (1) imagining how others will act out the roles of the social positions they occupy, (2) imagining how others view their social worlds, and (3) evaluating one's self from the perspectives of others: significant others, reference groups, and the generalized other, that is, engaging in reflexive role-taking.

Role-taking is a process that humans engage in to understand others; therefore, it is an essential component of the symbolic interactionist research project of ethnography. "[T]he student must take the role of the acting unit whose behavior he is studying. Since the interpretation is being made by the acting unit in terms of objects designated and appraised, meanings acquired, and decisions made, the process has to be seen from the standpoint of the acting unit" (Blumer, 1969, 86). A contemporary interactionist ethnographer wholeheartedly agrees. "It is only through conversing with the other and attempting to experience the situation of the other through extended role-taking activity that one may tap into the life-worlds of the other on a more adequate (accurate, sustained, and comprehensive) basis" (Prus 1996, 23). The goal of role-taking in everyday life, as it is in ethnography, is "the task of achieving intersubjective understandings of the people participating in the settings under construction" (Prus 1996, 103).

Self-Indication

Self-indication is a process that entails indicating objects to oneself, "a moving communicative process in which the individual notes things, assesses them, gives them a meaning, and decides to act on the basis of the meaning. It is through this process that the human being constructs his conscious action" (Blumer 1967, 141-42). Individuals, through self-indication, through interpretation, through defining the situation, are not held hostage by their reference groups or their identity. Reference groups and identities provide us with tendencies, propensities, or proba-bilities to act in certain ways, but the most important process influencing behavior in the immediate situation is the process of self-indication. "At best the tendency or preparation to act is merely an element that enters into the developing act—no more than an initial bid for a possible line of action" (Blumer 1955, 63).

This selectivity in our responses eclipses social determinism. Instead of inter-nal drives or external social forces controlling our behavior, self-indication is a countervailing power. Self-indication allows us to make history, not be made by history. It allows freedom, spontaneity, and novelty. "The process of self-indication stands over against [drives] just as it stands over against the social factors which play on the human being" (Blumer 1967, 143).

Blumer claims not to ignore social structure, but rather views it as a stage in which there is plenty of room for improvisation. "Structural features, such as 'culture,' 'social structure,' 'social stratification,' or 'social roles,' set conditions for their action but do not determine their action" (Blumer 1967, 146). What Blumer is arguing for is the dialectical nature of action. It is bounded by social structure, but human beings construct and can change that structure. This dialectic would now come under the terms structure and agency.

What we must never lose cognizance of is that the social world is mediated by the actor's self and mind. Self and mind are processes through which we define, interpret, and then respond to the immediate situation.

The denial of self and mind are attributable to social scientists over-generalizing Darwin's argument that human beings are interconnected with animals lower on the phylogenetic order. A methodological stencil arose where explanation of "man's action grew out of the studies of the salivation of dogs and the maze-behavior of rats" (Warriner 1970, 48). Behaviorism is the touchstone example.

This type of thinking has been classified as the naturalistic fallacy, a belief that the human world is similar to the one found in nature. Humans, however, do not live by the "law of the jungle." We create laws and norms. We are constrained by those social forms, but we can also change them ourselves, without waiting eons for biological evolutionary change. The naturalistic fallacy gave rise to social Darwinism. Such thinking also represents the fallacy of zoomorphism, of attributing animal characteristics to humans. Humans are qualitatively different, a difference in kind and not just in degree. Concepts such as culture, interaction, groups, learning, intentionality, meaning, and consciousness are at the core of social science analysis. When such concepts are not brought to bear in explaining human behavior, reductionism prevails. But more damaging to science, what triumphs through such fallacious reasoning is a deformed image of human nature. The point is that the social must be analyzed at the level of the social.

That the mind actively constructs the world it responds to is a distinction that goes back to Kant (1965, 126 and 147; emphasis in original), who argued that we could not even experience the world without a priori categories which impose form (primarily space and time) on the world of experiences.

Concepts of objects in general thus underlie all empirical knowledge as its *a priori* condition. The objective validity of the categories as *a priori* concepts rests, therefore, on the fact that, so far as the form of thought is concerned, through them alone does experience become possible.

Thus the order and regularity in the appearances, which we entitle *nature* we ourselves introduce.

Kant thus formulated, on the basis of the above premises, his famous dictum: "thoughts without content are empty, intuitions without concepts are blind" (Kant 1965, 93). Warriner echoes Kant's notion: "without perception there is no experience; without experience there is no perception" (Warriner 1970, 77). Percepts become concepts, but concepts influence what we perceive. This is a dialectical process. Conceptualizing is a way of giving meaning to social objects. We respond to objects on the basis of the meaning they have for us; therefore, before we can respond we must attribute meaning to the object. Conceptualizing an object is locating it within a meaning context that allows us to respond to the object on the basis of the meaning that has emerged during the minded activity of conceptualization.

The conclusion that the mind is active and that reality is a phenomenological one is attributable to Kant's argument. Because we have a priori concepts, the mind actively engages in constructing the world. And because we construct the world through a priori categories (minded activity; self-indication) we are not responding to things-in-themselves but only to phenomena, only to social objects which have been mediated to us by our a priori concepts. That is what is meant by the social construction of reality. In order to know things-in-themselves, one would have to argue that we perceive the world objectively. Such an argument entails a passive-mind theory—the argument of the objectivist, copy theorist, or empiricist.[2]

Interactionists are thus idealists who believe that the world as encountered is constructed by human beings. They are also *realists* in the sense that they believe in a real world that exists. This real world can be different from how it is defined by ourselves or by anyone. Interactionists are thus not solipsists. Interactionists argue that people construct the world in terms of how they experience and define the world. They also believe that a real world exists and that we may define it differently, may experience it differently. Such notions are, of course, embedded in Thomas's concept of the definition of the situation.

Interactionists, then, maintain that there is ontological realism (a real world exists independent of us) as well as epistemological constructionism (we selectively respond to a small part of that real world). But epistemological constructionism does not entail judgmental relativism (the notion that all versions of reality are equally justifiable). That is the error of postmodernism. Just because the world that we know is constructed by us does not entail that everyone's construction is equal to everyone else's. A priori (logic) and a posteriori (empirical evidence) justifications must still persuade us that one interpretation of the world, or the facts, is more justified than someone else's. For the symbolic interactionist, a priori concepts are a process of minded activity. They include perspectives, reference groups, and conceptual and terminological frameworks for interpreting the world of stimuli before response is initiated. They become part of ourselves, our consciences, through the process of internalization. We interiorize the attitudes and beliefs of those whom we respect or who are of significance to us. This internalization provides us with sensitizing orientations to the entire realm of social life. "The processing within the actor of the sensory imputes produces a *perception* whose content characteristics are attributed to the external world, but which is in its immediate content character a product of the internal world of the actor" (Warriner 1970, 62; emphasis in original).

The dialectic between, on the one hand, mind and self as being-always-becoming, and on the other, social structure and role expectation as circumscribing social facts external to us and independent of our will, is the inescapable ground of everyday interaction. This dialectic has manifested itself in many debates: realism versus nominalism, materialism versus idealism, reification versus reductionism, behaviorism versus mentalism and so on.

Tiryakian has summed up this dialectical process, emphasizing the interplay of site and situation. Site may be objective reality, but situation and what the individual self indicates or takes into account is a mental phenomenon. "The notion of situation has a phenomenological status that differentiates it from the physicalistic notion of the environment. The site is a physical locale of potentiality, but the situation is an actualization of the locale as a result of the meaning the person finds in it" (Tiryakian 1968, 84).

Even though Blumer, Warriner, and Tiryakian acknowledge this dialectical process of social life, their writings tend to ignore social structure as soon as such an acknowledgment is made. The concept of definition of the situation, or self-indication, does not fully explain behavior inside bureaucratic, large-scale organizations that constrain our lives in myriad ways.

We also must differentiate between choice and self-indication. Self-indication means that we indicate situations to ourselves and then act accordingly. Understanding the social structure, or constraints, of situations we face is one of the things we may indicate to ourselves. Self-indication does not imply that we have unbridled human freedom. Coming to terms with the realities of life under corporate capitalism—that our choices and life-chances are limited—is one of the things that we had better indicate to ourselves if we are to adapt to an economy of relentless revolutions in the production and exchange of commodities. The process of minded activity is fundamental to social life and can be used to understand how the actor incorporates an account of the social structural and normative constraints encountered in everyday interaction. For example, indicating to ourselves the norm of obedience to authority is so powerful that even in a situation where we "know" we are possibly harming someone, two-thirds of us will administer a lethal dose of electricity to another human being who is screaming to be let out of a test situation (Milgram 1965).

Notes

1. The concepts of contemporary SI are well suited to analyze the behavior of people influenced by such social institutions as the media. At times, though largely in the past, interactionists have described behavior but failed to criticize, for example, with whom we identify, or the consequences of certain types of identification. They failed to see the disastrous consequences the new social institutions can have on our lives. With the recent work of Norman K. Denzin, a critical analysis of everyday life, using the concepts of SI (and others theories), has moved SI out of the phase of just analyzing behavior to its current status as one of the most critical perspectives in sociology. SI no longer has an "astructural" bias.

2. But for a contemporary critique of a priori concepts see J. L. Austin "Are There a Priori Concepts?" in his *Philosophical Papers* (Oxford: Oxford University Press, 1979), 32-54.

Part III

Socialization

10

Interactionism and the Child:
Cahill, Corsaro, and Denzin
on Childhood Socialization

Socialization was a foundational concept in sociology, but it has been less empha-sized in recent discussions of symbolic interactionism. From 1890 to 1934, the concept of socialization developed toward an interactionist perspective in the works of William James (1890, 1892), James Mark Baldwin (1895, 1897, 1910), Charles Horton Cooley (1902, 1908, 1909), John Dewey (1906, 1922), and George Herbert Mead (1934). Herbert Blumer (1937, 15) termed this perspective "symbolic interaction."

A number of questions emerge from the study of socialization: How do infants become human through a socially grounded process from which emerges a self, mind, conscience, identity, and the ability to engage in social interaction? How do we become like all other human beings, like some other human beings, and like no other human beings (Kluckhohn and Murray 1948, 35)? How does culture become internalized (i.e., enculturation) and individuality emerge? Needless to say, this process presupposes the existence of culture, which itself arises out of social interaction.

Cooley (1902, 1908) studied his own children to assess the self-objectification process, thereby formulating such concepts as the looking-glass self, and the way in which sentiments, especially self-esteem, are socially derived through our imagination of others' judgments. Yet the symbolic interactionist paradigm did not come to fruition until Mead, heavily influenced by James and Cooley, formulated a more elaborate theory of the self-as-object. His theory emphasized that the self develops through the social and cognitive processes of role-taking and language acquisition, and this proved to be a foundational perspective for American sociology. A framework for theorizing childhood socialization had been established. A symbolic interactionist research agenda emerged with the publication of John F. Markey's ([1928]1978) and W. I. Thomas and D. S. Thomas's work (1928). Subsequent research, however, primarily focused on adult socialization. Thus, until the 1970s, children and their social worlds were slighted in symbolic interactionist scholarship.

My focus is on the processes of socialization in early childhood and peer culture. Still, this area is too vast and unwieldy to cover without further circumscribing this chapter by limiting my review to three notable scholars—Spencer E. Cahill, William A. Corsaro, and Norman K. Denzin—who have had little critical attention paid to their work on childhood socialization.[1] There are other symbolic interactionists working in this field, but this chapter is directed to an in-depth exposition of a few scholars, rather than an extensive review.

Denzin's (1971, 1972, 1977, 1979, 1982) dialectical conceptualization of the emergence of self and mind is a comprehensive contribution from a symbolic interactionist perspective. Cahill's (1980, 1983, 1986a, 1986b, 1987, 1989, 1990, 1994) research generates insights into the self-acquisition and gender-identity process, utilizing the work of Mead, Garfinkel, and Goffman. Corsaro draws not only on the seminal work of Cooley and Mead but also on the theories of Piaget, Vygotsky, Youniss, and, especially, Aaron Cicourel. In various publications, Corsaro and his associates (Corsaro 1979a, 1979b, 1985, 1986, 1988, 1992; Corsaro and Eder 1990; Corsaro and Rizzo 1988, 1990) have examined the concept of peer culture and its influence on the genesis of self, mind, and collective identity. Corsaro, who refers to his "interpretive theory of childhood socialization," shares with Denzin and Cahill the following similarities: a critique of the stage model of development, a strong emphasis on the idea that children are active in their own socialization, rather than just passive vessels internalizing an adult-given normative order, and the view that socialization is a collective process (i.e., one entailing social interaction). Corsaro (1992), however, has extended the symbolic interactionist perspective through his conceptualization of "interpretive reproduction," which is explored in a later section devoted to differences.

My purpose is to review how these interactionists conceptualize socialization and the emergence of peer culture during childhood—its period of maximum efficacy. A summary of the Cooley-Mead heritage, from which most interactionist work on socialization derives, launches the chapter. The authors' work shares thematic similarities which will be organized under the following rubrics: (1) stages: automatic or contingent? (2) play and games, (3) peer groups and peer culture, (4) gender identity, and (5) public behavior. Clarifying issues in the structure-agency dimensions of social life, these works are reconceptualizing socialization theory by emphasizing its collective rather than individual aspects.

The Cooley-Mead Heritage

Taking the attitude of the other, role-taking, is the process through which children are socialized and develop selves. The mechanism of role-taking is language and, dialectically, language acquisition is a product of socialization through imitation at first, and then taking the role of the other.[2] Language is learned behavior,[3] but it is dependent on the size, form, and structure of the human brain.[4] Interactionists regard language, both verbal and nonverbal, as a conversation of symbolic gestures. These gestures have, as their defining characteristic, the ability to call out in a speaker and a listener shared understandings.

With names and labels (language), we are able to step outside of our selves as subjects and see our selves as others do (reflexive role-taking)—that is, as objects. We become conscious of our selves (reflective self-consciousness) and separate our selves from others (Lindesmith, Strauss, and Denzin 1988, 45). Additionally, we behave toward our selves as objects: planning, initiating, controlling, and refraining from action. Other objects, and our selves as objects, are symbolically constituted entities. Through the social conventions of language, we do not passively receive, or directly "see," objects, but actively constitute them as objects-as-they-appear-to-us. Interacting with other objects and our selves as objects, as symbolic representations, we engage in symbolic interaction. Without the acquisition of language, one cannot view or act toward one's self as an object. And until the self becomes an object to itself through language, it cannot develop. Role-taking and language acquisition are inseparable, unquantifiable, and unprioritizable processes of self-objectification and self-development.

Significant others are influential in this role-taking process; by internalizing their perspectives, the child socially constructs a self. Significant others are a looking glass; their view of us has much to do with how we view ourselves. Role-taking and language acquisition are embedded in one's relationship with significant others, peer groups, and the community at large. They link the child to the family, other primary groups, and the world beyond. Thus, the heart of socialization is interaction and negotiation. The ability of children to acquire language and manipulate symbols endows those so socialized with the capacity for agency.

Stages: Automatic or Contingent?

Denzin (challenging Piaget) and Cahill (challenging no one in particular) question the natural progression of developmental stages, even the one interactionists (following Mead) advance—the sequence of the play and game stages. "The movement from one stage to another is contingent on the development of sufficient language skills and on the presence of interactive experiences" (Denzin 1977, 89). "Nowhere does Mead attach age specifications" to the play and game sequence, and "implicit in [Mead's] formulations is the suggestion that some persons may never progress to the generalized other phase of taking the other's attitude" (Denzin 1977, 163). Cahill (1986a, 170) shares with Denzin the view that "childhood socialization does not consist of empirically discrete, easily identifiable stages." There is a "sequential pattern" to this process, and one can give names to the elements of that process, but these names are merely "analytic constructs" (Cahill 1986a, 170). Corsaro (1985, 73) accepts aspects of Piaget's model, yet he is critical of stages because of their linearity. Rather than discard stages, Corsaro's (1985, 74) interpretive model "extends the notion of stages by viewing development as a productive-reproductive complex in which an increasing density and reorganization of knowledge marks progression." This interpretive model, as did Cooley's and Mead's, attends to the importance of language. "Central to the reproductive view is the belief that language provides a socio-cognitive apparatus for the child and others to use. Language and discourse become the most critical tool for the child's construction of the social world" (Corsaro 1985, 74). Self-development, dependent on language acquisition, is thus problematic.

Denzin's rejection of Piaget's[5] stage theory, which, to him, entailed biological determinism, advances another differentiating tenet of symbolic interactionism: the age at which the self dawns. Social behavior, which presupposes a self, emerges earlier than previously thought. Cooley tied social behavior to the use of personal pronouns, while Allport linked it to understanding one's personal name or identity (Denzin 1977, 92). But Denzin's (1977, 96) ethnography on preschool children establishes that "children are social interactants far before the appearance of systematic pronoun usage, even before names are fully understood." The self is also adduced by "behaviors [that] go beyond verbal declarations," since much nonverbal behavior, also, is used "to communicate self" (Denzin 1972, 309). Denzin (1977, 21) argues that "by the age of three children are able systematically to take one another's roles, present definitions of self, construct elaborate games, and manipulate adults in desired directions." The emergence of self and mind is not determined by stages of growth, nor by attained age at which maturational processes allegedly "take off." Its course is shaped by environmental factors, the most significant of which is the character of the processes of interaction involving the child. Yet the distinguishing sign of selfhood is that the child "must be able to see himself as both object and subject" (Denzin 1972, 306).

As noted above, Denzin observes that three-year-olds "are able" to engage in social interaction, and it is important to consider that phrase. A self and mind at the age of three are problematic; stultifying environmental factors can vitiate the expression of agency. What is critical for Denzin (1977, 1982) is not alleged stages of development tethered to chronological age, but *interactional* age and experience; thus, the pace and progress one makes toward self-development and language acquisition is contingent.[6] How fully the child's self, identity, or conscience develop (that is, whether they are marred or enhanced) is contingent upon the social context of socialization. In short, context dispenses interactional life-chances, which lead to "differential levels of reflexivity" (Denzin 1972, 299). If children experience exceptional interaction, then the self emerges more rapidly than previously understood in the role-taking process characterizing interaction. Outstanding interaction and differential reflexivity are evidenced by sophisticated language behavior as well as the use of personal pronouns and personal names.

Play and Games[7]

Play and games contribute fundamentally to the emergence of self and mind by cultivating the ability to take the roles of others (Denzin 1977, 143). They function as forms of anticipatory socialization, through which children learn to interact with each other. Play and games are similar in some respects, but they are different from each other in fundamental ways. Games constrain by rules, authority, space, and time; play promotes creativity. Both furnish essential learning experiences that are required for adult life.

Games are forms of social interaction performed by one or more participants. They familiarize children with rules, engender skill acquisition, and habituate them to competition and cooperation, as well as authority, goals, plans of action, and chance, all of which significantly contribute to the unfolding of adult lives (Denzin 1977, 150). Children are swiftly exposed to the fact that life is not fair. An awareness of inequality tinges consciousness early, not only through variation in skill but also through aleatory factors beyond human control. The power of social constraints is imparted through the experience of being assigned "undesirable roles" to play; through realization that winners and losers are virtually inevitable in any game; and through recognition that time, place, and circumstance govern life-chances (Denzin 1977, 150). Games also involve pretense, bluffing, alignments, even rule breakers and cheaters—all part of everyday adult life.

Play is much less structured than games. Pretense characterizes play; skill and chance are less requisite. All the authors emphasize that play promotes cooperation and creativity, through which children actively construct their own social worlds. Corsaro's project underscores play's shared, collective, and interactive features, maintaining that it is in peer play that children develop a sense of social identity as children (Corsaro 1985, 66).

Cahill, expanding on Goffman's (1959) work, highlights how play helps children learn to fashion their gender identities and appearance through the management of "personal fronts." Since gender recognition is anatomically concealed, and often misidentified by both adults and peers, sartorial displays and bodily adornment signify to the world one's gender identity. Children conceive of such items as hats and bows as signifying gender, ignoring anatomical features, even when visible (Cahill 1989).

Cross-dressing is a process of learning appearance management and sex-appropriate gender display. Adults scrutinize such behavior and direct their children to more suitable sartorial symbols. Even peers criticize overwrought cross-gender exhibitions. Girls are allowed more sartorial freedom, while boys whose attire smacks of femininity are ridiculed. This is the beginning of a long march through childhood, where boys dissociate themselves from anything feminine, thereby contributing to the social reproduction of gender and the sexist evaluation of women in adult life.

Sartorial requirements enhance and limit behavioral repertoires. Girls are instructed to be careful about how they play because of how they are dressed. Gender-socialized behavior (e.g., play) is then adduced as evidence of human nature, justifying the sexist treatment of boys and girls.

One type of play is "spontaneous fantasy." It involves "becoming" all types of creatures (both people and animals) and the creation of social worlds "through [the child's] manipulation and animation of various play objects and materials" (Corsaro 1986, 91). Spontaneous fantasy is different from role-play proper. In this form of activity, children create novelty by expanding on the inspirational behavior of peers, thereby providing an ever-spiraling social world of imagination and invention.

Corsaro (1985, 193-208; 1986, 91) has found that three tension-saturated themes dominate this type of play: lost-found, danger-rescue, and death-rebirth. Through these themes, play teaches serious lessons for adult life. These fantasies generate play during which the skills of interpersonal behavior (for example, cooperation, trust, gratitude, and coping with anxiety) are sharpened. Two essential adaptive skills, the "control" of fear and the ability to "communally share" this control with peers, is produced. Spontaneous fantasy stimulates training in strategies for coping with the uncertainties, dilemmas, quandaries, and exigencies of everyday life with responses such as contingencies, plans of action, novelty, cooperation, and leadership. Children acquire these interactional skills through "communicative strategies," or "discourse abilities," such as turn-taking and topic selection, thereby establishing group cohesion (Corsaro 1986, 98-99). Thus, children's construction of social worlds through spontaneous fantasy underscores how children, through language, play an active role in their own socialization. And, dialectically, by participating in spontaneous fantasy, children develop language skills (Corsaro and Rizzo 1988, 880).

Besides spontaneous fantasy, Corsaro's (1985, 219-50; 1988) comparative ethnography of American and Italian nursery schools has led him to identify another common pattern of play: approach-avoidance. The structure of the approach-avoidance routine involves a "threatening agent" (monster) who is identified, approached, and avoided (Corsaro 1988, 5). Corsaro contends that in this routine, where threat is personified, children are learning how to cope with fear by devising escape plans. Furthermore, he (1988, 9) argues that, collectively, these routines generate communicative strategies that prepare the child for the adult world. Two communicative skills that children learn are interpretation and role-taking, whereby they "link specific signals or cues (voice intonation, facial expression, avoidance behavior, and so on) to shared knowledge about monsters, mad scientists, etc., to participate competently in the routine" (Corsaro 1985, 71). Children learn to control their environment so that they are not victims of it. Other lessons include the formation of friendship and taking care of oneself without adult interference (i.e., independence).

Cahill, Corsaro, and Denzin realize that play is an *adult* term for children's social interaction. It has the trivializing connotation that the interaction is not serious. Their respective ethnographies enable them to assert that play is reflective work by children and requires a self in order to be accomplished. In fact, play is children at work; it "involves such serious matters as developing languages for communication, defining and processing deviance, and constructing rules of entry and exit into emergent social groups" (Denzin 1977, 185). Thus, a child's world is not totally derivative from the adult world; children construct their own peer culture.

Peer Groups and Peer Culture

The most significant public arena for children is the peer group, through which a peer culture is produced. Corsaro (1992, 162; 1988, 3) defines a peer culture as "a stable set of activities or routines, artifacts, values, and concerns that children produce and share." A routine is an element of peer culture that is repetitive; it is a joint production, and it is predictable. Peer culture emerges through interaction in which children appropriate adult culture but transform it so that it fits the situation at hand, as exemplified in a "garbage man" routine that was even transmitted to the following year's class (Corsaro 1985, 250-54). Appropriation and transformation are clearly adducible from "animal family" role-play, whereby children, through shared knowledge of family role-play, adopt an external culture and alter it to mesh with the context of the ongoing peer group (Corsaro 1985, 105-20). They reproduce representative family performances—such as the enactment of power differentials—but recast them in order to produce recognizable but imaginative behavior (that is, novelty). A cross-cultural example is provided by Corsaro and Rizzo's (1988) research on another adult cultural routine specific to Italian culture: the *discussione*. Again, children appropriate adult culture and transform it so that the *discussione* is suitable for the needs of a peer culture. A form of public debate emerges among three or more children that involves making claims and counterclaims, stating beliefs, arguing, and disputing the history of shared experience. *Discussione* consists of the dramatization of opposition, where each child engages in a stylized ritual of providing "supporting evidence for one's positions within the debate" (Corsaro 1988, 886). The *discussione* is a verbal performance that spawns sophisticated communication skills, solidarity, and friendship. Children acquire social knowledge, interpersonal skills, and the ability to create social worlds through this ritual of debate. Through cultural routines, children exemplify their ability to role-take and role-make.

Corsaro's (1985, 272; emphasis in original) research has revealed two themes of peer culture: children's attempt to "gain *control* over their lives through the *communal production* and *sharing* of social activities with peers." Two major activities socially organize peer interaction: access to social participation and protecting interactive space, and both of them are initiated by children's conceptions of friendship (Corsaro 1985, 122-70). This parallels Denzin's (1977, 155) finding that "play is limited by the number of persons present and by the relationships the players have with one another." Access rituals allow children to gain entry to ongoing play in a peer culture. Corsaro enumerates many strategies that children use to enter and exit an interaction sequence. The most common feature of children's access strategies is that they are indirect and nonverbal, while adult access rituals tend to be direct and verbal. Children may imitate the ongoing behavior, circle the interaction until invited to participate, make reference to friendship, or just enter. Being defined as either a friend or not is one basis for inclusion or exclusion—a way of protecting interactive space. As children mature, they engage in more direct and verbal access strategies, such as greetings, questioning participants, or just requesting access.

Gaining access is no easy affair; sometimes children have to employ several access strategies before gaining entry to ongoing interaction. In the protection of interactive space, children establish play areas and activities, thereby dissuading others from entering the areas or engaging in the play. Children exclude others through five resistance strategies: no justification given, reference to arbitrary rules, specific claims to ownership of objects or play areas, justification based on space available or number of people already involved, and denial of friendship (Corsaro 1985, 128-31). Corsaro (1979a, 330) argues that children protect interactive space because of its fragility. By studying the transition from indirect to direct access strategies, one can discern the emergence of communicative competence, especially the art of negotiation.

Corsaro's (1979b, 53) research reveals how status[8] is a ubiquitous aspect of peer culture, especially in "language use." Children clearly "display knowledge of status as power" (Corsaro 1979b, 57). Cross-status interaction between superordinate and subordinate is typified by the superordinate's use of imperatives. Subordinates use informative statements, requests for permission to do something, and entreaties to engage in joint action. Same-status interaction—among superordinates or subordinates—is characterized by tag questions and requests for joint action. A tag question such as, "We're playing army, right?" is meant to confirm intersubjectivity or a shared definition of the situation. Since children recognize status as power, higher-status interactants are able to maintain control over the flow of interaction. They exert authority by giving orders, receiving deference, and (here the research is only suggestive) inflicting "discipline scripts" (Corsaro

1985, 77-100).

Deviance is also a part of peer cultures. Corsaro (1985, 255-68; 1992, 173) draws on Goffman's (1961) concept of "secondary adjustments" to describe the ways children actively resist adult rules and expectations—ways that constitute the underlife of the nursery school. Secondary adjustments contribute to children's sense of self, identity, and, especially for Corsaro, their collective identity qua children vis-à-vis adults. Nursery schoolers "worked the system" by resisting the rules concerning play areas and materials, guns and shooting, bad language, and clean-up time. The social knowledge they gain through resisting adult norms and organizations will help them with analogous aspects of working the system as adults: office politics, climbing the corporate ladder, and the general dissemblance of contemporary life.

By participating in peer culture, friendships are seasoned and interaction skills are honed. Children develop "solidarity," "mutual trust," and "communal sharing." Taking the role of others cultivates children's ability to share intersubjectivity and cooperate at joint action, collective definitions of the situation, and the construction of common meanings through which social worlds are built. Peer cultures are constituted in which children not only reproduce but also challenge and transform the world of adults so as to achieve self-control and a measure of autonomy, two defining characteristics of agency. Communicative competence or discourse ability (at turn-taking rules, access rituals, and role-playing) are matured in peer cultures, where we find the child's active contribution to his or her own socialization (Corsaro 1986, 84).

Gender Identity

Through taking the role of the generalized other, a child learns the rules of public conduct and acquires skill in applying those rules in everyday interaction (Cahill, 1986a, 164). Social control must be largely self-control in a democratic society that promotes civility, liberty, and freedom. Cahill's research sets out to answer the question how one acquires self-regulation by emphasizing the emergence of gender identity, a fundamental aspect of self and society.

One learns to act, think, and feel either as a male or female. Gender development is a process of recruitment into a gender identity. External genitalia, of course, do not provide the cultural equipment necessary so that one is recognized as masculine or feminine; such recognition involves a process of social construction. Consequently, interactionists reject essentialism, the idea that gender identity is biologically determined in favor of the theory that identity is socially anchored (Cahill 1980, 125; 1983, 2).

Caretakers, especially those connected with schools, recruit children into gender identities so that they internalize gender ideals and exhibit a range of competence at displaying those ideals in everyday behavior (Denzin 1971, 67). Self-regulation through gender socialization means a more or less loose conformity to gender ideals and rules of conduct that display masculinity or femininity (Cahill 1986a, 166).

Cahill uses five analytical constructs to depict gender identity formation: acquiescent participation, unwitting participation, exploratory participation, apprentice participation, and bona-fide participation. Gender recruitment begins during acquiescent participation, wherein people respond in socially prescribed ways to infants (investing them with masculine or feminine characteristics), even though, physically, newborn males and females are nearly identical (Cahill 1980, 1983, 1986a). These differential responses constitute acquiescent identity construction. The infant is encouraged to identify either as male or female. Others act as its looking glass, and as they respond to it, so does it respond to itself (Cahill 1980, 128).

Gender identity is constructed as others reproduce sexually differentiated behavior by reinforcing interaction that is in keeping with gender ideals. The social construction of gender continues as children respond to others' expectations in a process of unwitting participation—a process that centers on children's active, but unaware, participation in fashioning gender.

In Cahill's third construct, exploratory participation, children refine their ability to self-regulate as they label themselves, explore and affirm identities, and try to support their claims with appropriate behavior. During this experience, children become actively self-conscious agents. Cahill (1983, 5), suggests, following Denzin, that the self-labeling process now becomes important in the ripening of gender identity. The child reacts to his or her self as others would by trying to "confirm" or "ratify" the identity of male or female. Gender confirmation dwells in others' responses. If the child elicits gender-appropriate reactions, then he or she is treated as a boy or girl; gender identity is established. In order to elicit the confirming responses, the child models same-sex others from a variety of referents, such as TV, movies, stories, and parents (Cahill 1980, 1983, 1986a); however, in this media era, parents may be less influential as significant others (Cahill 1983, 8-9).

Claims and behavior are not always supported by others. This teaches children that they should be circumspect with their identity avowals and behavior. In other words, the labeling of behaviors as gender-appropriate is a matter of social control and the social reproduction of gender (Cahill 1983, 10-11; 1986b, 304; 1989). Children must behave as others expect them to; otherwise, they may not have their gender identities ratified. What the child considers appropriate will depend on the cues and expectations she or he has learned from the adults, peers, and general culture in her or his social world. During this period of interaction, the most important affirmation is one of "big boy" or "big girl," since the child tends to want to discard the label of "baby," a despised identity (Cahill 1986b, 302). As a result of labeling by others, as well as self-labeling, there is a strong relationship "between language practices and gender identity acquisition" (Cahill 1986b, 297).

During apprentice participation, which corresponds to our everyday notion of preadolescence, children interact in same-sex peer groups and maintain "gender segregation boundaries" (Cahill 1994, 464). Their commitment to behavioral displays of masculinity or femininity become subtle, sophisticated, and solid.

Bona-fide participation refers to interaction that is usually, though not necessarily, coterminous with the biological changes at puberty. Children perfect their competency at social skills, especially at what Cahill (1986a, 179) refers to as "heterosocial skill" (which is displayed by such activities as dating).

In large measure, children learn to become self-regulating participants in society by displaying masculine and feminine behavior, thereby conforming to the gender ideals of society and claiming a gender identity. Gender-segregation behaviors are rehearsed in childhood and performed in adulthood (Cahill 1994, 467). Yet both structure and agency are clearly visible as each generation modifies gender ideals, for example, through innovative sartorial expressions. Today, some men wear earrings while some women wear suits; however, a man wearing make-up and a dress would be deviant in any corporation.

Public Behavior

Cahill (1987, 1990) and Denzin (1971) also have emphasized the arduous task of socializing children to the normative expectations of behavior in public places. Drawing on the work of Durkheim and Goffman, Cahill describes the rituals necessary to constitute and maintain civil society. Parents or caretakers must instruct children in public etiquette and the ceremonies necessary to maintain a moral order. Children are not considered morally responsible people; therefore, they must be accompanied, while in public, by an adult who is held morally liable. Taking children to public places is a socializing experience (and often a harrowing one) for both the adult and child. The child must be taught the rules of public behavior. Since these rules are "unspoken," the child can learn only through a hands-on experience, such as by practicing public behavior under the tutelage of a caretaker and observing how others in the situation behave. If the child does not conform to the normative expectations of public etiquette, then the caretaker must discipline the child, since others stand ready to reaffirm society's expectations if the caretaker is found to be incapable of doing so. Any irresponsibility on the caretaker's part will elicit negative sanctions from the surrounding adults as well as the label associated with a negative moral identity. A child who misbehaves shapes the moral identity of the parent or caretaker; the young child is excused, though older children also are held morally accountable. Thus, children are not allowed to participate freely in public life but are under constant scrutiny so that they do not disrupt it. Until a child can behave in public—signifying that he or she has internalized the moral order—the child will be held captive by his or her parents. Allowing one's child to gambol in public expresses faith that one's child is bridled by the normative order against untoward acts.

Similarities

All three scholars celebrate the fact that socialization is not a "structurally determined process whereby the values and goals of social systems are instilled in the child's behavior repertoires" (Denzin 1977, 2-3). This emphasis does not deny that, to some extent, children are cultural, social, historical, political, and economic products (Denzin 1977, 15-27). These theorists acknowledge that social structure circumscribes human agency, but they argue that structural constraints are not deterministic. The tension between these two aspects of socialization is explored in the following section.

Socialization reproduces gender ideals, boundaries, and behavior, just as it reproduces the "natural and moral order" of society (Cahill 1986a, 181). One can draw the inference that injustice is embedded in gender socialization: it obstructs women's achievement by restricting access to many areas of life, a restraint justified by ideologies which misconstrue gender as a biological construct. Cahill's work shows us how adults forget that children and adults coauthor gender, thus empowering it over us. Implicitly, Cahill parallels Marx: we make religion but lose sight of our creation, thereby engendering a process of alienation. The theme of reification is implied in that theorizing gender as nature or heredity induces neglect of the fact that what is humanly constructed can be undone or transcended.

Injustice also can be inferred from Denzin's (1971, 68-69) work on the cooling-out function of schools. Socializing lower-class children for failure through reflected appraisals so that the students' self-image is one of incompetence, schools reproduce negative moral identities along with stratification. With the ideology of meritocracy internalized, children schooled to failure blame themselves for current problems and a dismal future.

Schools are not the only organizations that govern language acquisition, self-development, and minded behavior. Denzin (1977, 128) noted that "a child's speech repertoire reflects the character of her larger speech community." Children deprived of adequate interaction, in this case socialization within a suitable speech community, suffer a diminished capacity for language acquisition and self-development. Interaction at home, in a peer group, and at school can be salubrious or detrimental, emancipating or stunting. The caliber of such interaction is the primary factor contributing to the content of socialization and the pace of self-development. Caretakers can either enhance or shatter a child's self-esteem. Likewise, schools can take capacities and either cultivate them into abilities or harrow them into deficiencies. These contingencies help explain the differential pace of self and mind formation, as well as the impairment, or even absence, of such abilities. Thus, the child's world is profoundly unjust; though capable of agency, children cannot choose the quality of their speech communities nor the circumstances from which their selves emerge. Since the ability to acquire language and manipulate symbols is requisite for the emergence of the self, minded behavior, and social interaction, it follows that cultural capital, reflected in one's speech repertoire, legitimates and reproduces power and inequality in a meritocracy.

Cahill's work implies additional injustices. Adults do not have to observe the same rituals of public etiquette toward children that children are expected to observe toward adults. Children may be stared at and spoken to; they may have their public space invaded, and they may be discussed and commented on by surrounding adults. More often than not, they are treated as nonpersons. The ceremonial order is a mortifying one for children—one unintentionally designed to promote deviance. Children resist an unjust order when they "are not expected to do unto others what is done unto them, but what others instruct and encourage them to do" (Cahill 1987, 318-19).

These authors emphasize that socialization is an active process, accomplished through taking the attitude of others. While significant others are influential, because of their function as the child's first looking glass, children contribute to the social construction of their own worlds. Witness their participation in the formation of peer cultures through which they transform what is at hand into castles, spaceships, alien worlds—into make-believe social worlds where monsters lurk and heroes save the day. Climbing bars can be defined as a prison, a burning house, a restaurant, a circus, a home, or a den (Corsaro 1985, 184). This is the most fundamental example of bricolage. Like some South American writers, children create a world of magical realism; their play and peer culture are full of personification, anthropomorphism, zoomorphism, and animism; it is a world of the sacred and the profane.

Corsaro and Denzin focus on play and games that teach children numerous interactional strategies. These strategies cultivate their communication competence as well as develop their selves, minded behavior, and gender identity. Play and games anticipatorily socialize children into hierarchy, rules, chance, competition and cooperation, intersubjectivity and community, and the fact that life is not always fair.

Differences

Denzin and Cahill subscribe solely to the interactionist, or constructionist, approach. Corsaro (1992) has extended this paradigm; he regards "interpretive reproduction" as his signal advance over constructionism. It underscores that children act on their environment and participate in social worlds where they socialize each other; it stresses that children attempt to gain control over their world by communally appropriating, resisting, and reproducing the adult world, instead of simply imitating adult culture. Corsaro emphasizes children's transformative power through their appropriation of adult culture, creatively interpreted and reproduced within peer culture. He also highlights children's culture making that is nonderivative from adults. In contrast, Cahill's work on children's gender identity and public behavior and Denzin's work on speech communities emphasize the environmental, internalization, and social reproduction aspects of socialization. The socialization process entails a tension between continuity and change. Acquiring competence as a social actor involves a dialectic between the role-taking (reproductive/thesis) and role-making (productive/antithesis) qualities of the self (synthesis). Symbolic interactionism has always conceptualized this dialectic as an *inter*generational process. What Corsaro's project underscores is that becoming a social actor is also a process of *intra*generational routines in a progression of peer cultures. Both orientations acknowledge the interplay of structure and agency in the making of selves.

Corsaro's expansion (1992, 165, 168) was influenced by Giddens's (1984) work on structuration and Goffman's (1974) notion of "keying," a process in which meaningful activity from a primary framework—say, adult culture—is reframed and transformed into something else within peer culture. Corsaro's (1992, 169) research illuminates the point that socialization is creative as well as reproductive, thereby accentuating the agentic, role-making, and problematic aspects of everyday life—the foundations for emergence and novelty. Children transform culture even as they are socialized by it. Thus, Corsaro is reconceptualizing childhood socialization. To some extent, children make themselves through their own institution of peer culture. This connects his work to that of Marjorie Harness Goodwin (1990, 308) and Barrie Thorne (1993, 176), who argue that socialization theory has privileged internalization and viewed children as those "who are acted upon more than acting" (Thorne 1993, 3). Goodwin's (1990, 283) ethnography has shown that children not only shape themselves but also shape others through peer interaction. Thorne argues that for too long socialization has conveyed the idea that adults are active while children are passive. Children are not just learners; they are more than passive, incomplete, or incompetent adults; they are makers of fashion, gender, social identity, and selves. "There is much to be gained by seeing children not as the next generation's adults, but as social actors in a range of institutions. Children's interactions are not preparation for life; they are life itself" (Thorne 1993, 3).

While Denzin is critical of Piaget's stage model, Corsaro elaborates on it. According to Denzin, that model is nondialectical; it fails to take into account the macrostructural environment and the microstructural influences on the pace, or even eventual appearance, of self and mind. Thus, Denzin believes that minded behavior and self-formation via interaction must be probabilistically and indeterminately conceptualized.

Corsaro's work is set apart by his endorsement of equilibrium (Piaget's concept) as the motivation that propels children along the developmental hierarchy. As children develop, how do they make themselves? Like Piaget, Corsaro (1985, 280) argues that "learning should be viewed as a process of compensation resulting from children's continual attempts to deal with problems, confusions, and ambiguities in their life worlds." Encountering various intrusions, children seek equilibrium-maintaining activities within "a series of peer cultures," which propel them to cognitive advancement and adulthood (Corsaro 1985, 281; 1992, 171). Denzin and Gerald Handel see interactional experience as something much broader than a series of peer cultures, which warrants a further critique.

Critique

Handel (1990) has criticized Corsaro and Rizzo's work on peer cultures, arguing that they tend to minimize other sources of childhood socialization, particularly adults and the family. Handel (1990, 463) contends that a reader may come away with the notion that, to understand childhood socialization, one focuses only on peer cultures, analyzing the "language that children use when interacting with agemates." According to Handel, Corsaro and Rizzo construct an argument based on four polarities in which one side is privileged. In the first polarity, sociologists versus developmental psychologists, Handel criticizes the ambiguity in the authors' work for not specifying the importance of internalization. The second polarity, collective versus private, concerns the fact that collective processes of socialization are privileged over the private.[9] What about private play or the way children construct playthings on their own? The child versus adult is the third polarity. Here, Handel calls for balanced treatment of the effects that children have on adults and the effects that adults have on children. The fourth polarity, peer group versus family, can be used to critique not only Corsaro's work but also that of Denzin and Cahill. Where is the family in the childhood socialization process? Corsaro's claim that cultural routines originate in peer groups may be misleading if there is no prior study of the family. Handel's observation that children learn their first cultural routines in the home is sensible and points to a misleading gloss in Corsaro's methods. A comparative method should assess whether peer play expresses routines arising from family life or the peer group.

Social structure is not adequately researched in peer play and friendship formation. Goodwin's (1990, 49) ethnography of a peer group of working-class black children and the social organizational features of their talk—in stories, gossip, and argument—shows that, in the absence of structural constraints or directives from caretakers, girls and boys spontaneously talk to and play with one another. Goodwin's peer group consisted of an unfocused gathering in which gender asymmetry was generally absent. She found that many activities promote equality and solidarity (Goodwin 1990, 284-85); nevertheless, children segregate when conflict arises over what is defined as exclusively girls' or boys' play. Eder and Hallinan (1978) observed that girls' dyadic friendships were more exclusive than boys' (that is, girls rejected newcomers more frequently). Boys' play tends to require a larger number of participants, which helps to explain their orientation toward nonexclusivity. Teachers may reinforce gender separateness, however, through notions of what is appropriate play for girls and boys. Furthermore, children who are already cognizant of gender ideals may self-select gender-typed play (Eder and Hallinan 1978, 238). When the structure of the situation was an open classroom, boys and girls interacted together more often. Thus, context (interaction other than play) and structure (the open classroom) are factors that must be taken into account (Eder and Hallinan 1978, 247). Different types of play may lead to differentially valorized social skills. If males acquire group-leadership skills while females acquire skills at self-disclosure, then their play is socially reproducing gender inequality (Eder and Hallinan 1978, 247). This theme is further amplified by Eder and Parker (1987, 209) in their study of the effects of extracurricular activities: sports socialize males to competitiveness, achievement, and aggressiveness; cheerleading socializes females to the importance of attractiveness, glamour, and emotion management.

Additional attention to the structural dimensions of conflict is needed. Thorne (1993, 161) notes that teachers structure conflict into academics, which "ratified the gender divide by pitting boys against girls in math and spelling contests." This "harness[es] gender rivalry as a motivation for learning," debases competition into "hostility," and reproduces "polarization," by associating gender with opposition, antagonism, and conquest. Classrooms, the cafeteria, and playgrounds have "gendered turfs," which create two distinct social worlds wherein teachers "police gender boundaries" and aides "shooed children" away from places they thought exclusively girls' or boys' territory (Thorne 1989, 74-76). Thus, Thorne's (1993, 161) ethnography reveals how gender-segregated academic contests and play, structured by teachers and school aides, "perpetuates an image of dichotomous difference" and "encourages psychological splitting." These findings corroborate Cahill's insights. School practices that divide boys and girls institutionalize gender struggle. Extrapolating from how girls and boys are differentially directed (Cahill 1983, 1986a, 1986b, 1989; Eder and Hallinan 1978; Eder and Parker 1987), we come to understand how a gendered opportunity structure arises that reproduces inequality across generations (power, education, occupation, and income).

Future research should be directed at two arguments currently permeating public debate: (1) the declining effect of parents on children (the decline in family values argument) and (2) the increasing effect of media on children (or, to highlight agency, how children define media representations). Corsaro's (1985, 61) argument that "children are continually exposed to the adult world by the media (especially television)," grows in gravity since "children's initial exposure to media events and consumer goods in the family is often intensified in peer culture" (Corsaro 1992, 172).

Another underexplored topic is the role of schools in the socialization process. Aside from nursery school, Denzin, Cahill, and Corsaro have little to say about schools as agents of socialization. Thorne's (1989, 1993) account of gender play and Eder and Parker's (1987) study of extracurricular activities demonstrate that schools wield important influence over socialization.

Conclusion

All three authors have theorized dialectical accounts of their research: Cahill on recruitment to gender identity, Corsaro on the productive and reproductive aspects of peer-culture routines, and Denzin on the influence of interaction and language acquisition for self-development. They have shown that children, in their appropriation and transformation of adult culture, construct selves, gender, social identities, and peer cultures. No longer playing bit parts on the proscenium, children now appear center stage in that collective rather than individual, sociological rather than psychological, drama known as socialization. The inspirational work of Denzin, Cahill, and Corsaro provides a powerful platform for the continued study of childhood socialization, and it represents a significant advance in symbolic interactionist theory.

Notes

1. Whether Corsaro considers himself an interactionist is unclear; however, his approach is compatible with symbolic interactionism.

2. I thank an anonymous reviewer for reminding me not to gloss over this dialectical relationship.

3. The definition of language is one source of differences between developmentalists and symbolic interactionists. The latter do not define language as solely adult speech. Denzin (1977, 95), following Blumer, defines language as a set of "significant indicative gestures." The meaning of gestures arises out of the interaction process itself. Children engage in significant indicative gestures long before they master articulate speech.

4. Again, I thank an anonymous reviewer for reminding me of this point.

5. In 1977, Denzin presented a highly controversial interpretation of both Chomsky and Piaget, charging them with biological determinism. At issue, according to Denzin, is Piaget's argument for the "invariant character" of "specific ages for cognitive development" (Denzin 1977, 119). Denzin contends that the rate of self-development is contingent upon interactional experiences, nurturance by significant others, and environmental features. Children are either blessed or impaired by the world into which they are born. According to Denzin, Piaget views children under the age of seven as egocentric—unable to take the attitude of the other—and therefore inept in social behavior. Denzin's observa-

tion of play and games convinced him that Piaget's argument on the age of the appearance of the self and social behavior is erroneous. Piaget maintains that games with rules rarely appear before the age of seven. Denzin (1977, 117, 162) submits that this "clearly pre-judges the cognitive and interactive skills of the young child" and that Piaget's model "is irrevocably embedded in a biological image of cognitive development." Corsaro (1985, 54) believes that Denzin has misread Piaget, underscoring that it is equilibrium or equilibration that is "the central force which propels children through the stages of cognitive development." According to Corsaro, Piaget's model is "probabilistic" and concerned with how children compensate with activities when confronted with external intrusions. In fact, Piaget's equilibration model is interactive and therefore "should not be seen as a form of biological determinism" (Corsaro 1985, 54). Denzin (1977, 77) also disputed Chomsky's claim that there is deep, innate knowledge that shapes the language-acquisition process. According to Denzin, transformationalists (those adhering to Chomsky's principles of transformational grammar) maintain that a cognitive structure in the brain provides humans with a Language Acquisition Device (LAD). Denzin argued that learning disappears in this hypothesis, since the LAD is alleged to be an inherent structure that impels children to acquire language. But Denzin's views have apparently changed in regard to both Chomsky and Piaget. This is evident in the following statement where Denzin and his coauthors comment on the work of E. O. Wilson: "Wilson notes that prominent social scientists such as Chomsky, Piaget, and Kohlberg have theories of language, cognitive development, and moral development, respectively, that are consistent with sociobiology in that they posit an innate, genetic underpinning to child development. Children, they contend, go through certain stages in their development because they are genetically predisposed to do so. We regard this as a careless misreading of Chomsky, Piaget, and Kohlberg" (Lindesmith, Strauss, and Denzin 1988, 31-32).

6. In a statement derived from Sullivan (1953), Denzin (1972, 307) offers the following hypothesis, which is still a potential gold mine for research: "It would be predicted that the more complex the interactional world of the child is, the more rapid would be the genesis of self, and the closer in time would be the self and other differentiation." Rose Laub Coser (1991, 85) agrees: "Where social relationships are complex—that is, where we have different things in common with people occupying different positions—we are challenged to develop more complex mental abilities." Basil B. Bernstein's (1971) research on speech communities is also relevant, especially his concepts of elaborated and restricted codes in language socialization and their role in the social reproduction of class. See also William Labov (1967) on class stratification and English usage.

7. I am *not* referring to Mead's notion of the play and game stages. Mead was referring to two stages of development tied to different role-taking activities. In these stages the self and mind emerge. In the play stage, one can take the role of significant others, but only one at a time. In the game stage, one can take the roles of several others simultaneously. Ultimately, of course, the self and mind have fully emerged when one can take the role of the generalized other, that is, the abstract perspective of a group or society. In contrast, Cahill, Corsaro, and Denzin are merely referring to children at play and playing games.

8. During adolescence, other differentiations arise within peer cultures (Corsaro and Eder 1990, 208-13). Friendship takes on more seriousness and diversity occurs along attitudinal lines, so that peer groups now have more within-group similarity than those of early childhood. In addition, class distinctions arise, with middle-class peer groups based

on interests and working-class peer groups based on loyalty. Gender markers and conflict escalate. Among male adolescents, language activities such as "ritual insulting," "teasing rituals," "storytelling," and "gossip" intensify group solidarity and the formation of shared definitions of the situation. These language practices establish domination, and parallels can be drawn to Foucault's (1967) notion of discourse formation.

9. Corsaro (1992, 160) states, "I found myself studying collective, communal, and cultural processes." His (1985, 122) ethnography did not provide the opportunity to study solitary play: "children who found themselves alone consistently attempted to gain entry into one of the ongoing peer episodes."

11

Socialization and Emotions

The current SI position on emotions, plus recent research from within that general framework, is briefly sketched here.

It has been claimed that the sociology of emotions, especially the SI perspective on emotions, is growing rapidly (Palmer 1994, 424-35). The field of study has been divided into two branches: the organismic and constructionist perspectives (Adler, Adler, and Fontana 1987). The constructionist view, how "physiological processes are molded, structured, and given meaning," is the focus of the following review (Adler, Adler, and Fontana 1987, 225).

The Social Construction of Emotions

Probably the best contemporary statement of the social constructionist view has been put forth by Shott (1979, 1323).

> Within the limits set by social norms and internal stimuli, individuals construct their emotions; and their definitions and interpretations are critical to this often emergent process. Internal states and cues, necessary as they are for affective experience, do not in themselves establish feeling, for it is the actor's definitions and interpretations that give physiological states their emotional significance or non-significance.

Constructionists argue that local moral orders, values, norms, beliefs, socialization experiences—in general, culture—mediate our "relatively undifferentiated substratum of physiological arousal" from which emotions are constructed (MacKinnon 1994, 125). Rom Harré argues that "historians and anthropologists have established conclusively that there are historically and culturally diverse emotion vocabularies [so] that it follows that there are culturally diverse emotions" (Harré 1986, 10). Physiological arousal has no set meaning, that is, the arousal is given meaning—named as a specific emotion—through the definitional process. Again, a basic interactionist tenet is that human behavior is qualitatively different from the stimulus-response pattern. "The mediating role of cognitive appraisal and interpretation produces considerable variation in individual response to emotion-instigating situations, because of variation in the personal relevancy of situations and the appropriation of cultural grammars of emotions" (MacKinnon 1994, 125-26). Actors define and respond in a variety of ways to physiological arousal. This does not mean that there are no cultural and social influences, but that consciousness allows humans some control over their feelings. Positivists argue that culture and structure are so powerful that a modal emotion response is given to stimuli (MacKinnon 1994, 126). Rom Harré (1986, 12), in opposition to the positivists, contends that humans live in unique emotion worlds: "There can be little doubt that, even if there are some universal emotions, the bulk of mankind live within systems of thought and feeling that bear little but superficial resemblances to one another."

An emotion is a self-feeling (Denzin 1984, 3); yet, just as others are always already implicated in the view of self, others, "emotional associates," are always already implicated in emotions. "All experiences of being emotional are situational, reflective, and relational. A person cannot experience an emotion without the implicit or imagined presence of others" (Denzin 1984, 3). The influence of the group upon human behavior is thus exemplified in emotion behavior, that is, emotions are grounded in the larger social surround—an interpretative repertoire from which to draw (Potter and Wetherell 1987)—yet defined with reference to others, present or imagined, in the immediate situation of experience.

Reflexivity

The following paragraphs outline Rosenberg's (1990) recent statement of the SI perspective on emotions. He argues that the foundation of emotions is physiological but that through human reflexivity we attribute meaning to organismic processes to define, control, and manipulate our emotions. Reflexivity is the actor's ability to refer to his or her experience. In the construction of emotions we interpret physiological arousal and in the process name an emotion. Emotions are socially constructed through interaction between an actor and her or his social habitat. One's interpretation is affected by previous and ongoing socialization. Reflexivity affects any state of arousal subject to interpretation in three fundamental and transforming ways: emotional identification, emotional display, and emotional experiences.

Physiological arousal does not constitute an emotion; arousal must be interpreted and given meaning. An emotion is the result of the interplay between arousal and cognitive interpretation. Identification of an emotion is problematic because arousal is often ambiguous: "different emotions may have similar manifestations" (1990, 5). For example, fear and joy may be the same physiologically. At times we have two or more emotions (for example, fear and excitement). It is only through understanding our situation and experience reflexively that we can define our emotions as one or the other, or both, expressing ambivalence. There may be no differentiating physiological marker between fear and excitement. Another problem in identifying emotions is that we define feeling idiosyncratically: "internal experiences are unique and incommunicable" (1990, 5). There may be no word, or we may not know the word, for what we are feeling. An additional difficulty in interpretation is that we may be uncertain of our feelings.

The social environment, also, affects our cognitive interpretation of any arousal state. People, through causal assumptions acquired during socialization, define these states. We know that during certain situations the arousal that we notice should be normatively defined. Cultural expectations contribute to the defining process by providing socialized actors an "emotional logic." Certain events—for example, funerals, celebrations—demand certain emotions. Failing to make this culturally induced logical connection between arousal and interpretation is dangerous deviance: "Society takes this emotional logic very seriously. Failure to adhere to it constitutes one of the defining features of mental disorder" (1990, 6).

Rosenberg also believes that emotions are causes of behavior. One may attribute falling asleep to boredom, or cheering at a football game to excitement. One observes one's behavior, the circumstances under which it occurred, and then attributes an emotion as the cause.

Referent others, too, are used to infer the nature of our arousal. We conform to a "social consensus," that is, we tend to interpret our initial arousal according to how others are defining their emotional experience. States of arousal are emotionally defined so that they correspond to a "cultural scenario." Love may be one's emotional identification for feelings and physiological processes experienced around a potential partner that match cultural criteria. The point is that the interpreting process is affected by socialization and cultural scripts. There is an element of social constraint in the interpreting process.

Rosenberg asserts that emotions have "action implications": we act according to how we have interpreted our emotions. This is a restatement of the Thomas Axiom: things defined as real are real in their consequences. But, insightfully, Rosenberg (1990, 7) points out "because of these action implications people may be motivated to avoid emotional interpretations that have threatening consequences." Action implications may guide the interpretation of emotions.

Emotional display is quite different from emotional designation. It involves agency in both the exhibition and concealment of emotions. Rosenberg (1990, 8) locates emotional display "squarely in the realm of dramaturgy or impression management." It entails producing "intended effects" on others so that they interpret the situation in accordance with how one is emotionally staging the scene.

People engage in emotional display for a variety of purposes. One is to convince others that one is a moral actor, so, for example, one may display grief over someone's death when one is really quite happy. To violate normative expectations would be deviance and would prompt negative sanctions. Hochschild (1979) writes of "feeling rules," a phrase now part of the sociological lexicon. We are "emotional actors." Revealing or concealing emotions through such tools as verbal devices, facial expressions, and the use of physical objects helps us manipulate situations and others' impressions in order to achieve desired ends. Those beguiled by the fabrication of emotions pay a price. Televangelism, for example, is just one area where people's inability to attend to the speciousness of emotional dissembling has cost billions. In an age of commercialized emotions, pseudo-gemeinschaft and hucksterism are a way of life, such as in sales. So prevalent are these features of contemporary life that they have become personified as stock characters in novels and films. This has brought on the postmodern temperament of suspicion and doubt, which pervades human relationships and makes us cynical.

Emotional experience is not so easy for the individual to effect and can be outside one's control. We can display emotions, convey the proper expression to others to support social situations and social roles, but can we directly manipulate emotional experience, how we actually feel? Rosenberg (1990, 10; emphasis in original) contends that "people unable to exercise direct control over their emotional experiences adopt the strategy of attempting to control the *causes* of these experiences."

A mental cause is central to the notion that "how we think affects how we feel," a major insight of the cognitive theory of depression. If we want to control our emotions, then we attempt to control our thoughts. Thus, as active agents we can indirectly alter, or attempt to alter, emotional experience. We can also do this through "selective exposure," by avoiding that which depresses and seeking that which brings joy. Rosenberg can be faulted for contending that this process is not "difficult." One cannot have selective exposure or easily think positive thoughts, for instance, if one has lost a child, a farm, or a job.

Another way to alter emotional experience is through the body. We can exercise, drink alcohol, and take drugs—all producing physiological arousal—to try to bring about the desired experience. We can do this because the body—to the self-reflexive actor—is an object of manipulation. The self-reflexive human being actively defines and produces emotional identification, emotional display, and emotional experience.

The most significant collection of papers in the new sociology of emotions is David D. Franks and E. Doyle McCarthy's edited volume *The Sociology of Emotions: Original Essays and Research Papers* (1989). The following offers a review of how some sociologists are drawing links between emotions and the social and cultural context of late capitalist Western society. I begin by outlining those of their theoretical insights consistent with SI and then make brief comments on the research papers.

McCarthy maintains that a sociology of emotions can be built out of traditional social psychology and the sociology of knowledge: "Each views mental structures as manifestations of particular cultural and social developments; each conceives social factors as intrinsic to mentality" (1989, 51). The logical place to start for McCarthy is to expand on the work of Mead.

Emotions are social emergents that develop in social relations. The fact that emotions are socially embedded in group processes explains their commonality (we all share in group processes) and their differences (we all belong to different groups and social worlds). Emotions are situationally constituted and thus vary according to the diversity of situations encountered, by class, race, gender, society, and culture. Emotions are thus not biological, personal, or universal in mode of expression. Emotions are a product of socialization and social interaction, and thus McCarthy's argument (1989, 68) correctly notes that Cooley's position "of unsocialized feelings is theoretically indefensible."

As Franks and McCarthy (1989, xix) caution, there may be universal emotions, such as anger, "but this in no way undermines the argument that emotions are cultural and historical ways of experiencing and acting capable of considerable variation in both what is felt and in the meaning of what is felt."

Gordon (1989, 115) agrees with McCarthy's view and goes on to note that the interpretation of emotions is also socially embedded, "Sociology's most significant insight into emotions may be that individuals interpret emotional experience within socially constructed frameworks of meaning." Gordon (1989, 115) contends that there exists an "emotional culture"through which people "communicate, perpetuate, and develop their knowledge about and attitudes toward emotions." In our emotional culture, actors define the meaning of an emotion by attributing it to either an institutional or impulsive orientation.

The institutional meaning of an emotion centers on control over one's feeling and expression, conforming to norms, values, and collective standards. The impulsive meaning of an emotion centers on one's spontaneity, lack of inhibition, and abandon. Our society has both institutional norms and impulsive ones. We should express emotion according to certain institutional standards, say, at a funeral. But an individualistic culture cultivates impulsive expressions as a way of self-discovery. Even impulsive emotion is not divorced from social embeddedness, however. "From a sociological standpoint, impulse is not antithetical to self-control: standards and techniques for being impulsive are socially learned and negotiated" (Gordon 1989, 128). Gordon (1989, 132) concludes that the social construction of emotions cannot be conceived of as a personal process; it is guided by social norms, vocabulary, beliefs, and our entire emotional culture. This emotional culture guid   es our emotional expressions whether we define and give meaning to our emotions through an institutional or an impulsive orientation. Again, here we notice SI's interpretation of human behavior dialectically, as a process involving both constraint and agency.

Emotions and Gender

Hochschild explains that "different cultural prisms for men and women" can affect the way a couple interprets gratitude. This can affect their relationship, for "crucial to a healthy economy of gratitude is a common interpretation of reality, such that what feels like a gift to one, feels like a gift to the other" (1989, 96). But couples, because of gender differences, interpret reality differently.

Hochschild focuses on how changes in the economy, where (according to her) women hold 80 percent of the new jobs since 1980, have not produced the corresponding cultural shift to accommodate women's lives at home. She employs William Ogburn's concept that there is a "cultural lag" in sanctioning, supporting, and encouraging men to work at home. This gender "culture lag" is in behavior and attitudes, for when it comes to housework and childrearing, men still believe they are "women's work" and hence do not participate in the social reproduction of the household.

Hochschild dichotomizes gender culture into a traditional view and an egalitarian one. Where men and women fall in their attachment to one of these views will shape the way they define gratitude for certain social acts. Their views will also shape the quality of their relationship, how they feel about the spouse: warm and grateful or cold and resentful.

In a traditional family, if a man helps out at home, this may be viewed as a gift by the husband and received as one by the wife. If the wife works outside the home, this may be intended as a gift by the wife and felt as one by the husband. A family such as this, interpreting reality the same way, can have a rich economy of gratitude.

In an egalitarian family, traditional gift giving over providing income or social reproduction of the household is changed. Men do not view their wives working as a gift but as a social expectation. Women do not view their husbands doing housework or childrearing as a gift, since men are now expected to share in the social reproduction of the household as well as the financial maintenance of it. If both interpret reality this way and both engage in corresponding behavior (that is, sharing financial responsibility and social reproduction), this too may bring about a happy household. Gifts that are given over and above expectations will engender gratitude.

Problems arise when couples misperceive and misreceive gifts because of their attachment to different gender cultures. The problem is that men are, by and large, attached to masculine culture, resulting in spousal exploitation; for example, women who work full-time still do 80 percent of the housework and childrearing. Hochschild (1989, 102) reports that men's acceptance of women working, an androgynous economy, has not generated an androgynous culture in the home, that is, men doing housework; consequently, men evade taking responsibility for their share of the social reproduction of the household.

> The most common form of "mis-giving" occurs when the man offers a traditional gift—hard work at the office—but the woman wants to receive a "modern" gift—sharing child-rearing and housework. Similarly, the woman offers a "modern" gift—more money, while the man hopes for a traditional gift—like home cooking. As external conditions create a "gender gap" in the economy of gratitude, they disrupt the ordinary ways in which a man and woman express love.

Obviously, because our economy necessitates a dual income to stay financially afloat, women will be giving modern gifts, but men (who adhere to traditional gender culture) will not be reciprocating. The unrequited condition will cause only bitterness and resentment and adversely affect the marriage. Men will not feel gratitude for their wives working to the extent that they will share in the social reproduction of the household. Women will feel no gratitude for an occasional "helping out" approach. Different interpretations of reality will lead to an impoverished economy of gratitude.

As Hochschild notes, women are adapting to their changing environment, the economy, but men are not adapting to their changing environment, women. The tenacity of traditional culture impedes men's progress, for work has always had high value but housework has never been esteemed; therefore, "these changes are likely to feel to women like moving "up" and to men like moving "down" (Hochschild 1989, 109).

Hochschild has shown how cultural variation influences the emotion of gratitude. What one defines as a gift, and what a gift means, that is, how one responds to it, depends on how it is interpreted through the constraint of a gender culture and the social context of a changed economy.

Managing Our Emotions and the Emotions of Others

Hochschild's (1979, 1983) research also has established that we employ "feeling rules" to manage our emotions. Emotional labor "requires one to induce or suppress feeling in order to sustain the outward countenance that produces the proper state of mind in others" (Hochschild 1983, 7). Flight attendants and bill collectors must engage in emotional display (that is, to commercialize their emotions)—a facade of cheerfulness or a posturing of aggressiveness, further alienating workers.

Thoits (1996, 86), inspired by Hochschild, has researched how we "manipulate the feeling of others" in order to obtain "solidarity, behavioral compliance, social change, and/or identity change." Environmental surroundings, such as lights and music, can be used to set a mood; yet, Thoits is mainly concerned with interpersonal emotion-management techniques. At a psychodrama center, Sisyphus, devoted to changing people's behavior, identity, or whatever personal problem was bothering them, Thoits observed such techniques as (1) enactment of one's personal problems in a group setting; (2) provocations, whereby one's conflicts were exaggerated by other members, including through "physically aggressive acts" and "verbal attacks"; and (3) physical-effort techniques such as pounding and whipping pillows in order to "stimulate intense negative emotions" so that in the process a "meaning [is attached] to the object being pounded/whipped/beaten" (Thoits 1996, 91-97). These techniques were ostensibly to facilitate emotional release, such as venting and catharsis so that a participant would come to an "insight" (Thoits 1996, 98). After these negative emotions, such as sadness or despair, had been released, other emotion-management techniques were used to facilitate positive emotions. Group supportive acts and individual comforting behaviors involved either the group or an individual in hugging, holding, rubbing, or massaging participants who had gone through catharsis so as to facilitate social acceptance. Variations in these techniques (to promote identity change or group solidarity) have been used in total institutions: drug treatment programs, on political prisoners, and in the military services (Thoits 1996, 105). They are not just used to resocialize, but used by all of us to socialize each other." Considerable experimental and observational evidence shows that even small children know how to use provoking and comforting to alter other children's emotional states" (Thoits 1996, 106). Attempts to manipulate the emotions of others through these or other techniques probably occur in all "encounters marked by conflict or attempts to persuade" (Thoits 1996, 106). We can generalize this even more by noting that interactants influence each other's emotional experience, that emotional experience is a socially constructed event (Staske 1996).

Other Emotions

Clark (1989) used a multiplicity of research techniques to study sympathy. She found sympathy to be an emergent of social interaction and that sympathy rules vary by subculture.

A way of feeling is socially embedded in and representative of an age, which is analogous to classifying an age according to a *Weltanschauung* or *Zeitgeist*. Clanton (1989, 179) thus suggests that "patterns of emotional experience change in response to changes in society and culture. " He uses this tenet of the sociology of emotions to explore the way jealousy is conceptualized and experienced in two different time-frames.

In the first time frame, 1945-1965, jealousy is conceptualized as proof of love, natural, and good for marriage. In the second time-frame, 1970-1980, jealousy is conceptualized as unnatural, a product of learning that should be unlearned and is bad for marriage. Jealousy becomes a human defect, a product of low self-esteem. Clanton traces the social roots of this change in mentality to changes in love relationships. He argues that in the 1950s and early 1960s, the emphasis was on "relationship commitment or togetherness." In the 1970s the emphasis was on "personal freedom" in marriage and relationships. The goal of personal freedom is seen as "part of a larger trend in favor of more freedom, more experimentation, and a more positive view of pleasure" (Clanton 1989, 187). He views the social roots of this conceptual change in jealousy as part of the counterculture and youth culture that was burgeoning in the 1970s. Again, the thesis of the sociology of emotions is to conceptualize emotions as embedded in history and culture.

Weigert and Franks (1989) attribute the emotion of ambivalence to the ongoing change, incompleteness, competing ideologies, multiple interpretive frameworks, and complexity of contemporary society. Our culture promotes ambivalence through contradictory values and symbolic forms expressed in the mainstream and a counterculture. Social organizations engender ambivalence through their formal adherence to universalistic norms but their practice of informally operating on particularistic ones. The contemporary family breeds ambivalence, since members find it hard to reconcile personal and group goals. An individualistic culture supports personal achievement, and yet it also socializes us to be committed to our families. There are interactional ambivalences, for example, when we question if we are acting toward another on the basis of sex or love. Gender culture produces ambivalence in females: should they work, should they rear children, or should they try to do both? Contradictory messages are given to women currently socialized in the United States.

Weigert and Franks characterize ambivalence as the modern temper, an existential condition.[1] There is no authority to legitimize absolutes, this is a postmodern theme that echoes back to Nietzsche. Since we are responsible for the world and our actions, since there are no more supernatural guidebooks that can provide succor for our existential loneliness and isolation, this leaves us with uncertainty, angst, and ambivalence as to what is believable, what is the good society, and what is the good life. Now that we know we are the authors of our world, that knowledge costs us certainty and security: "The post-modern context generates intense ambivalence as a paradoxical concomitant of the human control over, and responsibility for, nature, society, and self" (Weigert and Franks 1989, 220).

Swanson (1989) maintains that virtues and emotions, such as honesty, courage, gratitude, temperance, humility, meekness, justice, repentance, kindness, forgiveness, faith, hope, and love, are socially constituted. When we role-take, we not only internalize a cognitive perspective on the world (a way to think) but we internalize an affective framework as well (a way to feel). Culture socializes us to both ways of thinking and ways of feeling, which, of course, will vary by subculture and other traditional variables.

Franks (1989, 154) outlines "how human interpretation of affective behaviors

reflects and maintains power structures and stratification systems." In this structural analysis, Franks points out the way asymmetrical resources in relationships,
such as power and status, influence battered wives to define the situation as their
own fault. Victims, the powerless in general, are more accurate at role-taking. In
this process, the powerless often adopt the standpoint of the other. This is especially the case in close personal relationships. In the case of battered women, this
may lead to self-accusation rather than attributing the cause to where it surely
belongs, to a violent and inexcusable display of emotion.

The sociology of emotions is growing, leading to new methods of inquiry. Ellis
(1991a, 1991b) has contended that an untapped way sociologists can study how
people define emotions is through introspection. She maintains (1991b, 125) that
SI and the new sociology of emotions should focus on "studying emotions emotionally, examining our own emotions, and concentrating on introspective narratives of lived experience." A sociological introspection of others or self can also
reveal the cultural influence on the interpretive process. Ellis uses introspection to
study her own and others' emotions, noting how norms and situations require
emotional display, how emotions can be mixed, contradictory, and redefined. She
also illustrates, through self-reports and the reports of others, how emotions are
controlled and managed, and the strategies for doing emotion work.

Ellis (1991b, 139) argues that "advancing the case for an emotional sociology
does not mean arguing against empiricism or rigor." She is following a venerable
history in SI methodology, arguing that one can incorporate scientific and human-
istic methods to explore subjectivity.

Palmer (1994) has recently highlighted the social constructionist position
through humans' ability to attribute emotions to animals (anthropomorphism). He
(1994, 430-32) also researched nurses, who attribute emotions and "personalities"
to neonates in what he called "emotionalized anthropomorphic reactions." These
neonates had "severe medical problems and [were] hanging onto life by a thread."
One doctor ordered a nurse not to touch a neonate considered near death, but the
nurse, believing the baby was experiencing feelings, acted on her definition of the
situation. The baby recovered and the doctor felt guilty.

Summarizing, we observe that emotional frameworks are internalized just as
are cognitive frameworks, and that, therefore, emotions have social and cultural
roots that vary historically. One can define an epoch by a characteristic or representative emotion, such as ambivalence, or notice the effect a changing social
context has on the appraisal of an emotion such as jealousy.

An Examination of the Emotions
of Resentment and *Ressentiment*

By Bernard N. Meltzer and Gil Richard Musolf

A voluminous literature, chiefly by psychologists and philosophers,[2] deals with the closely related emotional experiences of resentment and *ressentiment*. However, very little has been written about the commonalities and divergences between these two terms. Given certain important differences in their interpersonal and societal implications, it is worthwhile to examine the emotions typically designated by the terms. We shall begin such an examination by surveying conceptions of the nature of resentment and of *ressentiment*, delineating the similarities and differences between them. We shall then consider the social contexts within which each of them is considered likely to arise. Finally, we shall discuss views of the likely social consequences of the occurrence of each, in the course of which we suggest a modification of classic views of *ressentiment*.

Although this section is basically an effort at conceptual clarification, we also present some supplementary empirical data. Consisting of eighty-four personal experience narratives written by students in sociology classes, these essays are not used inductively to derive generalizations, but illustratively to help elucidate various ideas. Students were asked to write a description of "a brief or long-term situation in which you have felt resentment against someone or something." In their description, students were to indicate "(a) What you resented, (b) Why you felt resentment, (c) How long you felt resentful, (d) Other people in the same situation who felt resentful, and (e) What you did, if anything, to express your resentment." The age and gender of each narrator were also requested. The resultant essays, expectably, chiefly relate to problems arising out of relations between roommates, family members, and romantically involved individuals, as well as different racial groups.

Resentment

In common usage, "resentment" refers to a feeling of displeasure induced by being insulted, offended, or deprived. Thus, it is typically a reaction to slights or affronts, to assaults, whether mild or severe, upon one's self. Inescapably, this reactive feeling is based on the actor's definition of the insult, slight, sense of deprivation, or other felt injury as unwarranted, unjust,—the result of wrongful conduct or unfair institutions.[3] In the familiar words of Erving Goffman (1967), "one's face is a sacred thing" (31) and "as sacred objects, men are subject to slights and profanation" (27). Illustrating a common, obvious form of felt injustice is a report by one of our essayists.

> In the last four and a half years, I have been resentful towards my girl friend's family for treating me different because I'm a different race from them. . . . The reason I felt resentment is because a person can not decide what race they will be and I was being discriminated [against] for just that. . . . They treated me bad for no reason. (Male, 24 years old)

Resentment, Murphy and Hampton (1988, 56) point out, is "a protest against the demeaning action but also a defense against the action's attack on one's self-esteem." For resentment is a reaction to treatment that is defined as disrespectful, contemptuous, spiteful, or insolent, and thus tending to lower one in the eyes of others (see Barbalet 1998 for a fuller discussion of this point). Like the reflexive emotions of shame and embarrassment, resentment is a reaction issuing from discreditation; however, unlike shame (discredited self) and embarrassment (discredited self-presentation), which involve adverse self-judgments, resentment is a consequence of explicit or implicit adverse judgments by others. The object of this reaction is, as Haber (1991, 48) points out, "the defiant reaffirmation of one's rank and value in the face of treatment calling them into question." Again, drawing upon insights from Goffman (1967, 31), as "a ritually delicate object," the self prompts those who define some action as disparaging "to lead themselves into duels." Certainly, some of the actual duels occurring historically were prompted by resentment. As we shall later show, however, such retaliatory action is not always the case in resentment and is even more unlikely in *ressentiment*.

In this initial characterization of resentment we do not intend to reify the emotion; as we shall later show, this emotion—like all others—is identifiable only as it arises in certain social situations. Today, most sociological treatments of emotions accord with McCarthy's (1989, 67) caution against the entification of emotions, that is, the view that they exist as entities that can be defined and observed apart from their cultural and ideational contexts. In fact, as Franks (1985, 165) asserts, "The name we give to an emotion reflects the particular aspect of [a] situation that we selected for focus."

Several other emotions have often been conflated with resentment despite some differences. Anger, for example, Haber (1991, 30) points out, shares the element of displeasure, but, unlike resentment, it does not necessarily involve absence of justification. Similarly, Rawls (1971, 533) holds that envy shares with resentment a sense of hurt or loss, but lacks a moral principle for its arousal. These differences, however, are somewhat obscured by the frequent occurrence of both anger and envy (as well as fear) as concomitants or, even, components of resentment. Both Nietzsche and Scheler specify that *ressentiment* (a form of resentment that we shall soon describe) comprises feelings of hatred, wrath, envy, revenge, and the like.

Additionally, Haber (1991, 37) characterizes resentment as primarily confined to injury to oneself (or someone closely related), while viewing injury to others not closely related as inciting indignation. Interestingly, the Abonwari of Papua New Guinea (Telban 1993) lack words for such general terms as emotion and thought, as well as for jealousy, envy, and self-pity, which are referred to as "not being cared for" (or "feeling bad"); however, the various forms of "not being cared for" are viewed as wrongful treatment by others and give rise to feelings termed resentment.

Complicating the conceptualization of resentment is the fact that we find it useful to distinguish both a generic meaning (which we have delineated above) and a specific meaning for it. In its generic sense, resentment can be usefully treated—as we shall soon indicate—both as a short-term form (for which we retain the designation "resentment") and a long-term form (which, following Nietzsche [1887] (1956), we designate *ressentiment*). For reasons of convenience, and to avoid confusion, we shall use "resentment" as the specific, fleeting form of the emotion, as opposed to *ressentiment*. One of our narrators voiced an illustrative experience of this form:

> In my sophomore year , , , my roommate was sloppy, dirty, and wouldn't help clean her mess. . . . I confronted her about it and she threw a fit about us not caring about her feelings. A very heated argument occurred and she stormed out of the room and I haven't seen or heard from her since. (Female, 21 years old)

Such usage differs from the employment, by some scholars, of the two concepts as synonymous (see, for example, Solomon 1995; Gerth and Mills 1953; Betz 1991; Yankelovich 1975; Reiser 1993; Ashforth 1992).

Most treatments of resentment have focused on its arousal in interpersonal situations. Moreover, such arousal tends to issue from incidents of put-downs, rebuffs, slurs, snubs, insults, and other relatively minor injuries. The resultant resentment is likely to be transitory, as described in phrases such as "taking umbrage" or "feeling piqued." In contrast, *ressentiment* is more likely to persist and to become intensified.

Ressentiment

The concept *ressentiment* was introduced in a special technical sense by Nietzsche [1887] (1956) and was developed sociologically by Max Scheler [1915] (1961). No English (or German) word adequately expresses the same nuances of the term—nuances giving it a breadth and depth of meaning absent from resentment. While French-language dictionaries we consulted define the term simply as resentment, a few English-language dictionaries that include it define it in such ways as the following:

> A feeling of bitter anger or resentment together with a sense of frustration at being powerless to express this hostility overtly. (*Webster's New World College Dictionary* 1997)

> An oppressive awareness of the futility of trying to improve one's status in life or society. (*Random House Dictionary* 1967)

> A generalized feeling of resentment and often hostility harbored by one individual or group against another, especially chronically and with no means of direct expression. (*The American Heritage Dictionary*, abridged 1982)

These definitions refer to two noteworthy features of *ressentiment* that differentiate it from the conventional meaning of resentment: (1) the protracted (chronic) character of the emotional experience, and (2) powerlessness to take retaliatory action against its sources. These elements—as well as other, nondefinitional features—merit further treatment.

For both Nietzsche [1887] (1956) and Scheler [1915] (1961), *ressentiment* is a generalized, chronic feeling that involves both a desire for revenge against its perpetrator(s) and failure to express the revenge in direct action. The essays of several narrators exemplified this element, designating as agents of wrongful conduct coaches who play favorites, racist society, and inaccessible abandoning fathers. This failure reflects a sense of powerlessness vis-à-vis the agent (person, group, or institution) of the inciting injury or offense. As Scheler [1915] (1961) puts it, *ressentiment*-related revenge is distinguished by two essential characteristics. "First of all, the immediate reactive impulse . . . is . . . checked and restrained, and the response is consequently postponed to a later time and to a more suitable occasion. . . . This blockage is caused by the reflection that an immediate reaction would lead to defeat, and by a concomitant pronounced feeling of 'inability' and impotence" (46).

In like manner, Nietzsche [1887] (1956) refers to *ressentiment*-linked passivity and impotent revenge in such expressions as the following: "the rancor of beings who, deprived of the direct outlet of action, compensate by an imaginary vengeance" (170); "the impotent and oppressed" (172); and "the weakness of the weak, which is after all his essence, his sole and inevitable reality" (179). Revenge, according to Scheler (1961, 50), becomes transformed into *ressentiment* the more it is directed against lasting circumstances that are deemed injurious but beyond one's control. In some cases, the circumstances constitute an abstraction, such as "the establishment," "the system," "the government," or "the economy"—all seen as especially invulnerable. In any event, the circumstances are felt to be beyond one's control. Thus, Solomon (1994) points out, power—or the lack of it—is a crucial component of this emotion. If this is so—and it appears to comport with our personal experiences and observations—we should expect directly vengeful actions to occur chiefly when the agents of acts engendering either resentment or *ressentiment* are of lower status (and power) than the aggrieved. Strangely, however, while viewing *ressentiment* as entailing repressed, impotent desires for revenge, Scheler (1961, 177n4, 196n54) appears to contravene this view by also attributing the French Revolution to an "enormous explosion of *ressentiment*." Scheler did not consider it necessary to explain what could be viewed as a contradiction in his monograph; later studies, explored below, fill in what he implicitly suggests but leaves unexplained.

In some instances the *ressentiment* is so widespread as to take a collective form, that is, to affect a structural category of people within a society. Thus, subordination on the basis of class, ethnicity, gender, or sexual orientation may become a source of *ressentiment*. Nietzsche [1887] (1956) referred to those who suffer from a "slave morality," and Scheler [1915] (1961) held the petit bourgeoisie and various other status groups (other than the nobility) to be subject to *ressentiment*. As we shall later see, Nietzsche saw *ressentiment* as linked with both Judeo-Christian religious doctrines and egalitarian-socialistic ideologies, while Scheler associated this sentiment with membership in the bourgeoisie, as well as with particular social roles.

The indefinitely prolonged time lag between felt injury and redress-oriented reaction to its agent is another crucial component. Sugarman's (1980) *Rancor against Time: The Phenomenology of Ressentiment*, a rare differentiation between resentment and *ressentiment*, emphasizes this point. Typifying this feature of long duration, the following reported experience of a student also includes no action to avenge herself:

> I resent the fact that my "father" never wanted anything to do with me. . . . [O]nce I was born he was out of the picture [i.e., abandoned the family]. I don't know much about him. And he doesn't know anything about me. He never even took the time to find out. (Female, 18 years old)

A similar failure to retaliate against the agent(s) of wrongful treatment is demonstrated in the following student report:

> The only resentment I have had in my life is toward my parents for the reason of always comparing me to my sister, who always was an "A" student. . . . I felt resentment because no matter how good I did they always compared me to my sister's grades. . . . The only resentment I show is by not telling my parents how I do in school. (Male, 19 years old)

The time lag is usually related to the ongoing, lasting nature of many injustices leading to *ressentiment*—as opposed to the more sporadic, isolated acts usually eliciting resentment—as well as to feelings of impotence. Solomon (1994), reviewing Nietzsche's ideas, indicates that the long-term repression or suppression of acts of revenge tends to greatly intensify *ressentiment*. Illustrative of such intensification is the following comment by a Korean battered wife: "Until he comes back at night, I can't sleep. I can't eat. I can't rest. I hate and hate. . . . For 14 years of our marriage, this feeling has built up. . . . I just want to kill him" (Cho 1987, 249; cited in Denzin 1989, 57).

We see here an instance of the relentless re-experiencing of impotent vengeful feelings. *Ressentiment*, then, "is a long-term, seething, deep-rooted negative feeling toward those whom one feels unjustly have power or advantage over one's life" (Rollins 1996, 237). The emotion becomes an obsessive, smoldering, simmering, and festering sense of wounded self-esteem and desire for revenge. By contrast, according to Nietzsche, the immediately direct responses—or even indifference—to affronts, which characterize the "Master" class, leave no lasting impress.

Finally, *ressentiment* shares with resentment a crucial moral aspect, a sense of being denied what we believe is our just due. John Rawls (1971) suggests that this feeling presupposes equality and, as such, is linked with our sense of justice. He asserts that, "If we resent our having less than others, it must be because we think that their being better off is the result of unjust institutions, or wrongful conduct on their part" (533).

Contexts of Resentment and *Ressentiment*

Nietzsche categorizes people into two "classes," the Master/Aristocratic/Noble class and the Slave/Common/Herd class, both of which designations relate more to character than social strata. For him [1887] (1956), membership in the Slave class (comprising the common, wretched, poor, lowly, sick, and ugly—in short, those with fewer resources) is derived from the personal attributes of individuals,[4] "utterly denying the origins in economic exploitation of all discontent from below" (Dowling 1984, 133). This social-Darwinist perspective extolled the merits of a Master class that Nietzsche believed deserved their superior positions and their monopoly of resources. Nietzsche's argument, Antonio (1995) correctly holds, is an "antisociology." Absent the cognizance of structural impediments to achievement, Nietzsche's antisociology censures emancipatory projects and egalitarianism, while ridiculing sociology's matrix—the Enlightenment grand narrative of progress, rationality, science, consensus, and democracy (9-10)—for engendering "cultural mediocrity and mass discipline" (20). Nietzsche champions, instead, the need for "restoring authority, hierarchy, and cultural domination under a new rank order of values and leadership" (28). His essentialist conception of the "weaker," ineffectual segments of the population as ineluctably prone to *ressentiment* is somewhat modified, however, by the role he assigns Judeo-Christian doctrines as creations of the emotion. As we shall later see, Nietzsche claims that these doctrines both emerge from and reinforce *ressentiment*.

In contrast to Nietzsche, Scheler (1961), saw *ressentiment* as deriving socially, from various statuses and roles. Primary among these was membership in the bourgeoisie, particularly the lower-middle-class strata, comprising artisans, lower-level public officials, and small-business proprietors. Additionally, Scheler stressed the importance of types of social stratification as sources of *ressentiment*. While societies marked by clearly demarcated rank orders tend to foster comparisons only within each stratum, those where relatively free social mobility prevails encourage competition within the whole system, with people comparing their lot with that of higher strata—thus engendering the likelihood of *ressentiment*.[5] Scheler (1961, 24-27) also situates the likelihood of the occurrence of *ressentiment* within certain specific positions in the social structure, such as those of women, especially unmarried women, the elderly, priests, and others who experience recurrent situations in which they must repress negative affects such as revenge. To these we can add racial and ethnic minorities and other subordinate groups that are susceptible to continuing affronts.

Implicit in Scheler's discussion is the role of cognitive elements in the elicitation of *ressentiment*. Neither structural nor situational features per se—but *agency*, based on definitions of these features by actors—elicit the emotion. Both resentment and *ressentiment* are "based not on personal involvement so much as personal *insight* in the disjuncture between social rights and social outcomes" (Barbalet 1998, 137; emphasis added). Thus, Murphy and Hampton (1988, 55; emphasis in original) remind us: "[O]ne resents only *culpable wrongdoings* (i.e., *responsible wrongdoings*)." Hence, several cognitive conditions are presupposed for the arousal of either resentment or *ressentiment*. As Fischer and Ravizza (1993) assert, acts that may ordinarily give rise to resentment may be interpreted by the "wronged" party in ways that *inhibit* the emotion. For example,

when jostled by a crowd, . . . your resentment might be inhibited if you are too tired or busy or fearful, or simply inured to life in the big city. . . . In contrast, you might think the other was pushed, didn't realize, didn't mean to. . . . These things would provide reasons for the inhibition of resentment. (Fischer and Ravizza 1993, 122-23)

Similarly, Watson (1993, 122) points out that we are likely to inhibit resentment if we deem the "wrongdoer" to be acting uncharacteristically because of extraordinary circumstances, or as psychologically abnormal or morally underdeveloped such as children, being under great strain, being psychotic, being hypnotized, or having been unfortunate in one's formative circumstances. In other words, we tend to excuse or forgive otherwise resentment-inducing actions when the agent is seen as not being responsible for his/her injurious behavior (see Strawson 1974; Watson 1993 for discussions of this point). In other words, as in many other kinds of situations, we tend to excuse acts that are "accidental," unintended, nonmalicious, or otherwise lacking in *mens rea*.

Several students of *ressentiment* link its occurrence with the experience of career failure. Shaeffer (1988), in a highly conservative defense of the economic status quo, states:

> When a civilization experiences [significant economic] growth over a period of decades or centuries, those who have contributed the least develop powerful resentments as they find themselves significantly behind those who have worked, saved, risked, and prospered. (8)

In like vein, studies by Nordstrom, Friedenberg, and Gold (1965, 1967), purporting to follow Scheler, attribute the arousal of *ressentiment* to failure in the competition for achievement, as in the following assertion: "Ressentiment begins when an angry individual feels an oppressive sense of impotence which he cannot imagine actively transcending. This impotence results from his having lost out in competition with others over the course of his life" (1967, 13).

A number of research studies of resentment and *ressentiment* recognize social contexts in which they appear.[6] Following are a few examples: adverse relations between youth and their fathers (Ball 1964); unfair workings of a civil service system (Ospina 1996); erosion of confidence in national institutions (Yankelovich 1975); view of a black protest group's leadership as ineffective (Owens 1975); perceived unfairness of affirmative action policies (Lynch and Beer 1990); interpretation by members of each gender of unjust advantages held by the other gender (Reiser 1993); definition by men that women receive undeserved "special treatment" (Liff and Cameron 1997); responses of nurses to violence and threats from impatient patients in an emergency clinic (Akerstrom 1997).

Consequences of Resentment and *Ressentiment*

Nietzsche [1887] (1956) viewed *ressentiment* as embodying an intense desire for revenge, as did Scheler (1961). Both also stressed the inability of those experiencing *ressentiment* to rebel against the agents of their unjust treatment, who are more powerful. *Imaginary* or symbolic revenge, however, may often take the place of actual retaliation.[7] Such revenge may underlie a transformation of values, a substitution of new, attainable values for those which appear unattainable.

For Nietzsche [1887] (1956), the Judeo-Christian morality embodies this transformation of values, protecting the weak against the strong and promising both equality and salvation to the downtrodden. The notion of charity, and expressions such as "The meek shall inherit the earth" and "Turn the other cheek," embody this morality. This "slave morality," emphasizing equality, selflessness, meekness, humility, altruism, sympathy, pity, prudence, mercy, and other qualities Nietzsche considers signs of weakness, represent a transmogrification of the noble/aristocratic/ master qualities of self-assertion, daring, creativity, passion, dominancy, pride, and desire for conquest. Nietzsche [1887] (1956) sketches this transformation in the following terms:

> [People are] transmuting weakness into merit. . . . Impotence, which cannot retaliate, into kindness . . . submission before those one hates into obedience to One of whom they say that he has commanded this submission—they call him God. The inoffensiveness of the weak, his cowardice, his ineluctable standing and waiting at doors, are being given honorific titles such as patience; to be *unable* to avenge oneself is called to be *unwilling* to avenge oneself—even forgiveness. . . . And there's some talk of loving one's enemy. (180-81)

As for Scheler [1915] (1961), he described the transformation of Christian morality, since as early as the thirteenth century, in which such bourgeois moral values as the following have triumphed: cleverness, quick adaptability, a sense of the "calculability" of all circumstances, economy, and a desire for security.

Both Nietzsche and Scheler viewed *ressentiment* as productive of the repression of spontaneity and self-expression—by Christian teachings, according to Nietzsche, and by the petit-bourgeois no-risk mentality, according to Scheler. (Ironically, the values of self-denial and productive discipline, which Weber saw as integral to the Protestant Ethic and the inception of the spirit of capitalism, helped to bring forth Nietzsche's ideal normative order, one that extols rugged individualism and laissez- faire.) Nordstrom, Friedenberg, and Gold (1965, 1967), in studies of *ressentiment* among administrators and teachers in secondary schools, purport to link this emotion with such repression, as asserted in the following comment:

> Institutional arrangements will be regarded as *ressentiment* to the degree that they are designed to facilitate external control of impulsive behavior . . . at the expense of disciplined self-expression, and to minimize opportunities for demonstration of specific personal excellence. (1965, 2)

Given this negative characterization—a prevailing evaluation—of *ressentiment,* it is not surprising to learn that Sartre (1965, 14) describes those who experience the emotion as individuals who "establish their human personality as a perpetual negation." Augmenting the negative view of this emotion is a widely held view among scholars that both resentment and *ressentiment* tend to be base, dastardly emotions resorted to by thin-skinned individuals and seekers after excuses for failure, that these emotions are often felt irrationally, on occasions in which one has *not* been morally wronged. Thus, Solomon (1995) refers to a "vindictive" emotion, frequently a personal, petty, disproportionate reaction to a slight; Ortony, Clore, and Collins (1988) write of a "distasteful" emotion; and Adam Smith

[1759] (1969) designates a "disagreeable" passion.[8] On the other hand, Solomon (1994), elsewhere, takes a more positive view of *ressentiment*, pointing out that it often entails compassion for others in the same situation, and its implicit sense of injustice may lead to corrective action; thus, *ressentiment* can be seen as an expression of "the socially responsible insistence of the community on justice and justification" (124). Similarly, Haber (1991) argues that resentment can be a form of personal protest that expresses regard for oneself, for others, and for the normative order (48). Moreover, Haber (1991, 82) holds that a display of resentment may serve as an instrument of individual or social change. In fact, the historian Hippolyte Taine (cited in Jameson 1976, 201) sought to explain revolutions in terms of underlying *ressentiment*, and Jameson (1976) contends that this emotion is the very *content* of revolutions. In the same vein, various scholars have asserted that "the individual of *ressentiment* is a potential revolutionary" (Vaneigem 1979, 9) and that "our revolutionaries are men and women of resentment" (Solomon 1995, 266).[9] Thus, Merton (1957, 155) maintains that "organized rebellion may draw upon a vast reservoir of the resentful and discontented as institutional dislocations become acute." In the light of such characterizations, the role of the political agitator is readily recognized as that of raising consciousness of unjust treatment (where such consciousness is absent), inducing *ressentiment* (where the emotion is absent), and organizing resistance to the recurrence or continuation of unjust treatment. Moreover, Folger (1987) claims that revolutionary ideologies can help to *create ressentiment*. That *ressentiment* can be used to initiate (and sustain) revolution argues against the more passive—and contemptuous—conceptions held by Nietzsche, Scheler, and their many followers.

Short of rebellion or revolution, those experiencing *ressentiment* may seek retaliation in safer and more subtle ways. As the following excerpt from a student essay reports, resentment or *ressentiment* may issue in complaints to the source of the felt wrong:

> In 1997 the . . . Department of Civil Service changed their hiring process. For college graduates, this means that an [employing agency] will key in the degree(s) they are looking for to fill a specific employment position. Prior to 1997 my undergraduate degree qualified me for *numerous* jobs. . . . I have been resentful since 1997 when I realized the limits that [the change imposed on me]. . . . I have expressed my concerns to Civil Service Personnel. (Female, 49 years old)

An even more forceful form of retaliation is reported by another student, as follows:

> [In high school,] the varsity [basketball] coach fired my [highly esteemed junior varsity] coach based on her sexual preference. . . . We (several players on the team, along with our parents and lawyers) got the varsity coach fired, . . . still what he did will always be in my mind. (Female, 18 years old)

The familiar example of slaves in America "clumsily" breaking their hoes and other farm implements can also be cited here. Scott (1985) offers a less well-known illustration: the constant, circumspect struggle—through techniques of evasion and resistance—by peasants in Malay against their oppressors. On the level of acts by individuals, it is our impression that many instances of arson, vandalism, and keying of car exteriors are occasioned by feelings of resentment or *ressentiment*. Less dramatic instances of retaliation abound. In Germany, according to Betz (1991), the two ends of the political spectrum reflect a climate of political *ressentiment* fueled by the failure of established parties to confront new issues: while the Greens emphasize preservation of the natural environment, the new right urges the protection of national and cultural identity. Closer to home, Schuman and Krysan (1996), ascribe to *ressentiment* the contribution of funds by residents of three Michigan counties to the far-right gubernatorial campaign of David Duke in Louisiana. The formation of Russian nationalism in the last third of the eighteenth century is attributed by Greenfeld (1990) to a combination of admiration and *ressentiment* toward the West. Still another study (Nehring 1997, 40) considers much popular music, especially with angry lyrics (e.g., hip-hop and rap music) to be "purely creative, imaginary acts of revenge" in the youth culture, inspired by *ressentiment* but conceivable as marginal forms of rebellion. And, surely, the underlying sources of such social movements as the struggles for black rights, gay/lesbian rights, and women's rights include this often-maligned emotion.

The foregoing paragraphs argue for rejection of Nietzsche's and Scheler's views of *ressentiment* as essentially a form of resignation and, as such, opposed to active endeavors to avenge or redress the wrongs inducing it. We would modify these views by contending that passivity, or inactivity, may be a frequent, but not immutable, component of *ressentiment*, depending on the total social context. Rather than a necessarily perdurable state, *ressentiment*-related passivity may at times become a lengthy, dynamic, *transitional* stage between treatment defined as wrongful and retaliation or rectification.[10] That is, ressentient individuals or groups may come to define the inducing agent as either intolerable or no longer overpowering and, therefore, susceptible to acts of revenge or revolt. A classic literary illustration of this point is to be found in Shakespeare's *Julius Caesar*. In the following quotation (part of a litany of defects), Cassius, filled with *ressentiment* over his subordination to Caesar, describes Caesar's physical weakness, thereby opening the door to a view of Caesar as less than omnipotent and thus vulnerable to overthrow:

He had a fever when he was in Spain,
And when the fit was on him, I did mark
How he did shake—'tis true this god did shake.
His coward lips did from their colour fly,
And that same eye whose hand doth awe the world
Did lose his lustre; I did hear him groan.

Ay, and that tongue of his that bade the Romans
Mark him and write his speeches in their books,
Alas, it cried, "Give me some drink, Titinius,"
As a sick girl, Ye gods, it doth amaze me
A man of such a feeble temper should
So get the start of the majestic world
And bear the palm alone. (*Julius Caesar*, Act I, Scene ii)

Thus, *ressentiment* may issue in action when the conditions from which it derives become defined as mutable and defeasible, that is, when corrective action is perceived to be practicable.

Conclusion

We have discussed conceptual differences between two emotions subsumed by resentment, one of which we portray as a relatively simple feeling and the other as somewhat more complex. By "resentment" (the simpler form) we have indicated what is usually a short-term reaction to affronts to the self.[11] By *ressentiment*, on the other hand, we have (following Nietzsche and Scheler) denoted a chronic feeling of affront linked with vengeful desires that cannot be readily consummated. While resentment can occur in any situation of social interaction (including, of course, interpersonal interaction) in which one's self is assailed by others, *ressentiment* tends to be induced by more durable, intense, and, on occasion, abstract sources, including social-structural features.

Contrary to the views of both Nietzsche and Scheler, who saw *ressentiment* as engendering reluctant resignation and passivity, we have followed the lead of a few scholars who point to *ressentiment* as a potential source of individual and, especially, collective action and social change. This latter view renders *ressentiment* an emotion with possible significant societal consequences.

Nietzsche gives this idea a different twist, claiming that a set of doctrines, Christianity, bred from *ressentiment*, has had profound effects on the normative order of Western civilization. Further research might examine convergences between Nietzsche's ideas (as well as Scheler's) and Weber's Protestant Ethic thesis, both of which concern the reciprocal influences of ideas and emotions, on the one hand, and society and culture, on the other.

Notes

1. For a thorough study of mixed emotions from an SI perspective, see Andrew J. Weigert, *Mixed Emotions: Certain Steps toward Understanding Ambivalence* (Albany: State University of New York Press, 1991). See also Thomas Scheff and Suzanne

Retzinger, *Emotions and Violence* (New York: Lexington Books, 1991).

2. Literary critics, too, have given attention to these emotions; illustrative of these are Jameson (1976) on the novels of George Gissing; Beauchamp (1982) on a Jack London work; Pinkerton (1970) on Katherine Ann Porter's portrayal of black *ressentiment*; Bertonneau (1998) on *The Bostonians*; Horne (1990) on *Dombey and Son*; and Weisberg (1972) on Hamlet's indecision.

3. Cooley's (1922, 269-70) brief treatment of resentment as the product of injury to one's self-feeling omits the necessity of a sense of injustice or unfairness. Thus, he mentions resentment evoked by being caught in a lie, being observed in an act of cowardice, or becoming the recipient of charity or pity.

4. Similarly, in his analysis of the important role of *ressentiment* in the life of the Roman emperor Tiberius, Marañon (1956) treats the emotion as a deep-seated personality trait, its usual onset in adolescence, that becomes "the director of our behavior, of our slightest reactions" (9).

5. Runciman's (1972) distinction between *egoistic* relative deprivation (feelings of being deprived relative to fellow in-group members) and *fraternal* relative deprivation (feelings that one's in-group is deprived relative to some out-group) is called to mind here.

6. Note that several scholars cited here do not differentiate between resentment and *ressentiment*.

7. Weigert (1983, 348) speculates that vandalism and arson by juvenile delinquents against schools, parks, graveyards, and so forth, may be expressions of *ressentiment* through attacks on and defacements of symbols of adult society.

8. Marañon (1956, 9) quotes Don Miguel de Unamuno as follows: "Among the deadly sins resentment does not figure, and yet it is the gravest of all." Marañon (1956, 10-17) goes on to maintain that the following array of undesirable traits are associated with resentment (which he conflates with *ressentiment*): lack of generosity, poor endowment with the capacity for affection, of mediocre moral quality, timidity, incapacity for gratitude, hypocrisy, lack of understanding, and (in men) sexual failure, physical imperfection, and asthenic body type.

9. However, citing Lukacs, Frank (1992, 100) points out that "Nietzsche . . . discovered that the whole class consciousness of the proletariat is a [*ressentiment*] of slaves," thereby putting a different "spin" on these ideas.

10. Cynicism, too, may initiate inaction. As Goldfarb (1991, 20) reminds us, the widespread conviction that "forces behind the scenes completely control the human order" stands for proof that "there is little or nothing ordinary mortals can do about it." It would appear that such cynicism-related passivity is unlikely to disappear or diminish as long as the cynicism itself remains. However, who among us does *not* know cynics who have become "born again" idealists?

11. A preponderance of the personal experience narratives we collected described instances of this type, although this is not clearly reflected in the few illustrative reports we have used.

12

Gender and Power

A cardinal SI tenet is that gender is a social construction that varies by culture, history, social class, race, family, and sexual orientation. Just as significant is the centrality of socialization to gender construction. These tenets are widely shared among sociologists.

The following introduction—that for most of human history men have lived on the hill of society while women have lived in its hollows—is not to chronicle a passion narrative but to acknowledge an incontrovertible conclusion: it has been a man's world. A world of male domination carries indelible and profound repercussions for gender socialization. History, structure, and culture shape socialization as penetratingly as do the family and the peer group. Socialization and the contingencies that structure it are constitutive of our humanity. The universality of the one and the particularity of the other are what make each generation, each individual, both communal and unique.

Structure: The Androcentric World

In every period of history, at every level of society, in every androcentric, especially militaristic or fundamentalist, culture, women have been abused and mutilated—whether from circumcision, "honor killing," suttee, purdah, footbinding, the burning of witches at the stake, wife auctions, rape, sexual harassment, domestic violence, the culturally enforced wearing of either a chador or burka, or the culturally rushed wearing of almost nothing at all, including culturally induced eating disorders such as anorexia nervosa and bulimia, and, until the last few tics of the Western clock, a denial of property rights and suffrage every-where; scapegoated for the evils of the world—whether because of Eve, Pandora, Helen of Troy, home wreckers, or single parenthood; and theorized as inferior—whether by Freud, scientific sexism, panreligious dogma, or the myths, folktales, and fairytales that enshrine patriarchy. Men, as gods, kings, and captains of industry, make the world. In old men's tales men must *cherchez la femme*, in modern cinema men are seduced by the femme fatale of film noir, and in politics men are driven mad by the dragon lady or Lady MacBeth fulminating "are you a man?"—gosh, whether in Genesis, by genetics or genitalia, women have only undone men and their worlds.

"Image is everything." From classical antiquity to the postmodern world women are represented as seductress, temptress, and vamp: Delilah who cuts off Samson's hair, Solomé who orders the decapitation of John the Babtist for her dance, Judith who saves the Jewish nation by beheading the Assyrian general Holoferness, Bathsheba who corrupts the virtuous David, and Matty Walker who manipulates the smitten simpleton to kill for her and then double-crosses him in Lawrence Kasdan's *Body Heat*. Women's story (as written by men) has been the erotic thriller.

As pantheons became monotheistic patriarchies, an Asherah, Astarte, Athena, Ishtar, or Isis became idolatry. Paganism and mystery cults evolved into a revealed religion. God, the creator of the universe, emerged a father and a single parent; the goddesses of the Levant and Mesopotamia became mythology.[1]

Public authority has been attired in robes, gowns, suits, diadems, helmets, tunics, togas, birettas, miters, and uniforms. Women have rarely worn these; some are still forbidden for them to wear. To be sure, women have been veiled in more ways than one, though few of us have bowed to bonnets or babushkas.

Women have been bared to androcentric interpretation and display—whether in art, religion, literature, philosophy, law, or the current male gaze of contempo-rary cinema. Androcentric interpretation and culture have created masculine institutions and structures of domination where women had to (and still do) strug-gle for access, recognition, inclusion, equity, and equality. Innumerable laws, such as the Code Napoleon, barred women from almost any participation in public life. A masculine perspective and its concepts—a gender ideology—have been applied to interpret the past and the present in order to justify the history of male domina-tion, gender inequality, and contemporary sexist practice. For most of human history we have not so much reflected as deflected on women. They have been invisible, well documented in the "herstory" accounts. Power is in the hands of those who interpret. The pen has done more violence than many swords. Until recently, men have been privileged to wield both.

Patriarchy, Hegemony, and Feminism

Patriarchy is a male-dominated system of power, privilege, and prestige justified by sexist ideology. Patriarchy can range from cultures in which it is less severe (though still extensive) such as in the United States, to cultures in which everyday life is a form of terroristic misogyny, such as it was in Afghanistan under the Taliban. When the norms, values, beliefs, institutions, discourses, social practices, relations, and arrangements, that is to say, when most aspects of everyday life are enveloped in a ruling-class culture that is seen as "natural,"—accepted by the oppressors and the oppressed alike as the way life is and should always be—then one is living under the condition of hegemony.[2] In a hegemonic culture, dominant ways of life support a system in which alternatives—to most members of society—are inconceivable. Ruling-class practices are seen as "human nature," "natural," "normal," "given," "commonsensical," "right," "innate," "inevitable," "eternal," "biological," "God-given," and inviolate. The sociological tenet that behavior, beliefs, and arrangements are socially constructed, maintained, and altered is indiscernible. It is the pervasiveness, permeation, penetration, and persuasiveness of ruling-class ways of life and ideas woven into the social fabric of society and the behavior and beliefs of its members that constitutes hegemony. Hegemony is thus part of the subjectification process, a way of socializing people to become subjects with a particular mentality or consciousness, a devised way to interpret and understand (and therefore behave in) the world. Language structures consciousness (the Sapir-Whorf hypothesis) so that what we have no name for we cannot see or come to know; in contrast, what is meaningful to us, we may devise many names for, making fine distinctions. If the ruling class provides our language, that is, our concepts, theories, and interpretations, then it supplies the structure of our consciousness. Since the way to "see" the world is through ruling-class eyes, hegemony impairs critical consciousness and social transformation. Hegemony is a process that operates as though all agents of socialization seek as their "hidden curriculum" the "universalization of ruling-class interests." Social control is achieved through the manufacture of consent; that is to say, through internalizing and identifying with ruling-class ways of thinking, being, and doing, society's members come to believe that the system is legitimate; moreover, coercion is thereby obviated. The downtrodden may not only have allegiance to such a system but also may even staunchly defend a system that causes their own misery and alienation—a condition known as false consciousness. Hegemony is analogous to a Clingon cloaking device: it renders the colonizers (of the mind, in this case) invisible. Hegemony thus contributes to the social reproduction of power, privilege, and prestige by eclipsing transformative interpretations and practices, namely, equality.

However, hegemony—an oppressor's dream and an oppressed's nightmare—is a situation that is never totally achievable. The notion that the cultural and institutional order are drenched in ruling-class discourses and practices, that social life is always already patterned with no exit or no escape, flies in the face of ongoing reform and revolution everywhere. Gramsci (1971) realized that the oppressed can form counterhegemony, revolutionary discourses, and practices. Feminism is a paradigm example. As Marx first enlightened, struggle is as much about subjectivity as it is about stratification; revolution is as much about reification as it is about repression. While ruling-class practices are certainly privileged, they are not eternal. New forms of subjectivity, of consciousness, are ongoing. Additionally, the meaning of any object depends on how people define and interpret it, and in today's postmodern society, interpretations are endless. People are never passive to the ideas and social practices of a ruling class. Foucault (1979) cautions that wherever there is power there is resistance. Ruling-class practices and ideas are contested at every turn. "When Eve span and Adam delved, who was then the gentleman," sang the English peasants who revolted in 1381. Slaves sabotage their instruments, mock their masters, and escape their captors—even rising up like Spartacus to kill those who shackle them. Minions are mischievous, students rebellious, children disobedient, and every dog has his day. Every social policy ever proposed runs smack into a Mack truck of opposition, an anvil chorus of nay sayers. Recalcitrance (even wildness, at times) rules the day. Life is rife with conflict. Actors possess agency and can penetrate through dominant interpretations with ideas of their own, ideas that engender a reconstructed consciousness and, it is hoped, structural transformation. Structures of interpretation and thought, and the social practices they support, are never so entrenched, embedded, or eternal that they cannot be unmasked and thereby overcome. The subjugated make history. In fact, everyday life—the feminist movement itself—exemplifies the ongoing process of social transformation. Feminism has furnished a language to reconstruct consciousness (deconstructing notions of masculinity and femininity grounded in biological determinism and the myth of the vaginal orgasm, for example) and a praxis to transform sexist social practices so that patriarchy (in the West, at least) is contested (though resistance, backlash, and new ways that science can sidle up to sexism can arise). As Jean-Paul Sartre stated, existence precedes essence. There is no essential male or female, no essential masculinity or femininity, no maternal instinct, no testosterone-driven aggressiveness sans culture. Masculinity and femininity are clay in the culture's hands. Whatever our world has been, is, or will be, we are the makers of it. Social life is a process between structure and agency. Structures not only oppress—like the Rolls Royce limousine in the opening scene in Mel Brooks's *Life Stinks* that sprays gutter water on the homeless—they also awaken with anger. A plaque placed on the Titanic at the bottom of the ocean warns that unless we are ever vigilant the unthinkable can happen; likewise, resistance to repression by everyday human beings worldwide can make the unthinkable (equality) happen. It is in our hands. Let us look at some structural dimensions first.

The inequality of women is currently a cultural universal. In the United States, women who work full-time all year long still earn only 75 percent as much as men do (Wright and Jacobs 1994, 511). Women are not only financially disadvantaged compared to men, but, in addition, bear the brunt of poverty. The gender/poverty ratio was 1.30 in 1991, "which means that women were 30 percent more likely to be poor than men" (Casper, Garfinkel, and McLanahan 1994, 594). The phrase "the feminization of poverty" characterizes the discrete social worlds that men and women live in. The political system has had until very recently almost no representation from women. "At the current rate of increase at which women are being elected, we will have parity with men in a short 342 years" (Wolf 1994, 14).

Androcentric cultures have authorized a gendered division of labor. For millennia women were confined to the private sphere of domesticity: childbearing, childrearing,[3] housecleaning, and nurturing. Then moving forward with glacier speed, women entered the public sphere where they were relegated to jobs from which most men would flee as though from the plague, the "pink-collar ghetto." When women entered the competitive, professional world, they either had to abandon reproduction or were chastised for leaving their children at home. Only recently has criticism subsided against women who want a professional career and children. If women choose both, they will be stifled in their career by trying to fulfill two roles, since the "second shift" at home dissipates the energy necessary for a high-powered career. Men have not shifted gears to enter the domestic sphere in any significant degree. Still, so many women pursue the children/career option that the phrase "the Mommy track" has been penned to typify it. The Mommy track means a near-nil chance at climbing the rungs of the corporate ladder. Even without children, advancing to the CEO position is so rare that it is as though the corporate world had sanctioned Salic law, the ancient Frankish proscription forbidding women to inherit land. The dearth of opportunities for women near though not at the top has coined the proverbial metaphor of the "glass ceiling," one can see the top but not enter it. When women do enter fields dominated by men, the men leave: "male flight." A number of studies have reported that the feminization of occupations has led to a deterioration in the status and earnings of those occupations. There is a debate as to whether the profession was in decline in status and earnings before women entered or that women entered, prompting management to lower wages. In any event, a sex-segregated occupation, dominated by males, becomes resegregated, dominated by females (Wright and Jacobs 1994). Status and wages drop through the floor. If the occupation is not resegregated, a gender realignment leads to internal stratification, where men have higher-level jobs and women lower-level ones, a process of ghettoization (Wright and Jacobs 1994). Also, empirical evidence supports the conclusion that "the more women in an occupation, the less both its male and female workers earn" (Marger 1999, 310). Additionally, "women are underrepresented in power positions even in fields that they numerically dominate, like nursing and librarianship" (315).

The history of some of the greatest cases of the U.S. Supreme Court has centered on issues of sexual discrimination.[4] To name only a few: *Minor v.*

Happersett (1875) was a case involving Virginia Minor, president of the Missouri Woman Suffrage Association, who was denied the right to vote because she was a woman. Women's suffrage was not settled until 1920 with the passage of the Nineteenth Amendment to the U.S. Constitution. Job bias was the issue in the 1971 case of *Phillips v. Martin Marietta Corporation*. Ida Phillips was denied a job at Martin Marietta because she had preschool children, an explicit policy of the corporation. The corporation had hired men with preschool children. The *Frontiero v. Richardson* (1973) case involved Susan Frontiero, who was a lieutenant in the U.S. Air Force with a dependent husband. The air force had argued that only men could have dependents (a stereotype?) and so did not give Lieutenant Frontiero any dependent allowance. She sued, citing sexual discrimination. One of the latest, *Rotary International v. Rotary Club of Duarte* (1987), involved the case of a local rotary club admitting three female members, which went against the policy of Rotary International. The International kicked the local Rotary out. Were women being treated as second-class citizens? These are just a smattering of some of the cases involving sex discrimination issues that have come before the highest court in the land. How would you have decided them?

Defiance, contempt, and slight regard for culture, roles, laws, practices, and institutions deemed patriarchal and injurious has been center stage in feminist theory[5] for the past three decades. The feminist revolution has been televised. It has thoroughly transformed gender identity, the family, the workplace, and the culture. In politics, corporations, and education, change (though too slow) is ongoing so that "the place of women in American society is decidedly different from what it was just a short time ago" (Marger 1999, 316; see also 316-22). Changes are still being, and still need to be, wrought.

The history and contemporary manifestation of structural and institutional gender inequality has only been briefly explored here. This chapter centers on how men and women come to be, how their being in the world is developed and reproduced. Scholarship is ablaze as to how much men and women—qua being—are essentially categories, variations, or a mold. Scholarship about sex and gender has had a history of those who maximize differences and those who minimize them.[6] Ideology has muddied both absolutist approaches. But men and women being in the world is, as yet, particular. Culture enforces (though less and less) gender scripts. Gender scripts are defined and negotiated. No human is a robot to the gender scripts of his or her society. Every status or position in society has embedded within it certain cultural expectations about appropriate behavior for that status. Sociologists define this expected behavior as roles. There are gender roles that men and women are socialized, that is, expected, to play. But that is only half the story. Humans also engage in role making, they not only socially reproduce their culture but, in addition, create new culture in the process of daily interaction. Socialization is not solely passive; all humans take an active part in their own socialization. Agency, negotiation, collective action, and role making (the case of gender bending, for example) transform our culture, make social history. Scholarship will continue to scrutinize what is contributed to our behavior by biology, culture, socialization, and structure and agency. We now note the disreputable beginnings of research on sex and gender.

Difference Maximizers

Early research attempted to establish innate and immutable psychological and behavioral differences between the sexes, labeling one, male, as superior and the other, female, as inferior. This history is similar to attempts to concoct differences of biological and cultural superiority among classes and races, the ideological justification of inequality, exploitation, and oppression. The history of this specious academic theorizing has been unmasked as scientific racism.

Janet Shibley Hyde (1990) has provided a history of sexual inferiority research, such as the measurement of cranial capacities to detect female intelligence by phrenologists and neuroanatomists. During the 1880s, for example, arguments were advanced that the brains of females and males were different, "that females had smaller heads and smaller brains than males, that brain size was a direct indication of intelligence, and that women must therefore be less intelligent than men" (1990, 56). Let us look as just one shining example of this early "research," a statement by Gustave Le Bon.

> In the most intelligent races, as among the Parisians, there are a large number of women whose brains are closer in size to those of gorillas than to the most developed male brains. This inferiority is so obvious that no one can contest it for a moment; only its degree is worth discussion. All psychologists who have studied the intelligence of women, as well as poets and novelists, recognize today that they represent the most inferior forms of human evolution and that they are closer to children and savages than to an adult civilized man. They excel in fickleness, inconstancy, absence of thought and logic, and incapacity to reason. Without doubt there exist some distinguished women very superior to the average man, but they are as exceptional as the birth of any monstrosity, as, for example, of a gorilla with two heads; consequently we may neglect them entirely. (Le Bon 1879, 60-61, quoted in Gould 1981, 104-5)

Unbelievable! Well, believe it. To be sure, Gustave Le Bon's pronouncement is a candidate for a social theory version of Ripley's *Believe It or Not*. Unfortunately, such pontifications could be found ad nauseam from the history of social thought. As Stephen J. Gould's research proves (1981), such absurdities were scientific gospel, especially in the strange careers of craniometry and phrenology.

Lewis Terman, who first tried but eventually failed to find biological differences in intelligence between blacks and whites, did not believe that there were biological differences in intelligence between the sexes (Hyde 1990, 58).

From the 1930s, with the development of L. L. Thurstone's Primary Mental Abilities test, there emerged the field of differential psychology. Since then, there has been a focus on sexual differences in verbal, mathematical, and spacial ability (1990, 58). What possesses these researchers to seek difference and define whatever the difference is that females have, if any, as inferior? There is no need to belabor the point that the belief in biological inferiority dies hard. I shall rest my case with Dr. David Reuben's comments on the biological deterioration of women after menopause.

> The vagina begins to shrivel, the breasts atrophy, sexual desire disappears. . . . Increased facial hair, deepening voice, obesity. . . . Coarsened features, enlargement of the clitoris, and gradual baldness complete the tragic picture. Not really a man but no longer a functional woman, these individuals live in the world of intersex. (Reuben 1969, 292, quoted in Fausto-Sterling 1992, 110-11)

Difference Minimizers

Since the early 1980s, there has been prolific research that reevaluates these long-standing and accepted genetic and/or psychological differences. Hyde (1990, 61-63) summarized this literature, concluding that post-1980 research has now found no difference in verbal ability, that differences in cognitive ability are not large, and that the largest differences are in one type of spacial ability, mental rotation. No doubt research will continue to try to prove or disprove genetic sexual differences. But one avenue of research is clear, the socialization concept (especially for interactionists) is the primary research focus to understand and explain behavior.

From Sex to Gender

In the past twenty years sociological terminology has undergone a change. The term *sex roles* previously described behaviors men and women displayed due to familial and cultural socialization. That term is today reserved for behaviors exclusively biological: menstruation, pregnancy, lactation, erection, and seminal ejaculation (Lipman-Blumen 1984, 2).

Gender now describes the social construction of masculine and feminine behavior produced through socialization to our culture and its major institutions of family, education, and media. All masculine and feminine behavior not due to biology is now deemed due to the normative expectations that every society instills in men and women, that is, prescriptions and proscriptions on how they should act.

Sandra Lipsitz Bem (1983) has summarized a new account of sex typing, the process through which one develops masculine or feminine behavior. Three major theories on sex typing, psychoanalytic, social learning theory, and cognitive-development theory, have been dominant. Gender schema theory, a new model, has aspects of both cognitive developmental theory and social learning theory (Bem 1983, 603). It is also compatible with tenets of symbolic interactionism.

Gender schema theory argues that the child is active in learning cultural conceptions of masculinity and femininity. "A schema is a cognitive structure, a network of associations that organizes and guides an individual's perception" (603). Sex is a fundamental category of perception, as is race and social class. Sex as a cognitive structure, or any schema, allows one to encode incoming stimuli. It helps one define the situation, to attribute meaning to events and objects. A gender scheme is one that encodes information or stimuli as gender specific. Gender schema theory supports SI's contention that the world is composed of social objects, that through perception one constructs a world embedded in subjectivity (604).

Sex typing is derivative of gender-schematic processing (604). We define objects and events as masculine or feminine. "As children learn the contents of their society's gender schema, they learn which attributes are to be linked with their own sex and, hence, with themselves" (604). Many attributes are out there, for example, strong/weak, rational/emotional, but the child self-selects ones appropriate for her or his sex. Through this process "children's self-concepts become sex-typed [and they perceive themselves to be] not only different in degree but different in kind" (604). According to Bem, children's self-esteem is grounded on how well they perceive themselves as matching the culture's gender schema (605).

Thus a gender schema functions as social control, for children recognize—cognitively process—attributes, behaviors, and objects as masculine or feminine and internalize/encode this information leading to culturally "appropriate" behavior. This whole process reproduces the prevailing gender schema (605). As long as the sexual division of labor remains culturally important in the socialization process, a belief that there are distinct masculine and feminine attributes will be reproduced, that is, stereotypes and sex typing will remain.

Nurturing has long been thought of as a behavior that women are biologically predisposed to, a behavior men are biologically incapable of or unsuited for. Rationality was a behavior that men were deemed to possess and that women were judged as biologically incapable of achieving. But today, most educated people understand that such behaviors were not the result of biological determinism—that "anatomy is destiny," to use Freud's phrase—but the outcome of socialization to cultural expectations of what is masculine and feminine behavior. Such notions about masculine and feminine behavior were never true in practice. Men have always been capable of irrationality and nurturance just as women have been capable of rationality and detachment.

Gender and Cross-Cultural Research

Gender is a historical construction. There are also class, racial, and cross-cultural variations in masculine and feminine behavior. What is normative in one culture, class, racial or ethnic group, or historical period may be deviant in another. Cultural expectations are continually changing.

Nancy Chodorow (1971), summarizing the conclusions of culture and personality theorists, notes that they argue "that there are no absolute personality differences between men and women" (173). There are regularities, however. In both primitive and advanced societies "girls seem to have an easier time of learning their adult role," though it is more complicated in advanced societies (182).

In contemporary Western society, the socialization process is fraught with conflict, centering on issues of being and doing. Chodorow concludes from her cross-cultural research on socialization that girls and women "are" while boys and men "do." For example, Karen Horney (quoted in Chodorow 1971, 182; emphasis in the original) states that

> the man is actually obliged to go on proving his manhood to the woman. There is no analogous necessity for her: even if she is frigid, she can engage in sexual intercourse and conceive and bear a child. She performs her part by merely *being*, without any *doing*. The man on the other hand has to *do* something in order to fulfill himself.

To support the being versus doing dichotomy, Chodorow (1971, 183) adduces Parsons's comments on female and male socialization, who suggested men must be successful, get promoted, and be providers. Simone de Beauvior, Bruno Bettelheim, and Margaret Mead are also cited as providing arguments that there has existed a long-standing belief that male identity centers on doing, while female identity revolves around being.

But Chodorow illuminates that women have always been doing, but that their doing has perpetually been undervalued. For example, Chodorow summarizes researchers who have studied power and inequality on the kibbutz. Women work as nurses, teachers, clean buildings and bathrooms, wash and repair clothing, and take care of sick children and the elderly. Yet their power, status, and privileges are far from equal. "Although they work harder and longer than most men in order to 'prove' themselves and their worth, the men continue to find it necessary not to recognize the value of her work or to accord women equal status" (185). On the kibbutz, as in society generally, what men do is seen as more important than what women do, and consequently, status and privilege accrue to those doing the "important" work, whatever that may be, which is usually what men are doing. For example, in Western society, men are largely physicians and that position is accorded high status. In Russia women are physicians and the occupation there has low status.

Chodorow (1971) reports that cross-culturally, the socialization of boys is less flexible than it is for girls. Boys cannot wear dresses, cook, or play with dolls, whereas girls can be tomboys, wear jeans, climb trees, play sports, and wear men's clothing (186). She cites many other examples. Cross-culture research also supports the argument that men's roles, or masculine identity, is more highly valued. Girls report that they would prefer male roles and occupations traditionally considered masculine. Boys do not favor traditional feminine careers (186-87). Cultures generally praise male activities and devalue female ones. Or, as has been pointed out in the case of physicians, cultures value whatever it is that men are doing, though if women are doing it, it is devalued.

One result is that female socialization, especially for Western societies, is not so straightforward. Women are socialized for two roles, one for traditional childbearing, childrearing, and housekeeping duties with the concomitant feminine behavior of passivity, compliance, and nurturance. Yet, in school they are taught to achieve and strive for success (190). Female socialization is fraught with conflicts, ambiguity, and ambivalence. "Should I pursue traditional devalued activities or a nontraditional valued one?" We know that as girls mature their former tom boy activities are frowned upon and they become "less successful in school and drop out of the role of equal participant in activities that they once held" (193). Research literature, as well as popular autobiographical accounts, is abundant with the status degradation ceremonies that women face when entering nontraditional careers. Interactionists have researched these issues through participant observation. We examine such research shortly.

A strong argument against biological determinism has also been made by Gilmore (1990). After reviewing the cross-cultural concept of masculinity, he argues that gender is a cultural construction. There may be consistency, even a preponderance, in cross-cultural ideologies of masculinity, but there is no universality. Invariant behavior within the species is necessary to prove biologically determined behavior. There are notable exceptions in masculine behavior in many societies, supporting the cultural constructionist view.

What is the recurring concept of masculinity deduced from Gilmore's cross-cultural research? A general image, or ideology, of masculinity centers on man as an impregnator, protector, and provider (223). Gilmore argues that this social and cultural construction of masculinity, or a "manhood ideology," is functional. Men, internalizing the masculine ideology, ensure that society adapts to its social environment. According to Gilmore, one function of manhood ideologies is to prevent or diminish regression, "the tendency to return to prior states of development, to evade reality" (228). Productivity, achievement, and performance, resonating through most cultures surveyed, is the hallmark of a "true" man.

But Gilmore's argument ignores the contribution of females to productivity, provision, protection, procreation, and societal adaptation. Gilmore's work can be faulted for implying that it is solely men who offer these contributions. Before industrialization, Thio argues, women were always economic providers.

On the farms of colonial America, men, women, and children helped produce the family's livelihood. The wife was typically an essential economic partner to the husband. If her husband was a farmer, she would run the household, make the clothes, raise cows, pigs, and poultry, tend a garden, and sell milk, vegetables, chickens, and eggs. If the husband was a skilled craftsman, she would work with him. Thus weavers' wives spun yarn, cutlers' wives polished metal, tailors' wives sewed buttonholes, and shoemakers' wives waxed shoes. It was after industrialization had been in full swing that women lost their status as their husbands' economic partners and acquired a subordinate status as housewives. (1991, 224)

It was not just during the agricultural period that women equally shared in production. As anthropologist McBroom (1992, 50) states: "Such a division of labor between woman the nurturer and man the provider is not typical of primitive cultures, where women supply a high degree of material income." Status loss was accompanied by a transmogrification of women's role.

Women's family role became centered on child care and taking care of men. This role involved more than physical labor. It was relational and personal and, in the case of both children and men, maternal. As women's mothering became less entwined with their other ongoing work, it also became more isolated and exclusive. (50)

And a change to an inferior role necessitated a gender ideology to justify it. "A 'cult of femininity' arose to justify female subordination on the grounds that women were naturally passive, nonaggressive, and nurturant, with no head for business" (50).

Gilmore deserves credit for revealing that men and masculinity are not the same everywhere. There are androgynous cultures for example, and his research suggests that culture far outweighs biology in influencing behavior. This has always been the SI position. To acquaint ourselves with the cultural variation in the masculinity concept, I explore some cultural conceptions of masculinity that are absent the typical machismo orientation displayed in many Western cultures.

Gilmore (1990, 201-19), relying on others' ethnographies, portrayed two peoples, the Tahiti of French Polynesia and the Semai of Malaysia, to contravene arguments of a universal cultural conception of masculinity, and by extension, biological determinism.

In Tahiti there is a lack of sexual differentiation and role playing; women have high status, occupational diversity, possess power, and participate in sports. Men cook, clean house, dance with other men, and are not compelled to prove their manliness.

Tahitian language is gender neutral, pronouns do not signify the sex of subjects or objects. Machismo is notably absent, that is, there is no obsession with protecting women or fighting foreigners. Possessiveness, or treating women as property, is unheard of. Cultural norms that induce men to strut, perform, or achieve material success, are lacking. Men have no male honor to defend, are passive, ignore insults, and are not vengeful. Gilmore concludes that, for Tahitians, masculinity/femininity are not separate concepts. The Tahitians are androgynous in behavior.

The Semai men are nonviolent, even nonaggressive. "The Semai believe that to resist advances from another person, sexual or otherwise, is equivalent to an aggression against that person" (Gilmore 1990, 211). Men and women are noncompetitive, yielding, and not possessive. "Semai men do not worry about honor, paternity, or social boundaries" (212). Sporting events or contests are absent, children are not disciplined, and property, or ownership, is an unknown concept or practice. "The sexual division of labor is preferential, not prescriptive or proscriptive" (216).

In both societies, men do not have to "prove themselves by taking risks," natural resources are plentiful, and external threats are absent or run away from. In fact, Gilmore concludes with a materialist argument, that the natural conditions of sufficiency are the prime variables in explaining the cultural variation.

Emancipation from the confinements of gender is embraced in the notion that behavior is changeable and that we can socialize our children to a horizon of behavior not available to most in past generations (because of the belief in biological determinism and cultural prescriptions and proscriptions). People are also capable of changing their selves, who they are and what they want to be and do. This is a fundamental SI tenet. To be sure, social constraints such as power, vested interests, disadvantages, and discrimination fetter us from becoming all that we might. But the recent sociological concept of gender will certainly provide men and women with arguments and options unavailable in the past.

Power, Gender, and the Sex-Gender System

Choice is a possibility, but vitiating choice is what Lipman-Blumen terms the "sex-gender system." Power is the essence of the sex-gender system. Men possess privilege, prestige, and satisfaction, and are "reluctant to relinquish" them (Lipman-Blumen 1990, 4). When a group, such as men, exclusively possess that which is privileged and prestigious, a power struggle will ensue once those oppressed try to change the balance of power.

Before we examine more closely how boys and girls are made and make themselves into a gender, it will prove insightful to review why power is embedded in the sex-gender system. Since Weber, power has been conventionally defined as the ability of a person, class, or organization to carry out its will and control the behavior of others despite resistance. This ability is based on ownership or control over resources, such as the means of production, means of administration, the means of communication, and, for women in particular, the means of reproduction. Power is also based on status and party. Power is legitimated by authority and is backed up by subtle coercion and, if necessary, savage force. If one has the goal of possessing positions of prestige and privilege, then one had better possess power as well, for, to be sure, there will be resistance by the disadvantaged and nonprivileged aware of the disparity. In this case, women who have attained gender consciousness of inequality can struggle to enlighten others and sound the clarion call for equality.

Padavic (1991) reports participant observation research that demonstrates how power reconstitutes gender in daily interaction within a hostile social context, the all-male, blue-collar work world. Gender is a process of negotiation, but inter-actants do not negotiate from equal positions; that is, men have more resources than women on the basis of historical and institutionalized positions of privilege. Work cultures that affirm masculinity provide another social constraint impeding women's integration into nontraditional jobs (Padavic 1991, 280). The symbolic production of masculinity and reified notions of what constitutes femininity are tenaciously guarded by men, since they both provide the only self-esteem enhancing, psychic rewards men receive from jobs that produce alienation. Men's belief that they are masculine doing masculine work that only "real men" can do—a self-defining though self-deluding label of superiority—allows them to define a situation of oppression (their job) as one of privilege.

Padavic's research was conducted at a coal power plant. At the plant, male bonding and masculinity production are accomplished through rituals of buying food and denigrating women through jokes, put-downs, and humiliating portrayals of nude women. Padavic chronicles the torments that men put women through when Padavic enters a previously all-male preserve, the blue-collar social world: teasing, pushing, being tossed back and forth in the air among workers, threats of bodily harm, and paternalism.

This treatment to assert dominance produced self-fulfilling notions of femininity. Padavic, to disprove stereotypes, acted in a way that created safety hazards, but more significant, the harassment created doubts in her mind as to whether she could perform the job. Through this treatment a "gender ideology" and stereotypical gender behavior are re-created. Traditional femininity was reconstituted in Padavic by men because they, as a group, were in a position of power to do so. When another female arrived who was physically and behaviorally opposite the feminine stereotype, she posed an immediate threat to masculinity. Since she did not affirm their notions of femininity, she was ignored, never helped, and despised.

Other SI scholars working in this tradition are Richardson (1986, 1988), who has researched the way a patriarchal society reproduces gender inequality even in extramarital affairs; Martin (1978), who has shown that in pursuing a job as a police officer women are relegated to a subordinate status and excluded from the mentoring process; Hammond (1980), who demonstrated that women medical students endure an unrelieved status-degradation ceremony; West (1984), who revealed that even a pinnacle status, such as physician, is no counter to the master status of gender, for women physicians are easily interrupted by their patients, as opposed to men; and Wolf (1986), who theorized how a culture of inferiority is internalized by women (and minorities and the poor) through the everyday process of role-taking from a patriarchal, racist, and classist generalized other. Women, having internalized the cultural myth of inferiority, socially reproduce gender ideology through false-conscious attitudes and behavior.

Steinem (1993) has told the story of how she was obstructed from doing her job as a journalist when she was refused access to interview her subject because the meeting was in a lounge. Those were the days when elite lounges were male-only bastions. "I was humiliated: Did I look like a prostitute? Was my trench coat too battered—or not battered enough?" (Steinem 1993, 23). The effect of such treatment in general, and in the particular cases above, is the destruction of self-esteem. It is damaged through the culture's unrelieved assault on females and everything that smacks of femininity. Steinem (53) reiterates a long-standing injustice: the structural condition of women is analogous to a Third World country: "low on capital, low on technology, and labor-intensive." The result is the internalization of inferiority. "The truth was that I had internalized society's unserious estimate of all that was female—including myself" (25).

For both men and women the socialization process leaves scars. Men are left with an unclear, unsure sexual identity. They must constantly prove their worth as providers. Insecurity is an incessant push push push toward success. Women are left with a devalued identity, a feeling of being left out of activities they might prefer to pursue. Women may internalize the ideology and image of inferiority (so pervasive in our media), resign themselves to a devalued occupation, or play the helper role to their husband's career. If they follow the nontraditional path, they will encounter hostility and opposition; though as many pursue this path, such hostility and opposition declines. Overcoming the toxic internalization of inferiority, from abusive parents to the venomous hierarchies of patriarchy, race, and class, is a process Steinem calls the "revolution from within." It is the recapture of self-esteem by the liberating power of seeing through one's own eyes, defining oneself, of not being interpreted, mentally colonized, and labeled by a misogynous culture, the male gaze, or an ideology masquerading as science. Gender imprisons. Procrustean beds never have been pretty sights.

Men and women engage in behavior that appears to be biologically determined solely because men and women, beginning from the cradle, are socialized to behave differently. The tendency to obscure this sociological insight induces us to define social behavior as biologically based. Innumerable cases abound where men are not rational or women nurturant to refute the argument that such behavior is a function of biology; though, there are ideological reasons why those in power would want women to believe that such is the case. An ever-changing and changeable pattern of socialization is the key to why men and women, and boys and girls, act as they do.

Becoming Boys and Girls: Family Socialization

It is now well known that the process of gender socialization begins at birth. Boys are wrapped in a blue blanket, girls in a pink one. Girls are socialized to play with dolls and cooking utensils, boys are socialized to construct buildings, use tools, and play with guns (Lindsey 1990, 36). The process of gender socialization affects behavior in all aspects of life, the "workplace, leisure activities, dress, possessions, language, demeanor, reading material, college major, and even degree of sexual experience and pleasure" (37).

The characteristics of children influence childhood socialization. Downey, Jackson, and Powell (1994, 36-46) have found that the sex composition of children affects how mothers socialize their children. Mothers will allow girls to do more gender-atypical domestic chores when there are no boys. The same holds true for sons in families with no daughters. Families with more sons than daughters are less likely to have mothers participate in the labor force, especially with preschool-age children. Downey, Jackson, and Powell suggest two reasons for this. One, parents the world over have expressed a preference for male children. "If sons are valued more than daughters, parents with more sons than daughters may consider it more crucial to provide personal care for their children rather than risk non-parental childcare" (Downey, Jackson, and Powell 1994, 37). Their second reason is that boys have more disciplinary problems and therefore obedience becomes an issue. Apparently, mothers reason that they can better discipline their sons and enforce obedience if they remain at home. Thus familial views on parenting are an emergent of the family situation—the actual experience of parenting—which is affected, in this case, by the structure of sex composition. Socialization is not determined but open to the characteristics of the family, that is, it is interactive. The characteristics of children help shape how their parents socialize them, providing us with an excellent example of the dialectical interplay between structure and agency in the emergence of behavior.

Lindsey (1990, 39) reports research that lacking a father at home during the years of primary socialization leads boys to learn masculinity by being told what they should not do, rather than what they should. Boys should not cry or act like sissies. The uncertain or vague notion of what a boy should do induces him to view and adopt stereotypical images of masculinity.

Interactionists argue that people actively participate in their own socialization process. Participation quickens with the emergence of gender identity. By the age of three, children begin to identify themselves as a boy or girl, to apply those labels to themselves, to select behavior appropriate with the label, and to make an emotional investment in that label or identity. Behavior organizes around gender identity (41). The most important socializing influence early on, of how traditional or liberating gender images are presented and enforced, is one's parents and family. SI states that people respond to social objects on the basis of the meaning that they have for them. Boys and girls mean different things to their parents; they are perceived differently. Lindsey (1990, 43) reports that sex typing of one's children begins immediately. "Parents are likely to describe sons as strong, firm, and alert, and daughters as delicate, soft, and awkward" (43). She goes on to describe research in which the social world of a girl is constructed differently from the social world of a boy: room decoration, toy selection, type of play between parents and child, boundaries on where to play, and type of play and games permitted (43-45).

At home, another powerful agent of socialization is television. Television socializes boys and girls with images and models of behavior that are "gender stereotyped" (52). This occurs not only in television shows where traditional gender roles are portrayed but also "commercials are blatant in creating desires for toys encouraging domesticity in girls and activity in boys" (53). Research has shown that the more children watch television the greater their gender stereotypes (232). We know that women are entering the workforce in increasing percentages, abandoning pink-collar jobs for professional ones, so that the notion of women solely interested in domesticity is distortive and a maladaptive image for both men and women.

Media Socialization

Certainly the media can socialize women to priorities other than domesticity. Lindsey (1990, 237-38) reports on research that studied 1940s images of women in the media when the war effort was in full swing. Screen images of women encouraged self-confidence, strength, ambition, independence, initiative, and competence symbolized by Rosie the Riveter. But "by the 1950s films reaffirmed the domestic subservience of women" (237). For example, even today, both print and broadcast advertisements are especially restrictive and traditional in their portrayal of who is responsible for a clean house. Household products are sold to women who are portrayed in the home, cleaning floors, kitchens, and talking to little men in toilet bowls.

Men are also depicted in stereotypical roles: breadwinners, cheating on their wives, incompetent with household cleaning machines or products, and inept at cooking or taking care of an infant. The positive stereotype is a man who is active, mature, competitive, successful, holding a prestigious job, wealthy, a fighter protecting country and family, virile, and, increasingly, as a sex object themselves (247-49).

Sex stereotyping has not gone away. Belknap and Leonard's 1991 study of sex stereotyping in commercial advertisements found that it is still pervasive. These researchers used expert opinion to select seven magazines that would represent modernism and traditionalism. They then content analyzed over 1,000 advertisements from *Good Housekeeping*, *Sports Illustrated*, *Time*, *Gentlemen's Quarterly*, and *Rolling Stone*, to replicate Erving Goffman's work on gender advertisements. They found "the portrayal of women was conventional, traditional, and stereotypical" (Belknap and Leonard 1991, 116). Social change is slow.

Media moguls, the captains of conscience, through cultural domination socialize us to define selective images as meaningful, that boys should be aggressive and that women should be passive. Children are especially vulnerable to this. Television is a powerful medium that provides symbols, referents, values, beliefs—norms in general that socialize. Corporate advertising campaigns shape thought, feeling, and behavior so that children, for example, demand gender-stereotypical toys. Even parents who may want to raise their children in a non-sexist atmosphere feel trapped as television usurps a place in the family. Television is a sort of cultural imperialism colonizing children with tantalizing images. Unless the tube is unplugged or regulated by parents, or children are taught the unreality of television and its commercial profferings, parents do not stand much of a chance in overriding its influence.

Hollywood has shown women which way madness lies. Susan Faludi (1991, 113) has impressively documented the themes Hollywood now propagates: "women were unhappy because they were too free; their liberation had denied them marriage and motherhood." Career women, those contemporary Regans and Gonerils, were driving husbands, but especially themselves, mad. Perhaps the most popular avatar of the woman driven mad due to no child or husband was the antagonist Alex Forrest in *Fatal Attraction*.

Faludi (1991, 129) illustrates how the "incompatibility of career and personal happiness" theme has inundated movies of the 1980s; movies such as *Baby Boom* and *Crossing Delancey*. Or that women who have babies are honored in such films as *Parenthood*, while "women who resist baby fever, by controlling their fertility or postponing their motherhood, are shamed and penalized" in films such as *Immediate Family* and *Another Woman* (132-33). Career women are simply demonized in such films as *Three Men and a Baby* and *Three Men and a Little Lady*, or they are brilliant but easily cozened in a film such as *House of Cards*.

Popular music is also extremely influential in socializing children, especially teenagers. Rock 'n' roll may be on the cutting edge, but it is far from portraying positive images of women. In fact, one can readily observe by watching MTV that rock music is reactionary and dangerous to women. Videos portray women, through lyrics and images, as sex objects, bimbos, or floozies, and open to violence and rape. One does not need to belabor the point that in rap music women are relegated to the status of bitches and whores by artists who have been so violently oppressed in our culture that their obliviousness to reproducing it is appalling.

School Socialization

Becoming socialized to masculine and feminine behavior is not limited to instruction from one's parents or television. Schools transmit children's secondary socialization to gender. Barrie Thorne (1989, 74) has researched the sex segregation practiced in elementary schools. Classrooms, the cafeteria, lines, and playgrounds have "gendered turfs." This creates two distinct social worlds.

Thorne, summarizing other research on the topic, contrasts the distinctiveness of these two worlds. The boys' social world was described as larger, involving age-heterogeneous groups, rough-and-tumble play, physical fighting, organized sports, direct confrontation and contests. Girls' social worlds have been less researched, but revolve around interaction in smaller groups, friendship pairs, cooperative and turn-taking behavior, telling secrets, and indirect expression of disagreement.

But like all aggregate summaries, Thorne notes the distortion in the two-world model. There is individual variation, some boys and girls display characteristics typical of their opposite gender. With classic sociological insight, Thorne critiques the two-world model for abstractions that separate characteristics from social contexts.

The danger in the abstraction is that we might "assume that males and females are qualitatively and permanently different" (74). Sex segregation exists, but boys and girls do play and work together. Knowing that they can is crucial for childhood socialization. If we believe girls and boys are qualitatively and permanently different, this can lead to discriminating socialization, reinforcing patterns of segregation rather than integration. For example, Thorne (1989, 76) notes that teachers "police gender boundaries" and aides "shooed children" away from places they thought exclusively girls' or boys' territory.

The question for Thorne is what social context and interaction processes bring boys and girls together, or keep them apart. The interaction between boys and girls in elementary schools is Thorne's focus of context and process. She conceptualizes the notion of "borderwork" as a form of "cross-sex interaction [which is] based upon and reaffirms boundaries and asymmetries between girls' and boys' groups" (76). Borderwork is interaction that nevertheless strengthens gender solidarity.

Thorne's research (76-79) discusses classroom and playground contexts that constitute competition, cross-sex chasing that affirms boundaries, rituals of pollution that label one gender as contaminated, and invasions that disrupt play and antagonize. These contexts (structures) and interactions fortify gender solidarity and inequality. The boys' playing field is up to ten times larger, boys invade girls' games much more than girls invade boys' games, and girls are more often labeled contaminating. Teasing rituals discourage boy-girl friendships and boys or girls participating in gender-typed games of the opposite sex. Socially controlled separateness is established early.

Boundaried interaction may be dominant but not ubiquitous. Thorne's research depicts "relaxed cross-sex interactions" that reduce gender solidarity, such as large group projects that promote cooperation, activities purposefully organized by teachers to include boys and girls.

Two implications for development (81-82) are crucial here: (1) childhood behavior that is sex segregated is not necessarily due to sex differences but to socially organized and situational variables, and (2) interaction patterns can be changed to promote integration. Thorne's insights are significant because childhood socialization is a learning process, a process that constitutes and fortifies patterns of gender solidarity and inequality. If boys' and girls' social contexts of development are different, though they do not have to be, then adult consequences follow. Childhood socialization that engenders hierarchies, status, and control promotes the institutionalization of inequality in adulthood. Women are given less space in our society, their work and talk is violated and interrupted, and they are seen as contaminating the workplace (79).

Lindsey (1990, 206-18) and Steinem (1993, 120-26) report research that at each level of education, women and men are stereotyped: kindergarten girls are directed to the minikitchen to learn to cook, set the table, and clean; elementary school textbooks still scarcely portray females in prestigious positions; males are the subjects of most stories; in high school there is still segregation in courses taken and encouragement for college preparation; in college women receive less faculty encouragement (though this happens at all levels), are overrepresented in the arts and humanities and underrepresented in sciences and mathematics; in graduate school fewer women gain access to the protégé system where a faculty mentor cultivates a talented graduate student; and, as professors, women are underrepresented in almost all areas, including administration.

A report by the American Association of University Women (1991) has argued that one of the main lessons that women learn in school is to undervalue themselves (Steinem 1993, 121). Women who attend a women's college retain higher levels of self-esteem, more often choose nontraditional subjects, complete their degrees, go on to graduate school, and remember college as a satisfactory experience (123).

The self is the most important concept in SI theory. How it is socially constructed is the essence of SI research. What we know, and what has been continuously backed up by research, is that expecting someone to do well enhances their self-esteem. We possess a looking-glass self. Role-taking from significant others or the generalized other that either champions or denigrates the self is foundational. The self can be enhanced, embellished, nurtured, or it can be systematically damaged. Home and school should be a palladium for the self. Even when it is against all odds that one can do well in school—single-parent family, impoverished school district—parents and teachers who expect children to do well cultivate high achievers (130). It is the Pygmalion effect.

The good news is social change is occurring and discrimination is lessening; "especially in the areas of college admissions, athletics and scholarships" (Lindsey 1990, 217). Social policy, specifically Title IX of the Educational Amendment Act of 1972, is engendering the change. The reason is that federal funds will be withheld from an educational institution if discrimination is adjudicated to exist. Things are changing, but clearly society has a long way to go.

Language and Socialization

Language is fundamental in the socialization process generally and crucially affects gender socialization particularly. SI argues that the development of language and the emergence of self, minded behavior, and role-taking abilities occur simultaneously.

Richardson (1989) argues that there are numerous ways that the English language contributes to a patriarchal society and to producing sexists, even if unintended. "*First,* in terms of grammatical and semantic structure, women do not have a fully autonomous, independent existence; they are part of man" (1989, 5; emphasis in the original). Instead of terms such as human beings, humanity, humankind, and humans, the term man has been used to include both women and men, in such phrases as mankind. Those who argue that women are included in this ignore vital human development insights. One is that "research has consistently demonstrated that when the generic man is used, people visualize men, not women" (5). This is especially crucial from the interactionist viewpoint because mental imagery is part of the role-taking process inherent in socialization. If one only role-takes from masculine images, especially if those images reflect privileged and prestigious men, then one will surely develop a distorted and limited image of women's capabilities and possibilities. Continuous role-taking and internalization of exclusively masculine mental images will hamper motivation and lessen self-esteem for girls. "One consequence is the exclusion of women in the visualization, imagination, and thought of males and females" (5).

The use of the pronoun "he" to cover men and women also creates the mental imagery of a man's world. Of course, "she" is used when referring to nurses, secretaries, and elementary school teachers. Changes in the language are important for enhancing self-esteem and for providing a sense of power, autonomy, or control over one's life.

Richardson also notes that the use of the word *lady* or *girl* can have a trivializing effect. She points out numerous phrases where the association of women with other stigmatized groups is commonplace. Another oppressive use of language is that "women are defined in terms of their sexual desirability (to men) [whereas] men are defined in terms of their sexual prowess (over women)" (7). Men are frequently defined in terms of their relation to the world, while women are defined in terms of their relation to men. Divorce is one example. What is a divorced man called? Richardson illuminates that many words referring to women go through the process of peroration, that is, they become obscene. For example, to insult a man, you can call him any number of names referring to women, or to his relationship with his mother. For example, any man who does not measure up to the cultural convention of masculinity may find himself labeled "effete," "un-manly," "effeminate," and "emasculated" (Gilmore 1990, 11).

Lindsey (1990, 47) recognizes that when men or women deviate from tradi-tional occupations there are linguistic markers to make note of the deviation: "female doctors" or "male stewardess." New linguistic conventions have sprung up to deal with exclusion of women. "She/he," "he" or "she," and "they" are ways to emphasize that both men and women are being discussed. "Ms." is a relatively new form of address so that the marital status of a woman remains unknown as it is for a man.

Women's insecure and inferior status is reflected in what are called tag ques-tions. A women can make a statement, assert a fact, but then, to avoid being la-beled aggressive, adds a tag such as, "It was a good movie, don't you think?" "It's a nice day, isn't it?" "As less assertive than declaratory statements, tag questions assume that women must ask permission for their feelings, likes, or dislikes" (Lindsey 1990, 48). Women, due to asymmetric power relationships, speak with words that hedge and qualify.

Gender and Identity

Lipman-Blumen notes that socialization to traditional gender roles continues through a process of cultural lag even after those patterns of behavior are no longer required (1984, 10). Cultural lag signifies that people are socialized to traditional cultural expectations of gender, and that those expectations prevail in the larger society long after they are no longer necessary, or even practiced.

This brings us to the notion of beliefs concerning proper masculine and femi-nine behavior. Beliefs are very powerful in propelling or retarding social change. Sociologists use the concept of ideology to refer to beliefs or belief systems. But they mean by the use of this term much more.

Ideology refers to a system of beliefs that defend and justify power and privi-lege. Since there are competing powerful interests, however, there are competing ideologies, though one system of ideology is usually dominant or prevails. Ideolo-gies of emancipation promote social change (Stark 1960).

Through socialization to a prevailing ideology, say, one that tried to defend and justify traditional notions of what is appropriate masculine and feminine behavior, we come to view such behavior as natural, rather than as socially and historically constituted. A belief in the naturalness or normalcy of such behavior masks the emerging and evolving character of gender. This process is given the fancy name of *reification* in sociology. Such taken-for-granted assumptions are what the French cultural critic Ronald Barthes has called myths. They serve to safeguard privileged and prestigious positions. For example, many in the past have argued that masculine and feminine behavior are biologically determined, invariant, and that that behavior should be reflected in the social structure: men in positions of power and women in positions of subservient or helper roles.

But ideology, though extremely powerful, cannot determine people's views of themselves forever. Interactionists always contravene with the argument that people are not determined, that they are not ideological dopes to roles, rules, and meaning. People create their own social worlds inside of structures, attach meanings to roles, rules, and engage in negotiation based on the meaning roles and rules have for them. They act on the basis of their definition of the situation, which may be to subvert roles, rules, and traditional notions of masculine and feminine behavior. People can bring about structural change.

One place where structure, gender, and identity are undergoing thorough transformation is at the professional workplace. As women entered the professional level in the past three decades, the workplace has been fraught with gender wars. Workplace culture entails a warrior ethos that is transforming traditional images of femininity. This male culture of work—competitive, self-sacrificing, all-consuming—backed up by male dominance and privilege, is, as yet, changing women's behavior more than women are changing it. Patricia A. McBroom in *The Third Sex: The New Professional Women* (1992), has chronicled this conflict and the requirements women must make to enter and compete alongside their hostile male colleagues in the self-denying, family-stifling, reproduction-repudiating, relationship-estranging, organizationally directed corporate world of high finance.

Battle-weary just to gain entrance into the corporate world, women were not unwitting participants to the hardships they would endure once grudgingly admitted. But as McBroom's study shows, they were caught unaware as to how severe those hardships could be and how thoroughly workplace culture, structure, and behavior would transform their definition of femininity and woman qua woman.

The women of McBroom's (1992, 7) study have undergone profound resocialization, since they were reared for domesticity but ended up pursuing a career.

> This new path is a third way of being in the world—that is, it borrows from the male and female past but belongs to neither. The result is to alter normal gender behavior for women so dramatically and so thoroughly that a new cultural form is created, identified in historical literature of the twentieth century as the New Women and identified here as The Third Sex.

McBroom documents how women's personal identity insidiously erodes the longer one is in the professional work world, and that what is eroding is their concept of femininity. Femininity is the self-image many of these women were originally socialized to; however, a professional image is the one they must now adopt. Many of the women define the two as incompatible. McBroom (47) lists a number of adjectives that define the feminine image: gentle, soft, weak, helpless, kind, warm, dainty, delicate, appealing, conniving, sweet, sensitive, pretty, accommodating, charming, and quiet, among others. The professional image of being a woman is associated with being strong, competent, assertive, responsible, proud, perceptive, powerful, and independent, among others. These two concepts center "the conflict women feel between the new and the old, the office and the home, the professional and the romantic identities. The words mark the changes in gender identity" (47).

Workplace ethics, or the lack of them, reshape women's values, norms, and behavior. A gender identity based on nurturance and communication is dysfunctional at the organizational level. Organizations want productivity and efficiency. Expediency, not justice, guides the accomplishment of tasks.

McBroom (59) argues that men socialized to abuse are functional at the workplace, or, at least, a workplace that has a warrior ethos. Men's socialization and gender identity meshes well with this workplace culture, women's does not. Men socialized to abusive patterns of communication and interaction reproduce those patterns at work. Women, to say the least, find surviving, let alone thriving, in such an environment consternating.

For millennia, the sexual division of labor has shaped and allowed this pattern to flourish. It is not a culturally unique pattern to Western civilization. "Typically, in cultures where men are culturally conditioned for war, they also dominate women, espouse religious beliefs focused on male gods, and are distant from their children because the gender spheres are separated" (60). These are war cultures. Men are required to kill and be killed. They are taught that the feminine is repulsive, and eventually grasp that they are unessential to the reproduction of life. Protection and self-sacrifice are necessary in a warrior world. Societies found it culturally adaptive to train men for these roles. The rituals and ceremonies necessary to produce living-death machines are brutal; indeed, they are torture.

This warrior culture, McBroom argues, has been transplanted to the workplace. The traditional sexual division of labor allowed it to go unchallenged; however, now women are trying to survive and challenge it at the same time. But until workplace culture is demasculinized, at least from the excessively brutal aspects of a warrior ethos, women will be at war with men and themselves. As McBroom (70) simply states "the unreconstructed women does not do well in a professional setting." She must unlearn one gender identity and learn a different one. She must eradicate one set of beliefs and adopt another, diametrically opposed. One cannot do this in a perfunctory or pro forma manner. Identity must become essence. She either is successful or crashes into the wall of masculine culture, a fatality. Women validate masculine culture by adapting, but they can resist and advocate as well; it is just that the latter necessitates endurance. Thus, workplace culture, while increasingly subject to feminization, is oppressive to women, since in order to stick around long enough to change the system, women have to change first.

The oppression is especially embittering, since that for many women, to compete and stay around, they have felt it necessary to forego reproduction. But as McBroom's study revels, one's social background is influential in such decisions. It was primarily women from patriarchal families who would not reproduce. The remembrance of an all-dominating male was too repulsive to engender a yearning for pronatalism. McBroom (96) argues that in a culture where two incomes for economic survival are a necessity, a patriarchal family is maladaptive. "In evolutionary theory, adaptation refers to differential rates of reproduction among competing species, and, in this study, patriarchal families were not producing any offspring." Women from matriarchal families were reproducing, though still below a national average. These women could master their jobs and have children. The crucial factor was that they chose husbands who were willing to nurture their children. These women also had the highest levels of self-esteem.

Even with a spouse willing to share childrearing, the gender identity of an all-caring mother has to fall by the wayside. Professional women, because of grueling schedules, still find that they have to put their children in day care, "violating one of the most widely held and cherished standards of the American middle class—that a woman should spend the first few years in full-time care of her own child" (139). Now there is certainly bad day care injurious to children, however, McBroom's (161) research has "found that there are few, if any, differences between infants in good day care and infants reared at home. But the day care must be good." In today's culture, then, the sharing family pattern is functional for adaptation.

The one major problem with women changing and men not changing their gender identity is that relationships can suffer. Feminine values contributed to a healthy family life. If both partners are aggressive, competitive, and achievement oriented, that is, if women have wrenched all traditional femininity from their selves, while men have obdurately refused to gain compassion and sensitivity, the marriage made in hell emerges. McBroom sounds the clarion call for humanizing the workplace and democratizing the family.

The Future

One of the ways we can measure the change in gender socialization in the past twenty-five years, specifically, conceptions of femininity, is to notice the change in women's behavior and attitudes toward family, marriage, and children. Women today plan to have fewer children; there are fewer unwanted births; family size is smaller; the period of mothering is shorter; women are having children later in life; adolescent mothers are increasing; more women are having no children; one-parent families are rising; female employment is growing among mothers of all ages of schoolchildren, particularly among mothers with preschool children; new types of female-headed households are occurring: never married, cohabitation, lesbian, and communal; and postdivorce stepfamilies are increasing (Gerson, Alpert, and Richardson 1984, 434-37). Compared to the 1960s, these trends are holding.

Gerson, Alpert, and Richardson report (1984, 438) that a family developmental framework around parenting/socialization has five stages: decision and preparation for parenting, transition to parenting, early parenting with preschoolers, middle parenting in the school years, parenting with adolescents, and later parenting with adult children and eventual grandparenting. These demographic trends influence all the stages of socialization. Because of changes in attitudes and conceptions of femininity, they report both positive and negative possibilities for the future. Decision making on whether to have a child has been influenced by feminism. Those who have sympathies with feminist thought are less likely to have children, while those who hold more traditional attitudes are likely to have children (439-40). The childbirth and the postpartum transition period is more difficult for women who had careers previous to mothering (444). For women who delay having children, there are welcome tendencies: healthier emotional environment, dependency of children is less, spouse participation is more, though parenting might be a more stressful period because grandparents may be too old to help in childrearing (444-45).

As a result of women in the workforce, alternative mothering is on the rise, such as family and institutional day-care providers. How this will affect childhood socialization generally, and gender socialization specifically, will be a research growth area. Women and men who want to work, a dual-career couple, can take some comfort in the attitude of a majority of family day-care providers. A 1990 study of family day-care providers has found that these providers use "mothering as a model for their involvement with children" (Nelson 1990, 591). They develop a "detached attachment" to the children, which requires emotional labor but is not as intense as mothering their own children (Nelson 1990).

One of Bem's (1983, 609) concerns is how one can raise "a gender-aschematic child in the midst of a gender-schematic society," that is, to reduce sexism, and artificial, culturally conditioned notions of masculinity and femininity. She presents a speculative scenario that may help. It centers on providing alternative schemata, that is, to resist or censure cultural messages about gender, to eliminate sex stereotyping, and to allow more freedom of choice in children's behavior (1983, 610-12). The purpose is not to create an androgyny—that boys and girls must be masculine and feminine—but an environment in which boys and girls believe and behave as though they can do anything.

Conclusion: The Dynamics of Myth and Power

Man, not always kind, is becoming decentered. Men are losing their roles as breadwinners, impregnators (an extremely small number of women are choosing to be artificially inseminated), and protectors, the three roles that Gilmore (1990) found as nearly cultural universals. Misogynous males are threatened, for the loss is one of power and privilege. That is one reason why the debate over gender is so mean-spirited, "this is a civil war for gender equality, and no ruling class has ever given away its power because it was the right thing to do" (Wolf 1994, xvii). Men need a theory of legitimation so as to argue that their position of authority and privilege is natural, meritorious, and justified. Their last bastion has been biology. Males full of fear and loathing need to argue that women and men are the way they are because of innate, immutable, biological differences. But the notion that gender is innate is a palpable absurdity, for behavior has changed dramatically in the past twenty-five years. It is this change in gender that threatened men find so alarming. If behavior is biologically determined, then biological determinists would have to argue that the biology, the genes of the species, especially women's, has changed within the past twenty-five years. What biological changes can account for such a dramatic shift in behavior? The explanation for changes in gender is that behavior is socially and culturally constructed. The past twenty-five years have ushered in enormous social and cultural change. Since biology is no longer the *legitimizing* palladium protecting the institution of masculine power and privilege, men are suffering a crisis in authority, what Habermas (1975) termed a legitimation crisis.

The championing of biology to retain power over women is analogous to the "biological warfare" by eugenists in the later part of the nineteenth and early part of the twentieth century. Power over and exclusion of eastern and southern immigrants finally failed to be justified by scientific racism; unfortunately, it took the Holocaust to awaken us all to the use of biology as a weapon of mass destruction. The sallow state of such lethal ideology was one ruddy triumph of social science in the twentieth century, though it is a precarious victory.

Male preserves are becoming extinct. Male bonding through conquering, oppressing, and being in charge is evaporating. Men are grasping at straws. What warrior likes to return home with no game at the end of the day? Where can men go from here? Naomi Wolf (1994, 22) argues that directions are as yet unclear.

> The inchoate despair and rage in many men come from lacking an alternative, positive image of masculinity. There is no fully articulated new male language with which to seek sex and love, feel self-mastery, communicate, have stature among other men, and recognize oneself as a successful member of one's gender.

If men have as yet no clear road to follow, women have their internalized oppression as an obstacle. Power and equality are there for women to take as long as they see themselves as human agents first. The structure of male oppression and the possibility of overcoming it provides an excellent example of the structure/agency dialectic. People who define the world as totally determined by others must wallow in the council of despair, an acquiescent victim instead of activist revolutionary. "Victim feminism is when we trap ourselves in a 'helpless victim' self-image that blinds us to our strengths. Women must stop thinking of themselves as the passive victims of history and understand that they can determine their own fate" (Wolf 1994, xvii, xv). Women, like other minorities, are an oppressed people. But oppression is not total determination and such a belief vaporizes human agency. "We tend to talk about obstacles as if they were insurmountable, as if we lived under a fascist state" (Wolf 1994, 51).

Certainly patriarchy is on the decline, despite backlashes. Families are moving, by sheer necessity, from the "male-ownership model of the family" to the "equal-partnership model" (Wolf 1994, 6). As long as there is capitalist patriarchy, however, women and poverty and women and power will be directly proportional. Gender equality does not mean class equality. "In a capitalist democracy, economic equality *with* men is not going to guarantee economic equality *among* women" (Wolf 1994, xxii; emphasis in the original).

The degradation of women is part of a larger process of negative valorization (dehumanization) that accompanies and legitimatizes stratification. Myths play a large role. They function to justify institutions and behavior. A myth is a discourse of power that represents and represses;[7] here, it provides ideological justification for inequality. We have many myths. We want so much power. Myth, through media, representations, constructs, or images, negatively valorize the powerless. Myth creates a public/official discourse of superiority and legitimation and, through internalization of those ideologies, a private discourse of inferiority and resignation, maintaining the consent of the governed. The social construction of the other is usually accomplished through binary opposition: we/them, superior/inferior, good/evil, on God's side/godless, the deserving poor/the undeserving poor, and male/female. These constructs are being deconstructed through feminist research, revealing their hegemonic functions; though, as Patricia Ticeneto Clough (1992, 15-16) has noted, some feminists have argued that deconstruction sans feminism abandons an oppositional voice substantiated by empirical science. These feminists suspect deconstruction of being another "masculinist discourse" to discredit the voices of the oppressed (15-16).

Resistance to patriarchy is taking place at all levels and in all institutions of society. Not only are women resisting but also all those whom Simone de Beauvoir theorized as others: the unrepresented, or only represented, through the constructs of power holders. Others resist by becoming others-for-themselves, rather than others-in-themselves. Demythologizing, debunking, and unmasking theory as a weapon of domination, along with theorizing their own understanding of themselves through class, gender, race, and Third World consciousness, others have gained power to claim attention, respect, and status. Power holders can (they are not passive to their loss of power) despair, repress, backlash, and contrive new theories to legitimate their oppression. To be sure, ideology is protean, new strains of this virulent virus will arise. *The Bell-Curve*, the latest mystification, demonstrates such resilience. Those who own the means of production own the means of mental production as well. As a species susceptible to symbolic manipulation in everyday life (performances, representations, and simulacra), we have been deceived, cozened, hoodwinked, bamboozled, had the wool pulled over our eyes, and been false-conscious pawns to power, privilege, and prestige. Ideology is a spring that catches its fair share of woodcocks. Rueful over the past, sanguine about the future, we must pin our hopes on vigilant scholarship and social resistance. The debate over gender will not go away soon, for the myth of innate inferiority—the ultimate discourse of power—will remain so long as does inequality. Equalize power and status, and the myths will crumble. Attack solely the myths, and power pulsates. Understanding does not entail transformation. Both structural transformation and a reconstructed consciousness are requisite for emancipation.

Notes

1. For two recent studies that discuss the ancient world, including its religions, see Robin Lane Fox, *Pagans and Christians* (New York: Knopf, 1989); and Donald B. Redford, *Egypt, Canaan, and Israel in Ancient Times* (Princeton, N.J.: Princeton University Press, 1992).

2. The concepts of patriarchy and hegemony are foundational to social theory and one can find discussions of them in any social theory text, dictionary of sociology, and almost any introductory sociology textbook. Not one theoretical idea here is my own. The paragraph is a compilation of ideas gleaned from reading about hegemony for years, emphasizing the most common notions. Nevertheless, Gramsci (1971), the theorist who developed the concept, Lefebvre (for his chapter on ideology and the sociology of knowledge) (1982), and Raymond Williams (1975, 1977) are excellent sources. Fruitful definitions for students (which also inspired my comments and phraseology, and from which I paraphrase) are found in David Jary and Julia Jary, *The HarperCollins Dictionary of Sociology*, New York: HarperCollins, 1991, and Gordon Marshall, *The Concise Oxford Dictionary of Sociology*, Oxford: Oxford University Press, 1994.

3. It should be noted that the concept of a child and that children need time to be raised is only a few centuries old. Children were usually thought of as small adults. In many countries children are harshly treated rather than nurtured during the period that Western culture has defined as childhood.

4. I have deliberately left much to the imagination as to how these cases were settled. They, as well as a host of other cases, provide electrifying sources of discussion on sexual discrimination. Students should look them up for a more thorough understanding of the issues and the politics of jurisprudence. For those students with a passion for scholarship, knowing the meaning of the following relevant constitutional terms will greatly enhance your understanding and the professor's amazement at your erudition: due process of law,

equal protection of the laws, and privileges and immunities. Title VII of the 1964 Civil Rights Act is also germane to this discussion. The source where I first read about these cases is lost to me.

5. Feminist theory is already being deconstructed as mainstream. Gay/lesbian scholars call for a critique of capitalist, patriarchal heterosexuality. Postfeminist studies are sprouting in many forms, but their main emphasis is on decentering heterosexuality as the normalized version of sexuality.

6. "[Some] theorists view both discourses as androcentric, because each accepts abstract, disembodied Man as the standard for women to be equal to or different from" (Stacey 1994, 482).

7. I draw on basic insights from Bronislaw Malinowski and Michel Foucault.

Part IV

Deviance

13

The Interactionist Conception of Deviance

SI scholars have contended that their theory may be applied to deviance as a special case of interaction. "General statements that hold true for the processes of interaction will therefore hold true for deviance, for deviance is but a special case of these processes" (Rubington and Weinberg 1973, vii). Howard Becker (1973, 178) has stated: "I intend the point I make to apply to sociological research and analysis generally, reaffirming the faith that the field of deviance is nothing special, just another kind of human activity to be studied and understood." The interactionist theory of deviance has grown first and foremost out of the work of Edwin Lemert and Howard Becker, but also through the work of such notable sociologists as John Kitsuse, John Lofland, David Matza, Frank Tannenbaum, Kai Erikson, Earl Rubington, Martin Weinberg, Jack Douglas, John DeLamater, Harold Garfinkel, Edwin Schur, Erving Goffman, and Eliot Freidson.

Probably the most famous statement of the SI position on deviance is Kai Erikson's (1966, 6; emphasis in the original):

> deviance is not a property *inherent* in any particular kind of behavior; it is a property *conferred upon* that behavior by the people who come into direct or indirect contact with it. The only way an observer can tell whether or not a given style of behavior is deviant, then, is to learn something about the standards of the audience which responds to it.

Howard Becker (1963, 9; emphasis in the original) has also written a trenchant analysis that concurs with Erikson's.

> *Social groups create deviance by making the rules whose infractions constitutes deviance,* and by applying those rules to particular people and labeling them as outsid-

ers. From this point of view, deviance is *not* a quality of the act the person commits, but rather a consequence of the application by others of rules and sanctions to an "offender." The deviant is the one to whom that label has successfully been applied; deviant behavior is behavior that people so label.

Deviance is in the eyes of the beholder with power. The powerful institute deviance as they legislate it, prohibit it, or label it. Becker (1963, 2) notes that rules are both formal ("enacted into law") and informal ("encrusted with the sanction of age and tradition"), but the rules he is primarily concerned with are "those kept alive through attempts at enforcement." The rules, because of power differentials, are intrinsically political; conflict prevails among various groups in society as to what the rules should be. Established rules are used as a social weapon by the powerful against the less powerful (Becker 1963, 18).

Also, because we belong to many different groups, rules are relative, ambiguous, and contradictory (Becker 1963, 8). An excellent example documenting the arbitrariness of deviance production is Arlene Daniel's (1973, 132-40) work on combat psychiatry. She illustrates how what may be defined as aberrations in civilian diagnosis may be ignored or defined as nonexistent in military psychiatry. Rule-breakers are not a homogeneous group; they share only being labeled and the attendant experience (Becker 1963, 10). The experience is shaped by how people react to the deviant. And how people react depends on who committed the act and "who feels he has been harmed by it" (Becker 1963, 12). Erikson (1966, 7) concurs: "whether or not a person will be considered deviant, for instance, has something to do with his social class, his past record as an offender, the amount of remorse he manages to convey," and so on. Because of power differentials, then, "differential enforcement on different categories of people" is a constant injustice (Becker 1963, 13).[1] Power holders produce the labels necessary to achieve status aggrandizement for themselves or status degradation for others. Power confers to the holder definitional hegemony and social control. According to Schur (1975, 290; emphasis in the original), the powerful can achieve: "(1) enhanced ability to avoid *unwanted labels*, (2) enhanced ability to *obtain wanted* labels, and (3) enhanced ability to impose labels on others." Labels can be applied ad hoc, whenever the situation calls for social control. As Erikson (1966, 22) states: "men who fear witches soon find themselves surrounded by them; men who become jealous of private property soon encounter thieves."

By exploring SI's position on the social construction and relativity of moral meanings we can gain an insight into this perspective on deviance. Other perspectives, the functional or Marxist, take a more absolutist position on the nature of deviance. The SI perspective argues that deviance is relative, arbitrary, dependent on cultural, temporal, geographical, and social class variables; it is always subjective and ephemeral, but never objective or perennial. Certainly, there are behaviors, those fitting the notion of *mala in se*, for example, that would be considered criminal in an absolutist sense even by interactionists. The incest taboo as a cultural universal would be an excellent example. Crime, however, is only a small part of deviance.

Deviance does not inhere in the act but is socially created through the process of social definition and societal reaction. This sociological insight is traceable to Durkheim, for whom a crime was whatever violated the collective consciousness. Deviant behavior is contingent upon others defining it as such. It is thus the societal response, not the behavior itself, which establishes that an act is deviant. Moreover, the definitions of deviance, and the sanctions levied, are not universal but "vary widely among conventional members of various subcultural groups" (Kitsuse 1973, 25). Even laws that we would expect to maintain consistency in sanctions may vary from one jurisdiction to another. Such is the arbitrary nature of laws. Such variation, of course, has not gone unnoticed. In fact, organizations have arisen to establish consistency among legal norms (laws) and penalties. The National Conference on Uniform State Laws is an example.

The Social Construction and Relativity of Moral Meanings

Morality is the foundation of the law, but society's support of one position or another on many issues is as temporary as a scaffold. Thus a society's morality manifests a mercurial nature, as does its oscillating concern over social problems. The only thing constant about moral boundaries is their perpetual flux.

One historical example of this "moral passage" from the profane to the accepted is the enactment and repeal of Prohibition laws. Robin Williams (1970) coined a phrase that became a part of the sociological lexicon, "a patterned evasion of norms," to describe the behavior of people reacting to laws that are resented and thus not well complied with. Contemporary moral passages can be seen in the struggle over the definition of abortion, euthanasia, drugs, homosexuality, single-parent families, and on and on. If morality were not subject to influence and change, there would be no current conflict over the definition and status of these behaviors. The fact that such behaviors are at the center of national debates underscores the interactionist position that most moral meanings, laws, and deviance are relative, a product of social construction. Deviance thus is a consequence of political struggle as well. Our normative order is politically constituted. The group that wields power defines the norms.

A number of theorists, many partial to SI and phenomenology, have elaborated not only on the relativity of moral meanings in contemporary society but also on the necessity to construct a dichotomy between good and evil. Jack Douglas advances the argument, following Durkheim, that evil or deviance will always be among us no matter how good we are. "If we do eradicate our present evils, we will simply construct new ones" (Douglas 1970, 5). In order to live in the good society we must eradicate the evil, and the good society always presupposes the necessity of evil, of crime, of deviance.

One of the determinants of morality, according to Douglas, is our incessant, intensive competition for social status, which requires that we degrade others so as to upgrade ourselves. The self competes for moral superiority vis-à-vis other individuals and groups. Those who are able to ascribe stigma to others and avoid stigma being cast upon themselves are assumed to be morally superior. Thus, part of life is a struggle for moral identity.

One of the obstacles in this competition for moral superiority is the extent to which we can determine the true identities of others. Before we can feel or ascribe any moral superiority to ourselves, we must ascertain the other's identity as accurately as possible; otherwise, embarrassment and the possibility of suffering a derogation of one's own self is likely. Such identity determination is facilitated by a hierarchy of moral selves parallel to economic and professional success. For example, in capitalist society to be wealthy is to be virtuous, to be poor is to be disreputable.

Another point advanced by Douglas is that morality is a contextual, situational emergent. Moral heterogeneity exists in almost all conceivable social interactions. We do not all share the same moral standards or the same precepts about what is a proper or improper course of action. The moral meaning of any action cannot be disembodied from the social context in which it occurs. An action may be moral under one condition and immoral under others. The morality or immorality of an action is situationally determined and problematic. But since argumentation or deliberation would be endless and interaction at a standstill, if moral debates on every action were pursued, we adopt a pragmatic morality: we agree to act in ways that will accomplish a workaday interaction to achieve immediate goals, a working morality.

Recent research by Reese and Katovich (1989) illustrates just how relative deviance can be. The timing of the act is everything. If an act is untimely, it can be labeled deviant, whereas the same act engaged in at a different time is viewed as normal. Reese and Katovich have researched alcoholism, where drinking at the wrong time elicits stigma. Otherwise, drinking is a cherished part of our recreational culture, a multibillion-dollar industry, and is presented to us in endless media advertising as a way to enjoy life, relax, and, of course, as an enhancer to sex or a disinhibitor of sexual standards. Drinking is far from intrinsically deviant, but because of context and timing it may become so labeled, stigmatizing the drinker.

Reese and Katovich (1989, 166-73) identify nine dimensions that make alcoholism a case of temporal deviance. Timing refers to when an act takes place. Taking a drink in the morning before work or church "is often a social cue of alcoholism and evidence that outside help may be required" (Reese and Katovich 1989, 166). Frequency concerns how often a person drinks. An alcoholic is someone who drinks too often. Duration centers on how long someone is drinking. An alcoholic is someone who cannot stop drinking or someone who seems to be always drinking. Tempo is the normative rate of an activity. An alcoholic is someone who drinks too fast. Pacing is allowing an activity to dominate one's time. "Problematic drinking is characterized by episodes during which too few non-drinking activities intervene" (Reese and Katovich 1989, 169). A violation of rhythm occurs when acts do not conform to normative notions about "periodicity." An alcoholic is someone who has a "rigid" pattern of drinking, such as, say, every weekend. Acts that violate notions of "sequencing" are ones where what has gone on before or is to go on soon are ignored in favor of the activity. The alcoholic drinks even after becoming drunk or if he or she is going to drive. The normative sequence of events is of no concern to the alcoholic. Synchronicity refers to acts that should not occur when one is doing other acts. Again, driving while drinking is an act that violates synchronicity. Drinking while at work is another example. Chronicity violations are ones that occur too soon or too late in life. Drinking while under the legal age is the prime example here.

Other SI scholars have been illustrating the relativity of deviance, especially society's trend to define deviance down, to destigmatize previously stigmatized activities. Irwin (2001) has researched the new meanings tattoos have in contemporary America, illustrating that deviance is a matter of negotiation and that tattooing has undergone a "dramatic moral passage" (50). Generally, Irwin believes that deviance defined downward is especially successful "when middle-class individuals take up particular deviant activities" (50). However, many Americans still view tattoos as "outrageous and unacceptable behavior" (58), violating "conventional values and norms regarding hygiene, beauty, decision making, and self-presentation" (67). Thus, middle-class individuals with corporate or academic careers need to purposely contribute to the redefinition of sporting a tattoo by "a set of legitimation techniques to help maintain their social status," a discourse of "stigma management maneuvers designed to repair identities during face-to-face interactions [through] fram[ing] tattoos within core mainstream norms and values" (50). Irwin's subjects obtained tattoos for a variety of reasons: to "rebel from or defy conventionality," to express "liberation, independence, and freedom," and, for males, to "construct a masculine identity" (55). Thus four legitimation techniques were employed to bring these desires to respectability: expressing "life transitions, skills, achievements, and personality traits. . . . By casting their motivations for tattoos within conventional frameworks, individuals were marking their passage through mainstream moral careers" (62). Ironically, in that process, "tattooees ended up confirming many of the norms and values they were initially trying to escape" (67). Irwin's research highlights that informal interactions can define deviance down, that is, destigmatize it, contributing to a moral passage in the culture.

Similarly, Bromberg and Fine (2002) illustrate the relativity of deviance through research on reputation, which can have a moral passage that runs full circle. Pete Seeger's reputation is a case in point. He became a celebrity as a folk guitarist, was then "villifi[ed] as a political subversive during the McCarthy era," and then forty years later, became "so beloved that the state would invest its considerable symbolic resources in honoring him" (1136). Structure and agency are involved: "[s]tructural conditions constrain how the past can be made relevant in the present. Rather than shedding the deviant label altogether, reputational entrepreneurs reshape the deviant label—and the facts behind it—as a badge of honor" (1139). Thus "reputations are radically malleable, even when the figure has not changed dramatically" (1151). This also illustrates the power of definitions of the situation and who gets to define them; in this case, "the power struggle among reputational entrepreneurs over who gets to shape reputations" (1151).

Hayes (2000) points out that indebtedness has undergone a changed social definition so that it is now a "normative status" (29). Also, the "low visibility of indebtedness makes it likely to go unnoticed and hence unlabeled by others" (30). This low visibility and the fact that it is normative to be in debt mean that it is harder to construct severe indebtedness as deviant. It even "helps people to ignore labeling efforts that may evoke shame" (38). In fact, today, pride may be the outcome of bankruptcy. Hayes reports on a person from Debtors Anonymous (DA) to illustrate the point. "Ted's struggle to make ends meet became a source of pride when members of his family reminded him that he did it for his children; thus the shame he should feel in his role as a debtor is offset by his pride in his role as a father who wanted the best possible education for his children regardless of the cost" (38). Our subjectivity allows us to stretch the definition of the situation so that in this case deviancy becomes heroic and shame is avoided. Shame usually comes, but that emotion is constructed through direct and indirect labeling by others in interaction, a slow process because of denial and the lessened stigmatization of debt.

Not only are there temporal and historical contexts that relativize deviance but cross-cultural ones as well (Scott 1970). A person who is labeled a pariah in one culture may be labeled a saint in another. And differences as to what constitutes deviance are found not just among the lay public, but ideologies as to what is deviant, or even criminal, vary among experts as well (Scott 1970).

Ideologies or theories of causality and cures of deviance vary among social scientists to the point of exposing salient contradictions. Not only are there differing views between disciplines such as sociology and psychology but also disputes within each discipline. And these professional disputes are not only intracultural but also cross-cultural. They vary greatly in societies of contrasting economic systems; that is, theorists in socialist and capitalist countries differ about the causes and cures of deviance. The experts' constructions of deviance are influenced by their country's economic structure and culture, and "the profession in which they are trained, the organizations for which they work, and the clientele on whom their meanings are imposed" (Scott 1970, 269).

Definitions of deviance proliferate proportionately with the number of groups or organizations connected in any way (including groups and organizations where the deviants themselves are in charge, such as Alcoholics Anonymous) with the financing of, or treatment procedures practiced in correctional, welfare, and rehabilitative institutes. Meanings of deviance are in no way univocal or static.

That deviance is always in historical flux is illuminated by recent essays by Moynihan (1993) and Krauthammer (1993). They offer a conservative argument that in recent years behaviors that have been "downrated" as deviant have become more common in societies where moral norms have been less enforced, allowing previous deviance to be redefined as generally acceptable. Conversely, moral positions formerly considered acceptable are now considered deviant. Homosexual activity is an example of behavior once defined as deviant that is now defined by many as acceptable behavior. In such instances where political pressure for legislative and court actions are sought and won, moral stigma not only has been reversed but may frequently fall on the enforcers of earlier definitions.

Even if an imputation of deviance is alleged by a labeler or accuser, the person or institution (court of law) must make it "stick." The actor may neutralize the charge, may give an account that annuls the accusation. Or, he or she may decide to change, admitting that he or she has been wrong or a sinner.

But what if one cannot change the behavior, what if one has only one face to present, one that is perpetually deviant? Fred Davis has attempted to analyze that type of interaction situation. For the visibly handicapped, sociability is always problematic, the impairment an obstacle to everyday interaction. The handicap condition seizes the attention of the normal, arousing them to engage in a "kind of reductionism [which] almost invariably cast[s] a pall on the interaction and embarrasses the recovery of smooth social posture" (Davis 1967, 195).

Davis argues that there are three stages necessary to unstrain the interaction. The process is normalization from the normal's point of view or deviance disavowal from the handicapper's point of view. The handicapper is viewed as inferior unless he or she can, vis-à-vis the normal, negotiate a redefinition of self. The normal can, of course, always win a competitive battle of moral identity, to the extent that moral culpability is still associated with any physical, mental, or economic deficiency, as it is in Western society. As Robert Scott (1970, 255) argues, "the mere possession of a stigmatizing condition or attribute [is] often viewed as prima facie evidence of God's punishment for one's sins." AIDS is the most prominent contemporary example.

The first stage of deviance disavowal or normalization is "fictional acceptance," whereby a "bare subsistence level of sociability" is maintained. Next is "facilitating normalized role-taking," whereby the normal takes the role of the other as a whole person rather than reduce the person to the despoiled aspect of his or her identity. The third stage is the "institutionalization of the normalized relationship," exhibited by the normal either "suppress[ing] his effective awareness of many of the areas in which the handicapped person's behavior unavoidably deviates from the normal standard" or joins "the handicapped person in marginal, half-alienated, half-tolerant, outsider's orientation to the 'Philistine' world of normals" (Davis 1967, 202-3).

Unfortunately, such deviance disavowal is ongoing, the handicapped person having to negotiate her or his status with every new interactant, a wearisome and anxiety-producing constant. Instead of the self competing for moral superiority, it is here competing for moral survival, for a greater than vitiated identity. The highest upscaling for the handicapper's self is, perhaps, to the negotiated status of "normal" among fellow interactants, a precarious status, with the danger of spoiled identity ever present. Any difficult situation might direct alter's attention to the saliency of the handicap, reducing ego from a "normal" person to a projection of his or her most vexatious and impaired feature.

The presentation of ourselves as moral creatures, as respectable citizens, guides our daily interaction, and, indeed, our action and goals are facilitated or blocked to the extent that we either attain or fail to attain audience acceptance of our respectability presentation (Ball 1970). As Donald Ball (1970, 332) reports from research in an emergency room, "respectability may become a life-and-death matter." Those defined by emergency-room staff as derelicts—vagrants, drunks, and so on—are not responded to with maximum life-saving efforts. Respectability and moral worth are emergents. The phenomenon requires both actor "conviction" and audience "acceptance" to sustain this definition of the situation (Ball 1970, 336).

Respectability management is thus a daily requirement of us all if we are to succeed in our pursuits, while failure to negotiate the respect of others will result in a social sanction continuum. Such sanctions might range from looks of displeasure to those of scorn and revulsion. Additional sanctions could include failing to win acceptance by or permission to engage in interaction with another, a group, or an organization; confinement in prisons and mental institutions; and, perhaps, ultimately, death.

In a socially stratified society, our status, and the statuses of the groups we belong to, possess differential respectability credentials. None of us possesses enough credentials to gain acceptance by any or all groups.

Accounts

One way we can try to retain credibility is to give an account of our behavior. Vocabularies of motive, as well as accounts, can be present before an act occurs in explanation of why we are going to engage in a certain act. But by and large, they are post hoc explanations of behavior. "An account is a linguistic device employed when an action is subject to valuative inquiry" (Scott and Lyman 1972, 405). Just as competition over moral superiority is ongoing, so is the confrontation between the labeler and the person labeled. Those labeled will initiate arguments, or present evidence, to render the label defeasible. The charge does not have to be serious; all types of accounts may be required for everyday interaction, for untoward behavior, where persons are competitors in "face games" (Scott and Lyman 1970). People offer accounts to escape stigmatization.

Accounts are excuses or justifications, stratagems to armor the actor against social ostracism. "Justifications are accounts in which one accepts responsibility for the act in question, but denies the pejorative quality associated with it" (Scott and Lyman 1972, 406). And "excuses are accounts in which one admits that the act in question is bad, wrong or inappropriate but denies full responsibility" (Scott and Lyman 1972, 406).

If the account is personally "honored" by the offended party, or adjudicated reasonable by a court of law, the actor has successfully negotiated his or her definition of the situation; if the account is viewed as hackneyed, insincere, or self-serving, then the actor's chances at "deviance disavowal," or neutralization, may prove inefficacious.

Accounts are honored or not honored for different reasons by different people. One must be aware of the "social circle" into which one is presenting an account and the "background expectations" of the social audience. Much depends on the situation to be explained. "Hence the 'normal' individual will change his account for different role others" (Lyman and Scott 1972, 415). Of course, people of power may avoid accounts or demand them with relative ease, while the socially powerless might be expected to proffer groveling accounts for the most trifling faux pas.

Accounts range from "saving face" after committing a slight blunder to defending oneself in a court of law for, say, child abuse or murder. When serious matters arise, like the latter situation, one's accounts are presented by professional account constructionists: attorneys at law. Also, other experts may take over and present accounts for you. Loseke and Cahill (1984) argue that experts on battering present accounts (those of excuses) as to why women stay with husbands who beat them up. Loseke and Cahill argue that the accounts presented are hardly scientifically credible, but resemble folklore. Staying with a battering husband is deviant behavior, so some account must be presented as to why this occurs. Women who are battered are deemed incompetent to present their own case, so professional experts have monopolized the definition of the situation by dismissing any account other than their own (Loseke and Cahill 1984).

What, then, is the major function of accounts? "Accounts are employed to restore fractured sociation, [to re-establish] a basis for the moral order and a solution to the Hobbesian question" (Scott and Lyman 1970, 111-14). Accounts reestablish a viable, working interaction when that interaction has been "strained" because of unexpected or untoward behavior.[2]

How do we construct accounts or vocabularies of motive? The same way we construct other minded activity, by "conversing" with our identified-with others, our reference others or groups. Reference others provide us with a vocabulary, or ideology, of motive. "Men discern situations with particular vocabularies, and it is in terms of some delimited vocabulary that they anticipate consequences of conduct" (Mills 1967, 357).

One of the contemporary problems of the self is identity conflict, and it is Mills who alerts us to this. We suffer anxiety not only over whom to identify with before an action is undertaken but also over whom to use as a referent in constructing an account. "In secondary, secular, and urban structures, varying and competing vocabularies of motive operate coterminously and the situations to which they are appropriate are clearly not demarcated" (Mills 1967, 363). We mentally converse with referent others and construct plans of action in which we anticipate approval and refrain from plans of action that would elicit censure, placing our moral identity in jeopardy. "Acts often will be abandoned if no reason can be found that others will accept. Diplomacy in choice of motive often controls the diplomat" (Mills 1967,

358). Vocabularies of motive must be normatively appropriate. They are a process of social construction, emergents from the situation. "Rather than fixed elements 'in' an individual, motives are the terms with which interpretation of conduct *by social actors proceeds*" (Mills 1967, 355; emphasis in the original).

Accounts and vocabularies of motive in a plural society are just as problematic as actions. Different status groups, classes, and ethnicities may require accounts or give accounts not wholly anticipated by other groups of contrasting status, class, morality, values, or beliefs (Scott and Lyman, 1970). Consensus does not prevail as to when minor infractions require accounts or even as to what constitutes a minor infraction in everyday interaction. Social change is so rapid, and the cultural spectrum of random interactants so broad, as to make both accounts and what action may incur them problematic.

We construct accounts that would be acceptable by those we identify with, but at times our accounts have to satisfy, or convince, a broader range of people, and we tailor our motive to correspond to the norms of the group in question.

> A satisfactory or adequate motive is one that satisfies the questioners of an act or program, whether it be the other's or the actor's. As a word, *a motive tends to be one which is to the actor and to the other members of a situation an unquestioned answer to questions concerning social and lingual conduct.* (Mills 1967, 358; emphasis in the original)

The killing of someone is questioned conduct, but justifiable homicide is an unquestioned answer, in the sense that it is perfectly acceptable to a court of law, the questioning in court (if that is one's defense) concerning only whether justifiable homicide or a different type of killing occurred, such as, say, premeditated murder.

There are two processes that occur in the construction of the moral meaning of a social act: (1) the preinitiation phase of the act, which occurs as an internalized conversation with one's reference group, as well as taking into perspective a relevant world of objects and ongoing activities (of course, one may literally talk to others as well) and (2) a post hoc emergent motive justifying or excusing that action if and only if that action is questioned, either by others or by the self. The motive is tailored to placate the individual or group pressing the valuative inquiry.[3]

Many research articles have probed people's accounts and vocabularies of motives. A recent SI research article by Scully and Marolla (1994) illustrates the process, one that includes justifications and excuses.[4] They interviewed convicted rapists in order to elicit how they constructed deviance disavowal. Those rapists who denied their acts by "presenting the victim in a light that made her appear culpable" constructed five justifications. These justifications included viewing the woman as seductress, the myth that women mean "yes" when they say "no," the myth that woman may resist but eventually enjoy it, the myth that nice girls do not get raped, and the justification that rape is really a minor offense (Scully and Marolla 1994, 166-70). These justifications not only are presented post hoc, but in addition have become so pervasive in the culture that they are used by the deviants in the commission of their crime. In fact, they are so popular as myths that they require no further explanation to the general public, they are self-explanatory. This tells us that we have a rape culture.

Scully and Marolla also report that other rapists admit what they have done but present an excuse for it. These excuses typically take the form that denies *mens rea* or that provides the rapist with some appeal to diminished responsibility. These researchers (1994, 171-76) identify three excuses: the use of alcohol and drugs, emotional problems, and the nice guy image. Again, these are thought of not only as post hoc but also, for example, in the alcohol and drug excuse, rapists believe that actually being intoxicated may reduce one's responsibility. Rapists may drink alcohol or take drugs beforehand with that as an excuse in mind if caught. These excuses are presented so that the behavior is seen as inconsistent with the self, so that some moral identity is retained. One is sick, or generally a nice guy, or just had too much to drink. But all in all, what has happened is viewed as an aberration rather than a characteristic of the self. Rapists know the rape culture well, and given the all-too-often reprehensible comments of judges and the verdicts of juries, they may well be able to diminish their responsibility or justify their action.

The social construction of respectability, of moral meanings, is a dialectical affair between actor and audience—though determined in part by the immediate situation—and the larger culture and social system. These larger aspects set the stage, are at times, perhaps, imponderable influences, but the actor and audience are still the final determining agents. It is the problematic nature and relativity of respectability and moral meanings that interactionist research has tried to illuminate. Good and evil are part of a political and cultural drama. What is "good" and what is "evil" depend on the political fortunes of power players.

Dramatizing Evil

SI research has not been as concerned with the etiology or the epidemiology of deviance, as have, say, the perspectives of functionalism and conflict theory, but with what are the social consequences bombarding the deviant by being so labeled. How evil is dramatized through the labeling process has been the major concern. Interactionists have studied the effects of labeling, or social typing—a process, both informal and formal—on the self. Specifically, what changes, if any, are there in the person's self-concept, identity, and self-esteem, and how do these internal transformations affect subsequent behavior? What consequences accrue to the individual labeled deviant after he or she has learned or identified with criminal/deviant behavior through social interaction or through a reference group; has engaged in a deviant act; has been perceived and caught in the deviant behavior; has been negatively sanctioned by an official agency of social control; and is developing or has developed a negative identity by internalizing or accepting others' responses to the deviant label? How does the label itself reflect social relations? What expectations, in reference to future conduct, can we have for someone labeled deviant? (Rubington and Weinberg 1973, 7)

Social inquiry is typically initiated after the deviant has been negatively sanctioned; that is, after the deviant has been labeled with a derogatory status or has undergone what Garfinkel entitled a "status degradation ceremony," or what Rubington and Weinberg referred to as being "socially reconstituted."

In SI research, the observations of the sociologist are to be focused on the *process* of societal reaction. Societal reaction is not a consideration to all rule breakers, but solely to those labeled as deviants (Becker 1963, 14). To be a deviant one must not only violate a norm but also be "caught" and singled out for specific treatment, a most important aspect of which is the labeling (social degradation) ceremony. Let us take a closer look at this process, from beginning to end.

Becker constructs four types of deviant behavior, as follows:

Table 13.1 Types of Deviant Behavior

	Obedient Behavior	*Rule-Breaking Behavior*
Perceived as Deviant	Falsely Accused	Pure Deviant
Not Perceived as Deviant	Conforming	Secret Deviant

The categories of the upper left and lower right are the ones of interest to Becker. There is a distinction here between norm violator and deviant. The lower right-hand category enlightens us that one may commit deviant acts but, through competence or luck, one may never be publicly labeled. As long as one is not perceived as deviant, one is not deviant in the sociological sense.[5]

Because one can be a secret deviant, the implication here is that one can engage in deviant acts without acquiring a deviant identity, since deviant identities (from the SI perspective) are a result of a public labeling ceremony (that is, unless the person forces a deviant identity on himself or herself).

Becker's typology also defines the category of those who suffer an unequivocal social injustice: the falsely accused. Since being deviant is a product of societal reaction, if one is reacted to and treated as a deviant, one is deviant in both Becker's and Kitsuse's sense of the term, regardless of the act in question.

Becker (1963, 23) also argues against multivariate analysis in noting that "all causes [of deviance] do not operate at the same time." He maintains that a sequential model of deviance is necessitated, rather than a simultaneous one. The ontological assumptions of the positivists, according to him, are not in harmony with reality.

In the sequential model, the deviant develops a career. The factors that influence mobility in this career are considered career contingencies. Career contingencies are the result of structure and agency.

One career contingency is commitment. Some people have vested interests (time, money, and reputation) in commitment to social norms. Others have "avoided entangling alliances with conventional society" (Becker 1963, 28). But the single most important variable leading to career deviance is "the experience of being caught and publicly labeled as a deviant" (31).

The status of deviant is a master status, that is, others will respond to this status and ignore other auxiliary factors or subordinate statuses (33). The process of becoming a deviant is set in motion, a process Becker believes is a self-fulfilling prophecy.

Becker's argument can be summarized as follows: (1) The deviant is cut off from previously ongoing social interaction. (2) Contranormative circumstances arise that the deviant had no intention of initiating. (3) The person becomes subject to stereotypical and repressive responses which may increase deviance. (4) Because of isolation from normal interaction the person may join a subcultural group of deviants and achieve solidarity but also solidify his or her deviant identity. (5) Association with subcultural groups fosters neutralization techniques and a justificatory ideology about one's deviance. Additionally, one is socialized on how to improve one's deviant career. The deviant repudiates conventional norms and mores. The subculture, like the primary groups we have discussed throughout this book, functions to create social solidarity and to contravene negative definitions of the group's behavior by the conventional world. But, also like the peer group, the subculture cannot prevent negative sanctions, either formally from agencies of social control or informally from the general public. Becker's notion of the process of becoming a deviant is similar to Lemert's ideas on the process of primary and secondary deviance, discussed shortly.

A recent SI research article (Brymer 1994) illustrates the process of becoming a deviant that supports Becker's understanding. Brymer describes the historical emergence of an illicit subculture of poachers, who support each other in their hunting of game animals. The subculture provides social solidarity so that the cooperative behavior of hunting can occur. An ideology about the delegitimacy of government's regulation of hunting is manufactured so that members can rationalize criminal behavior. This subculture of poachers who are connected through their crimes to each other must also maintain social control over members so that none of them reveals to authorities the extent of the criminal activity. The members must also adapt to ever more sophisticated surveillance attempts by authorities. Also, recruitment problems arise as children grow up and are exposed to conservationist ideology. Thus subcultures of deviance have their own careers, evolve in interaction with authorities whom they must evade, and must solve recruitment problems in order to continue.

The distinction between the deviant act before and after labeling has been a concern of Edwin Lemert, who has formulated the concepts of *primary* and *second-ary* deviance. Lemert is focusing on the processual nature of identity as a conse-quence of a symbolizing and stigmatizing act, that of public exposure. As long as the aberration is not great and the role socially accepted, the deviance is primary.

> The deviations remain primary deviations or symptomatic and situational as long as they are rationalized or otherwise dealt with as functions of a socially acceptable role. Under such conditions normal and pathological behaviors remain strange and some-what tensional bedfellows in the same person. (Lemert 1975, 169)

After societal reaction, however, the deviation is secondary.

> *When a person begins to employ his deviant behavior or a role based upon it as a means of defence, attack, or adjustment to the overt and covert problems created by the consequent societal reaction to him, his deviation is secondary.* (Lemert 1975, 170; emphasis in original)

Like Becker, Lemert emphasizes the processual nature of becoming a deviant through deviation, societal response, and acceptance of the role. Stigmatization leads to deviant-role acceptance.

We have mentioned the symbolic ritual of labeling, but have as yet to analyze its structure, process, and function. We also need to examine Erikson's concern of why there is no recredentializing ritual to establish and secure an individual's "readmit-tance" into mainstream society. Exactly, then, what sort of societal reaction are we talking about? What are its characteristics? Is it informal, formal, or both? Is it done by specific agencies or nonspecific ones? Is it primarily legalistic, judicial, political, or all of these? Is it patterned or random, private or public? If public, who are the social audiences? Essentially, how identifiable (and with what precision) are these symbolic ceremonies? And further, what is their effect: Do they function to frighten or otherwise disengage, or deter, the individual from deviance? Or do they have an unintended effect of closing off any route of action but the deviant path?

By reviewing a number of works on societal reactions to deviance, perhaps we can synthesize in some systematic manner the concatenated process that leads to a status-degradation ceremony.

The social control-process (unless a serious crime has been committed) begins as an informal one. The initial "social audience"[6] (generalizing here, of course) is nonprofessional, sharing a proximity of social space with the deviant, nuisance ridden, often related (especially in cases of alleged mental illness), and limited both in sanctioning and social typing efficacy. Consequently there is as yet no emergence of a deviant identity (unless the deviant types himself or herself).

The Private Regulation of Deviance

The private regulation of deviance may linger as a period of tolerance where sanctions are not invoked. Lemert (1973, 109) recognizes this in his article on the successive stages of exclusion whereby people within an organization acquire a paranoid label.

> [T]olerance by others for the individual's aggressive behavior generally speaking is broad, and is very likely to be interpreted as a variation of normal behavior, particularly in the absence of biographical knowledge of the person.

As long as no crisis situation develops, the societal reaction may be contained. The deviant cues that any social audience descries are not of sufficient magnitude to elicit closer scrutiny.

If the deviation worsens, then an intensification in societal reaction may ensue. In the study by Lemert, "spurious interaction" is initiated as an informal sanction. Among the other members of the organization who inhabit a proximity of social space with the deviant, a conspiratorial norm emerges whereby they avoid any meaningful or sustained interaction with her or him. The person becomes stereotyped or stigmatized, which entails a concomitant set of behavioral expectations (Schur 1971, 51). The deviant has been labeled with a master status (as indicated earlier) that overrides his or her other statuses and functions to justify the types of response others engage in with him or her: spurious interaction. As Becker points out: "Treating a person as though he were generally rather than specifically deviant produces a self-fulfilling prophecy. It sets in motion several mechanisms which conspire to shape the person in the image people have of him" (Becker 1963, 34).

The person labeled paranoid may accurately perceive that people are conspiring against her or him. Lemert (1973, 112) mentions how one office group discussed the character of an "unwanted associate" at the water cooler, arranged coffee breaks by telephone to meet without him, hummed the *Dragnet* theme when he approached, and established a rule to restrict interaction with him. Such conspiratorial behavior only reinforces any paranoia the person may have had and leads to an intensification of those actions for which he or she had originally been labeled.

The master status of deviant is so overwhelming that it begins to define the essence of the person. The deviant act and the person begin to merge into one identity. Frank Tannenbaum (1975, 162), in discussing juvenile delinquency, described this process as the "dramatization of evil." "There is a gradual shift from the definition of the specific acts as evil to a definition of the individual as evil, so that all his acts come to be looked upon with suspicion."

What occurs now may be subsumed under the notion of social ostracism. The community or organization in proximity to the deviant tries to have the deviant isolated or removed from their social world. This signifies the period of formal sanctioning, an in-house procedure, but is to be distinguished from official sanctioning by an agency of social control.

From Lemert's work on bureaucratic organizations, one can discern three types of social ostracism: transference, encapsulation, and dismissal. Management persuading an individual of alleged deviance to leave, and contingent on another department accepting him or her, is an example of transference. Encapsulation refers to the creation of a special status for the deviant so that he or she may be assigned duties in an isolated sphere responsible to only a few. The third type is dismissal from the organization.

It is because of the proximity between deviant and community that strategies of removal are initiated. Kitsuse's (1973) study concerning homosexuals reveals that, in the absence of proximity, such elaborate procedures are unnecessary. Their social worlds do not overlap, thus conflict either does not originate or is not sustained. Nevertheless, the person's behavior is redefined.

> By whatever form of evidence the imputation of homosexuality [read any deviant act] is documented by *retrospective interpretations* of the deviant's behavior, a process by which the subject re-interprets the individual's past behavior in light of the new information concerning his sexual [read any] deviance. (Kitsuse 1973, 22; emphasis in the original)

One notices the similarity of Kitsuse's retrospective interpretation with Mead's notion of understanding the past, that is, that one reinterprets the past in light of the present, which implies that one has gained some new insights about the past.

Johnson and Ferraro (1977) describe the victimization process in battered women, a result of a "turning point" after which the past is reinterpreted. The marriage and the husband are thoroughly redefined. Violence, which may have been thought of only as incidental to the marriage, is now seen as always having been at the center. What may have been acceptable for decades is now viewed retrospectively as a situation in which one has been the victim.

Tannenbaum (1975, 162) posits the need to view behavior as consistent, which augments Kitsuse's insight. "There is a persistent demand for consistency in character. The community cannot deal with people whom it cannot define. Reputation is this sort of public definition." As these authors note, the affected community goes into high gear to search for behavior that will corroborate the initial allegation of deviance. Edwin Shur (1971, 55) cites two examples (taken from the work of John Lofland) to illustrate the effort to locate supportive condemning information. One concerns Richard Speck, where favorable background information was covered on the back page of a Chicago newspaper, but any damaging information highlighted on the front page of the same paper. The second example concerns Charles Whitman, whose biography was inconsistent with his shooting spree atop a college tower in Texas. Whitman had been an Eagle Scout, served honorably in the armed forces, and had done well in college. Journalists, social scientists, and others usually provide some account which explains the behavior, perhaps serving the function of a need for perceived order in the social world. "When social and psychological explanations fail, one can always try biological or physiological ones. Regardless of the character of the account, Actor must be accounted for" (Lofland, quoted in Schur 1971, 55).

Another important finding of Lemert's study is that those who have the power to label might not have the necessary sanctioning efficacy. Within a particular social sphere of interaction, the deviant may resist attempts made to sanction her or him. The labelers may be powerless in dealing with the immediate situation. Lemert (1973, 111) cites various reasons for this impotence, such as: (1) the person's own power, (2) his or her special skills or information, (3) that exposure of incompetence may be an embarrassment for those who placed him or her in office, and (4) the person's ability to marshall outside power. The implication is that sanctioning power is inversely related to the power and status of the deviant.

Norman Denzin (1970) argues that the private regulation of deviance may occur largely unseen by the "public eye." This consequently extreme relativity in sanctioning and rule emergence has led him to develop a relational concept of deviance and morality.

Among dyads of intimate, face-to-face relationships, unique moral orders emerge. Denzin has studied marriage as an example of a social world largely closed to public scrutiny. Among the married, particular "symbol systems" emerge, specified rules of conduct prevail, a universe of discourse develops limited to two. In this private reality, it is hoped impregnable to outsiders, extremely relative interactional norms result in private sanctioning for violations of the relational moral order. This private sanctioning is rarely viewed by others, except, for instance, in embarrassing situations like a public argument.

Knowledge about the moral order is secret and carefully guarded. Impression management is orchestrated by both partners to stage a marriage identity. In any public interaction of the pair, both are vigilant to ensure that neither partner engages in any "misconduct" that would bring embarrassment, discreditation, or spoilage to their marriage identity. Sanctions may be so subtle as to be imperceivable by outsiders, evolved exclusively so as to caution one's partner when straying into private territory. Control over the situation is restructured by the more circumspect partner. "Poise" must be maintained.

If the marriage identity is spoiled, it might deteriorate the relationship. Private violations of the relational morality are usually mended by accounts, but transgressions of the larger moral order may sever the tolerance bond and necessitate the "betrayal" of the partner to an agency of social control.

Thus, as we have seen, a number of contingencies, or variables, may be operative in the stigmatization process as well as in the efficacy of sanctioning. Social ostracism may require outside help, a need to publicize the problem. Let us now turn to that stage in the development of the deviant's career.

The Public Regulation of Deviance

For whatever reasons, deviance that cannot be handled by those most immediately involved generates a decision to go public, to elicit outside help, usually by "calling the cops." Some examples are a family that no longer feels it can handle a "mentally disoriented" member, a neighborhood exasperated over a gang of juvenile delinquents, or parents who cannot control a child to their satisfaction. The power of the state is requested, an official agency of social control is solicited.

The social-control process now becomes political, for "rules are not universally agreed to. Instead, they are the object of conflict and disagreement, part of the political process of society" (Becker 1963, 18). A certain group has thus enlisted the power of the state to sustain their definition of the situation. Such an enlistment, or solicitation, attempts to legitimate the requesting person's values and condemn as improper or immoral the values of the person against whom action is sought. The state's decision to support one side or the other is thus a political decision, legitimating certain values and denigrating others.

The official agencies of social control now enter the "war of wills" whereby a legalistic function is achieved: boundary maintenance.

> Transactions taking place between deviant persons on the one side and agencies of control on the other are boundary maintaining mechanisms. They mark the outside limits of the area in which the norm has jurisdiction, and in this way assert how much diversity and variability can be contained within the system before it begins to lose its distinct structure, its unique shape. (Erikson 1962, 310)

The normative parameters of action are not all codified, but those the society collectively defines as important are selected out and codified. They are society's laws, and it is a violation of these that constitute the public regulation of deviance.[7]

Because deviance sensitizes us to behavior that is beyond the normative parameters of everyday interaction, it functions not to disrupt stability but to preserve stability (Erikson 1962, 310). We witness such behavior and thereby seek corrective measures to eradicate it. The deviant "informs us, as it were, what the devil looks like[,] he shows us the difference between kinds of experience which belong within the group and kinds of experience which belong outside it" (Erikson 1962, 310). The type of behavior that has a legal or medical referent stipulating official action upon its violation is the domain of concern to the official agencies of social control. But, as we have said, an action may transgress the boundaries of the community even though it has not necessarily been codified in a law or statute.

One paradox noted has been that when social-control agencies define their boundaries with precision, they may be engaging in the overproduction of a deviant population. The desire to stake out an area of jurisdiction leads agencies to "add elements to the [deviant] roles that may not have existed previously, and so encourage pulling new people into them" (Freidson 1973, 126). This is the practice of "empire building." The agencies' need for financial support may also lead them to define the deviant universe as larger than it actually is in order to receive the necessary funding (Freidson 1973, 126).

The actual deviant population is then somewhat immeasurable. The amount of deviance can be overproduced or underproduced, the regulating mechanism being the social-control machinery capable of processing deviants (Erikson 1966, 24-25). Erikson claims that deviancy will rise to the level of the social control capability of a community and thereby remain relatively constant (Erikson 1966, 24-25). Social control personnel will regulate the flow of deviancy depending on other exigent circumstances. For example, if more mental hospital beds are needed, then those already incarcerated will tend to have a speedier recovery rate; while if finances are in need and the supply of patients down, those incarcerated will tend to have complicated cases requiring longer periods of recovery, or the hospital staff will urge psychiatrists to make more referrals to their institution (Erikson 1966, 24-25).

Peter McHugh (1970, 61) argues that, generally, we downgrade others, or label them as deviants, on the basis of two commonsense rules or understandings of action. They are: (1) "a deviant act must occur in a situation where [an actor] can conceive that there were alternatives to that act, and, (2) it must be committed by an actor who knows what the alternatives were." There must be alternatives to the act, and the actor must possess intent at the time of the action; otherwise, one is exempt from responsibility.[8] If we can see that there were alternatives and that the actors intended their actions, then we degrade them by labeling them as deviant. There frequently are, of course, alternatives available to individuals even though they might not perceive their availability.

Deviants are considered to be those who fail to act properly where and when there were no impediments to acting properly. As McHugh states (1970, 72), "Failure itself is not deviance. Deviance is to fail in the absence of conditions of failure. The very same act would not be deviant if conditions of failure were present." Intent also must accompany the act: "a deviant is not one who happens to violate the rule, but one who defies it" (McHugh 1970, 76). As indicated earlier, deviancy is relative to the situation and the actor's frame of mind. "These are the criteria of meaning in a deviant act because they generate the content of the matter as deviant" (McHugh 1970, 83).

Society has created deviance not only by establishing rules but, especially, by a symbolic response. The symbolic response and the genesis of a deviant identity generate an almost iron-clad role; consequently, secondary deviance becomes a way of life. This process is summarized by Lemert (1975, 171) in eight steps.

(1) Primary deviation; (2) social penalties; (3) further primary deviation; (4) stronger penalties and rejections; (5) further deviation, perhaps with hostilities and resentment beginning to focus upon those doing the penalizing; (6) crisis reached in the tolerance quotient, expressed in formal action by the community stigmatizing of the deviant; (7) strengthening of the deviant conduct as a reaction to the stigmatizing and penalties; (8)

ultimate acceptance of deviant social status and efforts at adjustment on the basis of the associated role.

Thus, for interactionists, the particular behavior itself is decentered as an object of inquiry. As one critic of SI's position on deviance has stated: "those of this school come dangerously close to saying the actual behavior is unimportant" (Akers 1968, 463). The designation of deviance waxes problematic and relative, for even if an act constitutes a crime and the actor has manifested the two criteria of knowing of alternatives and still intending to do wrong, such a state of affairs may prevail for only a limited time and space. Moral passages on actions as either respectable or disreputable are ongoing and dynamic, as is portrayed in the labeling of drunkenness as at one time immoral, now, a sickness; gambling as illegal, then legal in certain states; the ongoing seesaw in the status of abortion; and so on (Gusfield 1967).

Status Degradation

According to Erikson (1962, 311), the dramatic, ritualized, public ceremony of officially labeling someone as deviant has three phases. The first phase is a "confrontation" between the deviant and the agency: a criminal trial or psychiatric case conference. In the second phase a "judgment" is rendered: a verdict or diagnosis. Finally, the last phase entails a "placement" and the attainment of a deviant role: a prisoner or patient. Most labeling theorists would concur with the following statement: "the dramatization of the evil therefore tends to precipitate the conflict situation which was first created through some innocent maladjustment" (Tannenbaum 1975, 165).

The specifics of this dramatized ritual have been focused on by Harold Garfinkel. He elaborates the conditions necessary for a successful degradation ceremony, that is, "those that are concerned with the alteration of total identity (Garfinkel 1973, 89). These ceremonies, according to Garfinkel, consist of any communication that will transform the "public" identity of a deviant into that of a lower status.

The most important characteristic of these ceremonies is that they are public, a medium through which moral indignation is expressed, functioning to "effect the ritual destruction of the person denounced" (Garfinkel 1973, 90). The old public identity is discredited, a new one is forced upon the person. "The other person becomes in the eyes of his condemners literally a different and *new* person. He is not changed, he is reconstituted" (Garfinkel 1973, 91; emphasis in the original).

The condemners also engage in retrospective interpretation. "What he is now is what, 'after all,' he was all along" (Garfinkel 1973, 91). A different motivational scheme explaining his or her behavior is substituted. A juvenile delinquent, for example, is no longer mischievous but evil.

The condemners also tend to be professionals operating within an organizational network. For example, "a court and its officers have something like a monopoly over such ceremonies" (Garfinkel 1973, 94). The task of the professional denunciator is accomplished when he or she has reordered "the definitions of the situation of the witnesses to the denunciatory performances" and has thereby transformed the public identity of the victim (Garfinkel 1973, 92). The person is no longer a mischievous child but a juvenile delinquent.

A theoretical debate is present within the sociology of deviance between those who believe that such ceremonies have a deterrent effect, and the labeling theorists, who contend that such ceremonies, paradoxically, only promote the very deviance they wish to eliminate. "Their very enthusiasm defeats their aims. The harder they work to reform the evil, the greater the evil grows under their hands" (Tannenbaum 1975, 164-65). The fate of the deviant after being stigmatized with a "spoiled identity" is not prosperous. Transforming someone's public identity, that is done to deter further deviance, in fact, inadvertently sets in motion the mechanism which leads to secondary deviance. The status-degradation ceremony functions to create a deviant career. The deviant may be successful at managing his or her spoiled identity, but, in all probability, the deviant's competence to do so may be virtually impossible, given that so many social factors encroach upon his or her plans of action. The most damaging factor is that her or his social self has been nearly destroyed.

Erikson (1966, 16) argues that, once labeled, an irreversible trend is set in motion.

> Now an important feature of these ceremonies in our own culture is that they are almost irreversible. Most provisional roles conferred by society—those of the student or conscripted soldier, for example— include some kind of terminal ceremony to mark the individual's movement back out of the roles once its temporary advantages have been exhausted. But the roles allotted the deviant seldom make allowance for this type of passage. He is ushered into the deviant position by a decisive and often dramatic ceremony yet is retired from it with scarcely a word of public notice. And as a result, the deviant often returns home with no proper license to resume a normal life in the community. Nothing has happened to cancel out the stigmas imposed upon him by earlier commitment ceremonies; nothing has happened to revoke the verdict or diagnosis pronounced upon him at that time.

Perhaps, severed from former social relationships and patterns of daily interaction—wife, family, friends, job—deviants somehow survive the looming isolation, alienation, and marginality of their opaque and now hollow worlds. The legitimate career contingencies collapse. The illegal career contingencies, since all others are exhausted, entice. The deviant drifts, lost to all integrating forces, abandoned flotsam in an anomic, alienated, and inhospitable world. Deviance commitment strengthens.

One alternative is realized. In escaping from this haunting psychological and social oppression, the person may seek out others so labeled. In a socially scarred subcultural group,[9] the person may again feel the soothing effects of being socially grounded, of social solidarity. The deviant away from home may feel at home again. At this time a deviant career, secondary deviation, has been manufactured. Seeking out other deviants may be necessary even after the deviant has "served his or her time," for, as Erikson admonished, there are no reentry rituals.

For example, recent research has shown that drug abuse is based on identity with other users (Anderson 1994). Abusers know they are "outsiders," the "them"; consequently, like-minded friends and a shared lifestyle are sought, which socially anchors these otherwise marginalized individuals. Identified-with others nurture a solidarity, binding addicts to kindred souls. If drug abuse is to be eradicated, then macrosolutions are needed that help the abuser sever attachment to a deviant culture and bond to mainstream society.

This is the conversion strategy behind a twelve-step or other protocol (such as Alcoholics Anonymous) where one in possession of a "spoiled identity" does not become even more socially deviant (as may happen with incarceration) and instead adopts a socially accepted renewed identity. But, of course, society needs to accept the former addict, or convict, if successful reentry is to be maintained.

Deviance is thus contingent on who you are, where you are, the historical and cultural times you live in, of whom your social audience is composed, and the relative power held between deviants and social-control personnel. The contingencies of movement along this career path comprise tolerance, informal sanctions, formal/political/official sanctions—including labeling in a ritual/routinized ceremony—and, finally, the possibilities for reentry into mainstream society.

The Self: Human Agency and Resistance

As discussed earlier, the social construction of our own mentality is dialectical, depending on how others respond to us and how we respond to others' responses. If we are responded to favorably, our self-esteem tends to be enhanced, but, as with official sanctioning, if we are responded to negatively our self-esteem tends to deteriorate, especially since a negative response tends to reify our deviant act into a master status. We become the act we have committed. We are responded to totally as deviant and thereby become totally what we have only engaged in partially; an act becoming transmogrified into an entity. A casual role becomes a permanent identity. This process of reification, Erikson believes (1966), is historically grounded in Puritan culture. Nisbet (1967, 484) agrees: theoretically we have not advanced, but rather appropriated a "secularized Puritanism." To talk about someone's act "almost as if we were talking about his occupation is precisely what the Puritans did mean by such a phrase: to characterize a person as deviant was to describe his spiritual condition, his calling, his vocation, his state of grace" (Erikson 1966, 198).

Labeling by a less significant force would be problematic and, more than likely, ineffectual in damaging our self-esteem or altering our self-image. The source of the label, its meaning to us, is critical. But a social-control agency is a powerful, at times a preponderant force, that can reconstitute the self.

The battle of the self over enhancement or derogation is not equally drawn, that is, society has more influence on or force over us than we do on it or on ourselves. Therefore it is hard to maintain a positive self-image in the face of societal oppression. The definition of our self is shaken because of the master status ascribed to us for whatever deviant acts we have been charged with committing. By a public status-degradation ceremony, the generalized other—our general frame of reference—becomes a negativity bombarding us. Negative imagery of ourselves is reinforced and thereby escalated by significant others. The old identity loses the battle. The only solution is retreat, to seek a referent, an ally, a subsociety where we can receive positive feedback, a countervailing construction of identity. But to secure the psychological succor we must solidify our commitment to our new compatriots. Such action only confirms and justifies the labelers' beliefs that they have acted wisely, that their scenario contained no surprise denouement. Labeling is a self-fulfilling prophecy.

Nevertheless, I can suggest one sequence of events—there are others—where internalization of a negative label or status may not result: the political or religious deviant, who may view such labeling as nonlegitimate. The legitimacy of the rule enforcers and rulemakers may be called into question; a legitimation crisis may exist. The social distance between deviants and their immediate oppressors may be oceanic. One may be so alienated from, disaffected with, or bent on the overthrow of the larger society and its rulers that laws hold no legitimacy. Revolutionaries may define deviance as resistance to an unjust social order: no justice, no peace.

Revolutionaries respond to society on the basis of the meaning it has for them, which is as a repressive social order in need of immediate overthrow. Since the generalized other is thereby delegitimized, or discredited, one substitutes a stabilizing reference group, say, revolutionaries, to maintain a positive self-image. Labeling, therefore, creates no certain effect, if any. The revolutionary may successfully neutralize any negative imputation. For example, Goffman noted that such convictions may survive even the onslaught of a total institution. "Strong religious and political convictions have served to insulate the true believer against the assaults of a total institution" (Goffman 1961, 66).

The religious or political reference group will sustain one's positive self-image and, perhaps, if the person is romantically inclined, even enhance it. Revolutionaries, or religious martyrs, believe they are working for a greater cause. Their moral code is deemed stronger, more righteous, more indignant, precisely because they define it as such. Situations defined as real are real in their consequences. Revolutionaries and religious true believers do not internalize oppressors' judgments, envisioning themselves as the future judges. These are the days of apocalyptic prophecy. Judgment day, the day of reckoning, where the meek will inherit the earth and the working-class finally unite, is conceived to be imminent. In addition, revolutionaries may be cognizant that the meaning of their action will be redefined as heroism if and when the revolution is won. Their action is oriented toward the future; hence, it is concerned not with how the contemporary society views them but with how postrevolutionary society will evaluate their action. Such an understanding is encapsulated in the notion that history is written by the victors.

Meanings of actions change, of course, as the social context changes. If one may symbolically reconstruct conformists into deviants who previously escaped official detection and sanctioning, there is no reason why one cannot symbolically reconstruct deviants into heroes as well. Such is the history and such was the fate of our own revolutionary heroes, many of whom were once jailed for their actions. As William James (1968, 46; emphasis in original) stated: "I am always inwardly strengthened in my course and steeled against the loss of my actual social self by the thought of other and better *possible* social judges than those whose verdict goes against me now." So must Antigone have thought when she defied Creon and buried her brother Polyneices.

A comment by Nietzsche, (*Daybreak* section 20; emphasis in original) who wrote on the historical, sociocultural, and class-based nature of morality, is trenchant:

> One has to take back much of the defamation which people have cast upon all those who broke through the spell of a custom by means of a *deed*—in general, they are called criminals. Whoever has overthrown an existing law of custom has hitherto always first been accounted a *bad man*; but when, as did happen, the law could not afterwards be reinstated and this fact was accepted the predicate gradually changed;—history treats almost exclusively of these *bad men* who subsequently become *good men!*

Nevertheless, the status-degradation ceremony usually imparts a socially degraded conception of oneself. The individual makes a choice, but the range of options is circumscribed, the plans of action are thwarted. The deviant interacts with others in mutual discomfiture, to the benefit of neither. Remember that, as Erikson mentioned, there are no delabeling ceremonies.

A heart-warming though rare case of triumphing over harsh negative labels is told by Joseph N. Sorrentino in his autobiography, *Up from Never*. Sorrentino, a former juvenile gang member robbed, stole, and flunked out of high school four times. As an adult he was imprisoned in a civilian jail and a military brig; he nearly killed two people with his fists, was dishonorably discharged from the marines, and drifted from one menial job to the next. Eventually, after redefining himself and changing his normative and comparative reference groups, he went back to night school and then on to the University of California at Santa Barbara, where he graduated magna cum laude. From there he went to Harvard Law School where he achieved the honor of valedictorian. Such a case tends to suggest that once actors have reached the stage of secondary deviance, their fate is not always doomed. Sorretino's case is an example of self-delabeling. Trice and Roman (1970) also report on apparent successful efforts by Alcoholics Anonymous to delabel and destigmatize formerly labeled alcoholics. Successful reintegration into American society by middle-class alcoholics (no percentage is reported) is achieved by Alcoholics Anonymous' promulgation of a view of alcoholism as an allergy, or disease, inflicting those susceptible to the illness. They also cast patients in the role of repentants who have suffered downward mobility but have now reaffirmed their commitment to American values and the norm of self-control.

The self thus is able to bounce back. It is resilient, even though it may have suffered harsh stigmatization. What seems crucial to self-destigmatization is a redefinitional process undertaken by the self, aided by a change in normative and comparative reference groups. As we have seen, minded activity involves role-taking from identified-with others and reference groups; once those change, behavioral change is likely. For the same reason, incarcerating people in prison with hopes of rehabilitation is futile. Inmates surrounded by prisoners are not likely to change their self-identity when no positive, law-abiding referent others are available. Expectations to the contrary can be entertained only by the most expedient and feckless of policymakers.

A superb example of how the self resists determination, however, is analyzed by the social historian Eugene Genovese. People, even in the face of oppression, are volitional and self-determining. If ever there was a social experience of structure dominating agency, it was the system of slavery. Yet even here slaves resisted, chiseling meaning into their lives, no matter how overwhelming the cement of oppression; they made a social world of their own. For example, Christianity was a means of social control, but the slaves were not the cultural dopes, passive vessels, or dupes their masters perceived them as. They reinterpreted the ruling class' definition of the situation through revolution-minded activity.

> The slaves and free coloreds were taking the message as they saw fit, not necessarily as the white missionaries intended. If Methodism did reduce the revolutionary thrust inherent in the African cults, the accommodation it provided was based on the principle of human brotherhood in Christ, which could be transformed into a rather bloody reformism by those with imagination. (Genovese 1974, 191)

We need only remember the religious inspiration of people like Denmark Vesey, Nat Turner, and Harriet Tubman to appreciate this point.

The notion that people are gullible recipients of hegemonic ideologies is challenged by Genovese's assertion that

> [there are] two major pitfalls in the evaluation of the religion of the southern slave quarters; the facile tendency to assume that the southern slaves passively absorbed a religion handed down from above and completely relinquished their African heritage without replacing it with anything new, and the mechanistic error of assuming that religion either sparked the slaves to rebellion or rendered them docile. (Genovese 1974, 183)

What the slaves socially constructed was: "a world-view sufficiently complex to link acceptance of what had to be endured with a determined resistance to the pressures for despair and dehumanization" (Genovese 1974, 183). It was through the slaves' construction of religion that they not only claimed their humanity but also that their religion became their most meaningful cultural construction. It gave them a sense of dignity, solidarity, self-respect; in general, it was a counterideology to the racist nonsense promulgated by plantation masters. Through resistance they created individual, as well as a collective, identities that enshrine human agency as a *sine qua non* of the human condition. "Born into language, culture, and race, and class, and gender politics, the subject is never fully autonomous" (Payne 1996, 3). That sentiment expresses the constraint of social forces. Marx's assertion that people make history, even though not just as they please, nor under circumstances of their own choosing, expresses the notion of resistance/agency. Thus, we must conclude that even though we cannot control the social conditions that confront us, we can, through social interaction, choose to defy structures of domination. That is the human condition, the dialectic between structure and agency. On this both Mead and Marx agree.

Notes

1. On this theme there is agreement between SI scholars and those whose ideas exemplify a radical, or Marxist, conceptualization of deviance and criminality. Chambliss, for example, argues that social control agencies are in collusion with members of the ruling class to insure that only the right categories of deviance are prosecuted. By such collusion "the law enforcers end up as crime producers" (Chambliss 1975, 177).

2. Accounts are justifications given to others to restore the flow of interaction. Self-justifications, a similar cognitive process, but ones given for a different purpose, have been studied by cognitive-dissonance theorists. The theory states that anytime we hold two discrepant conditions, a cognitive dissonance results driving us (psychologically) to achieve cognitive consistency. If we can externally justify a behavior or attitude we are not likely to change either our behavior or attitude. If we must internally justify our behavior or an attitude (external justification absent) then our behavior or attitude is likely to change in order to regain cognitive equilibrium. For a fuller discussion, see Elliot Aronson, *The Social Animal*.

3. This is a hyperrational description of human behavior, which ignores emotion in human activities. In everyday life emotion enters into action. The above material described the process of accounts analytically, as though separate from emotions.

4. These guilt-neutralization techniques were previously described by David Matza in *Delinquency and Drift* (New York: Wiley, 1964).

5. John Kitsuse extends the argument with the contention that if one perceives someone as deviant "but does not accord him differential treatment as a consequence of that definition, the individual is not deviant in the sociological sense" (Kitsuse 1973, 22).

6. Erikson's phrase "social audience" connotes rich imagery, almost a Big Brother atmosphere. The implication is that our behavior is always being watched by someone. Thus we all function to circumscribe the parameters of normative behavior, in a manner much analogous

to the ubiquitous chorus in Greek tragedy, which symbolized the normative structure of the community through which no actor's hubris went unremarked. In a very real sense we have become a disciplinary-carceral-panoptic society; a repressive gaze is incessantly focused upon us. See the works of M. Foucault, especially *Discipline and Punish: The Birth of the Prison* (New York: Pantheon, 1977).

7. At times, a norm may be violated without any law or statute as referent. The community then punishes behavior *not yet stipulated* as deviant by referring to an alleged deviant act that *is* stipulated.

8. What McHugh is saying here has been acknowledged practice in the criminal justice system. The actor must possess *mens rea*, or guilty mind. The actor must also be of sound mind; if the actor is found *non compos mentis*, then, of course, he or she may be sent to a mental institution instead of prison.

9. Criticism of the general use of the concept of subculture has been made by two inter-actionists. Gary Fine and Sherryl Kleinman have enumerated four criticisms: (1) subculture is treated as synonymous with the demographics of a population, thereby circumscribing a cultural spread; one does not enter a subculture in the way I intimated above, for that consti-tutes, instead, a subsociety; (2) since a subculture is not a subsociety there is no referent for the population which shares cultural knowledge or participates in a universe of discourse; neither case studies nor survey research adequately tap into or delineates this population; (3) there is no account of social change in the content of personnel of a subculture; across time and space culture is fluid, open to external influences, rather than a reified, material thing; people and information are highly mobile; and (4) a subculture is not a reified, preexisting system of values. It consists of norms and behaviors that emerge through interaction; it is dynamic and processual rather than a social fact external to individuals. Therefore, subculture is a social interaction network in which culture is diffused through transmission or conduit systems. A social network of interaction, whose participants share a universe of discourse is the referent of a subculture. The transmission or diffusion of culture is open, dynamic, and fluid due to (1) multiple groups membership; (2) weak ties linking individuals to a host of others (3) structural roles (that is, key people who traverse and interact among multiple groups); and (4) mass media diffusion whereby would-be esoteric knowledge is promulgated. Entry into and withdrawal from a subculture stems from identification, which serves to social-ize members.

14

Conclusion

People respond to objects based on the meanings these objects hold for them. Significant symbols are interpreted consensually—their meaning is shared—so that culture, intersubjectivity, and joint action are enabled. Nevertheless, symbols and situations can be interpreted and responded to differently so that there is novelty and emergence, as well as deviance, in social behavior. Since people tend to interpret before they act, they are volitional, purposeful, and meaning-conferring, even in circumstances that are socially structured; thus, SI posits that people are determining as well as determined, that social constraint and freedom are in perpetual dialectical motion. The socially derived self bestows on humans an adaptive capacity to respond in reasoned fashion to their environments. From this socially constructed self, behavior emerges from the I and the Me dialogue. The self describes a process of minded behavior, not a structure or an essence.

We are humble creatures, but not culturally or biologically determined automata, not myrmidons to authority, rules, or roles. The ideas of the ruling class are not necessarily the ruling ideas. Adding to the uncertainty of social action is that the self engages in a conversation of gestures between the I and the Me, which is further complicated by the fact that our Me's often have internalized ideology embedded in prevailing cultural constructs. Even some of the impulses of our I's are socialized. Nevertheless, our I's inject indeterminism into our actions. Consciousness allows us to interpret symbols de novo. Another complexity is that novelty and chance lurk in all potential acts. With these layers of intricacy, behavior is unlikely to be predictable or cause driven. Explanation is not meaningful if behavior is just positivistically calculated. Such tenets roil reductionists. Thus ethnographic research that reveals actors' defining, meaning construction, process, is suggested in the study of everyday life.

The influence of the group on human behavior is thoroughly incorporated within the perspective of SI. Significant others, peer groups, secondary groups, subcultural groups, all influence the self, as the self is constantly role-taking, incessantly internalizing the standpoints of others. The power of the group is also extended to institutions and the larger culture. The family, education, and the media exert significant force on the development and behavior of individuals. Moreover, even the meanings that people attribute to objects and events are influenced by the culture and ideology prevailing in the society. A definition of the situation is incapable of being made without taking others into account. That is the implication of role-taking: others, significant others, reference others, the generalized other, or groups in general with which we have some form of communicative contact exert sway in our definitions of situations and in the definition of our selves.

If the self is reflected and constructed in a looking glass, then the others whom we encounter can be esteem enhancing or esteem impairing. For example, this is the case for many women whose self-esteem and identity has been systematically destroyed by physically, mentally, or emotionally abusive husbands. If the generalized other is racist, sexist, and classist, then those who role-take from such a perspective can be influenced accordingly. This is the problem of the internalization of inferiority by minorities, the poor, and women. We are inescapably connected to others in social interaction (the microstructure), the groups and organizations that surround us (the mesostructure), and the larger social forces that impinge upon our lives and over which we have little control (the macrostructure).

Though behavior is inextricably socially influenced, this fact does not attenuate the complementary notion that we still are human beings with consciousness and thinking ability. Those in power frequently underestimate the feistiness and potential rebellion of people under their sway. We are not always acquiescent and equable. We may fight back against racism and sexism. We may engage in class struggle and gender wars. People fight for freedom and liberty all over the world. Social movements are an ongoing feature of social life, as is social change. Both the Civil Rights Movement and the women's movement were completely unpredicted by those in power. Wives who have had enough abuse may kill their husbands or, perhaps, cut off their penises. The emergent, novel, and unpredictable character of behavior creates afresh social life. It certainly was unforeseeable in our culture that an abused woman would cut of her husband's penis; otherwise, the whole country would not have been talking about it ad nauseam. People's behavior is simply amazing! That is why it is the stuff of gossip, rumor, scuttlebutt, the talk of the town, or that recent and ever-metastasizing institution in American life, the talk show.

SI is in agreement with existential philosophy that humans make society and selves. Self and society are projects, Darwinian ones with no unfolding toward any predetermined end. Unanticipated consequences of social action will ricochet us and society in unimagined ways. Making our selves and society through negotiation is subject to differential constraint—in the obvious case, those with money have more opportunity to make something of their lives and to leave their mark on society; that is the real injustice of stratification. Mystifying the problem and foiling social reconstruction, many possessing such opportunity define merit in ways that ignore power and privilege, thereby reproducing a society of unequal self-development. Structure circumscribes access and choice. Nevertheless, all social behavior involves a structure/agency dialectic that is incalculable. The warp and woof of any theory of human behavior would be sorely inadequate not to include both components.

One way to end this book and summarize our main argument—that in becoming human one is a dialectical creation of structure and agency—is to think about how long the dialectical view of struggle and overcoming has been with us.

The notion that there are forces that constrain our lives is an old one. Before the advent of sociology, which began with the European Enlightenment, people attributed events beyond their control to supernatural causes. Religion and mythology try to make sense of events and give meaning to life in such a way. The Hindu notions of a juggernaut and karma both express forces capable of overpowering our lives. Remember the Greek myths of the Morae, or Fates, three invisible old women who influenced our life history. Clotho spun the thread of life, Lachesis measured it, and Atropos, when she saw fit, would cut the thread of life with her "abhorred shears." Fortune had her wheel which she would spin. The Greeks felt that someone was pulling the strings of life, or that someone held an object on which our life-chances depended: the myth of Althaea's brand. The Greeks knew that they were not the masters of their fates or the captains of their souls, but their mythology is rich with heroes choosing courses of action. Heracles, Orpheus, Castor and Pollux, Peleus, all Greek heroes who sailed with Jason in his quest for the Golden Fleece, battled the odds. These argonauts had many forces to encounter: Harpies, Clashing Rocks, and Scylla and Charybdis. In the *Odyssey*, Odysseus wandered for ten years, making choices every step of the way, though not always the right ones. Heracles (or the Latin Hercules) was the most famous hero of all. He had twelve tasks, the Labors of Hercules, that he had to do for King Eurystheus. I shall not go into these, for accounts of them are readily available. These twelve tasks are analogous, *mutatis mutandis*, to social obstacles that we all must confront. Against all odds, Hercules was able to complete the tasks. He used his ingenuity, cleverness, and thinking ability to define the situation in a way that allowed him to plot a course of action that led to triumph. Not all of us have to perform Herculean tasks, but adversity is a test, and (from Shakespeare) many times ennobler, of the human spirit; for fortune's blows do crave a noble cunning. And for many of us, who are buffeted by the power of race, class, and gender, life is analogous to a Herculean task, just to stay alive. We will encounter overwhelming forces in our lives, for if they are not there now, they will come. The self provides the readiness for this struggle. Resistance is born once selves develop. We can act and labor in ways that, it is hoped, preserve our dignity and integrity along the way. But because we are human we are fallible, succumb to temptation, violate precepts that we preach, and step over and on others in our quest for success; thus is much deviance to be sympathetically understood.

One plays the hand one is dealt, one can make a heaven out of hell or a hell out of heaven, or the more recent proverb, if life gives you lemons, make lemonade. The hand, hell, and lemons are all analogous to obstacles over which we have no control. Playing the hand, making lemonade, or making heaven out of hell all express the adaptive and transcending qualities of the human self. We are communal and individual, Me's and I's, respectively. Such is the drama of social transformation.

Interactionism and Social Policy

If we are to improve the social condition of humanity, then the institutions of learning are paramount. Since a human being's situation-in-the-world is always in the process of becoming, the world itself is always in the process of becoming. Through improving the institutions through which people learn, and through which they acquire a self, mind, and human nature, we simultaneously improve humanity's potentiality as we improve society.

If human beings have the potential for self-change, if human beings' situation in the world can continuously evolve and is an emergent process, then advocating for social intervention and new institutions of education and socialization to guide human intelligence toward social reconstruction is theoretically justified from the perspective of SI. If individual effort can make a difference, then will not collective and institutional effort make even more of a difference in our lives? If humans are purposeful and determining in their behavior, then they create the world around them and can socially reconstruct that world as well.

In conclusion, I have argued that SI arose as a perspective to challenge both biological determinism and behavioristic psychology, and in so doing reconceptualized human nature and behavior within a sociological orbit. The theme of voluntaristic nominalism is so strong in early interactionism that the framework generally equated self-change with social change. Mead, for example, held that the individual has a virtually infinite capacity to change and thereby to change society, and that equality of opportunity would improve the individual's life-chances to achieve his or her full potential. Mead had not unmasked the myth of meritocracy. Power, privilege, hegemony, ideology, and other structures of domination (racism, classism, and sexism, for example) were ignored by most early interactionists, but they are now attended to.

SI contributed evidence and a perspective to show that biology was not destiny, and that human nature was profoundly social.The self and mind can emerge only as the capacity for role-taking and language acquisition develop through internalizing the perspective of others into the cognitive process of the human being, constituting the influence of the group on human behavior, motivation, and perception, making social control self-control, and rewarding all (who do not have an impaired capacity for role-taking) with a conscience. Instead of being internally or externally determined, human consciousness allows people to respond selectively to stimuli. Human behavior is varied because stimuli are not inherently meaningful but are, instead, symbols to be interpreted. Interpretation emerges out of social interaction awash in a cultural and historical milieu. Humans thus live in a symbolic environment where interaction, institutions, and society are constituted by the shared gestures, symbols, and meanings that give pattern and regularity to behavior. Humans cannot be explained in terms of a hereditarian conception of behavior and intelligence, or a behavioristic psychology; rather, they need to be understood in terms of the subjective meanings and definitions people attach to social objects. One triumph of SI is that an adequate account of social behavior can no longer remain ass-eared to that music.

References

Adler, Patricia A., Peter Alder, and Andrea Fontana. 1987. "Everyday Life Sociology."
Pp. 217-36 in *Annual Review of Sociology*, ed. W. R. Scott and J. S. Short. Palo
Alto: Annual Reviews.

Aiken, H. D. 1962. "Pragmatism and America's Philosophical Coming of Age." Pp.
47-81 in *Philosophy in the Twentieth Century*, vol. 1, ed. W. Barrett and H. D.
Aiken. New York: Random House.

Akers, Ronald L. 1968. "Problems in the Sociology of Deviance: Social Definitions
and Behavior." *Social Forces* 46: 455-65.

Akerstrom, Malin. 1997. "Waiting: A Source of Hostile Interaction in an Emergency
Clinic." *Qualitative Health Research* 7: 504-20.

Akindele, F. 1990. "A Sociolinguistic Analysis of Yoruba Greetings." *African Language and Culture* 3: 1-14.

Allport, G. W. 1937. *Personality*. New York: Holt.

Allport, Gordon W. 1961. *Pattern and Growth in Personality*. New York: Holt,
Rinehart and Winston.

Almagor, M., A. Tellegen, and N. G. Waller. 1995. "The Big Seven Model: A Cross-
Cultural Replication and Further Exploration of the Basic Dimensions of Natural
Language Trait Descriptions." *Journal of Personality and Social Psychology* 69:
300-307.

Altheide, David L. 1984. "The Media Self." Pp. 177-95 in *The Existential Self in
Society*, ed. J. A. Kotarba and A. Fontana. Chicago: University of Chicago Press.

———. 1985. *Media Power*. Beverly Hills, Calif.: Sage.

———. 1988. "Mediating Cutbacks in Human Services: A Case Study in the Negotiated Order." *The Sociological Quarterly* 29: 339-55.

———. 2000. "Identity and the Definition of the Situation in a Mass-Mediated Context." Symbolic Interaction 23: 1-27.

———. 2002. "Children and the Discourse of Fear." *Symbolic Interaction* 25: 229-50.

Andersen, Margaret L. 1993. *Thinking about Women: Sociological Perspectives on Sex
and Gender*. New York: Macmillan.

311

Anderson, Tammy L. 1994. "Drug Abuse and Identity: Linking Micro and Macro Factors." *The Sociological Quarterly* 35: 159-74.

Anonymous. No Date. "The Principal Features of the Social Psychology of George Herbert Mead."

Antonio, Robert J. 1995. "Nietzsche's Antisociology: Subjectified Culture and the End of History." *American Journal of Sociology* 101: 1-43.

Aronson, Elliot. 1976. *The Social Animal*. San Francisco: W. H. Freeman.

Ashforth, Blake E. 1992. "The Perceived Inequity of Systems." *Administration and Society* 24: 375-408.

Austin, J. L. 1978. *How to Do Things with Words*. Cambridge, Mass.: Harvard University Press.

Baldwin, James Mark. 1910. *The Story of Mind*. New York: D. Appleton.

―――. 1968. *Mental Development in the Child and the Race*. Introduction by Vahan D. Sewny. New York: Augustus M. Kelley.

―――. 1973. *Social and Ethical Interpretation in Mental Development*. New York: Arno Press.

Bales, Robert F. 1966. "Comment on Herbert Blumer's Paper." *American Journal of Sociology* 71: 545-47.

Ball, Donald N. 1970. "The Problematics of Respectability." Pp. 326-71 in *Deviance and Respectability: The Social Construction of Moral Meanings*, ed. Jack D. Douglas. New York: Basic Books.

Ball, Donald W. 1964. "Covert Political Rebellion as Ressentiment." *Social Forces* 43: 93-101.

Barbalet, J. M. 1998. *Emotion, Social Theory, and Social Structure: A Macrosociological Approach*. Cambridge: Cambridge University Press.

Barnet, Richard J. 1973. *Roots of War*. Baltimore: Penguin Books.

Barnet, Richard J., and Ronald E. Müller. 1974. *Global Reach: The Power of the Multinational Corporation*. New York: Simon and Schuster.

Bassis, M. S., R. J. Gelles, and A. Levine. 1991. *Sociology*, 4th ed. New York: McGraw-Hill.

Bates, Alan, and Nicholas Babchuck. 1961. "The Primary Group: A Reappraisal." *The Sociological Quarterly* 2: 181-91.

Bateson, G. 1958. *Naven*, 2nd ed. Palo Alto: Stanford University Press.

Bazzanella, C. 1990. "Phatic Connectives as Interactional Cues in Contemporary Spoken Italian." *Journal of Pragmatics* 14: 629-47.

Beard, Charles A. 1914. *A Contemporary American History*. New York: Macmillan.

Beauchamp, Gorman. 1982. "Resentment and Revolution in Jack London's Sociofantasy." *Canadian Review of American Studies* 13: 179-92.

Becker, Howard. 1963. *The Outsiders*. New York: Free Press of Glencoe.

―――. 1967. "Becoming a Marijuana User." Pp. 411-12 in *Symbolic Interaction: A Reader in Social Psychology*, ed. Jerome G. Manis and Bernard N. Meltzer.

Boston: Allyn and Bacon.

———. 1970. "Whose Side Are We On?" Pp. 201-17 in *The Sociology of Sociology*, ed. Larry Reynolds and Janice Reynolds. New York: David McKay.

———. 1973. "Labeling Theory Reconsidered." Pp. 177-208 in *The Outsiders*, ed. Howard Becker. New York: Free Press.

Belknap, Penny, and Wilbert M. Leonard II. 1991. "A Conceptual Replication and Extension of Erving Goffman's Study of Gender Advertisements." *Sex Roles* 25: 103-18.

Bem, D. J., and A. Allen. 1974. "On Predicting Some of the People Some of the Time: The Search for Cross-Situational Consistencies in Behavior." *Psychological Review* 81: 506-20.

Bem, Sandra L. 1983. "Gender Schema Theory and Its Implications for Child Development: Raising Gender-Aschematic Children in a Gender-Schematic Society." *Signs: Journal of Women in Culture and Society* 8: 598-616.

Ben-David, Joseph, and Randall Collins. 1966. "Social Factors in the Origins of a New Science: The Case of Psychology." *American Sociological Review* 31: 451-65.

Benet, V., and N. G. Waller. 1995. "The Big Seven Model of Personality Description: Evidence for Its Cross-Cultural Validity in a Spanish Sample." *Journal of Personality and Social Psychology* 69: 701-16.

Berger, P. L. 1963. *Invitation to Sociology*. Garden City, N.Y.: Doubleday.

Bernard, L .L. 1924. *Instinct: A Study in Social Psychology*. New York: Holt.

Bernstein, Basil B. 1971. *Class, Codes and Control*. London: Routledge and Kegan Paul.

Bertonneau, Thomas F. 1998. "Like Hypatia before the Mob: Desire, Resentment, and Sacrifice in *The Bostonians*." *Nineteenth Century Literature* 53: 56-90.

Betz, Hans Georg. 1991. *Postmodern Politics in Germany: The Politics of Resentment*. London: Macmillan.

Bledstein, Burton J. 1976. *The Culture of Professionalism: The Middle Class and the Development of Higher Education in America*. New York: Norton.

Blumer, Herbert. 1937. "Social Psychology." Pp. 144-98 in *Man and Society*, ed. E. Schmidt. Englewood Cliffs, N.J.: Prentice Hall.

———. 1955. "Attitudes and the Social Act." *Social Problems* 3: 59-65.

———. 1966a."The Sociological Implications of the Thought of George Herbert Mead." *American Journal of Sociology* 71: 535-44.

———. 1966b. "Reply." *American Journal of Sociology* 71: 547-48.

———. 1969. *Symbolic Interactionism: Perspective and Method*. Englewood Cliffs, N.J.: Prentice Hall.

———. 1971. "Social Problems as Collective Behavior." *Social Problems* 18: 298-306.

———. 1980. "Mead and Blumer: The Convergent Methodological Perspectives of Social Behaviorism and Symbolic Interactionism." *American Sociological Review*

45: 409-19.

Borgatta, E. F., and M. L. Borgatta, ed. 1992. *Encyclopedia of Sociology*, 4 volumes. New York: Macmillan.

Boring, Edwin G. 1963. *History, Psychology, and Science: Selected Papers*. New York: Wiley.

Boutilier, R. G., J. C. Roed, and A. C. Svendsen. 1980. "Crises in the Two Social Psychologies: A Critical Comparison." *Social Psychology Quarterly* 43: 5-17.

Bramson, Leon. 1961. *The Political Context of Sociology*. Princeton, N.J.: Princeton University Press.

Braverman, Harry. 1961. *Labor and Monopoly Capital*. New York: Monthly Review Press.

Brigden, Susan. 2000. *New Worlds, Lost Worlds: The Rule of the Tudors, 1485-1603*. New York: Viking.

Bromberg, Minna, and Gary Alan Fine. 2002. "Resurrecting the Red: Pete Seeger and the Purification of Difficult Reputations." *Social Forces* 80: 1135-55.

Brown, P., and S. C. Levinson. 1987. *Politeness: Some Universals in Language Usage*. Cambridge: Cambridge University Press.

Brown, P., and S. Levinson. 1978. "Universals in Language Phenomena: Politeness Phenomena." Pp. 56-310 in *Questions and Politeness: Strategies in Social Interaction*, ed. E. N. Goody. Cambridge: Cambridge University Press.

Brymer, Richard A. 1994. "The Emergence and Maintenance of a Deviant Sub-Culture: The Case of the Hunting/Poaching Sub-Culture." Pp. 363-76 in *Symbolic Interaction: An Introduction to Social Psychology*, ed. Nancy J. Herman and Larry T. Reynolds. Dix Hills, N.Y.: General Hall.

Burkhardt, Frederick. 1984. "*Foreword to Psychology: Briefer Course*" by William James. Cambridge, Mass.: Harvard University Press.

Burton, D. 1980. *Dialogue and Discourse*. London: Routledge and Kegan Paul.

Butler, J. 1990. *Gender Trouble: Feminism and the Subversion of Identity*. New York: Routledge.

Byrnes, H. 1986. "Interactional Style in German and American Conversation." *Text* 6: 189-206.

Cagle, Van M. 1989. "The Language of Cultural Studies: An Analysis of British Subculture Theory." Pp. 301-13 in *Studies in Symbolic Interaction*, vol. 10, ed. Norman K. Denzin. Greenwich Conn.: JAI Press.

Cahill, Spencer E. 1980. "Directions for an Interactionist Study of Gender Development." *Symbolic Interaction* 13: 123-38.

———. 1983. "Reexamining the Acquisition of Sex Roles: A Social Interactionist Approach." *Sex Roles* 9: 1-15.

———. 1986a. "Childhood Socialization as a Recruitment Process: Some Lessons from the Study of Gender Development." Pp. 163-86 in *Sociological Studies of Child Development*, ed. Peter Adler and Patricia Adler. Greenwich, Conn.: JAI

Press.

———. 1986b. "Language Practices and Self Definition: The Case of Gender Identity Acquisition." *The Sociological Quarterly* 27: 295-311.

———. 1987. "Children and Civility: Ceremonial Deviance and the Acquisition of Ritual Competence." *Social Psychological Quarterly* 50: 312-21.

———. 1989. "Fashioning Males and Females: Appearance Management and the Social Reproduction of Gender." *Symbolic Interaction* 12: 281-98.

———. 1990. "Childhood and Public Life: Reaffirming Biographical Divisions." *Social Problems* 37: 390-402.

———. 1994. "And a Child Shall Lead Us? Children, Gender, and Perspectives by Incongruity." Pp. 459-69 in *Symbolic Interaction: An Introduction to Social Psychology*, ed. Nancy J. Herman and Larry T. Reynolds. Dix Hills, N.Y.: General Hall.

Callon, M., J. Law, and A. Rip. 1986. *Mapping the Dynamics of Science and Technology: Sociology of Science and Technology in the Real World*. London: Macmillan.

Camic, Charles. 1986. "The Matter of Habit." *American Journal of Sociology* 91: 1039-87.

Carey, James. 1987. *Media, Myths, and Narratives: Television and the Press*. Beverly Hills, Calif.: Sage.

———. 1988. *Communication as Culture: Essays on Media and Society*. London: Unwin Hyman.

Casper, Lynne, Irwin Garfinkel, and Sara S. McLanahan. 1994. "The Gender-Poverty Gap: What We Can Learn from Other Countries." *American Sociological Review* 59: 594-605.

Cassirer, Ernst. 1944. *An Essay on Man*. New Haven, Conn.: Yale University Press.

Cattell, R. B. 1946. *Description and Measurement of Personality*. Yonkers, N.Y.: World Book.

Chaika, E. 1982. *Language: The Social Mirror*. Rowley, Mass.: Newbury House.

Chambliss, William J. 1974. "The State, the Law, and the Definition of Behavior as Criminal or Delinquent." Pp. 7-43 in *Handbook of Criminology*, ed. Daniel Glaser. Chicago: Rand McNally.

———. 1975. "The Political Economy of Crime: A Comparative Study of Nigeria and the U.S.A." Pp. 167-80 in *Critical Criminology*, ed. Ian Taylor, Paul Walton, and Jock Young. London: Routledge and Kegan Paul.

Chandler, Alfred D. Jr. 1962. *Strategy and Structure: Chapters in the History of the American Industrial Enterprise*. Cambridge, Mass.: MIT Press.

Charon, Joel M. 1979. *Symbolic Interactionism*. Englewood Cliffs, N.J.: Prentice Hall.

Chodorow, Nancy. 1971. "Being and Doing: A Cross-cultural Examination of the Socialization of Males and Females." Pp. 173-97 in *Woman in Sexist Society: Studies in Power and Powerlessness*, ed. Vivian Gornick and Barbara Moran. New York: Basic Books.

————. 1978. *The Reproduction of Mothering*. Berkeley: University of California Press.

————. 1989. "Family Structure and Feminine Personality." Pp. 43-58 in *Feminist Frontiers II*, ed. Laurel Richardson and Verta Zaylor. New York: Random House.

Chomsky, N. 1968. *Language and Mind*. New York: Harcourt Brace Jovanovich.

Cicourel, Aaron V. 1972. "Basic and Normative Rules in the Negotiation of Status and Role." Pp. 229-58 in *Studies in Social Interaction*, ed. David Sudnow. New York: Free Press.

Clanton, Gordon. 1989. "Jealousy in American Culture, 1945-1985: Reflections from Popular Literature." Pp. 179-93 in *The Sociology of Emotions: Original Essays and Research Papers*, ed. David D. Franks and E. Doyle McCarthy. Greenwich, Conn.: JAI Press.

Clark, Candace. 1989. "Studying Sympathy: Methodological Confessions." Pp. 137-51 in *The Sociology of Emotions: Original Essays and Research Papers*, ed. David D. Franks and E. Doyle McCarthy. Greenwich, Conn.: JAI Press.

Clough, Patricia Ticineto. 1992. "The Rhetoric of Sexual Difference and the Narrative Construction of Ethnographic Authority." Pp. 3-17 in *Studies in Symbolic Interaction*, vol. 13, ed. Norman K. Denzin. Greenwich, Conn.: JAI Press.

Cocchi, P. 1992. Review of *Small Talk: Analyzing Phatic Communion*, by K. P. Schneider. In *Journal of Pragmatics* 18: 373-93.

Collier, Gary, Henry L. Minton, and Graham Reynolds. 1991. *Currents of Thought in American Social Psychology*. Oxford: Oxford University Press.

Collins, R. 1987. "Interaction Ritual Chains, Power, and Property: The Micro-Macro Connection as an Empirically Based Theoretical Problem." Pp. 193-206 in *The Micro-Macro Link*, ed. J. C. Alexander et al. Berkeley: University of California Press.

Collins, Randall, and Michael Makowsky. 1972. "Erving Goffman and the Theater of Social Encounters." Pp. 202-14 in *The Discovery of Society*, ed. Randall Collins and Michael Makowsky. New York: Random House.

Cook, K. S., G. A. Fine, and J. S. House, eds. 1995. *Sociological Perspectives on Social Psychology*. Boston: Allyn and Bacon.

Cooley, Charles H. 1902. *Human Nature and the Social Order*. New York: Scribner's.

————. 1909. *Social Organization*. New York: Scribner's.

————. 1918. *Social Process*. New York: Scribner's.

————. 1922. *Human Nature and the Social Order*, revised edition. New York: Charles Scribner's Sons.

————. 1956. *The Two Major Works of Charles H. Cooley: Social Organization and Human Nature and the Social Order*. Glencoe, Ill: Free Press.

————. 1967a. "The Roots of Social Knowledge." Pp. 68-83 in *Symbolic Interaction: A Reader in Social Psychology*, ed. Jerome G. Manis and Bernard N. Meltzer. Boston: Allyn and Bacon.

————. 1967b. "False Separation of Individual and Society." Pp. 153-55 in *Symbolic Interaction: A Reader in Social Psychology*, ed. Jerome G. Manis and Bernard N. Meltzer. Boston: Allyn and Bacon.

————. 1968a. "The Social Self: On the Varieties of Self-Feeling." Pp. 137-43 in *Self and Social Interaction*, vol.1, ed. Chad Gordon and Kenneth J. Gergen. New York: Wiley.

————. 1968b. "The Social Self: On the Meanings of 'I.'" Pp. 87-91 in *Self and Social Interaction*, vol. 1, ed. Chad Gordon and Kenneth J. Gergen. New York: Wiley.

————. 1970. "Self as Sentiment and Reflection." Pp. 377-82 in *Social Psychology through Symbolic Interaction*, ed. Gregory P. Stone and Harvey A. Farberman. Waltham, Mass.: Xerox.

————. 1972a. "Looking-Glass Self." Pp. 231-33 in *Symbolic Interaction: A Reader in Social Psychology*, ed. Jerome G. Manis and Bernard N. Meltzer. Boston: Allyn and Bacon.

————. 1972b. "Primary Group and Human Nature." Pp. 158-60 in *Symbolic Interaction: A Reader in Social Psychology*, ed. Jerome G. Manis and Bernard N. Meltzer. Boston: Allyn and Bacon.

Corsaro, William A. 1979a. "'We're Friends, Right?' Children's Use of Access Rituals in a Nursery School." *Language in Society* 8: 315-36.

————. 1979b. "Young Children's Conception of Status and Role." *Sociology of Education* 52: 46-59.

————. 1985. *Friendship and Peer Culture in the Early Years*. Norwood, N.J.: Ablex.

————. 1986. "Discourse Processes within Peer Culture: From a Constructivist to an Interpretive Approach to Childhood Socialization." Pp. 81-101 in *Sociological Studies of Child Development*, ed. Peter Adler and Patricia Adler. Greenwich, Conn.: JAI Press.

————. 1988. "Routines in the Peer Culture of American and Italian Nursery School Children." *Sociology of Education* 61: 1-14.

————. 1992. "Interpretive Reproduction in Children's Peer Cultures." *Social Psychology Quarterly* 55: 160-77.

Corsaro, William A., and Donna Eder. 1990. "Children's Peer Cultures." *Annual Review of Sociology* 16: 197-220.

Corsaro, William A., and Thomas A. Rizzo. 1988. "*Discussione* and Friendship: Socialization Processes in the Peer Culture of Italian Nursery School Children." *American Sociological Review* 53: 879-94.

————. 1990. "An Interpretive Approach to Childhood Socialization." *American Sociological Review* 55: 466-68.

Coser, Rose Laub. 1991. *In Defense of Modernity*. Stanford, Calif.: Stanford University Press.

Coulmas, F. 1981. *Conversational Routine*. The Hague: Mouton.

Coupland, J., N. Coupland, and J. D. Robinson. 1988. "'How Are You?': Negotiating

Phatic Communion." *Language in Society* 21: 207-30.

Coupland, J., J. D. Robinson, and N. Coupland. 1994. "Frame Negotiation in Doctor-Elderly Patient Consultations." *Discourse and Society* 3: 89-124.

Coupland, N., J. Coupland, and H. Giles. 1991. *Language, Society, and the Elderly*. Cambridge: Basil Blackwell.

Coupland, N., K. Grainger, and J. Coupland. 1988. "Politeness in Context: Inter-generational Issues." *Language and Society* 17: 253-62.

Coutu, Walter. 1951. "Role-Playing vs. Role-Taking: An Appeal for Clarification." *American Sociological Review* 16: 180-87.

Cranston, M. 1967. "Liberalism." Pp. 458-61 in *The Encyclopedia of Philosophy*, vol. 4, ed. Paul Edwards. New York: Macmillan.

Cravens, Hamilton. 1978. *The Triumph of Evolution: American Scientists and the Heredity-Environment Controversy, 1900-1941*. Philadelphia: University of Pennsylvania Press.

Crozier, Michael. 1969. "Bureaucratic Organization and the Evolution of Industrial Society." Pp. 357-74 in *A Sociological Reader in Complex Organizations*, ed. Amitai Etzioni. New York: Holt, Rinehart, and Winston.

Crystal, D. 1987. *The Cambridge Encyclopedia of Language*. Cambridge: Cambridge University Press.

———. 1980. *A First Dictionary of Linguistics and Phonetics*. London: Deutsch.

Curti, Merle. 1980. *Human Nature in American Thought: A History*. Madison: University of Wisconsin Press.

Cuzzort, R. P. 1969. "Humanity as the Big Con: The Human Views of Erving Goffman." Pp. 173-92 in *Humanity and Modern Sociological Thought*, ed. R. P. Cuzzort. New York: Rinehart and Winston.

Daniels, Arlene. 1973. "The Philosophy of Combat Psychiatry." Pp. 132-40 in *Deviance: The Interactionist Perspective*, ed. Earl Rubington and Martin S. Weinberg. New York: Macmillian.

Darwin, Charles. No Date. *On the Origin of Species*. New York: Modern Library.

Davis, Fred. 1967. "Deviance Disavowal: The Management of Strained Interaction by the Visibly Handicapped." Pp. 189-204 in *Symbolic Interaction: A Reader in Social Psychology*, ed. Jerome G. Manis and Bernard N. Meltzer. Boston: Allyn and Bacon.

Davis, Kingsley. 1948. *Human Society*. New York: Macmillan.

Davis, Nanette. 1972. "Labelling Theory in Deviance Research: A Critique and Reconsideration." *The Sociological Quarterly* 13: 447-74.

———. 1980. *Sociological Constructions of Deviance: Perspective and Issues in the Field*. Dubuque, Iowa: Wm. C. Brown.

Degler, Carl N. 1970. *Out of Our Past: The Forces That Shaped Modern America*. New York: Harper and Row.

DeLamater, John. 1968. "On the Nature of Deviance." *Social Forces* 46: 445-55.

Denzin, Norman K. 1970. "Rules of Conduct and the Study of Deviant Behavior: Some Notes on the Social Relationship." Pp. 120-59 in *Deviance and Respectability: The Social Construction of Moral Meanings*, ed. Jack D. Douglas. New York: Basic Books.

———. 1971. "Children and Their Caretakers." *Transaction* 8: 62-72.

———. 1972. "The Genesis of Self in Early Childhood Socialization." *The Sociological Quarterly* 13: 291-314.

———. 1977. *Childhood Socialization*. San Francisco: Jossey-Bass.

———. 1979. "Toward a Social Psychology of Childhood Socialization." *Contemporary Sociology* 8: 550-56.

———. 1982. "The Significant Others of Young Children: Notes toward a Phenomenology of Childhood." Pp. 29-46 in *The Social Life of Children in a Changing Society*, ed. K. M. Borman. Hillsdale, N.J.: Erlbaum.

———. 1984. *On Understanding Emotion*. San Francisco: Jossey-Bass.

———. 1989a. "Reading Tender Mercies: Two Interpretations." *The Sociological Quarterly* 30: 37-57.

———. 1989b. "Reading/Writing Culture: Interpreting the Postmodern Project." *Cultural Dynamics* 2: 9-27.

———. 1989. *Interpretive Interaction*. Newbury Park, Calif.: Sage.

———. 1990. "Reading Cultural Texts: Comment on Griswold." *American Journal of Sociology* 95: 1577-80.

———. 1991. "Empiricist Cultural Studies in America: A Deconstructive Reading." *Current Perspectives in Social Theory* 11: 17-39.

———. 1991. *Images of Postmodern Society: Social Theory and Contemporary Cinema*. Newbury, Calif.: Sage.

———. 1992. *Symbolic Interactionism and Cultural Studies*. Cambridge, Mass.: Blackwell.

———. 1995. *The Cinematic Society*. New York: Sage.

———. 2001."Symbolic Interactionism, Poststructuralism, and the Racial Subject." *Symbolic Interaction* 24: 243-49.

De Vito, J. A. 1973. *Language: Concepts and Processes*. Englewood Cliffs, N.J.: Prentice Hall.

Dewey, John. 1906. *The Child and the Curricula*. Chicago: University of Chicago Press.

———. 1931. *Philosophy and Civilization*. New York: Minton, Balch.

———. 1957. *Human Nature and Conduct: An Introduction to Social Psychology*. New York: Modern Library.

———. 1961. *Democracy and Education*. New York: Macmillan.

———. 1972. "Mind, Experience, and Behavior." Pp. 328-30 in *Symbolic Interaction: A Reader in Social Psychology*, ed. Jerome G. Manis and Bernard N. Meltzer. Boston: Allyn and Bacon.

Dickens, D. R., and A. Fontana. 1996. "On Nostalgic Reconstruction in Interactionist Thought or, Realism as the Last Refuge of a Scoundrel." Pp. 181-92 in *Studies in Symbolic*, vol. 20, ed. N. K. Denzin, Greenwich, Conn.: JAI Press.

Digman, J. M. 1990. "Personality Structure: Emergence of the Five-Factor Model." *Annual Review of Psychology* 41: 417-40.

Ditton, Jason. 1980. *The View from Goffman*. London: Macmillan.

Douglas, Jack D. 1970. "Deviance and Respectability: The Social Construction of Moral Meanings." Pp. 3-30 in *Deviance and Respectability: The Social Construction of Moral Meanings*, ed. Jack D. Douglas. New York: Basic Books.

Dowling, William C. 1984. *Jameson, Althusser, Marx*. Ithaca, N.Y.: Cornell University Press.

Downey, Douglas B., Pamela Braboy Jackson, and Brian Powell. 1994. "Sons versus Daughters: Sex Composition of Children and Maternal Views on Socialization." *The Sociological Quarterly* 35: 33-50.

Duncan, Otis Dudley, and Leo F. Schnore. 1969. "Cultural, Behavioral, and Ecological Perspectives in the Study of Social Organization." Pp. 70-85 in *Sociological Theory: An Introduction*, ed. Walter L. Wallace. Chicago: Aldine.

Duranti, A., and C. Goodwin, eds. 1992. *Rethinking Context: Language as as Interactive Phenomenon*. Cambridge: Cambridge University Press.

Dykhuizen, George. 1973. *The Life and Mind of John Dewey*. Carbondale: Southern Illinois University Press.

Eder, Donna, and Maureen T. Hallinan. 1978. "Sex Differences in Children's Friendships." *American Sociological Review* 43: 237-50.

Eder, Donna, and Stephen Parker. 1987. "The Cultural Production and Reproduction of Gender: The Effect of Extracurricular Activities on Peer-Group Culture." *Sociology of Education* 60: 200-213.

Edwards, A. D. 1976. *Language in Culture and Class*. London: Heinemann Educational Books.

Elias, Norman. 1939 (1978). *The Civilizing Process*. Oxford: Blackwell.

Elkin, Frederick, and Gerald Handel. 1989. *The Child and Society: The Process of Socialization*, 5th ed. New York: Random House.

Ellis, Carolyn. 1991a. "Sociological Introspection and Emotional Experience." *Symbolic Interaction* 14: 23-50.

———. 1991b. "Emotional Sociology." Pp. 123-45 in Studies in Symbolic Interaction, vol. 12, ed. Norman K. Denzin. Greenwich, Conn.: JAI Press.

Ellyson, S. L., J. F. Dovidio, R. L. Corson, and D. L. Vinicur. 1980. "Visual Behavior in Female Dyads: Situational and Personality Factors." *Social Psychology Quarterly* 43: 328-36.

Encyclopedia of Philosophy. 1967 ed. S.V. "Behaviorism" by Arnold Kaufman.

Encyclopedia of Philosophy. 1967 ed. S.V. " Psychological Behaviorism" by Charles Taylor.

Entwistle, D. R., K. L. Alexander, A. M. Pallas, and D. Cadigan. 1988. "A Social Psychological Model of the Schooling Process over First Grade." *Social Psychology Quarterly* 51: 173-89.

Erikson, Kai T. 1962. "Notes on the Sociology of Deviance." *Social Problems* 9: 307-14.

———. 1966. *Wayward Puritans: A Study in the Sociology of Deviance*. New York: Wiley.

———. 1967. "A Comment on Disguised Observation in Sociology." *Social Problems* 14: 366-73.

Esterberg, Kristin G., Phyllis Moen, and Donna Dempster-McCain. 1994. "Transition to Divorce: A Life-Course Approach to Women's Marital Duration and Dissolution." *The Sociological Quarterly* 35: 289-307.

Eysenck, H. J. 1947. *Dimensions of Personality*. London: Routledge and Kegan Paul.

Faludi, Susan. 1991. *Backlash: The Undeclared War against American Women*. New York: Doubleday.

Farber, I. E. 1964. "A Framework for the Study of Personality as a Behavioral Science." Pp. 3-37 in *Personality Change*, ed. P. Worchel and D. Bryne. New York: Wiley.

Farberman, Harvey A. 1970. "Mannheim, Cooley, and Mead: Toward a Social Theory of Mentality." *The Sociological Quarterly* 18: 3-13.

———. 1975. "A Criminogenic Market Structure: The Automobile Industry." *The Sociological Quarterly* 16: 438-57.

———. 1980. "Fantasy in Everyday Life: Some Aspects of the Intersection between Social Psychology and Political-Economy." *Symbolic Interaction* 3: 9-21.

Faris, Ellsworth. 1936. "Review of *Mind, Self, and Society*." 41: 909-13.

Faris, Robert E. L. 1967. "Research in the Ecological Structure of the City." Pp. 51-63 in *Chicago Sociology: 1920-1932*, ed. Robert E. L. Faris. San Francisco: Chandler.

Faulkner, Harold. 1951. *The Decline of Laissez Faire, 1897-1917*. New York: Rinehart.

Fausto-Sterling, Anne. 1989. "Hormonal Hurricanes: Menstruation, Menopause, and Female Behavior." Pp. 291-306 in *Feminist Frontiers II*, ed. Laurel Richardson and Verta Taylor. New York: Random House.

———. 1992. *Myths of Gender: Biological Theories about Women and Men*. New York: Basic Books.

Feuer, Lewis S. 1953. "Sociological Aspects of the Relation between Language and Philosophy." *Philosophy of Science* 20: 85-100.

Fine, Gary Alan. 1984. "Negotiated Orders and Organizational Cultures." *Annual Review of Sociology* 10: 239-62.

Fine, Gary Alan, and Sherryl Kleinman. 1979. "Rethinking Subculture: An Interactionist Analysis." *American Journal of Sociology* 85: 1-20.

———. 1983. "Network and Meaning: An Interactionist Approach to Structure."

Symbolic Interaction 6: 97-110.

Fischer, John M., and Mark Ravizz. 1993. *Perspectives on Moral Responsibility.* Ithaca, N.Y.: Cornell University Press.

Folger, Robert. 1987. "Reformulating the Preconditions of Resentment: A Referent Cognitions Model." Pp. 183-215 in *Social Comparison, Social Justice, and Relative Deprivation,* ed. J. C. Masters and W. P. Smith. Hillsdale, N.J.: Lawrence Erlbaum Associates.

Foote, Nelson N. 1967. "Identification as a Basis for a Theory of Motivation." Pp. 343-54 in *Symbolic Interaction: A Reader in Social Psychology,* ed. Jerome G. Manis and Bernard N. Meltzer. Boston: Allyn and Bacon.

———. 1970. "Love." Pp. 319-27 in *Social Psychology trough Symbolic Interaction,* ed. Gregory P. Stone and Harvey A. Farberman. Waltham, Mass.: Xerox.

Foucault, Michel. 1967. *Madness and Civilization.* New York: Pantheon.

———. 1972. *The Archaeology of Knowledge.* New York: Harper Torchbooks.

———. 1979. *Discipline and Punish: The Birth of the Prison.* New York: Vintage.

Frank, Arthur W. 1992. "Can Sociology Swallow Nietzsche?" *Canadian Journal of Sociology* 17: 99-104.

Frank, Lawrence K. 1967. "Culture and Personality." Pp. 88-105 in *John Dewey: Philosopher of Science and Freedom,* ed. Sidney Hook. New York: Barnes & Noble.

Franks, David D. 1985. "Introduction to the Special Issue on the Sociology of Emotions." *Symbolic Interaction* 8: 161-70.

Franks, David D. 1989. "Power and Role-Taking: A Social Behaviorist's Synthesis of Kemper's Power and Status Model." Pp. 153-77 in *The Sociology of Emotions: Original Essays and Research Papers,* ed. David D. Franks and E. Doyle McCarthy. Greenwich, Conn.: JAI Press.

Franks, David D., and E. Doyle McCarthy. 1989. "Introduction." Pp. 11-20 in *The Sociology of Emotions: Original Essays and Research Papers,* ed. David D. Franks and E. Doyle McCarthy. Greenwich, Conn.: JAI Press.

Friedrichs, Robert W. 1970. *A Sociology of Sociology.* New York: Free Press.

Freidson, Eliot. 1973. "The Production of Deviant Populations." Pp. 125-27 in *Deviance: The Interactionist Perspective,* ed. Earl Rubington and Martin Weinberg. New York: Macmillan.

Fuchs, Stephan. 2001. "Beyond Agency." *Sociological Theory* 19: 24-40.

Garfinkel, Harold. 1972. "Studies of the Routine Grounds of Everyday Activities." Pp. 4-30 in *Studies in Social Interaction,* ed. David Sudnow. New York: Free Press.

———. 1973. "Conditions of Successful Degradation Ceremonies." Pp. 89-94 in *Deviance: The Interactionist Perspective,* ed. Earl Rubington and Martin Weinberg. New York: Macmillan.

Genovese, Eugene D. 1974. *Roll, Jordan, Roll: The World the Slaves Made.* New York: Vintage.

Gergen, K. J. 1992. *The Saturated Self.* New York: Basic Books.

———. 1996. "Technology and the Self: From the Essential to the Sublime." Pp. 127-40 in *Constructing the Self in a Meditated World*, ed. D. Grodin and T. R. Lindlof. Thousand Oaks, Calif.: Sage.

Gerson, Mary-Joan, Judith L. Alpert, and Mary Sue Richardson. 1984. "Mothering: The View from Psychological Research." *Signs: Journal of Women in Culture and Society* 9: 434-53.

Gerth, Hans, and C. Wright Mills. 1953. *Character and Social Structure.* New York: Harcourt Brace and World.

Ghiga, G. 1989. "Phatic Elements of Communication in Romanian Everyday Dialogues." *Revue Roumaine de Linguistique* 26: 45-52.

Gibbons, Don C. 1976. "Observations on the Study of Crime Causation." Pp. 68-86 in *Criminal Behavior and Social Systems*, ed. Anthony L. Guenther. Chicago: Rand McNally.

Gibbs, Jack P. 1966. "Conceptions of Deviant Behavior: The Old and the New." *Pacific Sociological Review* 9: 9-14.

———. 1972. "Issues in Defining Deviant Behavior." Pp. 39-68 in *Theoretical Perspectives on Deviance*, ed. Roberta A. Scott and Jack D. Douglas. New York: Basic Books.

Giddens, Anthony. 1984. *The Constitution of Society: Outline of the Theory.* Oxford: Polity Press.

Giele, Janet Zollinger. 1982a. "Women in Adulthood: Unanswered Questions." Pp. 1-35 in *Women in the Middle Years*, ed. Janet Zollinger Giele. New York: Wiley.

———. 1982b. "Women's Work and Family Roles." Pp. 115-50 in *Women in the Middle Years*, ed. Janet Zollinger Giele. New York: Wiley.

———. 1982c. "Future Research and Policy Questions." Pp. 199-240 in *Women in the Middle Years*, ed. Janet Zollinger Giele. New York: Wiley.

Giesen, B. 1987. "Beyond Reductionism: Four Models Relating Micro and Macro Levels." Pp. 337-55 in *The Micro-Macro Link*, ed. J. C. Alexander et al. Berkeley: University of California Press.

Gilligan, Carol. 1982a. "Adult Development and Women's Development: Arrangements for a Marriage." Pp. 89-114 in *Women in the Middle Years*, ed. Janet Zollinger Giele. New York: Wiley.

———. 1982b. *In a Different Voice.* Cambridge, Mass.: Harvard University Press.

Gilmore, David D. 1990. *Manhood in the Making: Cultural Concepts of Masculinity.* New Haven, Conn.: Yale University Press.

Glaser, Barney G., and Anselm L. Strauss. 1972. "Awareness Contexts and Social Interaction." Pp. 447-62 in *Symbolic Interaction: A Reader in Social Psychology*, ed. Jerome G. Manis and Bernard N. Meltzer. Boston: Allyn and Bacon.

Glaser, Daniel. 1972. "Criminality Theories and Behavioral Images." Pp. 482-97 in *Symbolic Interaction: A Reader in Social Psychology*, ed. Jerome G. Manis and

Bernard N. Meltzer. Boston: Allen and Bacon.

Godard, D. 1977. "Same Setting, Different Norms: Phone Call Beginnings in France and the United States." *Language in Society* 6: 209-19.

Goff, Tom W. 1980. *Marx and Mead: Contributions to a Sociology of Knowledge.* London: Routledge and Kegan Paul.

Goffman, Erving. 1952. "On Cooling the Mark Out: Some Aspects of Adaptation to Failure." *Psychiatry: Journal for the Study of Interpersonal Processes* 15: 451-63.

———. 1959. *The Presentation of Self in Everyday Life.* New York: Anchor Books.

———. 1961. *Asylums: Essays on the Social Organization of Mental Patients and Other Inmates.* New York: Anchor Books.

———. 1961. *Encounters: Two Studies in the Sociology of Interaction.* Indianapolis: Bobbs-Merrill.

———. 1963. *Behavior in Public Places: Notes on the Social Organization of Gatherings.* New York: Free Press.

———. 1964. "The Neglected Situation." *American Anthropologist* 6: 133-36.

———. 1967. *Interaction Ritual: Essays on Face-to-Face Behavior.* New York: Doubleday Anchor.

———. 1969. *Strategic Interaction.* Philadelphia: University of Pennsylvania Press.

———. 1971. *Relations in Public: Microstudies of the Public Order.* New York: Harper and Row.

———. 1974. *Frame Analysis: An Essay on the Organization of Experience.* New York: Harper and Row.

———. 1976. *Gender Advertisements.* New York: Harper and Row.

———. 1981. *Forms of Talk.* Oxford: Basil Blackwell.

———. 1983. "The Interaction Order." *American Sociological Review* 48: 1-17.

Goldfarb, Jeffrey C. 1997. *The Cynical Society.* Chicago: University of Chicago Press.

Goldman, Eric. 1955. *Rendezvous with Destiny.* New York: Vintage.

Gonos, George. 1977. "'Situation' versus 'Frame': The 'Interactionist' and the 'Structuralist' Analyses of Everyday Life." *American Sociological Review* 42: 854-67.

Goodman, E. 1997. "We Are Not a Nation of Character Actors." *Morning Sun* (Mt. Pleasant, Mich.), June 24.

Goodwin, Marjorie Harness. 1990. *He-Said-She-Said.* Bloomington: Indiana University Press.

Gordon, Chad, and Kenneth J. Gergen. 1968. *The Self in Social Interaction*, vol. 1. New York: Wiley.

Gordon, Steven L. 1989. "Institutional and Impulsive Orientations in Selectively Appropriating Emotions to Self." Pp. 115-35 in *The Sociology of Emotions: Original Essays and Research Papers*, ed. David D. Franks and E. Doyle McCarthy. Greenwich, Conn.: JAI Press.

Gossett, Thomas F. 1969. *Race: The History of an Idea in America.* New York: Schocken.

Gould, Stephen Jay. 1981. *The Mismeasure of Man*. New York: Norton.

Gouldner, Alvin.W. 1970a. "The Sociologist as Partisan: Sociology and the Welfare State." Pp. 218-55 in *Sociology of Sociology*, ed. Larry Reynolds and Janice Reynolds. New York: David McKay.

——. 1970b. *The Coming Crisis in Western Sociology*. New York: Avon Books.

Gove, Walter R. 1975. "The Labelling Perspective: An Overview." Pp. 3-20 in *The Labeling of Deviance: Evaluating a Perspective*, ed. Walter R. Gove. New York: Sage.

Gramsci, Antonio. 1971. *Selections from Prison Notebooks*. London: New Left Books.

Greenfeld, Lewis. 1990. "The Formation of the Russian National Identity: The Role of Status Insecurity and Ressentiment." *Comparative Studies in Society and History* 32: 549-91.

Grodin, D., and T. R. Lindlof. 1996. "The Self and Mediated Communication." Pp. 3-12 in *Constructing the Self in a Mediated World*, ed. D. Grodin and T. R. Lindlof. Thousand Oaks, Calif.: Sage.

Gross, N., W. S. Mason, and A. W. McEachern. 1958. *Explorations in Role Analysis: Studies in the School Superintendency Role*. New York: John Wiley and Sons.

Grossberg, Lawrence. 1986. "History, Politics and Postmodernism: Stuart Hall and Cultural Studies." *Journal of Communication Inquiry* 10: 61-77.

Gusfield, Joseph R. 1967. "Moral Passage: The Symbolic Process in Public Designations of Deviance." *Social Problems* 15: 175-88.

Haber, Joram Graf. 1991. *Forgiveness*. Savage, Md.: Rowman & Littlefield.

Habermas, Jürgen. 1971. *Knowledge and Human Interests*. Boston: Beacon Press.

——. 1979. *Communication and the Evolution of Society*. Boston: Beacon Press.

Hall, Peter M. 1972. "A Symbolic Interactionist Analysis of Politics." *Sociological Inquiry* 42: 35-75.

——. 1985. "Asymmetric Relationships and Processes of Power." Pp. 309-44 in *Foundations of Interpretive Sociology*, ed. H. Farberman and R. Perinbanayagam. Greenwich, Conn.: JAI Press.

——. 1987. "Interactionism and the Study of Social Organization." *The Sociological Quarterly* 28: 1-22.

——. 1997. "Meta-Power, Social Organization, and the Shaping of Social Action." *Symbolic Interaction* 20: 397-418.

——. 2003. "Interactionism: Social Organization, and Social Processes: Looking Back and Moving Ahead." *Symbolic Interaction* 26: 33-55.

Hall, Peter M., and Bradley W. Wing. 2000. "Book Review." *Symbolic Interaction* 23: 317-20.

Hall, Peter M., and Dee Ann Spencer-Hall. 1982. "The Social Conditions of the Negotiated Order." *Urban Life* 11: 328-49.

Hall, Stuart. 1979. "Culture, the Media and the Ideological Effect." Pp. 315-48 in *Mass Communication and Society*, ed. James Curran et al. Beverly Hills: Sage.

————. 1980. "Cultural Studies and the Centre: Some Problematics and Problems." Pp. 15-47 in *Culture, Media, Language*, ed. Stuart Hall et al. London: Hutchinson.

————. 1986a. "Gramsci's Relevance for the Study of Race and Ethnicity." *Journal of Communication Inquiry*. 10: 5-27.

————. 1986b. "The Problem of Ideology—Marxism Without Guarantees." *Journal of Communication Inquiry* 10: 28-44.

Hamilton, Peter. 1974. *Knowledge and Social Structure: An Introduction to the Classical Argument in the Sociology of Knowledge*. London: Routledge and Kegan Paul.

Hammond, Judith M. 1980. "Biography Building to Insure the Future: Women's Negotiation of Gender Relevancy in Medical School." *Symbolic Interaction* 3: 35-49.

Hampton, S. E. 1995. "Personality." Pp. 437-42 in *The Blackwell Encyclopedia of Social Psychology*, ed. A. S. R. Manstead and M. Hewstone. Oxford: Blackwell Publishers.

Handel, Gerald. 1990. "Revising Socialization Theory." *American Sociological Review* 55: 463-66.

Handlin, Oscar. 1973. *The Uprooted*. Boston: Little, Brown.

Hardert, R. A., et al. 1977. *Sociology and Social Issues*, 2nd ed. Hinsdale, Ill.: Dryden.

Harding, Sandra. 1991. *Whose Science? Whose Knowledge? Thinking from Women's Lives*. Ithaca, N.Y.: Cornell University Press.

Hardt, Hanno. 1986. "British Cultural Studies and the Return of the 'Critical' in American Mass Communication Research: Accommodation or Radical Change?" *Journal of Communication Inquiry* 10: 117-24.

Harré, R. 1986. *The Social Construction of Emotions*. London: Basil Blackwell.

Harré, R., and R. Lamb. 1986. *The Dictionary of Personality and Social Psychology*. Cambridge, Mass.: MIT Press.

Haverkate, H. 1988. "Toward a Typology of Politeness Strategies in Communicative Interaction." *Multilingua* 7: 385-409.

Hawley, Amos H. 1969. "Human Ecology." Pp. 64-70 in *Sociological Theory*, ed. Walter W. Wallace. Chicago: Aldine.

Hayakawa, S. I. 1947. *Language in Action*. New York: Harcourt, Brace and Company.

Hayes, Terrall A. 2000. "Stigmatizing Indebtedness: Implications for Labeling Theory." *Symbolic Interaction* 23: 29-46.

Hebdige, Dick. 1979. *Subculture: The Meaning of Style*. London: Methuen.

Helle, H. J., and S. N. Eisenstadt, eds. 1985. *Micro-Sociological Theory: Perspectives on Sociological Theory*, vol. 2. Beverly Hills, Calif.: Sage.

Herman, Thelma. 1943. "Pragmatism: A Study in Middle-Class Ideology." *Social Forces* 22: 405-10.

Herrnstein, Richard J., and Charles Murray. 1994. *The Bell Curve: Intelligence and Class Structure in American Life*. New York: Free Press.

Hewit, John P. 1991. *Self and Society: A Symbolic Interactionist Social Psychology*. Boston: Allyn and Bacon.

Hickman, C. A., and M. H. Kuhn. 1956. *Individuals, Groups, and Economic Behavior.* New York: Dryden.

Hinkle, Roscoe C. 1967. "Charles Horton Cooley's General Sociological Orientation." *The Sociological Quarterly* 8: 5-20.

———. 1980. *Founding Theory of American Sociology, 1881-1915.* Boston: Routledge and Kegan Paul.

Hinkle, Roscoe C., and Gisela Hinkle. 1954. *The Development of Modern Sociology.* New York: Random House.

Hintz, R. A., and D. E. Miller. 1995. "Openings Revisited: The Foundations of Social Interaction." *Symbolic Interaction* 18: 355-69.

Hochschild, Arlie Russell. 1979. "Emotion Work, Feeling Rules, and Social Structure." *American Journal of Sociology.* 85: 551-75.

———. 1983. *The Managed Heart: Commercialization of Human Feeling.* Berkeley: University of California Press.

———. 1989. "The Economy of Gratitude." Pp. 95-113 in *The Sociology of Emotions: Original Essays and Research Papers,* ed. David D. Franks and E. Doyle McCarthy. Greenwich, Conn.: JAI Press.

Hofstadter, Richard. 1969. *Social Darwinism in American Thought.* New York: George Braziller.

Hollinger, R. 1994. *Postmodernism and the Social Sciences: A Thematic Approach.* Thousand Oaks, Calif.: Sage.

Horne, Lewis. 1990. "The Way of Resentment in *Dombey and Son.*" *Modern Language Quarterly* 51: 44-62.

Hosticka, Carl J. 1979. "We Don't Care about What Happened, We Only Care about What Is Going to Happen: Lawyer-Client Negotiations of Reality." *Social Problems* 26: 599-610.

Hoult, T. F., ed. 1969. *Dictionary of Modern Sociology.* Totawa, N.J.: Littlefield, Adams.

House, J. S. 1981. "Social Structure and Personality." Pp. 525-61 in *Social Psychology: Sociological Perspectives,* ed. M. Rosenberg and R. H. Turner. New York: Basic Books.

———. 1995. "Social Structure, Relationships, and the Individual." Pp. 387-95 in *Sociological Perspectives on Social Psychology,* ed. K. S. Cook, G. A. Fine, and J. S. House. Boston: Allyn and Bacon.

Huber, Joan. 1973. "Symbolic Interaction as a Pragmatic Perspective: The Bias of Emergent Theory." *American Sociological Review* 38: 274-84.

———. 1974. "The Emergency of Emergent Theory." *American Sociological Review* 39: 463-67.

Hudson, Michael. 1972. *Super Imperialism: The Economic Strategy of American Empire.* New York: Holt, Rinehart and Winston.

Hunt, M. 1993. *The Story of Psychology.* New York: Doubleday.

Hutchinson, E. P. 1981. *Legislative History of American Immigration Policy 1798-1965.* Philadelphia: University of Pennsylvania Press.

Hyde, Janet Shibley. 1990. "Meta-Analysis and the Psychology of Gender Differences." *Signs: Journal of Women in Culture and Society* 16: 55-73.

Hymes, D. H. 1974. *Foundations in Sociolingustics.* Philadelphia: University of Pennsylvania Press.

Irwin, Katherine. 2001. "Legitimating the First Tattoo: Moral Passage through Informal Interaction." *Symbolic Interaction* 24: 49-73.

Jakobson, R. 1960. "Linguistics and Poetics." Pp. 350-77 in *Style and Language,* ed. T. A. Sebeok. Cambridge, Mass.: MIT Press.

James, W. 1890. *Principles of Psychology,* vol. 1. London: Macmillan.

James, William. 1968. "The Self." Pp. 41-50 in *The Self in Social Interaction,* ed. Chad Gordon and Kenneth J. Gergen. New York: Wiley.

————. 1970. "The Social Self." Pp. 373-77 in *Social Psychology through Symbolic Interaction,* ed. Gregory P. Stone and Harvey A. Farberman. Waltham, Mass.: Xerox.

————. 1980. *Principles of Psychology,* 2 vols. New York: Holt.

————. 1984. *Psychology: Briefer Course.* Cambridge, Mass.: Harvard University Press.

Jameson, Frederick. 1976. "Authentic Ressentiment: The 'Experimental' Novels of Gissing." *Nineteenth Century Fiction* 31: 127-49.

Jameson, Fredric. 1976. "On Goffman's Frame Analysis." *Theory and Society* 3: 119-33.

Jandy, Edward C. 1942. *Charles Horton Cooley: His Life and Social Theory.* New York: Dryden Press.

Janowitz, Morris. 1966. "Introduction." In *On Social Organization and Social Personality.* Chicago: University of Chicago Press.

Jary, David, and Gregory Smith. 1976. "An Extended Review of Frame Analysis." *Sociological Review* 24: 917-27.

Jennings, H. S. 1930. *The Biological Basis of Human Nature.* New York: Norton.

Johnson, John M., and Kathleen J. Ferraro. 1977. "The Victimized Self: The Case of Battered Women." Pp. 119-30 in *Existential Sociology,* ed. J. D. Douglas and John M. Johnson. New York: Cambridge University Press.

Jones, Susan Stedman. 1980. "Kantian Philosophy and Sociological Methodology." *Sociology* 14: 99-111.

Kahne, Merton J., and Charlotte Green Schwartz. 1978. "Negotiating Trouble: The Social Construction and Management of Trouble in a College Psychiatric Context." *Social Problems* 25: 461-75.

Kamin, Leon J. 1976. "Heredity, Intelligence, Politics, and Psychology: II." Pp. 374-82 in *The IQ Controversy,* ed. N. J. Block and Gerald Dworkin. New York: Pantheon Books.

Kant, Immanuel. 1965. *Critique of Pure Reason*. New York: St. Martin's Press.

Kanter, Rosabeth Moss. 1972. "Symbolic Interactionism and Politics in Systemic Perspective." *Sociological Inquiry* 42: 77-92.

Karp, David A., and William C. Yoels. 1979. *Symbols, Selves and Society*. Philadelphia: Lippincott.

Karpf, Fay Berger. 1932. *American Social Psychology*. New York: McGraw-Hill.

Kellner, D. 1992. "Popular Culture and the Construction of Postmodern Identities." Pp. 141-77 in *Modernity and Identity*, ed. S. Lash and J. Friedman. Oxford: Blackwell.

Kenrick, D. T., and D. C. Funder. 1988. "Profiting from Controversy: Lessons from the Person-Situation Debate." *American Psychologist* 43: 23-24.

Kenrick, D. T., and D. O. Springfield. 1980. "Personality Traits and the Eye of the Beholder: Crossing Some Traditional Philosophical Boundaries in the Search for Consistency in All of the People." *Psychological Review* 87: 88-104.

Kerber, Linda K., Catherine G. Greeno, Eleanor E. Maccoby, Zella Luria, Carol B. Stack, and Carol Gilligan. 1986. "On *In a Different Voice*: An Interdisciplinary Forum." *Signs: Journal of Women in Culture and Society* 11: 304-33.

Killian, Lewis M. 1985. "The Stigma of Race: Who Now Bears the Mark of Cain?" *Symbolic Interaction* 8: 1-14.

Kitsuse, John I. 1973. "Societal Reaction to Deviant Behavior." Pp. 16-25 in *Deviance: The Interactionist Perspective*, ed. Earl Rubington and Martin Weinberg. New York: Macmillan.

———. 1975. "The New Conception of Deviance and Its Critics." Pp. 273-84 in *The Labeling of Deviance: Evaluating a Perspective*, ed. Walter R. Gove. New York: Sage.

Kluckhohn, Clyde, and Henry Murray. 1948. "Personality Formation: The Determinants." Pp. 35-48 in *Personality in Nature, Society, and Culture*, ed. Clyde Kluckhohn and Henry Murray. New York: Knopf.

Kluger, Richard. 1975. *Simple Justice: The History of Brown v. Board of Education and Black America's Struggle for Equality*. 2 vols. New York: Knopf.

Kolko, Gabriel. 1967. *The Triumph of Conservatism*. Chicago: Quadrangle Books.

Kozol, Jonathan. 1991. *Savage Inequalities*. New York: HarperCollins.

Krantz, David L., and David Allen. 1967. "The Rise and Fall of McDougall's Instinct Doctrine." *Journal of the History of the Behavioral Sciences* 3: 326-38.

Krauthammer, Charles. 1993. "Defining Deviancy Up." *New Republic* 22 (November): 20-25.

Kroeber, Alfred. 1917. "The Superorganic." *American Anthropologist* 19: 162-213.

Krout, John A. 1971. *United States since 1865*. New York: Barnes & Noble.

Kuhn, T. S. 1962. *The Structure of Scientific Revolutions*. Chicago: University of Chicago Press.

Kuhn, Manford H. 1967. "The Reference Group Reconsidered." Pp. 171-84 in *Symbolic Interaction: A Reader in Social Psychology*, ed. Jerome G. Manis and Bernard N. Meltzer. Boston: Allyn and Bacon.

———. 1972. "Major Trends in Symbolic Interaction Theory in the Past Twenty-Five Years." Pp. 57-76 in *Symbolic Interaction: A Reader in Social Psychology*, ed. Jerome G. Manis and Bernard N. Meltzer. Boston: Allyn and Bacon.

Kuhn, Manford H., and Thomas S. McPartland. 1972. "An Empirical Investigation of Self-Attitudes." Pp. 112-24 in *Symbolic Interaction: A Reader in Social Psychology*, ed. Jerome G. Manis and Bernard N. Meltzer. Boston: Allyn and Bacon.

Kuhn, Thomas. 1970a. *The Structure of Scientific Revolutions*. 2nd ed. Chicago: University of Chicago Press.

———. 1970b. "Reflections on My Critics." Pp. 251-77 in *Criticism and the Growth of Knowledge*, ed. Imre Lakatos and Alan Musgrave. Cambridge, Mass.: Cambridge University Press.

LaBarre, Weston. 1975. "The Cultural Basis of Emotions and Gestures." Pp. 231-49 in *Introducing Anthropology*, ed. James R. Hayes and James M. Henslin. Boston, Mass.: Holbrook Press.

La Barre, W. 1954. *The Human Animal*. Chicago: University of Chicago Press.

Labov, William. 1967. *The Social Stratification of English in New York City*. Washington, D.C.: Center for Applied Linguistics.

Langer, Susanne K. 1957. *Philosophy in a New Key*. Cambridge, Mass.: Harvard University Press.

Lasch, Christopher. 1965. *The New Radicalism in America: 1889-1963*. New York: Vintage.

———. 1978. *The Culture of Narcissism: American Life in an Age of Diminishing Expectations*. New York: Norton.

Latour, B. 1987. *Science in Action: How to Follow Scientists and Engineers through Society*. Cambridge, Mass.: Harvard University Press.

Lauer, Robert, and Warren Handel. 1977. *Social Psychology: The Theory and Application of Symbolic Interactionism*. Boston: Houghton Mifflin.

Laver, J. 1981. "Linguistic Routines and Politeness in Greeting and Parting." Pp. 289-304 in *Conversational Routine*, ed. F. Coulmas. The Hague: Mouton.

———. 1975. "Communicative Functions of Phatic Communion." Pp. 215-37 in *Organization of Behavior in Face-to-Face Interaction*, ed. A. Kendon, R. M. Harris, and M. R. Key. The Hague: Mouton.

Lawler, James M. 1978. *IQ, Heritability and Racism*. New York: International Publishers.

Layder, D. 1997. *Modern Social Theory: Key Debates and New Directions*. London: UCL Press.

———. 1994. *Understanding Social Theory*. London: Sage Publications.

Leakey, Richard. 1994. *The Origin of Humankind*. New York: Basic Books.

Lecky, Prescott. 1968. "The Theory of Self-Consistency." Pp. 297-98 in *The Self in Social Interaction*, ed. Chad Gordon and Kenneth J. Gergen. New York: Wiley.

Lee, Raymond L. M. 1980. "Ethnic Relations in Interactionist Perspective: A Case of Ethnic Conflict in West Malaysia." *Symbolic Interaction* 3: 89-104.

Lee, S. C. 1964. "The Primary Group as Cooley Defined It." *The Sociology Quarterly* 5: 23-34.

Lefebvre, Henri. 1982. *The Sociology of Marx.* New York: Columbia University Press.

Leichty, M. G. 1986. "Social Closings." Pp. 231-48 in *Studies in Symbolic Interaction, Supplement 2: The Iowa School (Part A)*, ed. C. J. Couch, S. L. Saxton, and M. A. Katovich. Greenwich, Conn.: JAI Press.

Lemert, Edwin M. 1951. *Social Pathology.* New York: McGraw Hill.

———. 1973. "Paranoia and the Dynamics of Exclusion." Pp. 106-15 in *Deviance: The Interactionist Perspective*, ed. Earl Rubington and Martin S. Weinberg. New York: Macmillan.

———. 1975. "Primary and Secondary Deviation." Pp. 167-72 in *Theories of Deviance*, ed. Stuart H. Traub and Craig B. Little. Itasca, Ill.: F. E. Peacock.

———. 1979. "Beyond Mead: The Societal Reaction to Deviance." Pp. 426-35 in *Symbolic Interaction: A Reader in Social Psychology*, ed. Jerome G. Manis and Bernard N. Meltzer. Boston. Allyn and Bacon.

Lewis, J. David. 1976. "The Classic American Pragmatists as Forerunners to Symbolic Interactionism." *The Sociological Quarterly* 17: 347-59.

Lewis, J. David, and Richard Smith. 1980. *American Sociology and Pragmatism: Mead, Chicago Sociology, and Symbolic Interaction.* Chicago: University of Chicago Press.

Lewontin, R. C., Steven Rose, and Leon J. Kamin. 1984. *Not in Our Genes: Biology, Ideology, and Human Nature.* New York: Pantheon Books.

Liazos, Alexander. 1975. "The Poverty of the Sociology of Deviance: Nuts, Sluts, and Preverts." Pp. 250-72 in *Theories of Deviance*, ed. Stuart H. Traub and Craig B. Little. Itasca, Ill.: F. E. Peacock.

Lieberman, Leonard. 1970. "The Debate over Race: A Study in the Sociology of Knowledge." Pp. 388-405 in *The Sociology of Sociology*, ed. Larry T. Reynolds and Janice M. Reynolds. New York: David McKay.

Liff, Sonia, and Ivy Cameron. 1997. "Changing Equality Cultures to Move Beyond 'Women's Problems.'" *Gender, Work, and Organization* 4: 35-46.

Lifton, R. J. 1993. *The Protean Self: Human Resilience in an Age of Fragmentation.* New York: Basic Books.

Lindesmith, Alfred R., Anselm L. Strauss, and Norman K. Denzin. 1988. *Social Psychology.* Englewood Cliffs, N.J.: Prentice Hall.

———. 1991. *Social Psychology.* Englewood Cliffs, N.J.: Prentice Hall.

Lindsey, Linda L. 1990. *Gender Roles: A Sociological Perspective.* Englewood Cliffs, N.J.: Prentice Hall.

Lipman-Blumen, Jean. 1984. *Gender Roles and Power.* Englewood Cliffs, N.J.: Prentice Hall.

Longino, Helen E. 1990. *Science as Social Knowledge: Values and Objectivity in Scientific Inquiry.* Princeton, N.J.: Princeton University Press.

Loseke, Donileen R., and Spencer E. Cahill. 1984. "The Social Construction of Deviance: Experts on Battered Women." *Social Problems* 31: 296-310.

Lowie, Robert H. 1917. *Culture and Ethology.* New York: Horace Liveright.

Luckenbill, David F. 1979. "Power: A Conceptual Framework." *Symbolic Interaction* 2: 97-114.

———. 1988. "LeConte, Royce, Teggart, Blumer: A Berkeley Dialogue on Sociology, Social Change, and Symbolic Interaction." *Symbolic Interaction* 11: 125-43.

Lyman, Stanford M. 1984. "Interactionism and the Study of Race Relations at the Macro-Sociological Level: The Contribution of Herbert Blumer." *Symbolic Interaction* 7: 107-20.

Lyman, Stanford M., and Arthur J. Vidich. 1988. *Social Order and the Public Philosophy: An Analysis and Interpretation of the Work of Herbert Blumer.* Fayetteville: University of Arkansas Press.

Lynch, Frederick R., and William R. Beer. 1990. "'You Ain't the Right Color': White Resentment of Affirmative Action." *Policy Review* 51: 64-67.

Lyons, J. 1977. *Semantics*, vol. 1. Cambridge: Cambridge University Press.

———. 1968. *Introduction to Theoretical Linguistics.* Cambridge: Cambridge University Press.

MacKinnon, Neil J. 1994. *Symbolic Interactionism as Affect Control.* Albany: State University of New York Press.

Maines, David R. 1977. "Social Organization and Social Structure in Symbolic Interactionist Thought." *Annual Review of Sociology* 3: 235-59.

———. 1979. "Mesostructure and Social Process." *Contemporary Sociology* 8: 524-27.

———. 1982. "In Search of Mesostructure." *Urban Life* 11: 267-79.

———. 1988. "Myth, Text, and Interactionist Complicity in the Neglect of Blumer's Macrosociology." *Symbolic Interaction* 11: 43-57.

———. 1989. "Repackaging Blumer: The Myth of Herbert Blumer's Astructural Bias." Pp. 383-413 in *Studies in Symbolic Interaction*, vol. 10, ed. Norman K. Denzin. Greenwich, Conn.: JAI Press.

Maines, David R., and Joy C. Charlton. 1985. "The Negotiated Order Approach to the Analysis of Social Organization." Pp. 271-308 in *Foundations of Interpretive Sociology*, ed. H. Farberman and R. Perinbanayagam. Greenwich, Conn.: JAI Press.

Malinowski, B. 1943. "The Problem of Meaning in Primitive Languages." Pp. 296-336 in *The Meaning of Meaning*, 6th ed., C. K. Ogden and I. A. Richards. New York: Harcourt Brace.

Manders, Dean. 1975. "Labeling Theory and Social Reality: A Marxist Critique." *Insurgent Sociologist* 6: 53-66.

Mankoff, Milton. 1971. "Societal Reaction and Career Deviance: A Critical Analysis."

The Sociological Quarterly 12: 204-18.

Mann, M., ed. 1984. *The International Encyclopedia of Sociology.* New York: Macmillan.

Mannheim, Karl. 1936. *Ideology and Utopia.* New York: Harcourt, Brace and World.

Manning, Peter K. 1973. "Survey Essay on Deviance." *Contemporary Sociology* 2: 123-28.

———. 1976. "The Decline of Civility: A Comment on Erving Goffman's Sociology." *The Canadian Review of Sociology and Anthropology* 13: 13-25.

———. 1977. "Rules in Organizational Context: Narcotics Law Enforcement in Two Settings." *The Sociological Quarterly* 18: 44-61.

———. 1980. "Goffman's Framing Order: Style as Structure." Pp. 252-84 in *The View from Goffman,* ed. James Ditton. New York: Macmillan.

———. 1982. "Producing Drama: Symbolic Communication and the Police." *Symbolic Interaction* 5: 223-41.

Marañon, Gregorio. 1956. *Tiberius: A Study in Resentment.* London: Hollis and Carter.

Marger, Martin N. 1999. *Social Inequality: Patterns and Processes.* Mountain View, Calif.. Mayfield.

Markey, John F. [1928]1978. *The Symbolic Process and Its Integration in Children: A Study in Social Psychology.* Chicago: University of Chicago Press.

Marsh, D. 1989. "Review of *Small Talk: Analyzing Phatic Discourse,*" by K. P. Schneider. *Regional English Language Journal* 20: 88-89.

Martin, Susan E. 1978. "Sexual Politics in the Workplace: The Interactional World of Policewomen." *Symbolic Interaction* 1: 44-60.

Martindale, Don. 1960. *The Nature and Types of Sociological Theory.* Boston: Houghton Mifflin.

May, T. 1996. *Situating Social Theory.* Buckingham, UK: Open University Press.

McBroom, Patricia A. 1992. *The Third Sex: The New Professional Woman.* New York: Paragon Press.

McCall, G. J., and J. L. Simmons. 1966. *Identities and Interactions.* New York: Free Press.

McCall, Michal M., and Howard S. Becker. 1990. *Symbolic Interaction and Cultural Studies.* Chicago: University of Chicago Press.

McCarthy, E. Doyle. 1989. "Emotions Are Social Things: An Essay in the Sociology of Emotions." Pp. 51-72 in *The Sociology of Emotions: Original Essays and Research Papers,* ed. David D. Franks and E. Doyle McCarthy. Greenwich, Conn.: JAI Press.

McCrae, R. R., and P. T. Costa, Jr. 1997. "Personality Trait Structure as a Human Universal." *American Psychologist* 52: 509-16.

McDougall, William, 1908. *Introduction to Social Psychology.* London: Methuen.

McHugh, Peter 1968. *Defining the Situation: The Organization of Meaning in Social Interaction.* Indianapolis: Bobbs-Merrill.

———. 1970. "A Common-Sense Conception of Deviance." Pp. 61-88 in *Deviance and Respectability: The Social Construction of Moral Meanings*, ed. Jack D. Douglas. New York: Basic Books.

McKee, James B. 1993. *Sociology and the Race Problem: The Failure of a Perspective*. Urbana: University of Illinois Press.

McKenzie, R. D. 1924. "The Ecological Approach to the Study of the Human Community." *American Journal of Sociology* 30: 287-301.

Mead, George Herbert. 1934. *Mind, Self, and Society*. Chicago: University of Chicago Press.

———. 1967. *Mind, Self, and Society*. Chicago: University of Chicago Press.

———. 1972. *On Social Psychology*, ed. Anselm Strauss. Chicago: University of Chicago Press.

Meltzer, Bernard N. 1972. "Mead's Social Psychology." Pp. 4-22 in *Symbolic Interaction: A Reader in Social Psychology*, ed. Jerome G. Manis and Bernard N. Meltzer. Boston: Allyn and Bacon.

Meltzer, Bernard N., and Jerome G. Manis. 1992. "Emergence and Human Conduct." *Journal of Psychology* 126: 333-42.

Meltzer, Bernard N., and Gil Richard Musolf. 1999. "The End of Personality?" Pp. 197-221 in *Studies in Symbolic Interaction*, vol. 22, ed. Norman K. Denzin. Greenwich, Conn.: JAI Press.

———. 2000. "'Have a Nice Day!' Phatic Communion and Everyday Life." Pp. 95-111 in *Studies in Symbolic Interaction*, vol. 23, ed. Norman K. Denzin. Greenwich, Conn.: JAI Press.

———. 2002. "Resentment and *Ressentiment*." *Sociological Inquiry* 72: 240-55.

Meltzer, Bernard N., John Petras, and Larry T. Reynolds. 1975. *Symbolic Interactionism: Genesis, Varieties, and Criticism*. London: Routledge and Kegan Paul.

Meltzer, W. J. 1994. "Tourism and the Development of Capitalism in a Dominican Village." Ph.D. dissertation, University of Michigan.

Merton, Robert K. 1957. *Social Theory and Social Structure*, rev. ed. Glencoe, Ill.: Free Press.

Messinger, Sheldon L., Harold Sampson, and Robert D. Towne. 1970. "Life as Theater: Some Notes on the Dramaturgic Approach to Social Reality." Pp. 689-99 in *Social Psychology through Symbolic Interaction*, ed. Gregory Stone and Harvey A. Farberman. Waltham, Mass.: Xerox.

Meyers, D. T., ed. 1997. *Feminists Rethink the Self*. Boulder, Colo.: Westview Press.

Milgram, Stanley. 1965. "Some Conditions of Obedience and Disobedience to Authority." *Human Relations* 18: 57-75.

Miller, D. E., R. A. Hintz, and C. J. Couch. 1975. "The Elements and Structure of Openings." Pp. 1-24 in *Constructing Social Life*, ed. C. J. Couch and R. A. Hintz Jr. Champaign, Ill.: Stipes Publishing.

Miller, David. 1972. "Ideology and the Problem of False Consciousness." *Political*

Studies 20: 432-47.

———. 1973. *George Herbert Mead: Self, Language, and the World.* Austin: University of Texas Press.

Mills, C. W. 1951. *White Collar: The American Middle Classes.* New York: Oxford University Press.

Mills, C. Wright. 1964. *Sociology and Pragmatism: The Higher Learning in America.* New York: Paine-Whitman.

———. 1967. "Situated Actions and Vocabularies of Motive." Pp. 335-66 in *Symbolic Interaction: A Reader in Social Psychology*, ed. Jerome G. Manis and Bernard N. Meltzer. Boston: Allyn and Bacon.

———. 1975. *The Sociological Imagination.* New York: Oxford University Press.

Mischel, W. 1968. *Personality and Assessment.* New York: John Wiley and Sons.

Molotch, Harvey L., and Deirdre Boden. 1985. "Talking Social Structure: Discourse, Domination and the Watergate Hearings." *American Sociological Review* 50: 273-88.

Montag, L., and J. Levin. 1994. "The Five-Factor Personality in Model in Applied Settings." *European Journal of Personality* 8: 1-11.

Morgan, Leslie A. 1991. *After Marriage Ends: Economic Consequences for Midlife Women.* Newbury Park, Calif.: Sage.

Morris, Charles. 1937. *Logical Positivism, Pragmatism, and Scientific Empiricism.* Paris: Herman Et Cie Editeurs.

Morris, Richard B., and William Greenleaf. 1969. *USA: The History of a Nation.* Chicago: Rand McNally.

Moynihan, Daniel Patrick. 1993. "Defining Deviancy Down." *American Scholar* 61: 17-30.

Munch, R., and N. J. Smelser. 1987. "Relating the Micro and Macro." Pp. 356-87 in *The Micro-Macro Link*, ed. J. C. Alexander et al. Berkeley: University of California Press.

Murphy, Jeffrie G., and Jean Hampton. 1988. *Forgiveness and Mercy.* Cambridge: Cambridge University Press.

Murray, Susan B. 2000. "Getting Paid in Smiles: The Gendering of Child Care Work." *Symbolic Interaction* 23: 135-60.

Musolf, Gil Richard. 1992. "Structure, Institutions, Power, and Ideology: New Directions within Symbolic Interactionism." *The Sociological Quarterly* 33: 171-89.

———. 1993. "Some Recent Directions in Symbolic Interactionism." Pp. 231-83 in *Interactionism: Exposition and Critique*, 3rd ed., ed. Larry T. Reynolds. Dix Hills, N.Y.: General Hall.

———. 1994. "William James and Symbolic Interactionism." *Sociological Focus* 27: 303-14.

———. 1995. "Symbolic Interactionism and the State: From Reform to Radical Reconstruction." *Michigan Sociological Review* 9: 19-40.

———. 1996. "Interactionism and the Child: Cahill, Corsaro, and Denzin on Childhood Socialization." *Symbolic Interaction* 19: 303-21.

———. 2001. "John Dewey's Social Psychology and Neopragmatism: Theoretical Foundations of Human Agency and Social Reconstruction." *The Social Science Journal.* 38: 277-95.

Nagel, Joane. 2001. "Racial, Ethnic, and National Boundaries: Sexual Intersections and Symbolic Interactions." *Symbolic Interaction* 24: 123-39.

Natanson, Maurice. 1970. *The Journeying Self: A Study in Philosophy and Social Role.* Reading, Mass.: Addison-Wesley.

———. 1973. *The Social Dynamics of George Herbert Mead.* The Hague: Martinus Nyhoff.

Nathanson, Constance A., and Gerda Lorenz. 1982. "Women and Health: The Social Dimensions of Biomedical Data." Pp. 37-87 in *Women in the Middle Years,* ed. Janet Zollinger Giele. New York: Wiley.

Nehring, Neil. 1997. *Popular Music, Gender, and Postmodernism: Anger Is an Energy.* Thousand Oaks, Calif.: Sage.

Nelson, Cary, and Lawrence Grossberg. 1988. *Marxism and the Interpretation of Culture.* Urbana: University of Illinois Press.

Nelson, Margaret K. 1990. "Mothering Others' Children: The Experiences of Family Day-Care Providers." *Signs: Journal of Women in Culture and Society* 15: 586-605.

Nietzsche, Friedrich Wilhelm [1887]. 1956. *The Birth of Tragedy and the Genealogy of Morals.*Translated by Francis Golffing. Garden City, N.Y.: Doubleday.

———. 1968. *The Basic Writings of Nietzsche,* ed. Walter Kaufmann. New York: Modern Library.

Nisbet, R. 1966. *The Sociological Tradition.* New York: Basic Books.

———. 1967. "Review of Wayward Puritans." *American Sociological Review* 32: 484-85.

Noble, David W. 1967. *The Paradox of Progressive Thought.* Minneapolis: University of Minnesota Press.

Nordstrom, Carl, Edgar Z. Friedenberg, and Harry A. Gold. 1967. *Society's Children: A Study of Ressentiment in the Secondary School.* New York: Random House.

———. 1965. *Influence of Ressentiment on Student Experience in the Secondary School.* Brooklyn, N.Y.: Brooklyn College.

Novack, George. 1975. *Pragmatism versus Marxism.* New York: Pathfinder Press.

Omar, A. S. 1991. "Conversational Openings in Kiswahili: The Pragmatic Performance of Native and Non-native Speakers." *Kaswahili* 58: 12-24.

Ortony, A., G. L. Clore, and A. Collins. [1988] 1990. *The Cognitive Structure of Emotions.* Cambridge: Cambridge University Press.

Ospina, Sonia. 1996. *Illusions of Opportunity: Employee Expectations and Workplace Inequality.* Ithaca, N.Y.: Cornell University Press.

O'Toole, Richard, and Anita Werner O'Toole. 1981. "Negotiating Interorganization

Orders." *The Sociological Quarterly* 22: 29-41.

Owens, Raymond E. 1975. "Rubbing Raw the Sores of Discontent: Competing Theories and Data on Effects of Participation in a Black Protest Group." *Sociological Focus* 8: 143-59.

Padavic, Irene. 1991. "The Re-creation of Gender in a Male Workplace." *Symbolic Interaction* 14: 279-94.

Palmer, C. Eddie. 1994. "Human Emotions: An Expanding Sociological Frontier." Pp. 424-35 in *Symbolic Interaction: An Introduction to Social Psychology*, ed. Nancy J. Herman and Larry T. Reynolds. Dix Hills, N.Y.: General Hall.

Park, R. E., and E. W. Burgess. 1921. *Introduction to the Science of Sociology*. Chicago: University of Chicago Press.

Park, Robert E. 1967. *On Social Control and Collective Behavior*, ed. Ralph Turner. Chicago: University of Chicago Press.

Parker, John. 2000. *Structuration*. Buckingham, UK: Open University Press.

Parrington, Vernon Louis. 1927. *The Beginnings of Critical Realism in America*. New York: Harcourt, Brace.

Pavlidou, T. 1994. "Contrasting German-Greek Politeness and the Consequences." *Journal of Pragmatics* 21: 487-511.

Payne, Michael. 1996. *A Dictionary of Cultural and Critical Theory*. Cambridge, Mass.: Blackwell.

Peel, John. 1971. *Herbert Spencer*. New York: Basic Books.

Perinbanayagam, R. S. 1975. "The Significance of Others in the Thought of Alfred Schutz, G .H. Mead, and C. H. Cooley." *The Sociological Quarterly* 16: 500-521.

Perinbanayagam, R. S. 1991. *Discursive Acts*. New York: Aldine De Gruyter.

Pervin, L. A. 1985. "Personality: Current Controversies, Issues, and Directions." *Annual Review of Psychology* 36: 83-114.

Petras, John. 1968. "John Dewey and the Rise of Interactionism in American Social Theory." *Journal of the History of the Behavioral Sciences* 4: 18-27.

———. 1973. "George Herbert Mead's Theory of Self: A Study in the Origin and Convergence of Ideas." *Canadian Review of Sociology and Anthropology* 10: 148-59.

Piaget, Jean. 1926. *The Language and Thought of the Child*. New York: Harcourt, Brace Jovanovich.

Pickering, A. 1993. "The Mangle of Practice: Agency and Emergence in the Sociology of Science." *American Journal of Sociology* 99: 559-89.

Pinkerton, Jan. 1970. "Katherine Ann Porter's Portrayal of Black Resentment." *University Review* 36: 315-17.

Plath, Sylvia. 1982. "Letter to a Demon." *New York Times*. 18 April.

Potter, J., and M. Wetherell. 1987. *Discourse and Social Psychology: Beyond Attitudes and Behavior*. London: Sage.

Prendergast, Christopher, and J. David Knottnerus. 1990. "The Astructural Bias and

Presuppositional Reform in Symbolic Interactionism: A Non-interactionist Evaluation of the New Studies in Social Organization." Pp. 158-80 in *Interactionism: Exposition and Critique*, ed. Larry T. Reynolds. Dix Hills, N.Y.: General Hall.

Prus, Robert C. 1996. *Symbolic Interaction and Ethnographic Research: Intersubjectivity and the Study of Human Lived Experience*. Albany: State University of New York Press.

Quirk, R. 1962. *The Use of English*. New York: St. Martin's Press.

Quinney, Richard. 1975. "Crime Control in Capitalist Society: A Critical Philosophy of Legal Order." Pp. 181-202 in *Critical Criminology*, ed. Ian Taylor, Paul Walton, and Jock Young. London: Routledge and Kegan Paul.

Radloff, Lenore. 1975. "Sex Differences in Depression: The Effects of Occupation and Marital Status." *Sex Roles* 1: 249-66.

Rawls, John. 1971. *A Theory of Justice*. Cambridge, Mass.: Harvard University Press.

Reese, William A., and Michael Katovich. 1989. "Untimely Acts: Extending the Interactionist Conception of Deviance." *The Sociological Quarterly* 30: 159-84.

Reinhardt, J. M. 1937. "Personality Traits and the Situation." *American Sociological Review* 2: 492-500.

Reiser, Christa. 1993. "Gender Hostility: The Continuing Battle between the Sexes." *Free Inquiry in Creative Sociology* 21: 207-12.

Reynolds, Larry T. 1993. *Interactionism: Exposition and Critique*, 3rd ed. Dix Hills, N.Y.: General Hall.

Richardson, Laurel. 1986. "Another World." *Psychology Today* (February): 22-27.

———. 1988. "Secrecy and Status: The Social Construction of Forbidden Relationships." *American Sociological Review* 53: 209-19.

———. 1989. "Gender Stereotyping with English Language." Pp. 5-9 in *Feminist Frontiers II*, ed. Laurel Richardson and Verta Taylor. New York: Random House.

Riesman, D., N. Glazer, and R. Denney. 1950. *The Lonely Crowd: A Study of the Changing American Character*. Garden City, N.Y.: Doubleday.

Ritzer, G. 1980. *Sociology: A Multiple Paradigm Science*, rev. ed. Boston: Allyn and Bacon.

Robertson, I. 1987. *Sociology*, 3rd ed. New York: Worth.

Rock, Paul Elliot. 1979. *The Making of Symbolic Interactionism*. New York: Macmillan.

Rockwell, R. C., G. H. Elder Jr., and D. J. Ross. 1979. "Psychological Patterns in Marital Timing and Divorce." *Social Psychology Quarterly* 42: 399-404.

Rollins, Judith. 1996. "Invisiblity, Consciousness of the Other, and *Ressentiment* among Black Domestic Workers." Pp. 223-43 in *Working in the Service Society*, ed. Cameron L. Macdonald and Carmen Sirianni. Philadelphia: Temple University.

Rommetveit, R. 1974. *On Message Structure: A Framework for the Study of Language and Communication*. London: Wiley.

Rose, Arnold M. 1962. *Human Behavior and Social Processes*. Boston: Houghton

Mifflin.

Rosenberg, Bernard, and Norman Humphrey. 1955. "The Secondary Nature of the Primary Group." *Social Research* 22: 25-38.

Rosenberg, M., and R. H. Turner, eds. 1981. *Social Psychology: Sociological Perspectives*. New York: Basic Books.

Rosenberg, Morris. 1990. "Reflexivity and Emotions." *Social Psychology Quarterly* 53: 3-12.

Ross, Dorothy. 1991. *The Origins of American Social Science*. Cambridge: Cambridge University Press.

Ross, E. A. 1908. *Social Psychology*. New York: Macmillan.

Ross, Ralph. 1962. *Symbols and Civilization*. New York: Harcourt, Brace and World.

Rossides, D. W. 1993. *American Society*. Dix Hills, N.Y.: General Hall.

Roucek, J. S., and R. L. Warren. 1951. *Sociology*. Ames, Iowa: Littlefield, Adams.

Rowe, David C. 1994. *The Limits of Family Influence: Genes, Experience, and Behavior*. New York: Guilford Press.

Rubington, Earl, and Martin S. Weinberg. 1973. "General Introduction." Pp. vii-viii in *Deviance: The Interactionist Perspective*, ed. Earl Rubington and Martin S. Weinberg. New York: Macmillan.

Runciman, W. G. 1972. *Relative Deprivation and Social Justice*. Harmondsworth, UK: Penguin.

Sacks, H. 1995. Lectures on Conversation, vols. 1 and 2, ed. G. Jefferson. Oxford: Blackwell.

Sagarin, Edward, and Robert J. Kelly. 1975. "Sexual Deviance and Labelling Perspectives." Pp. 243-71 in *The Labeling of Deviance: Evaluating a Perspective*, ed. Walter R. Gove. New York: Sage.

Salazar, Alonso. 1990. *Born to Die in Medellín*. New York: Monthly Review Press.

Sartre, Jeán. 1965. *Being and Nothingness*. New York: Philosophical Library.

Scheffler, Israel. 1974. *Four Pragmatists: A Critical Introduction to Pierce, James, Mead, and Dewey*. New York: Humanities Press.

Schegloff, E. A. 1988. "Goffman and the Analysis of Conversation." Pp. 89-135 in *Erving Goffman: Exploring the Interaction Order*, ed. P. Drew and A. Wootton. Boston: Northeastern University Press.

Scheler, Max. [1915] 1961. *Ressentiment*. Ed., with an introduction by Lewis A. Coser. Trans. William H. Holdheim. New York: Free Press of Glencoe.

Schmitt, Raymond. 1974. "Symbolic Interactionism and Emergent Theory: A Reexamination." *American Sociological Review* 39: 453-56.

Schneider, K. P. 1988. *Small Talk: Analyzing Phatic Discourse*. Marburg: Hitzeroth.

———. 1981. "Topic Selection in Phatic Communion." *Multilingua* 6: 247-56.

Schuman, Howard, and Maria Krysan. 1996. "A Study of Far Right *Ressentiment* in America." *International Journal of Public Opinion Research* 8: 10-30.

Schur, Edwin. 1971. *Labeling Deviant Behavior: Its Sociological Implications*. New

York: Harper & Row.

———. 1975. "Comments." Pp. 285-94 in *The Labeling of Deviance: Evaluating a Perspective*, ed. Walter R. Gove. New York: Sage.

Schwendinger, Herman, and Julia Schwendinger. 1974. *The Sociologists of the Chair*. New York: Basic Books.

Scott, James C. 1985. *Weapons of the Weak: Everyday Forms of Peasant Resistant*. New Haven, Conn.: Yale University Press.

Scott, Marvin B., and Stanford M. Lyman. 1970. "Accounts, Deviance, and Social Order." Pp. 89-119 in *Deviance and Respectability: The Social Construction of Moral Meanings*, ed. Jack D. Douglas. New York: Basic Books.

———. 1972. "Accounts." Pp. 404-29 in *Symbolic Interaction: A Reader in Social Psychology*, ed. Jerome G. Manis and Bernard N. Meltzer. Boston: Allyn and Bacon.

Scott, Robert S. 1970. "The Construction of Conceptions of Stigma by Professional Experts." Pp. 255-90 in *Deviance and Respectability: The Social Construction of Moral Meanings*. New York: Basic Books.

Scully, Diana, and Joseph Marolla. 1994. "Rapists' Vocabulary of Motives." Pp. 162-79 in *Symbolic Interaction: An Introduction to Social Psychology*, ed. Nancy J. Herman and Larry T. Reynolds. Dix Hills, N.Y.: General Hall.

Seeman, M. 1997. "The Elusive Situation in Social Psychology." *Social Psychology Quarterly* 60: 4-13.

Senft, G. 1995. "Phatic Communion." Pp. 1-10 in *Handbook of Pragmatics*, ed. by J. Verschueren, J. Ostman, and J. Blommaert. Amsterdam/Philadelphia: John Benjamins.

Sennett, Richard. 1969. "Introduction." Pp. 3-19 in *Classic Essays on the Culture of Cities*, ed. Richard Sennett. New York: Appleton-Century-Crofts.

———. 1977. *The Fall of Public Man*. New York: Knopf.

Shaeffer, Robert. 1988. *Resentment against Achievement: Understanding the Assault upon Ability*. Buffalo, N.Y.: Prometheus Books.

Shalin, Dmitri N. 1988. "G. H. Mead, Socialism, and the Progressive Agenda." *American Journal of Sociology* 93: 913-51.

Shibutani, T. 1961. *Society and Personality*. Englewood Cliffs, N.J.: Prentice Hall.

———. 1967. "Reference Groups as Perspectives." Pp. 159-70 in *Symbolic Interaction: A Reader in Social Psychology*, ed. Jerome G. Manis and Bernard N. Meltzer. Boston: Allyn and Bacon.

———. 1981. *Social Processes*. Berkeley: University of California Press.

Short, James F. 1971. "Introduction." Pp. xi-xvi in *The Social Fabric of the Metropoles*, ed. James F. Short. Chicago: University of Chicago Press.

Shott, Susan. 1979. "Emotion and Social Life: A Symbolic Interactionist Analysis." *American Journal of Sociology* 84: 1317-34.

Silva, V. O. 1980. "Phatic Language: A Preliminary Contrastive Analysis between

English and Spanish." *Lenguaje y Ciencias* 20: 104-11.

Slater, Philip. 1970. *The Pursuit of Loneliness*. Boston: Beacon Press.

Smith, Adam. [1759]1969. *The Theory of Moral Sentiments*. New Rochelle, N.Y.: Arlington House.

Smith, Dorothy E. 1996. "Telling the Truth after Postmodernism." *Symbolic Interaction* 19: 171-202.

Smith, Ken R., and Phyllis Moen. 1988. "Passage through Midlife: Women's Changing Family Roles and Economic Well-Being." *The Sociological Quarterly* 29: 503-24.

Snow, David A. 2001. "Extending and Broadening Blumer's Conceptualization of Symbolic Interactionism." *Symbolic Interaction* 24: 367-77.

Sokal, Michael M. 1984. "Introduction to *Psychology: Briefer Course*" by William James. Cambridge, Mass.: Harvard University Press.

Solomon, Robert C. 1994. "One Hundred Years of *Ressentiment*: Nietzsche's *Genealogy of Morals*." Pp. 95-126 in *Nietzsche, Genealogy, Morality: Essays on Nietzsche's Genealogy of Morals*, ed. Richard Schact. Berkeley: University of California Press.

———. 1995. *A Passion for Justice: Emotions and the Origins of the Social Contract*. Lanham, Md.: Rowman & Littlefield.

Sorrentino, Joseph W. 1971. *Up from Never*. Englewood Cliffs, N.J.: Prentice Hall.

Sperber, I. 1990. *Fashions in Science: Opinion Leaders and Collective Behavior in the Social Sciences*. Minneapolis: University of Minneapolis Press.

Stacy, Judith. 1994. "The Future of Feminist Differences." *Contemporary Sociology* 23: 482-86.

Stark, Werner. 1960. *The Sociology of Knowledge*. London: Routledge and Kegan Paul.

Staske, Shirley A. 1996. "Talking Feelings: The Collaborative Construction of Emotion in Talk between Close Relational Partners." *Symbolic Interaction* 19: 111-35.

Steible, D. J. 1967. *Handbook of Linguistics*. New York: Philosophical Library.

Steinem, Gloria. 1993. *Revolution from Within*. Boston: Little, Brown.

Stewart, R. L. 1998. *Living and Acting Together: An Essay in Social Psychology*. Dix Hills, N.Y.: General Hall.

Stocking, George W. 1968. *Race, Culture, and Evolution*. New York: Free Press.

Stone, Gregory P., and Harvey A. Farberman. 1970. *Social Psychology through Symbolic Interaction*. Waltham, Mass.: Xerox.

Storrs, Debbie. 1999. "Whiteness as Stigma: Essentialist Identity Work by Mixed-Race Women." *Symbolic Interaction* 22: 187-212.

Strauss, A. 1969. *Mirrors and Masks: The Search for Identity*. San Francisco: Sociology Press.

———. 1972. "Introduction to *On Social Psychology*" by George Herbert Mead. Chicago: University of Chicago Press.

———. 1977. "Sociological Theories of Personality." Pp. 277-303 in *Current Personality Theories*, ed. R. J. Corsini. Itasca, Ill.: F. E. Peacock.

———. 1978. *Negotiations.* San Francisco: Jossey-Bass Publishers.

Strawson, Peter F. 1974. *Freedom and Resentment and Other Essays.* London: Methuen and Company.

Strong, P. M. 1988. "Minor Courtesies and Macro Structures." Pp. 228-49 in *Erving Goffman: Exploring the Interaction Order*, ed. P. Drew and A. Wootton. Boston: Northeastern University Press.

Stryker, S. 1968. "Identity Salience and Role Performance: The Relevance of Symbolic Interaction Theory for Family Research." *Journal of Marriage and the Family* 30: 558-64.

Stryker, Sheldon. 1980. *Symbolic Interactionism: A Social Structural Version.* Menlo Park, Calif.: Benjamin/Cummings.

Sugarman, Richard I. 1980. *Rancor against Time: The Phenomenology of "Ressentiment."* Hamburg: F. Meiner.

Sullivan, Harry Stack. 1953. *The Interpersonal Theory of Psychiatry.* New York: W.W. Norton.

Sullivan, Mercer L. 1989. *"Getting Paid": Youth Crime and Work in the Inner City.* Ithaca, N.Y.: Cornell University Press.

Sutherland, Edwin H., and Donald R. Cressey. 1970. *Criminology*, 8th ed. Philadelphia: Lippincott.

Swanson, Guy E. 1989. "On the Motives and Motivations of Selves." Pp. 3-32 in *The Sociology of Emotions: Original Essays and Research Papers*, ed. David D. Franks and E. Doyle McCarthy. Greenwich, Conn.: JAI Press.

Szymanski, Albert. 1978. *The Capitalist State and the Politics of Class.* Cambridge, Mass.: Winthrop.

Taft, J. 1987. "The Woman Movement and Social Consciousness." Pp. 19-50 in *Women and Symbolic Interaction*, ed. M. J. Deegan and M. Hill. Boston: Allen and Unwin.

Tannen, D. 1981. " Indirectness in Discourse." *Discourse Processes* 4: 221-38.

———. 1980. "A Comparative Analysis of Oral Narrative Strategies: Athenian Greek and American English." Pp. 51-87 in *The Pear Stories: Cognitive, Cultural, and Linguistic Aspects of Narrative Production*, ed. W. Chafe. Norwood, N.J.: Ablex.

Tannenbaum, Frank. 1975. "The Dramatization of Evil." Pp. 162-66 in *Theories of Deviance*, ed. Stuart H. Traub and Craig B. Little. Itasca, Ill.: F. E. Peacock.

Tanni, Francis A. J. 1976. "Transitions in Organized Crime: The New Mafia." Pp. 241-65 in *Criminal Behavior and Social Systems*, ed. Anthony L. Gurnther. Chicago: Rand McNally.

Tayler, Ian, Paul Walton, and Jack Young. 1973. *The New Criminology: For a Social Theory of Deviance.* London: Routledge and Kegan Paul.

Telban, Borut. 1993. "Having 'Heart': Caring and Resentment in Abonavari, Papua

New Guinea." *Etnolog* 3: 158-77.

Thayer, H. S. 1973. *Meaning and Action: A Study of American Pragmatism.* Indianapolis: Bobbs-Merrill.

Theodorson, G. A., and A. G. Theodorson. 1969. *Modern Dictionary of Sociology.* New York: Thomas Y. Crowell.

Thio, Alex. 1975. "Class Bias in the Sociology of Deviance." Pp. 272-91 in *Theories of Deviance,* ed. Stuart H. Traub and Craig B. Little. Itasca, Ill.: F. E. Peacock.

———. 1991. *Sociology: A Brief Introduction.* New York: HarperCollins.

Thoits, Peggy A. 1996. "Managing the Emotions of Others." *Symbolic Interaction* 19: 85-109.

Thomas, Jim. 1984. "Some Aspects of Negotiated Order, Loose Coupling and Mesostructure in Maximum Security Prisons." *Symbolic Interaction* 7: 213-31.

Thomas, W. I. 1966. *On Social Organization and Social Personality,* ed. Morris Janowitz. Chicago: University of Chicago Press.

———. 1972. "The Definition of the Situation." Pp. 331-36 in *Symbolic Interaction: A Reader in Social Psychology,* ed. Jerome G. Manis and Bernard N. Meltzer. Boston: Allyn and Bacon.

Thomas, W. I., and D. S. Thomas. 1928. *The Child in America: Behavior Problems and Programs.* New York: Knopf.

Thomas, W. I., and Florian Znaniecki. 1918. *The Polish Peasant in Europe and America.* Boston: Richard C. Badger.

Thorne, Barrie. 1989. "Girls and Boys Together but Mostly Apart: Gender Arrangements in Elementary Schools." Pp. 73-84 in *Feminist Frontiers II,* ed. Laurel Richardson and Verta Taylor. New York: Random House.

———. 1993. *Gender Play: Girls and Boys in School.* New Brunswick, N.J.: Rutgers University Press.

Tiryakian, Edward A. 1968. "The Existential Self and the Person." Pp. 75-86 in *The Self in Social Interaction,* ed. Chad Gordon and Kenneth J. Gergen. New York: Wiley.

Toffler, Alvin. 1981. *The Third Wave.* New York: Banton Books.

Travers, Andrew. 1982. "Ritual Power in Interaction." *Symbolic Interaction* 5: 277-86.

Trepagnier, Barbara. 2001. "Deconstructing Categories: The Exposure of Silent Racism." *Symbolic Interaction* 24: 141-63.

Trice, Harrison M., and Paul Michael Roman. 1970. "Delabeling, Relabeling, and Alcoholics Anonymous." *Social Problems* 17: 538-46.

Tronto, Joan C. 1987. "Beyond Gender Difference to a Theory of Care." *Signs: Journal of Women in Culture and Society* 12: 644-63.

Troyer, William. 1946. "Mead's Social and Functional Theory of Mind." *American Sociological Review* 11: 198-202.

Turner, Jonathan. 1985. *Sociology: A Student Handbook.* New York: Random House.

Turner, Jonathan H., Leonard Beeghley, and Charles H. Poivers. 1989. *The Emergence of Sociological Theory,* 2nd ed. Chicago: Dorsey Press.

Turner, Ralph H. 1956. "Role-Taking, Role-Standpoint, and Reference Group Behavior." *American Journal of Sociology* 61: 316-28.

———. 1962. "Role-Taking: Process versus Conformity." Pp. 20-40 in *Human Behavior and Social Processes,* ed. Arnold M. Rose. Boston: Houghton Mifflin.

———. 1967. "Introduction to *On Social Control and Collective Behavior,*" by Robert E. Park. Chicago: University of Chicago Press.

———. 1968. "The Self-Conception in Social Interaction." Pp. 93-106 in *The Self in Social Interaction,* ed. Chad Gordon and Kenneth J. Gergen. New York: Wiley.

———. 1976. "The Real Self: From Institution to Impulse." *American Journal of Sociology* 81: 989-1016.

———. 1995. "Foreword," *Sociological Perspectives on Social Psychology,* ed. K. S. Cook, G. A. Fine, and J. S. House. Boston: Allyn and Bacon.

Vaneigem, Raôul. 1979. *The Revolution of Everyday Life.* London: Rising Free Collective.

Vernon, G. M. 1972. *Human Interaction,* 2nd ed. New York: Ronald Press.

Visano, Livy. 1988. "Generic and Generative Dimensions of Interactionism: Towards the Unfolding of Critical Directions." *International Journal of Comparative Sociology* 29: 230-44.

Vold, George B. 1979. *Theoretical Criminology.* New York: Oxford University Press.

Waldron, Ingrid. 1997. "What Do We Know about Causes of Sex Differences in Mortality? A Review of the Literature." Pp. 42-55 in *The Sociology of Health and Illness,* 5th ed., ed. Peter Conrad. New York: St. Martin's.

Walker, Lawrence. 1984. "Sex Differences in the Development of Moral Reasoning: A Critical Review." *Child Development* 55: 667-91.

Wallace, Walton W. 1969. *Sociological Theory.* Chicago: Aldine.

Wardhaugh, R. 1993. *Investing Linguistics.* Oxford: Blackwell.

———. 1985. *How Conversation Works.* Oxford: Basil Blackwell.

Warriner, C. K. 1970. *The Emergence of Society.* Homewood, Ill.: Dorsey Press.

Watson, Gary. 1993. "Responsibility and the Limits of Evil." Pp. 119-50 in *Perspectives on Moral Responsibility,* ed. John M. Fischer and Mark Ravizza. Ithaca: Cornell University Press.

Watzlawick, P., J. H. Beavin, and D. D. Jackson. 1967. *Pragmatics of Human Communication.* New York: W. W. Norton.

Weigert, A. J. 1992. *Social Psychology.* Notre Dame, Ind.: University of Notre Dame Press.

Weigert, Andrew J. 1983. *Social Psychology: A Sociological Approach through Interpretive Understanding.* Notre Dame, Ind.: University of Notre Dame Press.

Weigert, Andrew, and David D. Franks. 1989. "Ambivalence: A Touchstone of the Modern Temper." Pp. 205-27 in *The Sociology of the Emotions: Original Essays and Research Papers,* ed. David D. Franks and E. Doyle McCarthy. Greenwich

Conn.: JAI Press.

Weinberg, Martin S. 1970. "The Nudist Management of Respectability: Strategy for, and Consequences of, the Construction of a Situated Morality." Pp. 375-403 in *Deviance and Respectability: The Social Construction of Moral Meanings*, ed. Jack D. Douglas. New York: Basic Books.

Weinstein, James. 1968. *The Corporate Ideal in the Liberal State: 1900-1918*. Boston: Beacon Press.

Weisberg, Richard. 1972. "Hamlet and Ressentiment." *American Imago* 29: 318-37.

West, Candace. 1984. "When the Doctor Is a 'Lady': Power, Status, and Gender in Physician-Patient Encounters." *Symbolic Interaction* 7: 87-106.

Wheaton, Blair. 1990. "Life Transitions, Role Histories, and Mental Health." *American Sociological Review* 55: 209-23.

White, Leslie A. 1940. "The Symbol: The Origin and Basis of Human Behavior." *Philosophy of Science* 7: 451-63.

White, Lynn, and John N. Edwards. 1990. "Emptying the Nest and Parental Well-Being: Evidence from National Panel Data." *American Sociological Review* 55: 235-42.

White, Morton. 1957. *Social Thought in America: The Revolt against Formalism*. Boston: Beacon Press.

Whorf, Benjamin Lee. 1956. "Language, Mind, and Reality." Pp. 246-70 in *Language, Thought, and Reality*, ed. John B. Carroll. Cambridge, Mass.: MIT Press.

Wiebe, Robert. 1967. *The Search for Order: 1877-1920*. New York: Hill and Wang.

Wiley, M. G. 1995. "Sex Category and Gender in Social Psychology." Pp. 362-86 in *Social Perspectives on Social Psychology*, ed. K. S. Cook, G. A. Fine, and J. S. House. Boston: Allyn and Bacon.

Wiley, Mary Glenn. 1991. "Gender, Work, and Stress: The Potential Impact of Role-Identity Salience and Commitment." *The Sociological Quarterly* 32: 495-510.

Williams, Margaret Aasterud. 1970. "Reference Groups: A Review and Commentary." *The Sociological Quarterly* 11: 545-54.

Williams, Raymond. 1975. *Television: Technology and Cultural Form*. New York: Schocken Books.

———. 1977. *Marxism and Literature*. Oxford: Oxford University Press.

Williams, Robin M., Jr. 1970. *American Society: A Sociological Interpretation*, 3rd ed. New York: Knopf.

Willis, Paul. 1977. *Learning to Labor: How Working Class Kids Get Working Class Jobs*. New York: Columbia University Press.

Wirth, Louis. 1969a. "Urbanism as a Way of Life." Pp. 143-64 in *Classic Essays on the Culture of Cities*, ed. Richard Sennett. New York: Appleton-Century-Crofts.

———. 1969b. "Rural-Urban Differences." Pp. 165-69 in *Classic Essays on the Culture of Cities*, ed. Richard Sennett. New York: Appleton-Century-Crofts.

———. 1969c. "Human Ecology." Pp. 170-79 in *Classic Essays on the Culture of*

Cities, ed. Richard Sennett. New York: Appleton-Century-Crofts.

Wolf, Charlotte. 1986. "Legitimation and Oppression: Response and Reflexivity." *Symbolic Interaction* 9: 217-34.

Wolf, Naomi. 1994. *Fire with Fire: The New Female Power and How to Use It*. New York: Fawcett Columbine.

Wright, Rosemary, and Jerry A. Jacobs. 1994. "Male Flight from Computer Work: A New Look at Occupational Resegregation and Ghettoization." *American Sociological Review* 59: 511-36.

Yankelovich, Daniel. 1975. "The Status of Ressentiment in America." *Social Research* 42: 760-77.

Young, K. 1944. *Social Psychology*. New York: F. S. Crofts.

Zeitlin, Irving. 1973. *Rethinking Sociology*. Englewood Cliffs, N.J.: Prentice Hall.

Zurcher, L. A. 1977. *The Mutable Self: A Self-Concept for Social Change*. Beverly Hills, Calif.: Sage.

Index

About the Author

Gil Richard Musolf is associate professor of sociology at Central Michigan University, where he teaches classical and contemporary sociological theory. He has published many articles on symbolic interactionism. He has also, of late, strayed into Shakespeare studies and recently published "Role-Taking and Restorative Justice: Social Practices of Solidarity and Community in Shakespeare's *Measure for Measure*" in *Contemporary Justice Review* (2002).